D1067423

MARIA EDGEWORTH
IN FRANCE
AND SWITZERLAND

R. L. Edgeworth, from a water-colour by John Comerford

MARIA EDGEWORTH IN FRANCE AND SWITZERLAND

Selections from the Edgeworth family letters

EDITED BY
CHRISTINA COLVIN

CLARENDON PRESS · OXFORD
1979

Oxford University Press, Walton Street, Oxford OX2 6DP
OXFORD LONDON GLASGOW
NEW YORK TORONTO MELBOURNE WELLINGTON
KUALA LUMPUR SINGAPORE JAKARTA HONG KONG TOKYO
DELHI BOMBAY CALCUTTA MADRAS KARACHI
NAIROBI DAR ES SALAAM CAPE TOWN

© *Oxford University Press 1979*

All rights reserved. No part of this publication may be reproduced, stored in a retrieval system, or transmitted, in any form or by any means, electronic, mechanical, photocopying, recording, or otherwise, without the prior permission of Oxford University Press

British Library Cataloguing in Publishing Data

Edgeworth Maria
Maria Edgeworth in France and Switzerland.
1. France—Social life and customs
2. Switzerland—Social life and customs
944.04′6′0924 DQ36 78–41114

ISBN 0–19–812518–6

Set, printed and bound in Great Britain by
Fakenham Press Limited,
Fakenham, Norfolk

PR 4646 .A53 1979b

gl

CONTENTS

Yankee 1980

DISCARDED 428738
William D. McIntyre Library
University of Wisconsin - Eau Claire

LIST OF PLATES

INTRODUCTION

1. *Maria Edgeworth and her Travelling Companions*

THE Irish novelist Maria Edgeworth (1768–1849) landed at Calais in October 1802. She was travelling in a family party with her father, Richard Lovell Edgeworth, her stepmother Frances Anne Edgeworth, and her stepsister Charlotte. The tourists who crossed the Channel in such large numbers after the Peace of Amiens mostly 'hurried about Paris from one *spectacle* to another, saw the opera, and the playhouses, and the masked balls, and the gaming houses, and the women of the Palais Royale [*sic*] and the lions of all sorts; went through the usual routine of presentation and public dinners, drank French wine, damned French cookery, and "came home content"'.[1] Their object was general sightseeing; the English abroad lived with the English and they went little into private French society. There were, of course, exceptions. Some visitors had specialized interests: Samuel Rogers, the banker poet, and the painter Benjamin Farington concentrated on the treasures of art assembled in Paris from the territories conquered by the French; scientists such as James Watt and Sir Charles Blagden were making contacts with the French *savants*; and writers of travel books were busy amassing direct information on post-revolutionary France. The Edgeworths published no book on their experiences, but they went abroad for cultural reasons, seeking 'des échanges de lumières et de talens', not only to see the sights but to frequent French intellectual society.[2] Most of the interest of their letters lies in their account of private life and of the people they met.

This was Maria Edgeworth's first journey to the Continent. Although she had already published what many would consider her best work—the children's stories in *The Parents' Assistant* (1796), the pioneering *Practical Education* (1798), and the regional novel *Castle Rackrent* (1800)—she was hardly, even in Great Britain,

[1] ME's *Leonora*, Letter X (*Tales and Novels* (1833), xiii. 32).

[2] D. J. Garat, *Mémoires de Suard* (1820), ii. 3; M. A. Pictet to RLE, 15 June 1802 (Edgeworth MSS.); M. A. Pictet to RLE, 15 Feb. 1802, and RLE to Pictet, 19 Mar. 1802 (H. W. Haüsermann, *The Genevese Background*, 61, 63).

a literary celebrity. Parts of *The Parents' Assistant* had been published in French in the Genevan periodical *La Bibliothèque Britannique*, extracts from *Practical Education* followed, and a full translation of the latter in book form was published in Paris and Geneva in 1800.[1] *Belinda* (1801) appeared in French in 1802, but although the translator remarked in his preface that nothing was more fashionable than the translation of an English novel, Maria Edgeworth herself reported that the fame of novels came and went very rapidly in Paris.[2] The Edgeworths had good literary introductions but it is unlikely that their works had brought them a wide reputation in France.

R. L. Edgeworth hoped that his eldest daughter, despite her thirty-four years, would find a husband on the Continent. She herself had no such expectation; a Swiss acquaintance described her, a little unkindly, as 'petite, laide, d'une tournure commune, et pâle à l'excès'; she was shy and, although she had been well taught, almost certainly she was not in 1802 the fluent and witty French speaker she later became.[3] Nevertheless Maria Edgeworth did receive her one and only proposal in December 1802. Her suitor was a Swede, Abram Niclas Clewberg Edelcrantz, a royal secretary and Keeper of the King's Privy Purse. He proposed, it seems, after less than a month's acquaintance, much too short a period for him to hope for a favourable reply from a daughter as exclusively devoted to her father as was Maria Edgeworth. Twenty years later she could still be moved to tears by a reference to this episode; it is clear that in retrospect she thought that she had been more in love than he had been, but the family in general did not care much for him and Mrs. Edgeworth considered that he would soon have become jealous of his wife's talents and would have exiled her from the court to live with his old mother in far-off Finland. One may feel some doubt whether she would really have been happy with a man so sharp-tongued,

[1] *Bibliothèque Britannique*, ix–xii (1798–9), xvi (1801) etc.; *Éducation pratique. Traduction libre de l'anglais de Maria Edgeworth par Charles Pictet de Genève* (1800).

[2] *Bélinde. Conte moral de Maria Edgeworth*, trans. Octave de Ségur (1802); *Leonora*, Letter XVIII (*Tales and Novels*, xiii. 56); see below, p. 25 n. 1.

[3] *Deux mois à Paris et à Lyon sous le consulat: Journal de Mme Cazenove d'Arlens*, ed. A. de Cazenove, 44; *Mem.* ii. 78. ME's French in her letters to her family is extremely careless. Letters to outsiders are careful but rather lifeless. Cf. her letters to Mme de Vindé (National Library of Ireland).

who showed so little taste for the home life which mattered so much to her.[1]

When Maria Edgeworth went to France for a second time in 1820 she was herself in charge of the party. Her much loved father, the dominating influence on all his family, had died in 1817, and she was slowly learning to become the initiative power among them. She organized this later visit mainly for the benefit of her two young stepsisters Fanny and Harriet, but also to avoid being at home at the time of the publication of her father's *Memoirs*; she was much more sensitive about his reputation than about her own. Extracts from the *Memoirs* were published in *La Bibliothèque Universelle* (formerly *Britannique*), but on investigation the French booksellers did not feel that a full translation would sell; on the other hand one of them clearly did think that he could sell a new novel by Maria Edgeworth herself.[2] Her stories, observant and witty, looked back to the no longer fashionable tradition of Voltaire and Marmontel, but with their realist social and economic background they also looked forward to the novels of Balzac: in Balzac's *Le Médecin de campagne* the tale of the old soldier resembles *Castle Rackrent* in manner, and the efforts of the doctor to rehabilitate a decaying village can be compared with the work of an improving agent in *The Absentee*.[3] By 1820 versions of all her books except *Castle Rackrent*, written in untranslatable colloquial Irish, had appeared in France and had apparently been popular; if she was not a literary lion, as she had been in England at least since her London visit of 1813, her name seems to have been quite generally known. In England she was much sought after for her conversation and she appears to have been able to convey something of the same 'perfume of wit' in her spoken French. The social success implied in the privately printed

[1] For this episode and for a full account of ME's life and literary career, see Marilyn Butler, *Maria Edgeworth, A Literary Biography*, esp. 192–5. See also ME to her sister Emmeline King, 13 Dec. 1847 (Edgeworth MSS.).

[2] *Bibliothèque Universelle*, xv (1820); and see below, p. 183. For ME's reputation in France, see Devonshire, *The English Novel in France* esp. chap. xiv. A French translation of *Manoeuvring* was nearly sold out in four months: Preface to *Ennui ou mémoires du comte de Glenthorn* (1812).

[3] The translator of ME's *The Modern Griselda* (1807) in *Les Deux Grisélidis* (1813) wrote (p. 9) that the principal merit of ME's stories was to be as little romantic as possible. M. Pierre Artur drew my attention to the resemblance in manner between Castle Rackrent and the tale of the old soldier in *Le Médecin de campagne*.

Memoir of Maria Edgeworth is probably exaggerated[1] and there is little external evidence on the subject; the authors of early-nineteenth-century *Mémoires* and *Souvenirs*, writing retrospectively, do not show much interest in foreign visitors. Nevertheless the Irish authoress and her family clearly had quite as many invitations as they could accept and the world in which they lived gave them plenty of scope for lively description.

Richard Lovell Edgeworth (1744–1817), Maria Edgeworth's father, despite very obvious faults, was the most interesting of his family both in character and intellectual range. He was a prosperous country gentleman from County Longford; half English, half Irish, both by birth and education, he was an improving landlord on good terms with his tenants but less popular with his own class. When he was younger he had been something of a radical, associated with the Irish Volunteer Movement both in its earlier and later, more extreme, phase, and now, in middle age, he had settled down as a liberal Whig who lived in a no man's land between Catholics and Orangemen. His former revolutionary sympathies were less important as a background to the French visit of 1802–3 than the intellectual interests acquired during his residence in England from 1763 to 1782. Soon after he left Oxford, at the time of his first marriage, he had become a member of the Lunar Society of Birmingham, an informal group of men interested in science and in the application of new theoretical discoveries to industrial processes. His chief scientific pursuit was engineering; as early as 1770 he took out a patent for what seems to have been a continuous track vehicle, he wrote *An Essay on the Construction of Roads and Carriages* (1813; French edn. 1827), he has a claim to be considered the real designer of the Macadam road, and with his 'machine for measuring the force exerted by horses in drawing ploughs and waggons and in giving motion to machinery of all kinds' he contributed to the eventual definition of horsepower by his Lunar Society friends Matthew Boulton and James Watt. He also spent much time in developing a semaphore telegraph.[2] Not content with all this, for over thirty years he had carried on educational research; he believed that educational principles

[1] The Edgeworths generally seem to have taken French compliments too literally.

[2] For RLE's scientific interests and achievements, see R. Schofield, *The Lunar Society*, 46–50, 261–2, 276–8, 410–12, etc.

should be deduced empirically from teaching children, rather than from abstract hypotheses. From the experience gathered in teaching his own large family he and his daughter Maria wrote *Practical Education*, published in 1798.

In 1772–3 he had paid his first visit to France and during a stay at Lyons was engaged in an elaborate project to divert the Rhône. He then learned to speak French fluently, with an extensive technical vocabulary which stood him in good stead among the scientific acquaintance he made in 1802–3. R. L. Edgeworth was a very energetic man, both in body and mind. Outside London, and in scientific circles he was generally found to be very lively company. Sydney Smith wrote of him as 'a man of the world and a great rattle; his conversation is very good and very full of information.'[1] But English 'Society' mostly regarded him as an egotistic and pompous bore who stood in the light of his better known daughter. His tendency to exaggerate and his outspokenness got him into trouble in France; in 1803 he was suddenly ordered to leave Paris, and this was not entirely, as he supposed, because of his relationship to the Abbé Edgeworth de Firmont, who had attended Louis XVI on the scaffold, but because of indiscreet talk, possibly criticism of Napoleon's policy towards the Swiss.[2]

Frances Anne Edgeworth (1769–1865), who married R. L. Edgeworth as his fourth wife in 1798, was the daughter of the Revd. D. A. Beaufort, the Irish topographer. Among the writers of the letters in this book she was the only one whose tastes and opinions had not been formed by Edgeworth and she was quite capable of standing up to him in argument even on a subject in which he was a specialist. She had had an excellent education which included some knowledge of science and very good French;[1] she also drew and was well informed about pictures. She was much less

[1] Sydney Smith to Mrs. Hicks Beach, 1 Apr. 1803: unpublished letter in the possession of Professor G. N. Ray, to whom I am indebted for permission to quote.

[2] J. G. Alger, *Napoleon's British Visitors*, 113. Sir John Edgeworth was great-grandfather to both the Abbé and to RLE. For RLE's life, see *Memoirs of* R. L. *Edgeworth* (1820); H. E. and H. J. Butler, *The Black Book of Edgeworthstown*; Marilyn Butler, *Maria Edgeworth*; Desmond Clarke, *The Ingenious Mr. Edgeworth*; Schofield, *Lunar Society*.

[3] Mme Cazenove d'Arlens, *Journal*, 44. Mrs. Edgeworth's grandfather, the Revd. Daniel Cornelis de Beaufort, had been minister to two Huguenot churches in London. In old age he lived with his son, Mrs. E's father.

doctrinaire than her husband and unobtrusively was a great influence on all the family, who had speedily become devoted to their new stepmother. At the time of the visit to France she had two baby daughters, Fanny and Harriet.

Charlotte Edgeworth (1783–1807), the fourth member of the party in 1802–3, was the second daughter of R. L. Edgeworth's third marriage. In 1803 Sydney Smith described her as 'very handsome and engaging'.[1] Her family regarded her as rational and unsentimental. Her sense of humour is apparent in her letters. Mrs. Edgeworth's brother, later Admiral Sir Francis Beaufort, fell in love with her, but she died of consumption when he was away on duty in 1807.

Of the two stepsisters who went to France with Maria Edgeworth in 1820, the elder was *Frances Maria* (*Fanny*, 1799–1848). She was pretty and reserved and apparently not spoilt by the excessive fondness of her eldest sister. When she went to France she had already paid two long visits to England in 1818 and 1819 and had only just recovered from a love affair with Lestock Wilson, whom she eventually married in 1829. Her younger sister *Henrietta* (*Harriet*, 1801–89), who had never before left Ireland, was the most practical and physically the most robust of her family, 'fresh and strong and deedy', as she was once described. Throughout her life her letters had a tart flavour, despite her warm heart, but the sometimes acid comments in the extracts printed below were partly due to a homesickness all the harder to bear because her youngest sister Lucy had been left desperately ill at Edgeworthstown. She married in 1826 the Irish antiquary, the Revd. Richard Butler. She was largely responsible for putting together the *Memoir of Maria Edgeworth*.

II. *The Edgeworths' social life in France and Switzerland*

One of the characters in Maria Edgeworth's *Leonora* (1806) wrote that he had 'had the good fortune to be admitted into the best *private society* in Paris . . . composed of the remains of the French nobility, of men of letters and science, and of families who, without interfering in politics, devote themselves to domestic duties,

[1] Sydney Smith to Mrs. Hicks Beach, 1 Apr. 1803.

to literary and social pleasures.'[1] This may be taken as Maria Edgeworth's own description of the circles in which she and her family spent most of their time in 1802–3, even if it underrates the public distinction of some of their friends.

Shortly after his arrival in Paris at the end of October R. L. Edgeworth met his old Lunar Society friend, the engineer James Watt, who introduced him to a number of people with scientific interests, including the great chemist Berthollet, and Prony, the director of the *École des Ponts et Chaussées*.[2] But the introductions which had the most permanent significance almost all came through the Anglophile Professor Marc Auguste Pictet of Geneva (1752–1825), who had visited Edgeworthstown in 1801. He was one of the editors of *La Bibliothèque Britannique*, a periodical which in this period was contributing much to the maintenance of English literary and scientific connections with the Continent. He was academically and politically one of the most important men in Geneva, then incorporated in France, and it was as a Tribune that he was in Paris in 1802–3. Later he became involved in French academic administration and was able largely to preserve the independence of the Academy of Geneva and to prevent its assimilation to the French system. Pictet was a *grand vulgarisateur* in the best sense; he was a good enough physicist and meteorologist to become an associate of the distinguished and select Society of Arcueil presided over by Berthollet.[3] Maria Edgeworth noted that M. de Serbellane in Mme de Staël's *Delphine* was supposed to be based on Pictet. However the description of a man with a calm and reserved manner and a delicate understanding of the feelings of others bears a greater resemblance to M. A. Pictet's brother, Charles Pictet de Rochemont.[4]

[1] *Leonora*: *Tales and Novels* (1833) xiii. 32; and see below, p. 38.

[2] Berthollet, Montgolfier, and Lavoisier had been acquainted with RLE's Lunar Society friends Boulton and Watt since the 1780s. Berthollet corresponded with Watt: Schofield, *Lunar Society*, 237–8.

[3] For M. A. Pictet, see *inter alia* J. D. Candaux, *Histoire de la famille Pictet*; C. Borgeaud, *L'Université de Genève*, ii; P. Köhler, *Mme de Staël et la Suisse*; M. Crosland, *The Society of Arcueil*; and Haüsermann, *The Genevese Background*.

[4] Paris Notebook; *Delphine* (1803), i. 56–7, Letter vii. In his own copy RLE marked with approval the passage 'un homme qui n'a jamais dit à la fin du jour un seul mot involontaire. Il ne faut pas attribuer cette réserve à aucun sentiment de dissimulation ou de défiance, mais à l'habitude constante de se dominer lui-même et d'observer les autres.'

The most important of Pictet's introductions was to the Delessert family. Étienne Delessert (1735–1816) was Swiss by birth, a banker who, after a period at Lyons (where Edgeworth had met him in 1772–3), had established himself in and near Paris with his bank, textile factory, and sugar refinery. Of his four sons, who shared in his business concerns, Benjamin (1773–1847), was the most distinguished. Like Pictet he was associated with the Society of Arcueil and in 1812 he discovered an economic process for making beet sugar, an invention of special value at that date because of the Continental blockade. He was a shy and reserved man and the Edgeworths preferred François, the second son. Maria Edgeworth's closest friend in France was the daughter, Mme Gautier (d. 1838). The *salons* of Mme Delessert and Mme Gautier both played a large part in the Edgeworths' social life. Mme Delessert was a strict, upright, Swiss Protestant, kindly and perhaps a little old fashioned.[1] Her compatriot Mme Cazenove d'Arlens, describing her hospitality, wrote 'le cercle est un peu noir, le salon antique'; the company however was distinguished. Brusque though her manners might seem, her daughter, the lively Mme Gautier, attracted to her house many of the same people. Her *salon* was frequented by members of the *Institut*, the Assemblies and the *Conseil d'État*, and the top ranks of industry, commerce and banking, as well as by her own countrymen from Geneva; at the time of the Concordat with the Pope she is described as having played the part of 'la providence visible de l'église de Calvin'.[2] Another *salon* with Swiss connections where much the same society was to be found was that of Mme Jacques Bidermann, wife of a wealthy banker and army contractor.[3] And again among the more wealthy of the Edgeworths' friends were M. and

[1] The old duchess in ME's *Leonora* was said to be 'something like Mme Delessert': ME to M. A. Pictet, 23 Sept. 1804 (Haüsermann, op. cit. 68).

[2] For the Delesserts and Mme Gautier, see Mme Cazenove d'Arlens, *Journal*, 44 ff., 55, 96, 107; Borgeaud, op. cit. ii. 140; Crosland, op. cit. 36; A. P. de Candolle, *Mémoires et souvenirs*, 63–7. Mme Gautier and her husband, recently dead, were great friends of Sir Samuel Romilly, who met and became a friend and correspondent of Maria Edgeworth in 1813: *Memoirs of Sir S. Romilly*, ed. Romilly; *The Romilly–Edgeworth Letters*, ed. S. H. Romilly.

[3] Both ME and Étienne Dumont describe boring readings there by Dureau de la Maille. For the *habitués* of the Bidermann *salon*, see Candolle, op. cit. 80–5; MS. Dumont 6, Bibliothèque Universitaire et Publique, Geneva; and ME's Paris Notebook.

Mme Morel de Vindé. M. de Vindé, originally a lawyer, had increased an inherited fortune by shrewd investment in new building in Paris. A man of wide interests in the arts and sciences, he had made a special study of agriculture, on which he wrote a number of papers, and he had also written a *Morale d'enfance* (1790) which ran into many editions. His wife was a singularly agreeable hostess—'no ostentation—no formality; but so easy, and so desirous that everybody round her should enjoy all the advantages of her wealth'.[1]

Not far from the Delesserts lived the Suards and the Pastorets, both eminent in slightly different ways for their hospitality. Mme Pastoret, gay, graceful, and witty, had acted as hostess for her uncle Dupont de l'Étang, in whose house the intellectual society of the *ancien régime* had gone on meeting even during some of the worst days of the Revolution. Her husband, a political moderate, like most of the Edgeworths' friends in 1802–3, and an early member of the *Institut*, became a senator in 1809. Later, after becoming strongly Royalist, he reached the summit of his career in 1829 as Chancellor of France. Mme Pastoret in her early life was *philosophe* in her outlook, but after the Restoration she became pious and Maria Edgeworth was amused to hear someone say 'Autrefois elle avait de l'esprit, mais elle est devenue Ultra [right-wing Royalist], dévote et bête'.[2] In 1801 she had set up a small school for children left at home while their mothers went to work and this is described in Maria Edgeworth's tale *Madame de Fleury*, which was partly written at Paris.[3]

In the same house, on another floor, lived J. B. Suard and his lively wife Amélie, 'aussi académiciens l'un que l'autre'. Suard, editor of *Le Publiciste*, was one of the last survivors of the *philosophe salon* of Mme Geoffrin, and, in very different circumstances,

[1] ME's *Emile de Coulanges: Tales of Fashionable Life* (2nd ser. 1812) v. 31–4 (passage abbreviated in later editions); Frénilly, François Auguste, marquis de, *Souvenirs*, ed. A. Chuquet (1908), 199.

[2] Frénilly, op. cit. 244; *Mem.* ii. 77; *Histoire de mon temps. Mémoires du chancelier Pasquier*, ed. E. A. G., duc d'Audiffret-Pasquier (1893). Though no name is given in the *Memoir* it is clear from Pasquier's account of her that Mme Pastoret must be meant.

[3] ME in the story puts the establishment of the school at the time of the Revolution. 'Fleury' was the name of Mme Pastoret's country house. For a description of Mme Pastoret, see *Madame de Fleury: Tales of Fashionable Life: Tales and Novels* (1833), x. 70.

still personnified its ease and charm. Modest and unambitious and full of common sense, he had early decided not to specialize: 'j'ai suivi mon penchant, j'ai beaucoup joui, et je n'ai rien sacrifié car je ne pouvais pas aspirer à la gloire d'un homme de génie, la seule qui eût pu me tenter.' Though Mme de Genlis wrote slightingly that at the Suards' house 'on dissertait et l'on ne causait point', their *salon* attracted people from all parties and from a number of countries. Suard's British acquaintance included Horace Walpole and Hume, Sterne, Wilkes, and Robertson the historian, whose *History of Charles V* he had translated.[1]

Even more agreeable to the Edgeworths was the Suards' oldest friend, André Morellet, 'le doyen de la littérature française' and 'the most reasonable of all the wits of France'.[2] He too was *philosophe* and he had written articles for the *Encyclopédie*, mostly on theology and metaphysics, as well as government economic pamphlets. He was elected to the *Académie Française* in 1785 and from that date had been concerned with the Academy's *Dictionnaire*, a work on which he was still engaged at the time of his death; he wrote to Maria Edgeworth in 1805 that grammar and etymology had been his favourite pursuits when he was young and they remained his chief enjoyment in old age.[3] The Edgeworths shared his interest both in the nuances of language and in political economy. During the Revolution Morellet had been forced to eke out his income with the badly paid labour of translating English books but his last years were made easy by the pension granted to members of the revived *Institut*, to which he was elected in 1803. Very much a man of the eighteenth century, he had little sympathy with the beginnings of romanticism—he wrote a strong criticism of Chateaubriand's *Atala*. He was said to resemble Voltaire in face though not in figure (he was a large man) and he had Voltaire's 'sourire caustique et plus que malin'. The

[1] Mme de Genlis, *Mémoires*, vi. 205; *Personal Recollections of the Duc de Broglie*, ed. R. de Beaufort, i. 41; A. Steinlein, *Bonstetten*, 243; see also Garat, *Mémoires de Suard*; Amélie Suard, *Essai de mémoires sur M. Suard* (*Bibliothèque de mémoires relatives à l'histoire de France,* N.S. ed. M. de Lescure (1881)), esp. 164; and Frénilly, *Souvenirs*, 140.

[2] ME's *Ormond: Tales and Novels* (1833), xviii. 347.

[3] Morellet to ME, 25 May 1805 (Edgeworth MSS.).

latter had nicknamed him *Mords-les*. In his genial old age however most people agreed on the charm of Morellet's conversation, so full of lively ideas and information.[1]

With these opportunities of access to intellectual French society the Edgeworths were passing their time so enjoyably that in January 1803, before his expulsion from Paris, R. L. Edgeworth was considering taking a house near the Luxembourg gardens and bringing over the rest of his family from Ireland.[2] There were two special attractions. As a Fellow of the Royal Society and a member of the Royal Irish Academy Edgeworth was invited to meetings of the *Institut*, and he was also made a corresponding member of the *Société pour l'encouragement de l'industrie nationale*,[3] which on a wider scale was pursuing the same interests as the Lunar Society to which he had belonged thirty years earlier. Among the active members of this society were Chaptal, the Minister of the Interior, Cuvier of the *Jardin des Plantes*, and Candolle, the Swiss botanist, and its secretary was the Edgeworths' friend Degérando. Edgeworth was also made welcome in the *salon* of Mme Lavoisier, widow of the great chemist who was guillotined in 1794;[4] he was thus meeting some of the best scientific company in Europe. A more general reason for the success of the Edgeworths' visit lay in the pleasure which they took in the art of conversation, in hearing others talk—and in talking themselves. (Long afterwards Harriet Edgeworth wrote of her father's 'over-value' of conversation.) They experienced in 1802–3 'the characteristic charms of Paris conversation, the polish and ease which in its best days distinguished it from that of any other capital'; words were used as enjoyable instruments upon which to play and not merely as a means of communication. The *salon* was not what it had been in the days of the *ancien régime* but it retained some of its former brilliance; Suard and Morellet, *habitués* of the *salon* of Mme

[1] Mme d'Abrantès, *Les Salons de Paris*, 286; Mme de Remusat, *Mémoires*, ed. P. de Rémnsat, i. 216; Frénilly, *Souvenirs*, 26, 39, 198, 215.

[2] The Edgeworths had originally intended no more than a two-months stay and at the New Year still meant to return home by the end of January.

[3] For this society, see Crosland, *The Society of Arcueil*, 179 ff. and Candolle, *Mémoires*, 131–3.

[4] For Mme Lavoisier, see M. Crosland, *Les Héritiers de Lavoisier* (Univ. of Paris, 1967), 24–6.

Geoffrin, still survived, although she herself was long dead.[1] In London in the early nineteenth century, for all the efforts of such hostesses as Lady Davy and Lydia White, with their 'esprit parties', there was no real counterpart of the French *salon*, nor is there to be found in English memoirs and letters of the period that sense of the value of style and elegance in conversation to which the French attached so much importance.[2] Mme de Genlis's comment on the *salon* of the Suards would have been impossible in an English setting. To the end of his life R. L. Edgeworth probably preferred Parisian to London society but his daughter commented that the Parisians were not such good listeners as the English and 'set more value on wit and less upon eloquence in conversation—far from wishing to go—or to see others go to the bottom of any subject in conversation, their motto universally was "*Glissez, mortels, n'appuyez pas*"'.[3] No doubt in the circles she was frequenting in 1802–3 there was not often cause for such a complaint, but the Utilitarian, Étienne Dumont, himself a noted talker, remarked that at Paris wit was treated as an end in itself, whereas in London it was an instrument of reason.[4]

Nevertheless what Harriet Edgeworth later called 'that evaporating lightness' of conversation was the great pleasure of the small parties in the *salons* which the Edgeworths visited in 1802–3. The Revolution had left the literary world and the old aristocracy mostly badly off and large parties and dinners were not much the fashion in Paris. Moreover Maria Edgeworth and her family were not frequenting *le grand monde* as they were to do in London ten years later. They write little of politicians and their friends in general avoided political conversation. But in 1820 to avoid

[1] *Memoirs of RLE* (2nd edn. 1821), 251, 261; ME's *Ormond*: *Tales and Novels* (1833), xviii. 351–5. In 1773 RLE may have visited the *salon* of Mme Geoffrin but the description of pre-revolutionary *salons* in *Ormond* probably owes something to the oral reminiscences of Morellet as well as to RLE's actual experiences; of the four hostesses named on p. 355 one, Mme de Tencin, was dead long before the 1770s, the period in which the novel is set. See also Mme de Staël, *De l'Allemagne* (2nd edn, London, 1813), i, chap. xi, De l'esprit de conversation.

[2] Holland House is the only possible exception, but because Lady Holland was a divorcée, few ladies visited there.

[3] ME to Harriet Beaufort, autumn 1815. The French phrase was inscribed on a print of skaters. Cf. Mme de Staël, *Considérations sur la révolution française* (2nd edn. Paris, 1818), iii. 271: 'L'art d'être aimable en France consistait à ne jamais épuiser un sujet.' See also Marilyn Butler, *Maria Edgeworth*, 207, for RLE's preference for Paris.

[4] Jnl. of E. Dumont, quoted in Köhler, *Mme de Staël et la Suisse*, 279.

politics in Paris was an impossibility. It was agreed by the French themselves as well as by English visitors that the *salons* had deteriorated after the Restoration, largely because of the excessive party spirit which had infected the women. Maria Edgeworth suggested that the political violence of the Parisian *belles* was 'merely to make themselves of consequence and to attract the attention of gentlemen'. Mme de Genlis described the result as 'une assemblée à l'anglaise—les Français dépourvus de politesse, de galanterie et d'agrémens.' 'Nous voici, ma chérie', said Mme de R-ze, 'nous voici toutes, plus enfoncées dans les horreurs de la politique que la chambre des communes et tout le parlement d'Angleterre.'[1] Ultra and liberal *salons* were equally at fault—and the less agreeable to foreigners. When she could, Maria Edgeworth tried to turn the conversation to the safer subjects of science and literature and with her witty talk and her 'happy art of unlocking the heart' she made friends on all sides and even captivated young men of fashion.[2]

Her new friends in Paris in 1820 were many of them Royalists, even from the Ultra party, rather to her sisters' regret; they appreciated the manners of the old nobility but thought poorly of their minds. The Edgeworths owed their acceptance in such circles partly to their distant relationship to the Abbé Edgeworth de Firmont, Louis XVI's confessor; he was a man justly admired for his courage and devotion, but it is difficult to believe that his very clerical Roman Catholic mind would have appealed to the elder branch of his family. None of them had ever met him, but C. S. Edgeworth, Maria's stepbrother, had recently published *Memoirs* of the Abbé and a French translation had gone into three editions.[3] The Edgeworths also benefited from introductions by Harriet, Countess de Salis, daughter of their father's old friend, William

[1] See below, esp. pp. 157–8 and ME's *Helen*, ii. 222–3; Mme de Genlis, *Mémoires*, vii. 10–11; Lady Morgan, *France*, 238. Cf. also ME to Joanna Baillie, 30 Mar. 1821 (Royal Coll. of Surgeons, Hunter Baillie letters): 'Even to shine in the salon they must be politicians and *deep thinkers* à l'anglaise . . . all at the same time talking, no one with common decency even appearing to listen, yet all hearing, Heaven knows how and answering all objections each triumphantly of his own opinion . . .'

[2] *Mem.* ii. 77–9; Lady Lansdowne to Lady H. Frampton in *Journal of Mary Frampton* ed. H. G. Mundy, 152.

[3] *Memoirs of the Abbé Edgeworth* (1815). The Abbé had been confessor to the Princess Elizabeth. In 1794 he was one of the few priests remaining in Paris and the Princess recommended him to her brother the King just before the execution.

Foster, Bishop of Clogher; it was through her that Maria Edgeworth was invited to the grand party of the Duchesse d'Escards at the Tuileries.[1] The letters of 1820, though much more lively than the earlier ones, thus often portray people intrinsically less interesting than those of 1802–3. It is unlikely that R. L. Edgeworth would have been content with so much of this kind of society.

One might suppose from the surviving letters from France that Maria Edgeworth now found her access to the Parisian intellectual world restricted; she no longer had the daily stimulus of her father's scientific and masculine tastes, Marc Auguste Pictet had gone home to Geneva and Morellet and Suard were dead, their style of writing completely out of fashion. This impression is misleading. She continued to meet old friends and made some interesting new acquaintance. In 1822 Harriet Edgeworth felt that she had seen enough to write home to her mother a comparison of London and Paris:

'Dr. Holland says that the French scientific society is pleasanter than the English. We did not see Gay Lussac or La Place so that we are not fair judges but the society at Mrs. Somerville's is more agreeable and much easier than that at Mme Cuvier's . . . I do not think either Mrs. Marcet or Mrs. Somerville polished in their manners but they are so good natured and have so completely the art of assembling and making happy about them all the cleverest people that one does not think of anything but liking it very much but their houses and Mr. Blake's are the best indeed the only very agreeable scientific society meeting places . . . Mme Gautier's dinners would quite bear a comparison with any of these three best meeting places but her dinners should rather be compared to Mrs. Marcets and Mme Lavoisiers to Mr. Blake's and certainly Biot—Prony—Arago—Gallois &c will balance Wollaston—Young—Sharp—Dr. Holland—and Humboldt—Chaptal—Camille Jordan—Garnier—against Warburton—Ricardo—Davy—Kater—Herschel &c &c without taking into account the different value of Mr. Blake Mrs. Marcet &c &c . . .'[2]

It may be noted that in Paris as in London the Edgeworths were more attracted by the scientists, the engineers, and the political economists than by figures of comparable reputation in the strictly 'literary' world.

[1] See below, pp. 112–13. [2] Harriet E to Mrs. E from London, 26 May 1822.

The surviving letters written from Paris describe a largely feminine society. After Maria Edgeworth and her sisters moved on to Switzerland in July the reverse is true. Moreover they now travelled about, making tours in French Switzerland, although they based themselves at Pregny, just outside Geneva. This was the home of their friends John Lewis Moilliet and his wife Amelia, daughter of the Lunar Society chemist James Keir. J. L. Moilliet, like his neighbour Dr. Alexander Marcet at Malagny and a number of other Swiss at this period, had made a career for himself in England, but after the Napoleonic wars were over he renewed his connection with his native town.[1] Harriet Edgeworth (Mrs. R. Butler) wrote many years later

> This was the Augustan age of Geneva. An unusual number of distinguished persons were living there at this period, and the mixture of English residents with passing foreigners from all parts of the world gave a piquancy to the reunions, which were sometimes in the freshness of the morning, breakfasts at different country houses, sometimes by moonlight on lawns sloping down to the shore of the lake . . . sometimes in the town houses of the Genevan residents.[2]

This appreciative description of course conveys only one side of the picture. Maria Edgeworth's critical faculties were not extinguished by her genuine pleasure in her new surroundings; she would probably have agreed with Mme de Staël who talked of Geneva as a place like a beehive where everyone made his cell exactly like everyone else's;[3] she found it a little limited—except when in the company of such men as Marc Auguste Pictet and his brother, Dumont, Candolle and other former *habitués* of Mme de Staël's house at Coppet.

Étienne Dumont was an old friend. He was a Genevan by birth, but had an influential career in three countries: in France as coadjutor of Mirabeau, in England as librarian to the first Lord Lansdowne, tutor to the third Lord and friend of all the Whig reformers, men such as Romilly and Mackintosh; finally he spent his last years in Geneva in public life, working for the establishment of utilitarian ideas there. For it is as a disciple of Bentham and the

[1] For the Moilliets, see *Letters from England*, xviii.

[2] *Mem.* ii. 122; cf. *Souvenirs du baron de Barante*, 158; Candolle, *Mémoires*, 402.

[3] Köhler, *Mme de Staël et la Suisse*, 371; Candolle, op. cit. 401.

popularizer of his theories on the Continent that his name is to be remembered.[1] Maria Edgeworth had first met him, briefly, in Paris in 1802, then in England in 1813 and 1818–19, and they had corresponded since 1807.[2] 'His society, always agreeable, was more than ever delightful at Geneva. He was proud of his country, enthusiastic in his taste for the fine scenery.' With his wit and his fund of literary anecdote he was excellent company and was particularly kind to the young; the tour which he went with the Edgeworths was the most enjoyable episode in their acquaintance.[3]

Perhaps the most interesting visit which Maria Edgeworth paid in Switzerland was to Coppet, which was still for her pervaded by the spirit of its dead owner, Mme de Staël. Mme de Staël was one of the most conspicuous literary personalities of the early 1800s, a forerunner of romanticism and, in her time, an important political influence. From the period of their first French visit until after the second her name frequently recurs in the Edgeworth correspondence. Egotistic, indiscreet in her loves and apt to seem meddlesome in affairs of state, Mme de Staël and her sayings and doings were a gift to the raconteur; she provided a great fund of good stories for her contemporaries. The Edgeworths collected them, perhaps a little maliciously sometimes and with a slight sense of rivalry; she was a greater lion than Maria, but, to be fair to the Edgeworths, they respected her genius; they sympathized with her political ideas, liberal but not radical, and they shared her interest in differences of national character and background, even if her emphasis on the emotions was alien to their more rational *philosophe* point of view. Mme de Staël had been even better as a talker than as a writer, but she languished without the stimulus of other clever people, '*une existence de représentation et de gloire*'; '*la solitude, me disait-elle un jour, est l'antichambre de la mort*', wrote

[1] See Jean Martin, *Étienne Dumont.* Bentham's theories made little impact in France and Dumont wrote to ME that 3,000 copies of his *Traités de législation civile et pénale* (1802) had been sold, almost all in Russia, Spain, and Portugal, but hardly any in France: Dumont to RLE, 4 Oct. 1806 (Bentham MSS., University College London).

[2] See below, 23; Maria Edgeworth, *Letters from England*, ed. C. Colvin, 49–50, 68–9, 83–4, 88–91, 93–4, 97, 116; Haüsermann, op. cit. 49–60, 93, 103–13, 116–9, 125–34, 137–52; *Dublin Review* cxlv (1909). Dumont's letters to ME are among the Bentham MSS at University College, London.

[3] *Mem.* ii. 123; Candolle, op. cit. 402.

Dumont.[1] Coppet, three years after her death, was owned by her son Auguste. There and elsewhere in Switzerland the Edgeworths met or discussed many of those who had enjoyed the generous warmth of her character and reflected back the brilliance of her conversation. Among them were Constant, her lover, and A. W. Schlegel, the German Romantic critic and tutor to her children, Candolle the botanist, her companion Fanny Randall, and her cousin and biographer Mme Necker de Saussure, together with the dry and reserved historian Sismondi and the amiable intellectual butterfly Charles Victor de Bonstetten, known in England for his connexion with Thomas Gray. Characteristically too Maria Edgeworth took an interest in the 8-year old Rocca, Mme de Staël's youngest child.

French scenes, French ideas, and French people are integral to the plots of four of the tales which Maria Edgeworth wrote between her two visits abroad—*Leonora, Madame de Fleury, Émilie de Coulanges*, and *Ormond*—and all four provide information about French social life supplementary to that given in the letters. Paris and Switzerland in 1820 left no such trace on her writing. There are a few Swiss and French references in the chapters of the three children's books, *Rosamond. A Sequel, Frank. A Sequel* and *Harry and Lucy Concluded.* In *Helen* there are a comment on the Paris Restoration *salons*, tantalizingly brief glimpses of Dumont, and a few minor references. But these are merely incidental. It is true that Maria Edgeworth published much less in the last twenty-nine years of her life than she had between 1800 and 1820, but she had always some literary project on hand and she made good use of the material gathered on her visits to England. In 1820 Paris and Switzerland did not provide the same literary stimulus and the letters of the second foreign visit are to be read for their own sake as pictures of people and manners, not for clues to her literary career.

III. *The letters*

'My mind has been so full of these letters since I have had them that I feel as if living in another world—a thousand times more interesting than any novel.' These words were written by Honora

[1] Dumont to ME, 20 Oct., 10 Dec. 1812 (Bentham MSS., U.C.L.).

Edgeworth in 1829, and about another Edgeworth,[1] but the sentiments in them were echoed by those who in 1867 were given copies of the privately printed *Memoir of Maria Edgeworth*.[2] Particular features singled out for praise were the letter of 1833 from Connemara,[3] that to Mrs. Stark outlining Maria Edgeworth's methods of writing,[4] and the letters from France. The Edgeworths themselves set a special value on the letters written away from Ireland: Honora Edgeworth in a note supplementary to her will directed that all her correspondence should be destroyed *except* the letters written by her eldest sister and her companions from France and from Scotland.[5] The letters covering the continental tours (and the Scotch tour) were filed by Harriet and Lucy Edgeworth separately from the annual folders in which they arranged the rest of their sister's letters.

In 1802–3, at the time of the first Paris visit, Maria Edgeworth's relations had hardly yet formed the habit of keeping all her letters. Relatively few of those from France survived and the editors of the *Memoir* made use of the letters of her travelling companions to fill out the tale. Similarly, although there was no lack of Maria Edgeworth's own letters, they completed the picture of the 1820 visit through the memories of Harriet, which she refreshed by reading her own letters of the period. The letters which the family wrote when they were abroad were in fact meant to be read as a series; no one person told the whole story and there is not much repetition. The tone and subject of the letters were of course varied to suit the addressee—Maria Edgeworth's letters to her Sneyd aunts in particular are pervaded by sentiment—but the whole collection was passed round the households at Edgeworthstown, at Black Castle, where R. L. Edgeworth's sister lived, and

[1] Honora E to Fanny E (Mrs. Wilson), 17 June 1829. The letters were from RLE's second wife to Mrs. Powys, and had been returned to the family after the latter's death in 1829. They no longer survive.

[2] Notebook of 1867 containing copies of letters of thanks for gifts of the *Memoir*.

[3] Published in full in *Tour in Connemara*, ed. H. E. Butler. The version in the *Memoir* is much abbreviated.

[4] *Mem.* iii. 147–60.

[5] An analysis of the surviving portion of the letters from ME to her sister Harriet shows that the latter destroyed almost everything except letters written away from Ireland and letters about authorship. In a letter of 15 Dec. 1832 Harriet wrote that she had in that year received thirty-seven full-length letters from her sister, not counting notes. Of these five survive; all but one concern *Helen*.

often also at Collon, where Mrs. Edgeworth's father D. A. Beaufort was vicar. To put together this book I have used the whole body of surviving letters. This not only provides a closer look at Maria Edgeworth's family, who had so strong an influence on her life and on her books, but also a more stereoscopic view of what happened.

As a letter writer Maria Edgeworth was obliged to start early; she was sent to boarding school when she was seven years old and her first surviving letter, of 30 March 1776, was only too clearly written under instruction.[1] Her father commented in 1778 'your last letter appeared to me more *en fille d'École* than your former letters—Indeed it is impossible to write without having something to say: at least it ought to be impossible.'[2] When the family settled down in Ireland in 1782, Maria Edgeworth, writing to a school friend, found much more to talk about. She was reading a very solid quantity of English and French literature and she had begun to make translations and to write plays and stories. Among the books she read were the *Letters* of Pope and Gray: 'What easy sprightly letters Greys [*sic*] are . . . they are not the stiff performance of an author written under the rod of Criticism and under the Presentiment that they would be published . . . All that I have ever seen of Pope's gave me that idea, the Style is too correct to be free, and the Wit is too labored to be pleasing . . .'[3] Maria Edgeworth's own letters improved immediately and thereafter right into her middle age their style owes a great deal to Gray, and perhaps to Mme de Sévigné, whom she also read with admiration. Indeed when compared with the spontaneous outpourings of her later life her family letters round the turn of the century seem charming and well-organized literary exercises, a sophisticated and much better version of the sort of thing which her sister Charlotte wrote from Paris. But such a style of writing is only possible when the writer has leisure and does not burden herself with a superfluity of facts to communicate, 'the things of most value to friends at a distance'. In Paris the family left much of the task of chronicler to 'Maria's superior powers' and she was obviously cramped by too little time for writing, too many tales to tell, and the need

[1] Marilyn Butler, *Maria Edgeworth*, 52.
[2] Ibid. 57.
[3] Ibid. 154.

to compress what she had to say on to too little paper (to save the cost of postage). Her letters are hardly expanded from her partially extant 'notes pour servir à l'histoire'[1] and have virtually no literary form. The best letter which she wrote on France in 1802–3 is that about Mme de Genlis[2] which, significantly, was composed during the leisure of her homeward journey. What she might have written if she had had more time can be seen in the lively accounts of Parisian society given in the letters of Mme de P— in the otherwise rather tiresome novel *Leonora* (1806).[3]

In the years which followed, Maria Edgeworth's style in writing to her family became gradually modified and the unconstrained and lively letters written in 1820 are a complete contrast to those of 1802–3. The reasons for the change are probably complex. Between 1800 and 1820 she was deeply involved in the education of the younger members of the family and in the management of the family estate, as well as in authorship, and she had less time to polish. She probably also felt less need to do so. As she reached the height of her career as a novelist she grew more fluent and confident in expressing herself. Moreover the bulk of her correspondence came to be not so much with the more formal older generation as with her own contemporaries and juniors. The fashion in letterwriting had been changing over the years. The 'artless and natural' ease of Gray's letters may have come to seem a little studied to the authors of the early nineteenth century, few of whom wrote to their family and friends at all in this manner. Her contemporary Étienne Dumont remarked 'l'âme de ce talent, c'est la facilité, l'abandon, écrire vite, avec confiance, servir tout chaud.'[4] Even in the eighteenth century, among Maria Edgeworth's immediate relations no one except her sister Charlotte and Dr. Beaufort made a conscious effort at epistolary elegance and some years before 1820 she indulged herself by abandoning it for something nearer the 'Irish freedom of manner' which she displayed in conversation.[5]

The folder of surviving letters from the 1802–3 visit now con-

[1] Paris Notebook.

[2] See below, pp. 96–102.

[3] *Leonora*: *Tales and Novels* (1833), xiii, 56–61, etc.

[4] Dumont to ME, 6 Sept. 1813 (Bentham MSS., U.C.L.).

[5] *Letters of Lady Louisa Stuart to Miss Louisa Clinton*, ed. J. A. Home, 1st ser., i. 251.

tains under thirty letters or fragments written by R. L. Edgeworth and Mrs. Edgeworth, Maria, and Charlotte. From the contents of Maria Edgeworth's notebook and from internal evidence it is clear that the series is by no means complete and many of the letters, closely written, faded, and occasionally crossed, on very large thin foolscap sheets, were already in bad condition by the mid-nineteenth century. The file for 1820 is much larger; it contains seventy letters or fragments of letters from Maria, Fanny, and Harriet Edgeworth. Both for 1802–3 and for 1820 the editors of the *Memoir* used a few letters now missing, but there are today further letters, not available to them, which have come in from other family collections. Less than half what is printed below has been published before.

Throughout the *Memoir* Harriet Edgeworth (Mrs. R. Butler) altered and embellished the texts—with considerable taste. To her Mason's *Life and Letters of Gray* still provided a standard. The Maria Edgeworth of the *Memoir* wrote more correct and graceful English, but her style lacked the sharp edge and vigour of the original letters[1] and many details of everyday life, now of historical interest, were naturally omitted as commonplace. Correction of some kind was reasonable; the letters were written with that 'happy negligence more attractive than accuracy' and the personal names were only too frequently wrongly spelt to the point of concealing identity. Like the earlier editors I have put the latter right where possible[2] and for ease of reading I have omitted some of the dashes used as punctuation and substituted full stops for others. I have also made corrections in the use of inverted commas and have broken up overlong sections of text into fresh paragraphs; Maria Edgeworth's use of paragraphs in her letters has little significance. Any conjectural or restored parts of the text are indicated by square brackets. The Edgeworths' spelling was not entirely standardized: they might for example write 'honor' or 'honour', 'salon' or 'sallon', 'conceive' or 'concieve'. Obvious slips of the pen both in French and English have been corrected but consistent and idiosyncratic spellings have been left

[1] Compare particularly the description of the party at the Collège de France on pp. 124–9 below with that given in *Mem.* ii. 58–60.

[2] Russian and Polish names, often misheard by the Edgeworths, have been standardized in the French form of their day.

unaltered. Empty square brackets indicate illegible words or gaps in the manuscript.

IV. *The Edgeworths' family correspondents*

Henry Edgeworth (1782–1813), R. L. Edgeworth's eldest son by his third wife, Elizabeth Sneyd. In 1802–3 he was in Edinburgh, studying medicine. He died of consumption after a lingering illness.

Charles Sneyd Edgeworth (1786–1864), R. L. Edgeworth's second son by Elizabeth Sneyd. He married in 1813 Henrica Broadhurst (Harriette). He became a lawyer but abandoned his profession after the death of his father in 1817. Thereafter he and his wife spent much of their time moving about England and the Continent in search of health. With Maria Edgeworth's help he published in 1815 *Memoirs of the Abbé Edgeworth*.

Honora Edgeworth (1791–1857), youngest daughter of R. L. Edgeworth and Elizabeth Sneyd. She married in 1838 Captain (later Admiral Sir) Francis Beaufort, brother of Mrs. Frances Edgeworth.

Lucy Jane Edgeworth (1805–1897), fourth daughter of R. L. Edgeworth by his fourth wife, Frances Anne Beaufort. For many years she suffered from a spinal complaint, but eventually recovered and married in 1843 Dr. Thomas Romney Robinson, F.R.S., of Armagh Observatory.

Mrs. Emmeline King (1770–1847), second daughter of R. L. Edgeworth by his first wife, Anna Maria Elers. She married in 1802 John King or König of Clifton, a surgeon from Berne who was assistant to her brother in law, Dr. Thomas Beddoes of the Pneumatic Institution, Clifton.

Mrs. Margaret Ruxton (1746–1830), sister of R. L. Edgeworth and wife of John Ruxton of Black Castle, near Navan. She stood almost in the relation of a mother to Maria Edgeworth, who was devoted to her.

Sophy Ruxton (1776–1837), elder daughter of Margaret and John Ruxton. She was Maria Edgeworth's closest friend and literary confidante outside Edgeworthstown.

Mary (1750–1841) and *Charlotte Sneyd* (1754–1822), sisters of Honora and Elizabeth Sneyd, third and fourth wives of R. L. Edgeworth. They lived at Edgeworthstown until the death of R. L. Edgeworth and intermittently after it. In 1802–3 they were being responsible for the Edgeworthstown household while R. L. Edgeworth and his wife were away.

The Revd. Daniel Augustus Beaufort (1734–1821), father of Mrs. Frances Anne Edgeworth. He was vicar of Collon and a distinguished Irish geographer.

Henrietta (*Harriet*) *Beaufort* (1778–1865), second daughter of D. A. Beaufort. She was the author of *Dialogues on Botany* (1819).

Louisa Catherine Beaufort (1791–1867), youngest daughter of D. A. Beaufort. She was author of an essay on the Round Towers of Ireland for which she was elected a member of the Royal Irish Academy.

Captain (*later Admiral Sir*) *Francis Beaufort* (1774–1857), younger son of D. A. Beaufort. He married as his second wife Honora Edgeworth. He was the author of *Karamania* (1817), a work written as a result of a survey of the coast of Asia Minor for the Admiralty. He later became Hydrographer to the Navy.

Elizabeth Waller (*Aunt Bess*) (d. 1835), sister of Mrs. D. A. Beaufort
For other members of the Edgeworth family, see Index.

v. *Acknowledgements*

My acknowledgements are first due to the writers of these letters for all the pleasure which they have given to me in making their acquaintance and that of the rest of their family. The Edgeworth family correspondence for the period up to 1817 is for the most part in the National Library of Ireland; the letters for the later period are in my possession. The National Library of Ireland kindly lent their collection to the Bodleian Library for me to use and the Huntington Library, California, was so good as to provide me with xeroxes of letters from Maria Edgeworth to Francis Beaufort. Miss Joan Gibbons most generously gave me letters written by Charlotte and Maria Edgeworth to Emmeline King (née Edgeworth).

The Edgeworth had a large diversity of interests and many people have patiently endured my questions and given me information for footnotes. Dr. T. H. Levere and Dr. G. L.'E. Turner have been particularly helpful over scientific problems and I should like also to thank Mrs. J. Alton, M. P. E. Artur, Mr. Giles Barber, Dr. Alan Bell, Dr. D. Bickerton, Mrs. L. Burnett, M. J. D. Candaux, Professor M. Crosland, Professor H. W. Donner, Dr. G. F. Ellis, Professor F. Haskell, Dr. M. C. Hurst, Mr. A. F. Martin, the late Dr. W. G. Moore, the Museum of Costume, Bath, Mr. W. O'Sullivan, Professor G. N. Ray, the Vicomte de Roquefeuil, Mrs. N. Selwyn, Mr. J. S. G. Simmons, Dr. R. Shackleton, Professor Paul Viallaneix, Dr. C. Westropp, Dr. H. Zawadzki, and the staff of the Bodleian Library and the library of the Taylor Institution.

My greatest debt is to Marilyn Butler and to members of my family who have throughout encouraged me and provided me with useful information of all kinds. Without their help this book could not have been produced.

VI. *Abbreviations*

E	Edgeworth
ME	Maria Edgeworth
RLE	Richard Lovell Edgeworth
Mem.	*A Memoir of Maria Edgeworth*, ed. Mrs. Edgeworth (privately printed, 1867)
Memoirs of RLE	*Memoirs of* R. L. *Edgeworth* (2nd edn. 1821)
Letters from England	*Maria Edgeworth: Letters from England*, ed. Christina Colvin (1972)
Paris Notebook	Maria Edgeworth's MS. notes of her Paris visit of 1802–3

References to Maria Edgeworth's novels are taken, where possible, from the 1833 Collected Edition.

1i Mrs Frances Edgeworth, from a pastel by Adam Buck, 1798

1ii Charlotte Edgeworth, from a water-colour by Adam Buck, 1787

1iii Maria Edgeworth, taken from the 1787 water-colour of the Edgeworth family by Adam Buck

FRANCE AND THE LOW COUNTRIES, 1802–1803

Maria Edgeworth to Sophy Ruxton

Brussels, 15th October, 1802

After admiring on the ramparts of Calais the Poissardes with their picturesque nets ugly faces and beautiful legs we set out for Gravelines with whips cracking in a manner which you certainly cannot forget. The stillness and desolation of the town of Gravelines can be compared only to that of the city in the Arabian [tales] where everybody was found turned into stone.[1] We had no amusement here except looking at the landlords pretty daughter and the fortifications, demilunes and curtains constructed by the celebrated Vauban—All which did not prevent the French from trotting through it.[2] The sight of little English gardens behind many of the houses in Gravelines excited my foolish wonder till my mother observed that all our English gardening was originally brought from Flanders. We left Gravelines in an equipage at which Sobriety herself could not have forborne to laugh. To our London coach were fastened by long rope traces 6 Flemish horses of different heights but each large and clumsy enough to draw an English cart or waggon; the nose of the foremost horse was thirty five feet from the body of the coach—their hoofs all shagged, their manes all uncombed and their tails all long enough to please Sir Charles Grandison himself.[3] These

Note. Identifications and biographical details of persons of importance to the narrative will generally be found in the Index.

[1] The story of Zobeide: *Arabian Nights Entertainments*; translated from the French of M. Gailland (London, 1785), 101 (Night lxiii).

[2] Demilune, a crescent-shaped outwork protecting a bastion or curtain wall. Curtain, the part of a wall connecting two bastions, towers, gates, etc.

[3] Richardson, *Sir Charles Grandison* (Shakespeare Head Press, 1931), i. 278 (Letter 36). The tails of Sir Charles's horses were not docked, but tied up when they were on the road. French post-horses, postillions, and posting arrangements regularly astonished English travellers (e.g. W. Shepherd, *Paris in 1802 and 1814*, 22, 28). There is an illustration of a top-booted French postillion in W. Roots, *Paris in 1814*, pl. III.

beasts were totally disencumbered of every sort of harness except one strap which fastened a saddle round their backs. High—high! upon their backs sat perfectly perpendicular two long waisted postillions in jack-boots and with pipes in their mouths.

The road from Gravelines to Dunkirk is through as ugly a country as you would wish to see. It appeared one vast flat common, without hedges or ditches or trees—tiled farm houses of equal size and similar form at even distances. All that the power of monotony can do to put a traveller to sleep is here tried, but the rattling and jolting on the paved road set Morpheus and Monotony both at defiance. To comfort ourselves we had a most entertaining 'Voyage par M. Breton dans les pays bas' to read and the charming story of Mlle Clermont from Mme de Genlis Petits Romans.[1] I never read a more pathetic and finely written tale.

Dunkirk is an ugly bustling town—strange looking *charrettes* driven by thin men in cocked hats—rope traces of course and horses at an immense distance from the carts—The window shutters of the shops turned out to the street and painted by way of signs with various commodities. A variety of things, amongst them little shirts and petticoats and corsets were fairly spread upon the ground on the bridges and in the streets. We stayed a whole day in Dunkirk to see all that was worth seeing; but that proved to be very little. The famous bason of Dunkirk,[2] about which there have been such disputes is not more worth disputing about than most of the other grand objects for which men cut one anothers throats. Voltaire once expressed his surprise at the French and English having waged war with each other for a few acres of snow (Canada).[3] He might with equal propriety have laughed at them for making war in a slop-bason. The pont-tournant[4] at Dunkirk is very well worth seeing and for those who have strong knees and have breakfasted it is worth while to climb the 264 steps of the

[1] J. B. J. Breton, *Voyage dans la ci-devant Belgique et sur la vive gauche du Rhin* (1802); Mme de Genlis, *Mademoiselle de Clermont* (*Petits Romans*, 1802).

[2] The harbour built in 1663 after Charles II had sold Dunkirk to the French. It was then intended to hold thirty ships of war, the beginning of the revival of the French navy: Voltaire, *Siècle de Louis XIV*, chap. vii. ME had been re-reading Voltaire just before her departure for France.

[3] *Candide*, chap. xxiii: 'ces deux nations sont en guerre pour quelques arpents de neige vers le Canada . . . elles dépensent pour cette belle guerre plus que tout le Canada ne vaut.'

[4] A bridge that can be withdrawn along one bank by being turned on a pivot.

tower. Whilst we were climbing, the town-clock struck and the whole tower vibrated and the vibration was communicated to our ears and heads in a most sublime and disagreeable manner—If anything that is sublime can be disagreeable. At the top of the tower we found a small room inhabited by the keeper—an old man in a dusty cocked hat. Over his chimney was pasted an arrêt interesting to us, as it discovered a similarity of fortune between him and my father. At the time of the English invasion this poor man was accused of having illuminated the tower and of having hung out lights to betray it to the enemy. Upon his trial it was proved that he had but a single candle in a lantern during the whole night—So Jean Baptiste Garcia and his son Louis Garcia were honorably acquitted. In times of popular commotion the mob is the same in all countries.[1]

We went to the play at Dunkirk. The playhouse was about as good as most of the playhouses in country towns in England but it was wretchedly lighted and not a tenth part filled. Two of the comic actors were good—The company all looked like rag-muffins or worse. A municipal officer who sat behind me and who looked as if his face and linen had been rubbed against a coalman's sack entered into conversation with me mistaking me for *Madame* as I looked so much the oldest of the party. 'Ah Madame il faut que je vous fasse voir une de nos jolies femmes de Dunquerque. Comment la trouvez-vous?' 'Mais . . . plutôt belle que jolie.' 'Eh—voilà une jolie femme—celle qui a la rose à sa coiffure.' 'Qui est-elle?' 'Ah Madame—c'est une femme du monde.'[2] As I looked stupid I suppose my municipal officer was determined to explain himself better and added 'C'est une femme publique—Et voilà une autre qui entre. (After a long pause) Madame a-t-elle jamais été à Paris?' 'Non Monsieur jamais.' 'Ah! Est-il possible?' Then I was no longer worth talking to.

At Dunkirk we entered what was formerly called Austrian Flanders or l'ancien Brabant. All things and persons began to look like Dutch prints and Dutch toys painted exactly in their proper colors; especially the women with their drop ear rings and

[1] See *Mems. of RLE* (1821 edn.) ii. 204–5. In 1798 RLE was supposed by an Irish mob to have illuminated Longford gaol as a signal to the French invaders. The Duke of York with British, Hanoverian, and Dutch troops had attempted to capture Dunkirk in the summer of 1793.

[2] Prostitute.

their necklaces like the labels of decanters and their long waisted, long flapped jackets of one color, and stiff petticoats of another. Even when moving the people looked like wooden toys set in motion by strings. The strings in Flanders must be of gold. The Flemings seem to be all a money-making money-loving people. They are just recovering their activity after the revolution. 'Ah Monsieur' said a man 'nous avions . . . Mais tout ce que nous avions qui valoit la peine de voir nous a été ravi—tous nos beaux tableaux sont à Paris!'[1] Paris seems to be the spoilt child of the revolution.

But we must not stay any longer making reflections at the ugly town of Dunkirk; we must go on to Bruges. The road 50 feet broad and solidly paved in the middle seems like all the French and Flemish roads to have been laid out by some inflexible mathematician. They are always right lines—the shortest possible between two points. The rows of trees on each side of these never ending avenues are of the ugliest sort and figure possible—tall poplars tripped almost to the tops as you might strip a pen; and pollarded sallies;[2] the giant poplar and dwarf sally placed side by side alternately—knight and squire. Between Dunkirk and Bruges we stopped at some post houses to change horses. The postmasters are kept in good order by the government—obliged to furnish horses always at a fixed price. The postillions have all badges like the badges in our charity schools strapped round their arms. They are numbered and registered and if they behave ill a complaint may be lodged against them merely by writing their names on the register which excludes them from a pension to which they would be entitled by the law if they behaved well for a certain number of years. Since I wrote this the postillions told us that the pension though promised is never paid—It is impossible to satisfy them. The maisons des postes are often lone wretched houses; in one of them I peeped into a grenier just like that described by Smollett in which the murdered mans body was concealed in the corner under a heap of straw.[3] At another post house we met with a woman calling herself a *servante* to whom we

[1] For an account of the removal of the Belgian pictures, see C. Gould, *Trophy of Conquest*, chap. ii.

[2] Willow trees.

[3] Smollett, *Travels through France and Italy* (1766), Letter xxxiv.

took not only an aversion, but a *horror*. Charlotte said that if she was to sleep in the room alone with this woman she should be afraid, not that she would cut her throat, but that she would take a mallet and hammer her head flat at one stroke. Do you remember the woman described in Caleb Williams—he wakens and sees her standing over him with an uplifted hatchet.[1] Our *Servante* might have stood for this picture.

Bruges is a very old desolate looking town which seems to have felt in common with its fellow towns the consequences of the revolution. As we had been charged very high at the Hôtel d'Angleterre at Dunkirk my father determined to go to the Hôtel de Commerce instead of l'hôtel d'Angleterre at Bruges. The Hôtel de Commerce is an old strange house which had been a monastery; the man-chambermaid led us through gallery after gallery upstairs and downstairs and turning to the right and left and all manner of ways [ ] bunch of keys in his hand, each key ticketted with a pewter ticket corresponding to the number of the bedchambers. There were 28 bedchambers—Thank heaven we did not see them all. I shall never forget the feeling I had when the door of the room in which we were to sleep was thrown [open]. It was so large and so dark that I could scarcely see the bed in a recess in the wall covered with a dark brown quilt. I am sure Mrs. Radcliffe might have kept her heroine wandering about this house for six good pages. If Margaret will put me in mind when we meet I will tell her more about the night we spent in this [room] and the footsteps we heard [overhead] in the g[arret] &c &c. It was just a house and just a night [to suit] Margarets taste [ ].[2]

In the morning we went to see the Central school.[3] It is in [an] old monastery and the church belonging to the monastery is

[1] William Godwin, *Caleb Williams* (OEN 1970), 231 (vol. iii, chap. iv).

[2] ME refers to Ann Radcliffe, author of *The Mysteries of Udolpho* (1794) and other 'cavernous, cadaverous tales'. Margaret was the younger daughter of ME's aunt, Mrs. John Ruxton. Some of their clothes were stolen from their room during the night: Charlotte E to Sneyd E from Brussels, 20 Oct. 1802, National Library of Scotland MS. 2722.

[3] Under a law of 1795 Central Schools were to be set up in every department to provide secondary education. Few were very successful and they were replaced under Napoleon by the *lycées* which gave a more traditional and disciplined education. For RLE's later views on Central Schools, see his *Essays on Professional Education* (2nd edn. 1812), 32–3.

[filled] with pictures collected from all the suppressed convents, monasteries and churches. Bonaparte has lately restored some of their pictures to the churches; but those of Rubens and Raphael are at Paris. The pictures in this church were all in confusion and the best thing I learnt was that John de Bruges[1] a native of this town is said to be the inventor of oil painting. The chambre de physique contained a good electrical apparatus[2] and an air pump, but no other machines of any consequence, in the cabinet of natural history there is a tolerably good number of stuffed birds and beasts considering that they have set about stuffing only within these two years—and there is a skeleton of a man who had been guillotined and the skin of a man who was guillotined—as fine thick white leather as ever you saw. If this secret were generally known I believe some men would literally go to war for one anothers skins. There is a good chambre à dessein at the École Centrale at Bruges where we saw *two* scholars drawing from antique busts and statues. There may be a pretty botanic garden for anything I can tell to the contrary; but it rained so hard that I could take only a vue d'oiseau of it from the upper windows. The preparations at all these écoles centrales which I have seen seem too vast and ostentatious. The people are just *beginning* to send their children to them. They are found too expensive and their number is to be diminished. The librarian of the École centrale at Bruges is an Englishman or rather a Jamaica-man of the name of Edwards. Bryan Edwards was his great friend and he was well acquainted with Johnson the bookseller, Dr. Aikin and Mr. and Mrs. Barbauld. He lived formerly at Warrington and it was at his house that Mr. Barbauld paid his addresses to Mrs. B. It was extremely agreeable to meet with people at such a distance from home who knew our friends so well. Old Mr. Edwards and his eldest son had often met Lovell at Johnson's[3] when they were in London about 3 years ago—they spoke of him quite with affection. The eldest son I think is something of a pedant but clever and the youngest, if I had a mind to flatter him very much, I might say

[1] Van Eyck.

[2] This consisted of a glass cylinder which was rotated against a silk cushion. It was connected at one end with a brass knob to which a chain was fastened leading to batteries.

[3] Lovell Edgeworth was RLE's eldest surviving son. Joseph Johnson was the Edgeworths' publisher.

was in his manner something like Henry.[1] The two sons spent the evening with us and they and their father, who is the most pleasing of the trio, accompanied us next morning part of our way to Ghent.

We went by the canal in a *barque* as elegant as any pleasure-boat that ever adorned the Thames. My father entertained the Edwards's with the history of his physiognomical guesses in a stage coach, by which he discovered the auctioneer, housekeeper &c &c.[2] The eldest son, like your Dr. in the county of Meath, piques himself upon telling characters by the hand-writing. He was positive my handwriting could not be that of a woman and then he came off by saying it was only the writing of a manly character—further still from the truth. We had an extremely fine day and the receding prospect of Bruges with its mingled spires, shipping and Windmills with the top of their giant arms moving above the trees gave us a pleasing example of Flemish landscape. Both the landscapes and the people in this country recalled the pictures of Teniers and the prints of Le Bas. We had good and agreeable company on board our Barque—the Mayor of Bruges and his lady—another frenchwoman of good family—and an old Baron de Triest of a sixteen-quartering-family. At the name of Mayor of Bruges probably you represent to yourself a fat, heavy, formal self-sufficient mortal, tout au contraire—M. Serret our Mayor was a thin gentleman of easy manners, literature, and amusing conversation—*Madame*—a Beauté de Province rather coquettish, intent upon pulling the black lace border of her black cap so as to shade her forehead in the most becoming manner. She twitched at it about a dozen times and opened her *ridicule*[3] I don't know how often to blow her pretty nose. M. Serret found us out to be the Edgeworths described by M. Pictet in his Journal Britannique. Since we came to France we have found Pictets account very useful; for at every public library and in every école centrale the Journal Britannique is taken and we have consequently received many civilities to be charged to the credit of that poor M. Pictet to whom I was so ungrateful.[4]

[1] Eldest son of RLE's third marriage.

[2] Later printed in *Irish Farmers' Journal*, iv. 117–18 (9 Dec. 1815), signed 'P.Q.'

[3] Reticule.

[4] See M. A. Pictet, *Voyage de trois mois en Angleterre, en Écosse et en Irlande*, 183–99. This was first published in *Bibliothèque Britannique*, xix (1802). J. Pinkerton in his *Recollections*, ii. 303, puts the circulation of monthly journals at no more than 500.

It was on a sunday when we arrived at Ghent and all the middling people of the town in their holiday clothes were assembled at the bridge and on the banks of the canal to see the *barque* arrive according to their custom. They made the scene very chearful. I do not know any English word that exactly translates the French *riant*. The old Baron de Triest, though he had not dined and tho' as he said of himself, *il avoit une faim de diable*, stayed to battle our coach and trunks through an army of custom-house officers. We stayed two days at Ghent and saw 'houses and churches' without number but no geese or turkies.[1] Here were some fine pictures by that Crayer of whom Rubens said 'Crayer! personne ne te surpassera!'[2] Do not be afraid my dear Sophy I am not going to overwhelm you with pictures, nor to affect to talk of what I do not understand but it is extremely agreeable to me to see paintings with those who have excellent taste and no affectation. At Ghent we went to the central school. Its library in a large church belonging to a monastery will be extremely fine and perishing cold when it is finished. A smart little librarian did us the honors of his town and we are obliged to him for getting the doors of the cathedral opened to us *at night*. We went in by moonlight and the cathedral had a sublime appearance. The lights were burning at the altar veiled from sight and our own monstrous shadows cast on the pillars added to the effect. The Verger took one of the tall candles to light us to some ancient monuments of white marble of exquisite sculpture. There were no pictures in this cathedral but it was finely painted in the manner in which the speakers room at the Temple is painted and by the master who taught de Gree.[3] This kind of painting seems to suit churches and to mix well with sculpture and statues. The little librarian thought he could never do too much in shewing his town of Ghent; and he walked my father almost to death . . .

[1] For houses and churches were to him geese and turkies;
He ate all and left none behind . . .
The Dragon of Wantley, 1. 29–30 (Percy's *Reliques of Ancient English Poetry*)

[2] Gaspar de Crayer (1584–1669), an Antwerp contemporary of Rubens.

[3] ME presumably refers to the paintings above the stalls, done in grisaille by Van Reyshoot in 1774. The 'Speaker' is Lord Oriel, last Speaker of the Irish House of Commons. In his grounds at Collon, co. Louth, he had a fine temple behind which he subsequently built a house. Peter de Gree (d. 1789) is mentioned by Mrs. E's father Dr. Beaufort as working on the temple in 1788 (Trinity Coll. Dublin MS. K. 6.59). I am indebted to Miss Anne Crookshank for the reference.

Maria Edgeworth to Charlotte Sneyd

Chantilly, 19th October, 1802

. . . We had a very agreeable journey through the Netherlands; and we spent four days very much to our satisfaction at Brussels. Of all the places I have seen since I came to France it seems the best calculated for the residence of English families; the country about it is beautiful and very like many parts of England. The town is full of elegant buildings and there are many charming public walks near, and in it. In the Place Royale, a handsome square, there are two excellent hotels L'hôtel d'Angleterre and l'hôtel de Flandres; we went to the latter, and we found that Mr. Chenevix and Mr. Knox were at the other. There are many fine churches and towers at Brussels and a few good pictures, but all the best pictures are gone to Paris, and if they were not I should not be able to describe them to you properly—and if I were ever so well able I should not be willing because all the descriptions of pictures and churches that I have ever read even by the hands of the best masters I have found tiresome. I have not however found it in the least tiresome to see the things themselves. . . . My father thought that it would be advantageous to us to see inferior pictures before those of the best masters that we might have some points of comparison and upon the same principle we went to two provincial theatres at Dunkirk and at Brussels but *unluckily*—I mean unluckily for our *principle*—we saw at Brussels two of the best Paris actors and actresses M. and Mme Talma. The play was Racine's Andromaque—imitated in English by the distressed mother.[1] Mme Talma played Andromaque and her husband Orestes—both exquisitely well. I had no idea of fine acting till I saw them and my father who has seen Garrick and Mrs. Siddons and Yates &c and Le Kain declares that he never saw anything superior to Mme Talma. We read the play in the morning—an excellent precaution—otherwise the novelty of the French mode of declamation would have set my comprehension at defiance. There was a ranting Hermione who had a string too tight round her waist—which made her bosom heave like the bellows of a bag pipes whenever she worked with her clasped hands against her heart to pump out something like passion. There was also a

[1] *The Distressed Mother* (1712), a tragedy by Ambrose Philips.

wretched Pyrrhus and old Phoenix whose grey wig I expected every minute would tumble off.

Next to this beautiful tragedy of Andromaque, the things that interested and amused me most at Brussels were—the dogs—not the lap dogs—but the dogs that draw carts and heavy hampers for their masters. Every day I beheld numbers of these traîneaux drawn by dogs—often four harnessed abreast and driven like horses. I remember in particular seeing a man standing upright on one of these little carriages and behind him two large hampers full of muscles; the whole drawn by four dogs. And another day I saw a boy of about ten years old driving four dogs harnessed to a little carriage laden with a parcel of goods almost as large as the boy. He crossed our carriage as we were going down a sloping street called La Montagne de la Cour without fearing our four Flemish horses and my father says if by any accident one of his dogs had stopped we must have gone over him. La Montagne de la cour is a very grand name and you may perhaps imagine that it means a Mountain, but be it known to you, my dear Aunt, that in le pays bas as well as in the County of Longford they make mountains of molehills. The whole road from Calais to Ghent is as flat and as straight as the road to Longford; but the inn keepers and postillions denominate every rising ground une montagne. We never knew when we came to a mountain except by the postillions getting off their horses with great deliberation and making them go a snails walk—a snails gallop would be much too fast. Now it is no easy thing for a French postillion to walk himself when he is in his boots. These boots are each as large and as stiff as a wooden churn and when the man in his boots attempts to walk he is more helpless than a child in a go cart; he waddles on dragging his boots along in a way that would make a pig laugh. As Lord Granard says, a pig may whistle though he has a bad mouth for it. I presume that *by a parity of reasoning*, as poor Mr. Duck[1] would say, a pig may laugh—But I must not talk any more nonsense but tell you facts, as facts my father says are always things of most value in letters to friends at a distance.

Fact 1st—We left Brussels last sunday (you are looking in your pocket book, dear Aunt Mary, I see you looking for the day of the month). The first place of any note we went to afterwards was

[1] Perhaps a reference to the self-educated poet Stephen Duck (1705–56).

Valenciennes—famous for the sieges it has stood and for its lace. We saw houses and churches in ruins the effects of English war and French Revolution—for Valenciennes has suffered both by internal and external enemies. It is as well as can be expected after both and recovering its industry but not its chearfulness. As to lace, tho' Valenciennes is very pretty we bought none recollecting that though Coventry is famous for ribbons and Tewkesbury for stockings yet only the worst ribbons and the worst stockings can be had at Coventry and Tewkesbury. Besides we are not expert in counting Flemish money, which is quite different from French, and puzzling enough to drive the seven sages of Greece[1] mad. Even the natives of the country cannot count it without rubbing their foreheads. With their wise English looking faces the Dutchmen stand counting in their hands and repeating 'Ç'a fait'—'Cela fait'—'Ah ç'a fait'—but what it is que ç'a fait they cannot make out under at least five minutes grace. For my part I fairly gave the point up and resolved to be cheated rather than go distracted. But indeed the Flemish are not cheats, as far as I have seen of them, though they love money best of all things next to their consciences. They would go to the utmost borders of honesty for a couronne de Brabant, or a demi couronne, or a double escalin or a single escalin, or a plaquette, or a livre, or a sou or a liard,[1] or for any of the vilest denomination of their absurd coin yet I do not believe they would go beyond the bounds of honesty with any one but an English milor—They are privileged dupes—No faith with heretics and no mercy upon English milors. A maid said to me at l'hôtel d'Angleterre at Dunkirk (the dearest inn we have been at) 'Ah Madame nous autres nous aimons bien de voir rouler les Anglois!' Yes; because they think the English roll in gold. My father has taken great pains to persuade people that he is not a Milor anglois and consequently he has not been forced to pay as such.

I beg your pardon my dear Aunt for detaining you so long at Valenciennes; now if you please we will go on to Cambray—famous for its cambrics, so called from Cambray—and for its

[1] Thales, Solon, Bias, Chilo, Cleobulus, Periander, and Pittacus, all noted for their pithy maxims.

[2] A *livre* was worth about 10*d.*, a *sou* a halfpenny, and a *liard* half a farthing. The *escalin* (Dutch *schelling*) and *plaquette* were small pieces of base money.

archbishop—the eloquent and amiable Fénelon. Bonaparte had so much respect for the memory of Fénelon that he fixed the seat of the present archbishoprick at Cambray instead of removing it to Lille as had been proposed. We saw Fénelon's head preserved in a church here, in an old bracket which but for his head deserved to have been burnt. How it escaped during the revolution is miraculous! But to return from the Archbishop of Cambray to Cambrics–Our hostess at Cambray was a dealer in cambrics and in them she seemed literally to have her being. Her whole soul was in her bale of *baptistes*. She was (in spite of cambric and Valenciennes lace of which she had a dirty superfluity upon her cap lined with pink silk) one of the very ugliest of the female species I ever beheld more hunchbacked [? than Mother-Bunch][1] but not half so entertaining, for she had not a story good or bad to tell us and besides she wore a huge shawl which if she had been as finely proportioned as the Venus de Medici would have destroyed all her charms in my fathers eyes. Notwithstanding all this my mother bought a piece of cambric from her for 4 Gs. and ½ and has marked two others to be sent to Paris if you and aunt Mary wish to have them. As I suppose she has written au long I say no more.

We were made amends for our ugly hostess by a most agreeable family who kept the inn at Roye where we stayed—a family whose ancestors had kept the same house for 150 years. The present landlord was a man of 68 his wife 60. He is an admirable [ ] she an excellent manager—both active and chearful—fond of one another and of their children—Their daughter a girl of twenty of a slight figure, vast vivacity in her mind and all her motions. She does all the business of the house and seems to love her father and mother, Papa! et Maman! better than anything in this world—except talking. My father formed a hundred good wishes for her—first when he heard her tell a story (which I will tell you some time or other) she used such admirable variety of action that he wished her on the stage—then when she waited at supper with all the nimbleness and dexterity of a female harlequin he wished that she was married to Jack Langan that she might keep the new inn at Edgeworthstown—But his last and best wish for her was that she could be waiting maid to you and my aunt

[1] The ale-wife in Dekker's *Satiro-Mastix* (1602). Several seventeenth- and eighteenth-century jest-books were named after her.

Mary. He thought she would please you both particularly, but for my part I thought she would talk a great deal too much for you. But this can never be brought to trial because her father and mother would not part with her for Pitts diamond[1] and she is too good to wish to leave them for any advantage to herself. My father offered to carry her in the carriage with us the next stage to see her sister who keeps the inn there but she would not go because her papa could not spare her. I am afraid I have tired you with histories of innkeepers and innkeepers daughters but in whatever rank of life I know you are interested for what is good.

In passing through a country I think it is dangerous for travellers to draw general conclusions relative to national characters or customs because they have not the means of judging. It is best therefore though it does not read so grand to state simply what we see. I *saw* today more windmills than I can count. I forgot to say that windmills abound on every hill and near every town in Flanders and they certainly enliven a country very much. I *saw* more horses than I can count drawing carts and waggons and each horse had a sheepskin ruff upon his collar. My father once looked out of the carriage window and exclaimed 'There is a sheep riding on a horse's back!—Oh no—I see now it is only one of those great sheepskins.'. They say that they use these sheepskins to keep the *withers* of their horses from the rain (I hope Mama's mare's withers and wind and back are all well). Besides sheepskins and wind-mills I *saw* today—not a peacock with a fiery tail[2]—but the ancient residence of the great Prince of Condé and of a long line of Princes famous for virtue and talents—the celebrated palace of Chantilly made still more interesting to us by having just read a beautiful tale of Madame de Genlis of which the scene is at Chantilly[3] . . .

After going through for an hour and a half a thick dark forest in

[1] One of the largest diamonds in the world. It once belonged to the grandfather of William Pitt, Earl of Chatham.

[2] I saw a Peacock with a Fiery Tail.
I saw a Blazing Sun that dropt down Hail.
I saw a Cloud . . .

The rhyme is printed in *A Little Book for Children* by T. W. (1702–12), and quoted in Harvey Darton, *Children's Books in England*, 60. It makes sense if the full stops are transferred to the middle of each line.

[3] The tale is *Mademoiselle de Clermont*.

which Virginia[1] might have lived secure from sight of mortal man, we came into open day and open country and from the top of a hill we beheld a mass of magnificent buildings shaded by wood. I imagined this was the palace, but I was told these buildings were only the stables of Chantilly. The palace alas! is no more. It was pulled down by the Revolutionists. The stables were saved by a petition from the war minister stating that they would make stabling for troops—to which use they are now applied. As we drove down the hill we saw the melancholy remains of the palace—only the white arches on which it was built covered with crumbled white stone and mortar. We walked to look at the riding house built by the Prince de Condé—a princely edifice! Whilst we were looking at it, we heard a flute played near us and we were told that the young man who played on it was one of the poor Prince de Condé's *chasseurs*. The person who shewed us the ruins [? had lost] some hundred pounds which he had earned in the Prince de Condé's service. He is a melancholy looking man of 60 years of age who during his whole life had been employed to shew the gardens and palace of Chantilly to strangers. He now shews their ruins and tells where the Prince and Princess once slept and where there were fine statues and charming walks. Pray read Mademoiselle de Clermont and when you have read it remember that we asked for l'Isle de l'amour and this poor man told us that it was once beautifully planted but now it is all destroyed! (We have had but one day's rain since we left you and one shower today to lay the dust. If we had picked weather we could not have had finer.)

At Chantilly we came into the usual road to Paris. Till then we had not gone a yard of the usual road from Calais and so much the better for us. My father says the road by Amiens is ugly beyond description. The country through which we came from Brussels was in most parts beautiful—planted in side-scenes in my father's manner[2]—you know what I mean—no straight lined hedges but

[1] A character in ME's *Belinda* (1801). Her story owes something to Bernardin de St. Pierre's *Paul et Virginie* (1787). She was a girl educated in seclusion by the hero of the story to be an ideal wife for himself.

[2] RLE had reorganized the Edgeworthstown grounds in the picturesque style after finding them in 1782 'laid out in the Dutch taste': *Mems. of RLE* (1821 edn.), ii. 7. Basically, the *jardin anglais* was asymmetrical, in contrast to the formal French garden, for example, as designed by Le Nôtre. The picturesque English garden of

serpentine hedges and indented groves. The English who can see nothing worth seeing in the country of France must certainly [look] with huge blinkers of prejudice but what is far more surprising the French themselves seem not to see the beauties of their own country but keep raving about Les jardins Anglois without perceiving that the best style of English park planting is put in practice throughout the whole of the Comté d'Artois &c. The parks about their châteaux are indeed all in bad taste guarded with grenadier poplars which they seem to prefer to the fine oaks and beech and elms which grow wherever they will let them grow. Even Chantilly does not seem to be layed out with good taste.

Paris—We arrived at this famous town of Paris about 3 o'clock today Wednesday and are lodged for a few days at L'hôtel de Courland but it is very dear and tomorrow my father sees M. Delessert fils to make arrangements . . .

Maria Edgeworth to Mary Sneyd

Paris, Hôtel de Courland, Place de la Concorde,
[Wednesday, 20 October, 1802]

. . . I forgot also to say (you know in forgetfulness there can be no order) that we entered Valenciennes just as the troops were marching to parade and that we saw an officer with furred waistcoat and furred pockets and monstrous moustaches which also looked like fur on his face. Altogether he looked very like the little Gibbon (see Shaws Monkeys[1])—only that the little Gibbon does not look conceited and he did. I forgot to tell you that I saw at Brussels a woman without stockings with lace on her cap finer and broader than you [ ].

I cannot *remember* anything else that *I have forgot*. Mr. Foster's two bulls are admirable but I am almost afraid to send them to Johnson because he complained so much and so justly of our sending perpetual corrections and additions whilst the printers

the late 18th century was very much less artificial in effect than the French version. For a comic description of the *jardin anglais*, see *Corresp. of Horace Walpole* (Yale edn.), xxxv, 125–6.

[1] Perhaps an illustration from one of the works of George Shaw, naturalist. Cf. T. Holcroft, *Memoirs*, i. 169.

were at work. The corrector of the press said with a heartfelt sigh 'I hope this list of Errata for Bulls will be the last.' My father has written a preface which I think you will like. I wish you were at this minute sitting beside me to hear it read[1] . . .

I wish I could send you in a frank a print which caught my eye in a shop window in Bond Street. At the bottom of it was written *Belinda*, or else indeed I never should have guessed that it had any relation to Belinda. The print is in a ladies memorandum book and if it was in your hands it would infallibly put you in a passion—that is into as great a passion as you can be put. Lady Delacour is a fat vulgar housekeeper and Belinda a stick worse a hundred times than sprawling Virginia.[2] In many booksellers shops at Bruges, Ghent and Brussels we found the translation of Belinda by Miss Edgewortz as they call her and print her. I have not yet had time to see whether it is well or ill translated. Cecilia and Evelina and Camilla and Mrs. Opie's Father and daughter and Ianthe written by Miss Clerke the granddaughter to the poor king of Corsica were everywhere.[3] You will I am sure be glad of this for when the Granddaughter of a king has spirit enough to write for her bread she deserves to be read. Ianthe was not I believe in any esteem in England, but the name of the author sells it in this republican country where I understand it is necessary to be careful what we write and say.

We are now in a magnificent hotel in a fine square formerly called 'Place de Louis Quinze'—afterwards 'Place de la Révolution'—and now 'Place de la Concorde'. In this square the guillotine was once at work night and day. Here Louis seize and Marie Antoinette died! &c Opposite to us is the Seine—and La Lanterne! On one side of this square are Les champs élisées; where the famous courtisanne de l'ancien regime drove her triumphal car with horses shod with silver.[4] What a mixture of things in this best of all possible worlds! Voltaire represented Paris by an image

[1] A reference to *An Essay on Irish Bulls* (1802) by R.L. and Maria Edgeworth. A 'bull' is an expression involving a ludicrous inconsistency unperceived by the speaker.

[2] The characters mentioned are all from ME's *Belinda*. The translation (1802) was by Octave de Ségur.

[3] Fanny Burney, *Evelina* (1778), *Cecilia* (1782), and *Camilla* (1796); A. Opie, *Father and Daughter* (1801); Clerke, *Ianthe*, translated in 1801 as *Ianthe ou la rose de Mont-Snodon et les cinq rivaux*.

[4] Cathérine Rosalie Gérard Duthé (1748–1830).

made of mud interspersed with precious stones.[1] As far as I have seen this seems to be not only an ingenious but a just emblem. In houses, in furniture, in dress, in everything here there is to English eyes and tastes a disgusting mixture of finery, and dirt. Exquisitely finished apartments in these grand hotels are to be had for money but as [left unfinished]

Mrs. Edgeworth to Charlotte and Mary Sneyd

Paris, 28 October 1802

. . . Mr. E seems to enjoy the best health and continues as well now that we are stationary as he was while we were travelling. He has excellent spirits and has had the pleasure of seeing many people of literature and merit eager to be introduced to Maria whose name is as well known in Paris as at Edgeworths town. You may remember to have heard him mention an abbé Morellet—a man of science to whom he was introduced the last time he was at Paris.[2] This very Abbé is alive still 75 years of age sprightly and polite and was the first man of letters to whom Mr. E and Maria were introduced! These are odd coincidences. Maria was told by him 'À Paris on lit votre livre sur l'éducation[3]—à Genève on l'avale—à Paris on admire vos principes—à Genève on les suit.' As yet we have seen but few people—those are amiable and pleasing. We have tolerably fixed our tiny establishment and have got pretty little lodgings at a reasonable price and a good job carriage. Most things are intolerably dear. Par malheur english manufactures are the fashion—printed Callicoes are twelve livres for an ell—plain muslin such as we bought in Dublin for seven shillings the yard is here 35 and 40 livres! But the fashions are worse than the prices. I will not touch upon that subject for fear of losing my temper and wasting paper . . .

[1] *Le Monde comme il va*: 'Il fit faire . . . une petite statue composée de tous les métaux, des terres et des pierres les plus précieuses et les plus viles; il la porta à Ituriel. "Casserez-vous, dit-il, cette jolie statue, parceque tout n'y est pas or et diamants?"'

[2] See Introduction, pp. xviii–xix; *Mems. of RLE* (1821 edn.), ii. 249–51; and ME's *Harrington and Ormond* (1817), iii. 253–68.

[3] *Practical Education* (1798).

Charlotte Edgeworth to Mrs. Emmeline King (née Edgeworth)

29 October 1802

. . . We stayed two or three days at the Hôtel de Courland and we are now lodging at small comfortable lodgings which are cheap and comfortable tho' not magnificent . . .

We got across the little sea in three hours and a half but I was so amazingly sick that I neither recovered the use of my fingers understanding or body for three days after we landed . . . I wish I had for there were several excellent figures. I did draw two which I hope I may have an opportunity of sending you along with all other scraps that are or may be. We sailed in company with Mr. Chenevix and Mr. Knox his companion. We landed just when the sun had resigned his powerful light to the moon which shone with uncommon splendor. Various sounds assailed our ears—French men speaking english and french—boys as at Holyhead eager to be employed—Passengers pushing their way thro' the croud on the beach. As we mounted the ladder from the ship—*Lift up your petticoat* says the man without whose assistance no earthly eloquence could have made me move my little finger. The most perfectly french looking man that I have seen since I came to France (M. Grandsire to whom we were recommended for lodgings guide and assistant) led us thro' the croud talking all the time, to a small office where my father had to put down his name. The scene was excellent, a graver man than a judge, at a desk listening with the utmost patience and attention to M. Grandsire, who with an infinity of words and gestures was translating my fathers explanation of the mode of writing his name—Four children at a round table eating bread and butter and calling out to their pretty young mother every minute, *à boire*, upon which she constantly opened a small cupboard and taking out a teapot held the spout to her young ones who each had a sup . . .

Here is my Paris journal . . .

21st—M. B. Delessert—banker—1 oclock walked to Les champs élisées and the rue de la révolution now called rue de la concorde—8 oclock in the evening went to see the Delesserts—M. and Mme Delessert their sons and nephews their daughter Mme Gautier her uncle charming family friendly, open and united—

Swiss—The uncle goodnatured friend of Lyons[1] . . . Ben Delessert is the young man who carries on a great part of the business. He is long pale goodnatured rather cold and swiss—Mme Gautier is fat enough fine eyes which she is capable of rolling like all french women. Mme Delessert is the most polite agreeable lively sensible goodnatured affectionate woman of sixty that I ever saw. You cannot think how much charmed I was with her the first evening that we went there for I had not the least expectation of seeing anything pleasant instead of which we found her and her brother and her son François Delessert all agreeable and entertaining. There were several other nephews and sons but they did not come forward. But now I must tell you what sort of a being François is, for whom we have all taken a violent fancy particularly my father and I because we see a strong likeness in him to Henry and to Henry in his merriest pin. He is aged two and twenty—Black hair black large lively eyes, profile like Henry's only a better chin—figure good but not extraordinary, lively in his conversation but not noisy . . .

[continued by Mrs. Edgeworth]
. . . We dined in company with the Swiss Ambassador the other day and he assured us that peace was quite restored at Berne and that not more than 10 lives had been lost in the affair there. The proclamation was modified and the Swiss submitted.[2] Perhaps Mr. King may like to hear this as it comes from what is considered here as good authority . . .

Charlotte Edgeworth to Harriet and Louisa Beaufort

30th October, Sneyd's birthday

My dear little girls—I beg pardon ladies—I should address you Honour'd and most respected Aunts. Pardon the intrusions of a

[1] RLE was at Lyons in 1772–3. See Introduction, p. xiii.

[2] Fighting had broken out between the supporters of the old cantonal and federal system of government and those of the unitary Helvetic Republic established under French auspices in 1798. The Helvetic authorities were driven from Berne in October and 'patriot' magistrates appointed, but after renewed intervention by the French these were removed and a modified constitution accepted. Emmeline's husband, John King or König, came from Berne.

niece who has the misfortune to presume to think she can in the least entertain you, or who can have the audacity to trouble the muscular power of four lovely eyes that will glance upon this paper.

Know then fair ladies that your humble servant is sitting by the most excellent wood fire in a small comfortable lodging, belonging to a man of the name of Verber—a german family a good man who can tell many pathetic stories relative to the Princess Elizabeth whom he knew from her infancy and who was a charming poor creature. This poor man and his wife came up into our little salle à manger and entertained as well as they could his eager audience with various accounts of the reign of terror. But the two speakers had the misfortune of ejaculating their stories in one breath and at the same instant. As soon as the vivacious husband began, the enthusiastic and more than vivacious wife commenced with fire in her eyes and unrestrained gesture, her recital. These people are very attentive and grant our requests for pillows or for candles or tables or any of the necessaries of their lodgers.

NB I should write this better if there were not my three companions writing at the same time on this most shaking of all shaking tables. We have four bedchambers filled with all the conveniencies that our hearts could desire, and we are as happy as absent friends can be, as we acquire new acquaintance every day who recieve us as friends, and whose conversation contains instruction or amusement or politeness or vivacity or sobriety, or all or one or two or three of these qualities, but always goodness.

Among the few who have all these qualities are our countryman the great Mr. Watt, and a M. Morellet—the most charming old man. Hariet we shall bring over with us when we return to you all a criticism on the little romance which you liked called Atala.[1] It will give you a specimen of the lively cleverness of the Abbé Morellet and I think will change your opinion of Atala. We are charmed with Mme Delessert. Oh she is such a sensible lively old woman, and a real mother to a fine family a real wife to a sensible man, a real companion to the meanest judges.

Published this day price 7 kisses a circumstantial account of the first visit of Miss Maria Edgeworth and her father mother and

[1] Morellet had criticized Chateaubriand's *Atala* (1801) for affectation, obscurity, and exaggeration.

sister to Mme Delessert—By Charlotte Edgeworth—Dedication to Miss Louisa Beaufort.
NB—In a few hours will appear the second visit paid to Mme Gautier daughter to the above respectable Lady of sixty three—Price 7 kisses and half a fervent embrace. The author hopes to be able to accomplish a work or works on a plan or plans sufficiently extensive to entitle her to a fervent embrace from each of her patrons beside the usual price of seven kisses, one on each feature and each hand (The second visit is dedicated to Miss Hariet Beaufort). You ought to be acquainted Ladies with this circumstance, that in France it is quite *ridicule* to shake hands, *we always* embrace. Moreover—I always repeat in the most contemptuous tone that puffed slieves are *si ridicule* and a sneer afterwards, just like our mantua-maker. Read any french story in the world and you will see how we like all ignorant strangers are surrounded by Les Marchands de mode &c &c &c &c
Now for the visit

Come come Maria it is eight o'clock, in our first visit at least to be punctual. Young Ben Delessert whom we saw this morning was extremely useful to us but I suspect that he is the only one of the family worth seeing. (M) Oh so I think. You know that Mme Gautier praised Prac Ed[1] so enormously to Lovell that she drove him absolutely out of the room. (C) Mme Gautier I suppose is a clever woman from what M. Pictet said, but vulgar I imagine. (FE) Yes thats just what I think. Arrived at l'hôtel Delessert à la rue Coq-Héron—(RLE) M. François open the door. You see the house is laid out just in the French manner—a large room from which is cut off an antichamber and a sort of hall above stairs. It has this great advantage, that when the door of the sitting room is open, the air that rushes in is not so cold as if it opened upon the stairs immediately.

Having passed thro' these two antichambers please to follow your prejudiced heroes and heroines to the door of the room which we knew was to contain beside those whom I have mentioned, sundry nephews and other sons of Mme Delessert. There was a tall screen which prevented your seeing the room any farther than the opposite wall; ranged between the folds of this screen was a row of squires whose bows were all prepared the minute that

[1] *Practical Education.*

the door was opened. Are these the nephews thought I. Oh yes certainly says probability—Now you see how they all spread over the room—'See millions blacken all the place.'[1] Who is that that seems so attentive to Miss E—who is deep already in conversation with Mme Gautier? Oh says probability (for this is a gentleman that constantly begins with Oh)—Certainly the favourite son of that good looking old lady who talks to Mrs. E and pours out the tea at the same time. Oh that is certainly Mme Delessert's favourite son, for whenever she wants some more water in the tea pot she always calls out 'Mon fils—mon fils François'—Upon which François starts without knocking down anything on his way, for the kettle. It is not so easy to steer among a parcel of gentlemen surrounding the fire with cups in hand and all thinking that few circumstances ought to give way to what is uppermost in their mind and which they produce to those about them in the form of conversation—A goddess much adored in all countries, but particularly in France.

Some stragglers like myself in the company who had not yet got into a knot took compassion upon me—seeing that I was like a wanderer in a large city and could only catch a sentence here and there from the various talkers that surrounded me. Ben Delessert took compassion upon me for which action I shall always defend him when attacked. I can tell you I cut a glorious figure—first attempt at any french beyond oui and non is a grand event so write it down in your pocket book—October the 21st. The goddess of conversation becoming warm with the fumes of tea and the fragrance of Grapes—All hearts expanded as each sentence fell. All talked yet all heard, and with hearing, all of our party at last became enraptured. Whether Mme Gautier's expectations were answered I can only guess by the consequences, which were that at parting for her house at Passy pretty early in our visit she invited Miss E and her friends to her maison de campagne on the Tuesday following, with various expressions of pleasure friendship gratitude and hopes for the future. Have I given you a sufficiently strong description of the excellencies of Mme Delessert? Well then her brother did me the honour to speak to me and as he spoke well and with great enthusiasm of Lyons[2] I had a

[1] Gay, *Fables*, 'The Turkey and the Ant', 1.12.

[2] See Introduction, p. xiii.

tripple cause for liking. That poor little fellow I have not seen since. When I said that all spoke, it was an irishmans all. There were various animals called cousins that wandered about the room, or stretched their long legs from their chair to the grate or across two chairs, or sat in mournful silence listening to the croud. I also was a mute as you may guess . . .

If we have taken a fancy for François Delessert how huge is that which we have taken for the Abbé Morellet. We met at Mme Gautiers. There was also a M. Dumont—a very sensible shrewd man who came in company with Lord Henry Petty who is travelling and to whom I believe he is tutor. There were two or three other gentlemen—I cannot answer for the degree of sense which each of them possessed. I cannot deny that one of them was reckoned a self sufficient talker—But altogether we were a happy set of 14 round a round table—Thus [sketch plan]—So you see that I have marked under our names and as we were seated so as that each had a great deal of conversation we were very happy. There are two or three that I have not mentioned. You will hear of them in time. M. Delessert is a very sensible old man. Mlle Turrettin is cousin to our Pictet who by the by is trotting to Paris as fast as possible. She has a great deal of information but she does not produce much more than her admiration of literature and Maria. Good by—I have something to say to Dr. Beaufort that I am in hopes will please him. *I am your affectionate CE*

I hope my dear Grandpapa that it will please you to hear that we went to see a gentleman today whose house was the most pleasant of any that we have seen since we left Ireland, and the most like your house at Collon;[1] not so clean but filled with such a variety of conveniences that it gives the idea of happiness—The Abbé Morellet's. An ink bottle hung to the door, mantle piece crouded with useful implements, books well arranged, in short everything convenient. In magnificent houses, everything is so contrived that the owners may waste their time as much as possible—Large rooms, suites of appartments, numbers of attendants and much ceremony, are all advantages to the unhappy nobleman, who would give up his title to be able to taste the pleasure of a small

[1] Dr. Beaufort was vicar of Collon. co. Louth. Cf. p. 176 below. The Edgeworths were fascinated by gadgets and machinery.

room, good fire, friends books and conversation. The Abbé Morellet is seventy four; he lives with his sister and his writing and books in an airy part of the town. He has a sort of screen with a shed over it, close by the fire; his books and papers are placed on little shelves in this screen, which surrounds his armchair—a table on one side of him on which he lays his desk when he is not writing, an arm which turns out to support his candle and which, as it has a joint, can be placed in any direction. His papers are all of the same size, and their titles are written on the back. On each side of the fire he has a book case—here and there hangs a desk which if turned upside down and hung by a hook to the shelf occasionally serves for a table. His screen folds and unfolds, runs on grooves in the floor.

The most curious circumstance relative to this family is that the niece, I wish it had been the daughter, of M. Morellet, was married to Marmontel, when he was exactly the age of my father when he married my mother—she was 25. Marmontel is dead, and he has left as a testimony of his gratitude to his wife, a little introduction to some of his works,[1] printed for his children and friends, expressing sentiments, and drawing a character so exactly suited to the sentiments of my father and the character of my mother, that it was most exceedingly touching. Mme Marmontel's mother has given us one of these, which she has kept I suppose for these last three years in her pocket book. We have not seen this lady yet and I am afraid we never shall because she lives so far from Paris.

It is several days since I began this letter, therefore many things have happened which have pleased us, among them a long visit from the Abbé Morellet, at which I wish you had been present, because his conversation is such as would please you particularly. I do wish you were here, there are so many that would like you and that you would like—There are so many beautiful buildings—but remember that your house is more comfortably furnished than the most comfortable we have seen.

Pray dear Grand Papa, humour me so much, as to be pleased with this little scrap of a letter, whether it is well or ill done, because I wish it and believe me to be your affectionate C Edgeworth

[1] See introduction to 1787 edn., edited by Née de la Rochelle.

November 2nd

We have seen a gentleman who has translated Belinda not only into french language, but french taste for he has altered the story. He intends to publish a translation which shall be literal. He is a very young gentlemanlike looking man and son to the Comte de Ségur who published the Memoirs of the court of Berlin.[1]

We saw yesterday one of the Elephants who shed tears when it met its companion. The companion is dead and they say that the poor animal has been very melancholy ever since. They have sent to Ceylon for another companion and I hope it will be happy, it is a very fine animal, easily frightened at noises. It was frightened at the noise of my mother laughing.[2]

[In Mrs. Edgeworth's handwriting] At the same place we saw one of the Savans who had been in Egypt. He complains bitterly of Lord Keiths barbarity and General Menou's but with tears hoped that his gratitude and that of his confrères might reach Sir S. Smith to whom they owed their safety their lives and preservation of their recueils[3] . . . We have met with much kindness on Maria's account who is treated quite as a little Ange tutélaire and her works as les loix de l'éducation en dernier ressort. When I tell my name and that I am related to l'auteur de l'incertitude[4] I find I am much respected—l'abbé Sicard calls me l'*auguste* épouse de M. E— . . .

[1] No second edition was published. Ségur's version is in some places a good deal condensed; French references are substituted for English, and in the conclusion the plot is altered by omitting Virginia's improbable marriage; she voluntarily resigns Hervey to Belinda and returns to the West Indies with her father. Octave de Ségur's father, Louis Philippe de Ségur, wrote *Histoire des principaux événements du règne de Frédéric Guillaume III, roi de Prusse* (1800).

[2] The male elephant for many years exhibited at the Jardin des Plantes died at the age of seventy in 1801 of *fluxion de poitrine: Magazin Encyclopédique* (1801), v. 116.

[3] This was Étienne Geoffroy-St. Hilaire (Paris Notebook). He refers to Sir S. Smith's conduct in 1801 in making the Convention of El Arish which permitted the French in Egypt to return to France. The agreement was directly contrary to his orders and Lord Keith disallowed it, although he said that the government would probably permit the French to return. Meanwhile however hostilities had again broken out.

[4] Mrs. E's great-uncle Louis de Beaufort wrote *Dissertation sur l'incertitude des cinq premiers siècles de l'histoire romaine*. The book was published anonymously at Utrecht in 1738 and with the author's name at The Hague in 1762.

Maria Edgeworth to Mary Sneyd

Paris, 31st October, 1802

My dear Aunt Mary, . . . As soon as we came to Paris we went up to the leads of the hotel de Courland from which we were told there was a fine view of Paris and so indeed there was—and the first object that struck us was the Telegraph *at work*.[1] This is as nearly as possible my father's. The first voiture de remise (job coach in plain English) that we got into belonged formerly . . . to whom do you think? To the Princess Elizabeth. Probably the Abbé Edgeworth had been in this very coach with her.[2] The coachman told us this history of the carriage. The master of the hotel however denied it and said it belonged to some Duke or Prince I forget who; but my father believes the coachman and thinks the master denied it only because he did not like to have it thought that he had *made* anything by the revolution. At all events we like best to believe the coachman because it is a singular coincidence. The hotel de Courland was so dear (apartments 28 and 36 guineas a month) that we were glad to get out of it. We are now in a private house very comfortable and with quiet good people. The master of this house was one of the King's guards—a Swiss. If I could draw plans well and as easily as little William I would draw you a nice plan of our rooms. We have one floor to ourselves—a pretty little dining room—2 bedchambers on one side of it opening into one another for Papa and Mama—two ditto on t'other side for Charlotte and Maria. In one respect the French houses are much more convenient than the English—they are so arranged that you can get in and out of all the rooms without passing through one to get at the other. There are strange little passages and odd back staircases and *ruelles*, or passages close to beds—my father says at first invented for purposes of intrigue but let their origin be what it would they are very convenient. The floors in the bedchambers

[1] RLE had designed a form of semaphore signalling as early as 1766 but made no attempt to establish an operating system until after Chappe's experiments in France. He tried unsuccessfully to get the Irish government to take it up in 1795 for defence purposes and in 1797 published a pamphlet entitled *A Letter . . . on the Tellograph and on the Defence of Ireland.* There are complementary accounts of this in *Mems. of* RLE (1821 edn.) ii. 159–73, 297–9, in Schofield, *Lunar Society*, 51, 409, and in A. Friendly, *Beaufort of the Admiralty*, chap. x.

[2] See Introduction, p. xxi n. 3.

are plaister—very cold. Thank you and aunt Cha— for woollen and fur shoes which are real comforts.

The day after we arrived at Paris M. Delessert's eldest son, he whom M. Pictet described as the French Rumford,[1] came to see us. As the room was full of smoke and as he only spoke of directions to places and persons I could not judge of him and I am told by all friends that I must suspend my *imaginations*. I can only say that he appeared reserved and stiff in his manners something like Lord Selkirk. He invited us to spend the next evening with his mother and sister. We went—found an excellent house—a charming family—with whom we felt as if we were perfectly acquainted after we had been in the room with them 5 minutes. Mme Delessert the mother—an elderly lady of about 60 has entirely won my fathers heart. She puts me in mind of the description he gave of the lady he saw in the old castle near M. de la Poypes.[2] He prefers her to every young and handsome Parisian he has yet seen—her species of politeness and conversation resembles that of my aunt Ruxton[3]—my father says so. After this I need not tell you how well I like her. I think I never loved any new acquaintance so well. Mme Gautier her daughter has fine large black eyes—the appearance and manners of a gentlewoman—very neatly dressed—not at all naked—people need not go naked here unless they chuse it. Mme Gautier is not so *engaging* as her mother; but very obliging and sensible and much more what is called a woman of the world. She is much connected with people of literature: Rousseau was a friend of this family: his letters (Martyn's) on Botany[4] were written for this lady . . .

My father did not present any of his introductory letters till yesterday, because he wished that we should be masters and mistresses of our own time to see sights, before we saw people. We have been at Versailles—melancholy magnificence!—at Le petit Trianon—elegant—poor Queen! We have been at the Louvre or as it is now called Le Musée to see the celebrated gallery of

[1] See Introduction, p. xvi.

[2] *Mems. of RLE* (1821 edn.) i. 287–9: she was a lady 'free from prejudice and party . . . fond of reasoning, yet averse from disputation; versed in literature, yet not anxious to display it.'

[3] RLE's sister.

[4] J. J. Rousseau, *Letters on the Elements of Botany*, trans. with notes and twenty-four additional letters by T. Martyn (1785).

pictures. I shall not attempt to describe any of them to you because I cannot describe them well and because I think most descriptions of pictures tiresome. I was entertained but tired with seeing so many pictures all to be admired and all in so bad a light that my little neck was almost broken and my little eyes almost strained out in trying to see them. We are to go again and again and when I am used to them—like Transfer I am sure I shall grow fond of them.[1] Those of Raphael, Rubens and Vandyke are in a room we have not yet seen so I have much admiration *to the good.* We were all extremely entertained and interested yesterday with seeing what are called les Monumens françois—all the statues and monuments of the great men of France—well arranged, according to their dates in the apartments of the antient monastery des Augustins. This would be a charming place (as my father observed) for children to learn history and biography and for artists to observe the progress of the arts—Practical Education forever! Here we saw old Hugh Capet with his nose broke and king Pepin with his nose flattened by time and Catherine de Medicis in full dress but in full beauty and Francis 1st and dear Henry the fourth[2] and more great men than my paper or my head will hold.

We have been to the Théâtre François and the théâtre Feydeau —both fine play houses—decorations superior to English and acting in general far superior—*in comedy*. In tragedy they bully and rant and throw themselves into academic attitudes too much. We were pleased with a little piece in which Gessner is introduced as the principal character—story like that of the fair penitent—only this is a real penitent.[3]

M. Pictet is expected in town every day—Mme Lavoisier and Mme de Staël and Princesse de Monaco ditto—ditto—ditto. Miss Williams is here—have not yet seen her. Mme de Genlis is here—have not seen her but shall. Lady Mount Cashel to whom Lady Moira gave us a letter is gone to spend some time in Languedoc—

[1] A character in Moore's *Zeluco* (1789), whose tastes were governed by what he became 'accustomed to'.

[2] These were the effigies of the kings of France removed from St. Denis.

[3] The Théatre Français was the home of the Comédie Française company and the Théatre Feydeau housed comic opera. The piece was perhaps *Gessner*, a 'comédie anecdotique' by Barré, Desfontaines, and Bourgueil, first performed in 1800. ME commented (Paris Notebook) 'bad company at the playhouse—dreadful smell—nosegays to hide'. *The fair penitent* (1703) was by Rowe.

sorry—but cannot help it—father has waited on Mr. Merry the minister Plenipotentiary or Chargé d'affaires at Paris. He was very civil—Lord Whitworth expected every day. Mr. Merry says he will certainly come in a day or two—will present father to Bonaparte. Whilst I was writing this Mr. Merry came to return my fathers visit and is now talking away at a great rate. . . . Adieu love me I am grateful to you. It is all I have at present to say for myself.

Richard Lovell Edgeworth to C. Sneyd Edgeworth

[n.d.]

The large buildings both public and private are built of large blocks of stone from the quarries of Montmartre near Paris. The stone is harder than Bath but it is easily cut with chizels and with stone hammers of different sorts—some pointed—some with edges like mattocks and some like those mattocks which have chizzle edges in our country [diagrams].

The generality of houses are built in a manner singularly convenient and expeditious. This same stone of Montmartre when burned in a reverberating furnace[1] heated with wood—which makes a stronger and cleaner fire than coal—becomes friable, that is to say frangible, that is to say to William[2] easily to be broken. It is carried in sacks from the furnace to the place where it is to be used. It must not be suffered to remain long in this state as its plastic power escapes. It must be kept dry and Oh wonderful! when it is reduced to fine powder by *bats* and short flails and tempered with water it becomes like plaister of Paris, fit to assume any form. It sets in a few minutes and by degrees becomes so hard as to defy the weather. It is not necessary to say that it must be covered from the wet at the top—else the rain would insinuate itself between the wall and the plaister and would expand when it froze and break the plaister from the wall. With this material they not only imitate hewn stone by covering the walls with it but cornices and mouldings and ornaments of all sorts are worked with it on the outside of the houses, precisely as they are formed amongst us withinside of our buildings with alabaster vulgo

[1] A furnace in which the flames are forced back upon the substance exposed to it. The stone referred to is gypsum.

[2] RLE's eight-year-old son.

plaister of Paris. Besides, this useful stone serves for mortar—indeed it is the only mortar that is used. It is made up from five minutes to five minutes with water in small *hods* and laid on with the hands in large lumps between the stones—the trowel is not so much employed as the natural organ. The mystery of this method of building is nothing more than this—their gypsum is of a stronger nature than ours and it bears the weather. They make their floors upon strong joists with lath and plaister and tiles or boards. They lay the joists as we do from wall to wall in the shortest direction. They nail laths on slips near the bottom of the joist. They plaister the ceiling on these laths—fill up the interstices from above between the joists with rubbish old mortar and some plaister. Over this they lay a coat of plaister and upon this tiles or boards.

Would you not suppose that walls built with ordinary stone, laid roughly to catch and hold the outside plaistering without any exactness—depending for their finish both as to the jambs and posts of their doors and windows upon plaister must be very cheap? No such thing—at 18 inches thick they cost 35 livres tournois per square toize. The toize is two yards french = 2 yards 2/13 english—the livre = to 10d. How much per perch of our measure—which is 21 feet long 1/6 thick and one foot high? I dont require the small fractions.

I should have told you above, that in moulding the cornices they do not use such little moulds as you have seen for inside work. As the cornices project sometimes 18 inches or two feet they are obliged to use moulds in proportion and they employ three or four or five men to force them along. It seems like magic to have a large cornice stuck up against the whole front of a house in an hour or two. The window stools are put in after the mason work is finished but not before the work is plaistered. That is the last operation. The roofs are loaded with oak timber, and constructed grossly—covered with tiles and frequently with fine slates about the size of our doublers,[1] which are brought from Artois by water. Their chamber doors are not so thick as ours—their locks execrable. Their hinges have however one convenience that ours have not—the pin of the joint is not rivetted in. It has a head by which it can be taken out; so that the door can be easily unhung.

[1] Probably the same as doubles, one of the smallest sizes of roofing slates.

None of the windows at Paris are hung as ours with pulleys &c—they open like doors in two parts. [diagram] One door shuts at the middle into the other by which means they are made close at the hinges and where they meet they are fastened by a good contrivance which [I] cannot describe at present.[1] The chimney pieces are low—in general without grates [ ] projecting mantles—the fuel wood, lying upon triangular bars about 3 inches high. I have sent you all this description my dear Sneyd because I had begun to write it for my own use and I thought when I had written half that I might as well send it to you where it would be safe against a future occasion . . .

Tonight for the first time we were at the grand opera.[2] The house is fine—the decorations magnificent—the spectacle or rather the drama absurd—an immense orchestra of excellent musicians—but we heard more noise than music—The dresses superb—the number of attendants and dancers prodigious—twenty or thirty of the dancers would be first rate anywhere else but when the younger Vestris appears you are instantly struck with the obvious superiority of his art and his powers. Mme Gardel appears still more excellent—such grace and lightness I never saw before. The dancing made amends for the rest of the representation which appeared to us tiresome in the extreme. I should not forget to tell you that the first Consul is upon a tour to the sea coasts—that I saw Cambacérès the second Consul at the Opera and that he is a very disagreeable figure in a broad-laced coat and his hair half powdered and his whole appearance mean and dirty and disagreeable. . . .

R. L. Edgeworth to Charlotte Sneyd

Paris, 18th November, 1802

Maria told you of M. and Mme de Pastoret; in the same house on another floor—for different families have entire 'apartments',

[1] A spagnolette bolt, running the whole height of the window and operated by a handle in the middle.

[2] At the Théâtre des Arts. Under Gardel this theatre was said to have supplied most of the principal cities of Europe with capital dancers: [Blagdon], *Paris as it was and is* (1803), 64, 67.

you observe the word, in one house—we met M. and Mme Suard: he is accounted one of the most refined critics of Paris, and has for many years been at the head of newspapers of different denominations; at present he is at the head of 'Le Publiciste'. He is prudent, highly informed, not only in books, but in the politics of different states and the characters of men in all the different countries of Europe. Mme Suard has the remains of much beauty, a belle [*sic*] esprit, and aims at singularity and independence of sentiment. Would you believe it, Mr. Day paid his court to her thirty years ago?[1] She is very civil to us, and we go to their house once a week: literati frequent it, and to each of them she has something to say.

At Mme de Pastoret's we met M. Degérando and M. Camille Jordan. Not Camille de Jourdan, the assassin, nor Camille Desmoulins, another assassin, nor General Jourdan, another assassin, but a young man of agreeable manners, gentle disposition, and much information; he lives near Paris, with his Pylades[2] Degérando, who is also a man of much information, married to a pretty sprightly domestic woman, who nurses her child in earnest. Camille Jordan has written an admirably eloquent pamphlet[3] on the choice of Bonaparte as first consul for life; it was at first forbidden, but the Government wisely recollected that to forbid is to excite curiosity. We three have had profound metaphysical conferences in which we have avoided contest and have generally ended by being of the same opinion. We went, by appointment, to Mme Campan's; she keeps the greatest boarding school in France, to meet Mme Récamier, the beautiful lady who had been nearly squeezed to death in London.[4] How we liked the school and its conductress, who professes to follow Practical Education, I leave to Maria to tell you. How we like Mme Récamier is easily told; she is certainly handsome, but there is nothing noble in her appearance; she was very civil. M. de Prony, who is at the head of the Engineers des Ponts et Chaussées—civil engineers—was

[1] Thomas Day, the eccentric author of *Sandford and Merton* (1783–9), and a great friend of RLE. For his search for a wife, see *Mems. of RLE* (1821 edn.) i, chaps. viii and ix.

[2] Pylades and Orestes, nephew and son of Agamemnon, were inseparable friends.

[3] *Vrai sens du vote national sur le consulat à vie* (1802).

[4] She had been in London earlier in the year.

introduced to us by Mr. Watt. I forgot to speak of him; he has just left Paris . . .
[MS. missing—printed from *Mem.* i. 132–4]

Mrs. Edgeworth to Mary Sneyd

Paris, 21st November, 1802

. . . That evening [Thursday, 17th November] we spent at Mme Delesserts—agreeably of course for her even chearfulness and good choice of company has the happiest influence on those who assemble at her house. Friday we saw Beauty riches, fashion luxury and numbers at Mme Récamier's. She is a charming woman surrounded by a groupe of adorers and flatterers in a room where are united wealth and taste—all of modern execution and ancient design that can contribute to its ornament. Maria will describe at length the strange mélange of merchants and poets—philosophers and parvenus—English—French—Portuguese and Brasilian which composed the company. We were treated with distinguished politeness and concluded the evening with taking us to her box at the Opera—where besides being in company with the most fashionable woman at Paris we saw a very fine Ballet and were seen by *Bonaparte* who sat opposite to us in a railed box through which he could see but not be seen. Saturday morning we saw the magnificent Salle of the Corps législatif and in the evening passed some hours in the agreeable society of Mme de Vergennes and her daughters. Sunday we were happy at home. Monday morning just as we were going out M. Pictet was announced. We neither heard his name distinctly nor recollected his looks—he is grown so fat and looks so well—more friendly no man can be. I hope he perceives that we are grateful to him for the flattering reception we have met with here.

The remainder of the morning was spent in the Gallery of pictures where we met Mr. Rogers the poet[1] and a Mr. Abercrombie who informed Maria that he was the man who carried to

[1] Author of *The Pleasures of Memory* (1792). Rogers said that he kept out of the way of the Edgeworths as their feelings were 'so little in unison' with his own: *Early Life of Samuel Rogers*, ed. P. W. Clayden (1887), 445. Rogers was concentrating on seeing pictures.

Ireland a letter from Miss Emma Sneyd about strawberry plants. The evening was spent with M. Pictet at his sisters—an agreeable and well informed widow with three handsome daughters. Tuesday we went to the National Library where we were shewn a large number of the finest Cameos Intaglios and Roman and greek medals—Many of the antiquities brought from Egypt—Busts Manuscripts &c—and in the evening we had again the pleasure of Pictets company and of the charming Mme Pastoret who was so obliging as to drink tea with us. Yesterday morning we had the pleasure of being at home when several ingenious and learned men called on us and consequently of hearing one of the most lively and instructive conversations on a variety of topics carried on for near three hours. As I think it is Mr. E's plan to knock you down with names I will enumerate these men whom Maria will hereafter teach you to distinguish—Edelcrantz (a Swede)—Molard—Eisenmann—Dupont—Pictet the younger. After they went we paid a short visit to the pictures—saw the salle du Tribunat and the Consuls apartments at the *Tuileries*. On the dressing table there were the busts of Fox and Nelson. At our return home we saw good François Delessert who is like Harry—and another man who was the man that took Robespierre prisoner and has made a Clock that is wound up by the action of the air on Mercury, like that which Mr. E invented for the King of Spain.[1] He told us many things which made us stare and some that made us shiver—and more that made us wish never to see him again.

The evening we went to Mme Suards. Dont imagine that these ladies are all widows—for they have husbands and in many instances the husband vaut mieux que la femme. At Mme Suards we met besides many ladies the famous Count Lally Tolendal and the Duc de Crillon. This morning Maria is gone with Pictet

[1] Dr. V. K. Chew (Dept. of Physics, Science Museum, S. Kensington) suggests that this may have been the clockmaker J. B. Duluc. Several members of the Lunar Society took an interest in clockmaking and for RLE it was a lifelong hobby. The clock mentioned here, wound up by atmospheric pressure, was probably a version of that invented in the 1760s by James Cox (d. 1788). The latter also invented a clock wound up by the opening and closing of a door; RLE made a version of this for his Irish home. I have been unable to trace any connection between RLE and the king of Spain, who had a famous collection of clocks. For RLE's clock-making, see Schofield, *Lunar Society*, 108, 129; *Memoirs of RLE* (2nd edn. 1821) i. 346–7, 378–9.

to the Abbé Sicard at the deaf and dumb[1] and Mr. E has staid at home to make a model of little Williams machine (dont tell William) . . .

All the persons from Geneva whom we have seen bear witness to the good employment of Lovells time and the excellence of his morals. Mr. John Foster writes that his time is equally and impartially divided between the best company and the best books. His residence at Geneva will I hope do him good and make him happy. The society seems to be peculiarly agreeable at Geneva and all the Genevese we have seen appear to have a peculiar expression of goodness in the manner and conversation. The Swiss are now in a most deplorable situation and will soon be forced to submit totally to the strong hand of power. They are an interesting people and the French here seem to sympathise with them very sincerely.[2] There are many fears that this business will produce another war with England but if that happens it will be more against the wishes and contrary to the interests of the French merchants than of the English who are sure of their present strength on the ocean. Mr. E has not seen Bonaparte yet for he has not had a review since we landed. In ten days there is to be one and Mr. E goes tomorrow to wait on Lord Whitworth as a previous step. It is a singular circumstance that Lord Whitworth the new ambassador has brought to Paris the same horses and the same wife and lives in the same house as the last Ambassador did eleven years ago. For he is married to the widow of the Duke of Dorset who was here then. In England many are the tales of scandal that have been related of the Consul and all his family but if they should reach your ears do not believe them. A lady told me it was vraiment extraordinaire qu'un jeune homme comme lui aît des moeurs si exemplaires—on peut dire qu'il est un autre Scipion[3] et d'ailleurs on ne s'attend pas qu'un homme soit fidèle à une femme qui est plus âgée que lui—mais si âgée aussi. Il aime la soumission plus que la beauté. S'il lui dit de se coucher à 8 heures elle se couche—s'il faut se lever à 2 heures elle se lève. Elle est une bonne femme. Elle a sauvé bien des

[1] L'Institution des sourd-muets in the Rue St. Jacques. Sicard had succeeded the founder, the Abbé de l'Épée, in 1790.

[2] See p. 19 n. 2.

[3] The Roman general Scipio Africanus Major, who refused to see a captive Spanish princess and returned her safely to her parents.

vies![1] Has Maria told you that she has had her Belinda translated into French—by a young Count de Ségur—a gentlemanlike and amiable young man of one of the most antient families of France married to a grandaughter of the Chancellor d'Aguesseau whose name I am sure you remember in many books—particularly D'Argenson's essays.[2] Many people support themselves by writing for journals and translating english books—Yet the price of litterature seems very low—and of all the necessaries of life very high. The influx of English has they say doubled the price of lodgings and of most luxuries. We seem to live very economically yet the sum of money at the end of each week is frightfully large. I think if I did not wish myself at home from affection and choice I should do so from Avarice . . .

R. L. Edgeworth to Charlotte Sneyd

Paris, 29th November, 1802

. . . 3rd Dec. Before I left Edgeworthstown I stated as one of my reasons for wishing at this period to take Maria abroad that it was the only probable means of giving her excellent qualities an opportunity of engaging a partner for the remainder of her life.[3] Yesterday a Swedish Chevalier (knight of one of the Swedish orders) a man of universal information polite manners and good character rich enough for a Swede 46 years old &c offered his hand and I most sincerely believe his heart to Maria. He had previously spoken to me and was by me referred to Maria. She objects with reason and kindness to his distant settlement. As her heart is still her own she may without injury to her future happiness take time to consider. It will give you and our dear Mary sincere satisfaction to be told that Marias good sense never appeared so much mistress of her imagination. She sees that she is truly respected and much liked in this country and the first offer should

[1] ME's informant was probably Mme de Vergennes, or her daughter Mme de Rémusat, lady in waiting to Josephine.

[2] René Louis de Voyer, marquis d'Argenson, *Essais dans le goût de ceux de Montaigne* (1785).

[3] See ME to Sophy Ruxton, 30 June 1802. The suitor was Abram Niclas Clewberg Edelcrantz. For this episode, see Introduction, pp. x–xi.

not be instantly accepted. I like the gentleman—and no selfish consideration—need I say so to you!—no selfish consideration shall on my part obstruct his wishes. I go this morning to make proper enquiries.

[In Maria Edgeworth's hand] My father has given me this letter to read. Let me assure you both my dear aunts that it was my wish to write to you myself but my father has done everything for me I could desire. No one can be more truly sensible of your kindness than I am.

[In R. L. Edgeworth's hand] We find the attention of the wise and good unremitting and no day passes without some acquisition of knowledge or some addition to our valuable acquaintance. Maria has made a little library from the presents of books which have been given to her—and she still preserves that sincere humility which is never puffed up by applause nor shrivelled by its being witheld from her. . . .

Maria Edgeworth to Mrs. Ruxton

Paris, Rue de Lille, no. 529,[1] 1st December, 1802

My dearest Aunt, I have been treasuring up for some time everything that I have seen and heard which I think could interest you and now my little head is so full that I must empty it or it will certainly burst. I wish I could talk instead of writing to you and I hope I shall soon have that delight. All that I have seen my dear friends at home has tended to attach me more firmly to you by the double effect of resemblance and contrast. Every agreeable person recalls you to my mind by some point of resemblance and everything disagreeable makes me exclaim How different from . . . &c &c. But you would rather have facts than sentiments perhaps. My father and mother and Charlotte and Maria are perfectly well in the first place and in good spirits—pleased with Paris but still more pleased with the idea of soon returning to our best friends and happy home . . .

M. Pictet arrived a few days ago. He gives up his whole time to us and seems to think of nothing but our interests and pleasures. Tell my aunt Mary that I am grown as fond of her favorite as her

[1] The number in the *quartier*, not the street.

heart could wish and have forgiven him for les *yeux baissés* and for bringing me home from Castle Saunderson &c. Indeed I did not know the extent of my obligations to him till I came to Paris. His account of us and his extracts in the Bibliothèque Britannique have been our introduction to all the most agreeable society we have enjoyed.[1] I had no idea of the manner in which men of letters and science are received here till I actually saw it. They mix with people of wealth and fashion—with the *nouveaux riches* and *les anciens nobles*. The latter are the most agreeable as you may well imagine. I wish I could paint all the people I have seen in little Williams magic lantern and shew them off for your amusement. With Mme Delessert and all her amiable family you are already acquainted from letters to aunt Mary and Cha. I must however add that my father thinks her like aunt Ruxton. At her house there is and has been for years meeting of the most agreeable and select society in Paris. She has the courage absolutely to refuse to admit either man or woman whose conduct she cannot approve. At other houses there is sometimes a strange mixture. To recommend Mme Delessert more powerfully still to you I must tell you that she was the friend or rather the benefactress of Rousseau—it is said that Rousseau was never perfectly good and happy except in her society. It was to her bounty that he owed his retreat in Swizzerland. She is generous and nobly charitable, but if it were not for her friends and her children who adore her, no one could ever find out half the good she does. One of her acts of beneficence is recorded in Berquins ami des enfans[2] but even her own son cannot tell us in which story it is, she has a collection of Rousseau's letters to her (Some of his letters to Mme Delessert you can see in the published collection). But I must stop or I shall fill the next page with Mme Delessert. Mme Gautier you are acquainted with; she gains upon our esteem every day. Her society like her mothers is literary, well bred and *select*.

Turn the handle of the magic lantern! Who is this graceful figure with all the elegance of court manners and all the simplicity

[1] Pictet, *Voyage de trois mois*, 193–4. He describes ME's shyness and 'les yeux baissés'. ME was away from home at the time of his first visit and had to be summoned back.

[2] A. Berquin, *L'Ami des enfans* (1782). The letters of Rousseau to Mme Delessert are probably those in *Lettres sur la botanique*. A general collection of his letters came out in 1803, but there is no evidence that ME saw it.

of domestic virtue—Don't you know her? She is Mme Pastoret. She was chosen for the preceptress of the Princess of [blank in MS.] in opposition to the wife of Condorcet an intriguing coquette and her husband had (I forget how many) more votes than Condorcet when it was put to the question who should be preceptor to the Dauphin at the beginning of the revolution. I must not tell you more of their history or I should have room for nothing else. Both M. and Mme Pastoret speak remarkably well—each with the species of eloquence which becomes them. He was president of the 1st assembly and at the head of the Kings council in the law department something like our Attorney General only of higher rank. The four ministers who were of the council at that time have all perished! He escaped by miracle or rather by courage.[1] He resembles my father in character more than anyone I have seen. As to Mme Pastoret I don't know any body to whom I can compare her except perhaps to Anne Nangle, who has something of Mme Pastoret's gracefulness. The Marquis de Chastellux speech exactly describes her 'Elle n'a point d'expression sans grâce et point de grâce sans expression.' She has two fine little boys to whom she is not a mere fashionable mother. I wish I had room here to describe her establishment for 28 poor children—the children of women who are occupied all day in the markets &c. They used to leave their children locked up or let them run about the streets. Now Mme Pastoret has provided them with a home and proper employments and she sends them home with their parents at night, that she may not destroy the tie of natural affection. I never saw any charitable institution that seemed to me so useful or that was half so touching. We saw all the little urchins at work in their small schoolroom opening on a little garden like that described in Shenstone's 'Schoolmistress'.[2] The children are under the care of a Soeur Françoise, as simple and good as any of the children. A little creature of ten months whose life she had saved lay with its weak head upon her shoulder whilst she was settling the plain work of her pupils—quite careless of the spectators. Nothing in this house was above the condition of the children—nothing could tend to give them ideas that might make

[1] ME in her Paris Notebook records Pastoret's history as told by himself.

[2] W. Shenstone, *The Schoolmistress* (1737 and 1742).

them afterwards discontented with their lot. In short we plainly saw that everything here was for use and nothing for ostentation.[1] A child of about six years old—I am sorry I began this story for I cannot stop.

Pray turn the magic lantern—Here come Mme Suard—with whom *it is said* Mr. Day was in love—and M. Suard a man of literature antiently of the French academy—Very good company in this house—for instance one night—The count (son of Duke) and countess de Crillon and sons—M. Lally Tolendal—exceedingly like father Tom—of an Irish family name Mullalagh which he softened into *Lally*—said to be more eloquent than any man ever heard to speak in France except Mirabeau—Marquis de Montmorency—a polite man of honor—worthy of his great name. Push on magic lantern. Here comes Boissy d'Anglas—a fine head! Such a head as you may imagine the man to have who restrained by his single courage the fury of the national assemblies when the head of one of the deputies was cut off and put on the table before him.[2] Next comes Camille Jordan—a man of virtue and eloquence, of pen, not of tongue. Dont mistake him for two horrid beings who resemble him in name. He was one of the Déportés.[3] Next comes M. de Prony directeur des ponts et chaussées—an excellent mechanic and mathematician (You do not desire to know more about him—but you would if you heard him speak. Little William would live in this man's pocket or up his sleeve).

Who comes next? Mme Campan—mistress of the first boarding school here—who educated Mme Louis Bonaparte and who professes to keep her pupils entirely separate from servants *according to the advice of Practical Education*[4]—paid us many compliments—is a woman of great address—makes up her goods just according as bespoke by parents—teaches drawing in a manner superior to anything I had any idea of from English schools—

[1] See ME's story *Madame de Fleury* in *Tales of Fashionable Life*, 1st series (1809), in which she describes Mme Pastoret's school. See Introduction p. xviii n. 3.

[2] In 1795, when Boissy d'Anglas was presiding over the Convention, an armed mob burst in carrying the head of Féraud on a pike. Boissy d'Anglas took off his hat and saluted, shewing no sign of fear. His courage deterred his colleagues from taking flight.

[3] Camille Jordan escaped to Germany just before the *coup d'état* of 18 Fructidor, although he was on the list of those to be arrested and deported.

[4] *Practical Education*, chap. iv, 'Servants'. This chapter was much criticized in England for impracticability.

could compare her with Mrs. Devis[1]—thought her superior—received from her a drawing in a gilt frame—will shew it you soon. Who do you think desired to meet and met us at Mme Campans? The beautiful Mme Récamier—invited us to dinner—her house said to be furnished in the best taste of any house in Paris—Very elegant and she does the honors well—very obliging manners—ambitious of the *suffrage* des gens d'esprit—at her dinner met the fashionable tragic and comic poet of Paris[2] and the richest man in Paris [Ouvrard] sat beside Charlotte!!! Went to the opera with Mme Récamier. She produces a great sensation whenever she appears in public—plays her part well with her veil particularly. I had often heard that a veil adds to beauty—here it almost creates it. She is certainly handsome very handsome but there is much of the magic of fashion in the enthusiasm she creates.[3]

Who comes next—Kosciusko—cured of his wounds—[simple][4] in his manners like all truly great men—met [him] at the house of a polish count and countess whose name [I] cannot spell—saw at the same time a beautiful princess [Jablons]ka or some such name and varieties of Polish pr[incesses]—There is a Russian Princess here who is always carried in and out of her carriage by two giant foot[men and a Russian] Prince so rich that [he seems not] to be able to spend his fortune and asks advice [how he shall do it. He never thinks] it seems of giving any of it away.

Who comes next—M. Deleuze who translated [the] Botanic garden[5] *as well* as it could be tra[nslated into] Fénelon-like prose. Who comes next? [ ] M. and Mme de Vindé [who

[1] Mrs. Devis kept the London school with ME had attended in 1781–2.

[2] The fasionable tragic poet was perhaps M. J. Chénier, but it is difficult to select the most famous among a number of now obscure poets.

[3] Charlotte E (29 Dec.) says of Mme Récamier: 'She is not exceedingly beautiful but she has charming and sweet manners and little affectation. She has not a great deal of *esprit* but quite enough.'

[4] The MS. of the latter part of this letter was clearly already damaged when the *Memoir* was being edited and it has since deteriorated further. The text has been partly reconstructed from *Mem.* i. 138–41. The list of people commented on also included Mme Cabarrus, M. and Mme Degérando and Sir Charles Blagden: 'O (the only Englishman [ ]—he gets in per favor of Count Rumford)'. RLE had known Blagden in London in the 1770s.

[5] Erasmus Darwin, *The Botanic Garden* (1789, 1791). Deleuze's translation was published in 1799/1800 as *Les Amours des plantes, poème en quatre chants, suivi de notes et de dialogues.*

have] a superb gallery of pictures—best concerts in Paris—and Library of 18 thousand volumes well counted and well arranged—and what charmed me more than either the books or pictures a little grandaughter of three years old very like my sweet Fanny with stockings exactly the same as those aunt Mary knit for Fanny and listing shoes precisely like what Fanny used to wear. She sat on my knee and caressed me with her soft warm little hands and looked at me with her smiling intelligent eyes. . . .
December 3rd. Here comes the brink of the last page and I have said nothing of the Apollo—of the paintings at the Museum—of the Louvre—Versailles—Le petit Trianon—La Monnaie—The Theatres—the Opera—The Abbé Sicard—Les sourds et Muets—L'Institution pour les aveugles—L'institut national and L'Hôpital des Invalides! What shall I do! I cannot speak of every thing at once and when I speak to you so many things always crowd upon [long erasure]

[Here my dear] aunt I was interrupted in a man[ner that will surprise you a]lmost as much as it surprised me [by the coming in of M. Edelcrantz] private secretary to the King [of Sweden, whom we have mentioned to you, of superior under]standing and mild manners, came[to offer me his] hand and heart. My heart you may [suppose cannot return his attachment] for I have seen but very little of [him and have not had time to ha]ve formed any judgment except [that I think] nothing could tempt me to leave my [own dear friends and my o]wn country to live in Sweden—[ ]ne would be materially injured by [ ] a mother who is old and dependant on him [. De]arest aunt I write to you the first moment [. I] am sure that except my father and mother no person in the world will feel so much interested in all that concerns me. I need not tell you that my father 'Such in this moment as in all the past'[1] is kindness itself —kindness far far superior to what I deserve—but I am grateful for it—and for yours my dearest aunt and friend. . . . Adieu—write to me pray . . .

[1] Pope, *Moral Essays*, i. 1.264.

Mrs. Edgeworth to Revd. D. A. Beaufort

1st December, 1802

As to M. Étache[1] I despair of being able to find him out. Military men are never seen in company—they live in a separate society and are not esteemed by the literary part of this little world. *Homme de lettres* is almost a profession and if a man can acquire that character he can with a small portion of esprit maintain it and at the same time have his company solicited by people of literature and men of pleasure. If a man of letters can dress himself decently he may find a dinner every day of the year and in accepting of it confer a favor upon each invitor. In that I think the manners of the two countries differ essentially—as well as in the interior regulations and arrangement of families. Husbands and wives apartments are quite separate—the breakfasts at different hours—their morning employments all separate. In the evening both are in society sometimes together and sometimes not. Since ridicules have been laid aside the husbands company is more necessary because he carries his wifes pocket handkerchief. A young man told me the other day que les maris sont devenus des meubles bien utiles cet hiver.

One meets but little gold in circulation. What there is consists of double and single Louis[2] of Louis 16th and 15th. There are no national banknotes under 500 francs and the private banks never issue any notes. They gave little canvas sacks of crowns. I felt like Gil Blas and his 40 crowns[3] when £50 worth of écus de 6 francs were put into my hands. It seemed an immense sum but it disappeared so soon that I could hardly believe I had spent it. At last however I convinced myself that no one had robbed me. Money seems much wanting. Nous sommes des Gueux—is the common phrase of all ranks—except the parvenus or *fournisseurs*[4] as they are called here. I was in company with the richest of these M. Ouvrard. I should like to see a little of that society too but we

[1] Anne de Beaufort, aunt to the Revd. Daniel Cornelis de Beaufort, Mrs. E's grandfather, married in 1684 a M. de l'Étache.

[2] A *louis* was worth 24 frs.

[3] Le Sage, *Les Aventures de Gil Blas de Santillane*, chap. ii: Gil Blas, given 40 ducats by his uncle, sets out to seek his fortune.

[4] Contractors.

could not without more expense of time and dress than they are worth.

Friday 3rd December

I had a great deal of conversation yesterday with M. Lasteyrie the president of the Agricultural Society here. He is a very pleasing benevolent man and has promised to give me for you an account of the process by which he has found means to preserve the flour of potatoes for 8 years in as good a state as the first day.[1] He has given Mr. E a little bag of the flour in its seventh year which seems good to all the senses. He told me that Normandy the Limousin but above all La Vendée produced the finest cattle. In La Vendée they have had cattle shews and prizes given for the best for 150 years. The three finest oxen at each shew were always killed and the meat of each sold at double the price for the finest—a third for the next and ¼ more for the last. They had names such as the Condé the Connétable &c and people invited their friends to dine with [them] pour manger le grand Condé ou le Connétable Bourbon. In the Limousin they still feed in summer because of the heat. In Normandy they always fatten in the field and are beginning to cultivate artificial grasses. In La Vendée they have plenty of natural grasses on the hills in winter—in the long extended marais in summer.

You are impatient to know Mr. E's opinion of the French Dictator but alas on that head your curiosity never will be satisfied for after taking all possible steps to secure his presentation after meeting with much civility from Mr. Merry and Lord Whitworth he gave up the idea intirely from motives of pure dislike to a man who could treat the wretched Swiss as he has done.[2] I cannot tell you how sorry I am . . .

Mrs. Edgeworth to Harriet Beaufort

Thursday, 6th December, 1802

My dearest Harriet . . . Since I closed my letter to my mother last saturday what have I seen? Why Sunday morning we went to M.

[1] See below, p. 68 n. 2.
[2] See above, p. 19 n. 2.

Bayen's cabinet de physique[1]—take notice no one goes to church or thinks of doing so. At M. Bayen's we met several people whose names you already know—Chenevix, Knox, Scott (son to Sir Hop), Irishmen—Edelcrantz (Swede)—Eisenmann (German) &c. An immense Electrical Apparatus occupies the middle of the room. The Battery contains 40 Squ. feet. It is connected with a conductor on the roof and is frequently charged with the electric contents of a cloud. He showed us many electrical wonders—impressions of various forms—explosions of various kinds. I had not the courage to touch the chain as the shock would have been tremendous but I admired a charge dispersed on the surface of a nonconducting plate on the ceiling with all the appearance of Blue and forked lightning—a lamp which was lighted mechanically by approaching tubes filled with hydrogen Gass—phosphoric bottles Barbary organs, musical glasses, old china fine enamel and much of the nonsense and some of science of Optics—were all to be seen in that little hot room. The master of the house is a very benevolent and obliging man who exhibits his collections and his inventions to strangers from pure good nature.

The evening of Sunday we spent with our dear Madame Pastoret—without exception the most engaging woman at Paris. Then we were introduced to the Comte et Comtesse de Crillon and their sons and to the celebrated *Boissy d'Anglas*. You will find his name often repeated in the early parts of the revolution—he was one of the chief of the Modérés who were afterwards called Royalistes. Monday morning M. Pictet breakfasted with us and we went to a M. Morel de Vindé who had invited us in the morning to see his gallery of pictures.[2] It is as I told him a charmant cabinet. To three feet high round the room which is 32 feet long

[1] This *cabinet de physique* was formed by the scientist Jean Bayen (1725–98). It is not clear who was now looking after it. For the electrical machine, see p. 6 n. 2 above. Phosphoric bottles were bottles containing calcium sulphide which glows in the dark after exposure to sunlight or to an electrical spark. A Barbary organ is a barrel organ, named after its inventor Barberi of Modena. The lamp was probably the Hydrogen Lamp invented in 1779 by Alessandro Volta. Such lamps were popular in *cabinets de physique*.

[2] M. de Vindé had inherited a fine collection of pictures etc. from a relation, M. Paignon d'Ijouval. He eventually sold the pictures to an English dealer: Frénilly, *Souvenirs*, 199; W. Buchanan, *Memoirs of Painting*, 372–3. ME describes his house in her *Émilie de Coulanges*: *Tales of Fashionable Life*, 2nd series (1812), ii. 31–3. The description is omitted in later editions.

are bookcases of yellow satin wood with doors of plate glass through which you see the finest editions of all the poets and superb collections of Engravings. From the top of this pretty book case to the Ceiling the walls are covered not crouded with excellent pictures of the best masters of the Flemish and French schools all of small size and highly finished. We saw a beautiful Cock painted in Fresco which was brought from the baths of Titus and a mosaic head dug up at Herculaneum. M. de Vindé's collection of fine prints is valued at 15,000 Louis. He has a pretty little daughter as little as Maria who is married and has two most beautiful nice little children whom she has just vaccinated.

Well from that house of wealth and elegance we went to David's *Atelier* in the Louvre and after going up 3 pairs of stairs found ourselves in a long gallery unplaistered unceiled yellow lights crossing it from broken arched windows—sometimes breaks in the side walls and rails through which you saw down to some passage beneath. And to this dirt inconceivable and smells abominable. At last we found our way up another winding staircase into a large handsome room where we saw the famous picture of the Horatii receiving their swords from their father and the other tableau more valuable still of the Elder Brutus when the body of that son whom he had condemned to death was just brought home. I also saw the Sabines. David is the best french painter but he is démocrate enragé.

We spent the evening with the Pictets charming sister Mme Lullin and her beautiful daughters. Friday morning we lost in talking to various visitors and evening we did not gain much by going to the opening of the philosophic lectures at the Lycée.[1] Wednesday we went to see the Hôtel de *Monnoie* (the Mint) which was built under the direction of Calonne and is indeed sumptuous as were all his plans. The Salle for public Lectures is 50 feet square 30 feet high supported by 4 pillars of Siena Marble at each side and a half one in the corners. We heard a lecture from M. Lesage the master of the Mint upon chemistry in which he endeavored to prove the old doctrine of phlogiston[2] and smiled with inconceiv-

[1] After 1803 *l'Athénée*. An institution founded in 1786 by the *philosophes* where learned lectures were given on a variety of subjects.

[2] Phlogiston, a hypothetical substance or principle formerly supposed to exist in combination in all other combustible bodies and to be disengaged by the process of

able self-complacency when he thought he had settled the minds of his audience on that important subject. We regretted very much the loss of an hour spent in listening to stuff which we were not to allow to settle in our heads. I was however ordered by Mr. Chenevix[1] and the rest of our company to go and make a compliment to M. Lesage who waited in the room for something of that sort. I said I could not tell such a lie for I never had been so ennuyée. At last they walked up en face de lui and I think I was very ingenious to be able to find out a compliment so équivoque that it pleased him and did not compromise my veracity. Here is a fine collection of specimens of stones and ores—all that is necessary for the study of mineralogy—and a nice little laboratory for the Assaying of metals. This place was as pretty and clean as a lady's boudoir. M. Lesage's study is more elegant than any lady's boudoir. Among the ornamental Morceaux that adorn it there is a curious figure made of some metal of which unfortunately I have forgot the name which is of a red vermilion colour but when exposed to the light is covered with a yellow oxyd like unpolished Gold leaf. The side that is in the dark remains red.[2]

In the apartments of M. Le Breton we saw Gérards original picture of Cupid and Psyche before they were animated by love who flutters over them in the form of a Butterfly.[3] The painting is very good but the idea is too recherchée to give me as much pleasure as the simple representation of Belisarius with one of his grandchildren which is also by the same artist. . . . But to finish my journal I must add that M. Le Breton Degérando and his wife dined with us and in the evening took us to the Lyceum to hear Delille recite some of his own verses. We heard him with

combustion. This theory of combustion had been demolished by Lavoisier. Members of the Lunar Society had been much preoccupied in phlogistical experiment in the 1780s and had been in general slow to accept Lavoisier's findings: Schofield, *Lunar Society*, 289.

[1] Charlotte E (29 Dec.) says that Chenevix was rather cold and awkward in manner 'does not know how to produce his wit and great cleverness.' In an undated letter written after her return home she also says that Chenevix 'was not in very high favor among the French literati for he had introduced his mistress as his wife at the time of the revolution.'

[2] A dichroic figure, possibly a gold compound.

[3] The butterfly represented not love but the soul. The Greek word psyche stands for both soul and butterfly (*Papilio brassicae*): *The Age of Neo-Classicism* (*Catalogue of the 14th exhibition of the Council of Europe*), 67. Mrs. Margaret Wind kindly drew my attention to this reference.

much pleasure and indeed if we had not felt it ourselves we must have caught some enthusiasm from the delighted crowd round us. I never heard such applause before . . .

Maria Edgeworth to Sophy Ruxton

Paris, Rue de Lille, no. 529,
8th December 1802

I take it for granted my dear friend that you have by this time seen a letter I wrote to my aunt a few days ago. To you, as to her, every thought of my mind is open. Believe me I know the value of your friendship, and ever since I quitted you it has been one of the most anxious wishes of my heart to prove to those who have loved me from my childhood that no change of place or circumstances [can make] my affection and gratitude for them vary a single point. Perhaps I have been too anxious and have been, as usual, my dear Sophy, a foolish self-tormentor. For instance when I had finished my last letter to my aunt I was going to have torn it to bits and to have written it over again because I found it contained only a list of the fine people and wits we had seen and I was afraid my aunt would think I made this list only from vanity and that I was *run away* with by a set of new acquaintance. My mother however stopped my tearing mania and made me send off my letter just as it was. Do you tell me the truth. Tell me whether any of these my imaginations were just? So much for folly—Now for love and wisdom. I have nothing new to tell you about our Swedish knight. I persist in refusing to think of leaving my country and my friends to live at the court of Stockholm &c &c and he tells me (of course) that there is nothing he would not sacrifice except his duty. He has been all his life in the service of the king of Sweden, has places under him, and is actually employed in collecting information for a large political Establishment.[1] He thinks himself bound in honor to finish what he has begun—says he should not fear the ridicule or blame that would

[1] Edelcrantz's foreign tour was concerned with the Swedish import and export trade. He was also to familiarize himself with European industry and agriculture. The large political establishment was perhaps the Kommerscollegium. Professor H. W. Donner kindly translated for me the relevant information from H. Gierow, *A. N. C. Edelcrantz*.

be thrown upon him by his countrymen for quitting his country at his age but that he should despise himself if he abandoned his duty to gratify any passion. All this is very fine and I must add reasonable—but it is reasonable for him only; not for me. I have not ever felt anything for him but esteem and gratitude and he says he could never be contented to be loved next to a father. I wish you were here! Write to me. It is a great while since I heard from you. Pray write. I need not I am sure beg you will not show this part of my letter to *anybody* except my aunt.

Now I will quit the dear chapter of self. Add to the list of remarkables and agreeables in my last—The count and countess de Ségur father and mother to our well bred translator—a charming couple—She, a beautiful Ninon de L'Enclos[1] of a grandmother—he a French nobleman of the old school who adds to agreeable manners a great deal of elegant literature. He repeated for us some beautiful domestic poems of his own composition.[2] He has promised to give them to me and of course you will have them. Malouet—the amiable and able counsellor of the king must also be added to your list. We met him yesterday. He has a fine countenance and like all great men simple manners—conversed freely with my father—not at all afraid of *committing* himself. In general I do not see any of that prodigious fear of *committing* themselves which makes the company of some English men of letters and reputation irksome even to their admirers. Mr. Palmer[3] the great man of taste who has lived for many years in Italy admiring fine pictures and statues is here and is very much provoked that the French should now see anything of what he has seen without stirring from Paris. Mr. Rogers the author of the pleasures of memory[4] is here—a man of taste and literature. We see Mr. Chenevix and Knox and Seymour sometimes. I do not at present recollect any more persons to add to your list, so I will go on to *things*.

I shall not pretend to say much to you about pictures or statues for I would rather that you and my aunt should think I had not one

[1] Anne (Ninon) de Lenclos (1620–1705), a celebrated courtesan who retained her charm well into old age.

[2] Louis Philippe de Ségur published in 1801 *Contes, fables, chansons et vers*.

[3] Perhaps Roger Palmer of Rush, co. Dublin, where he had a fine picture collection. I am indebted to Sir Ellis Waterhouse for this suggestion.

[4] See p. 33 n. 1.

ounce of taste than that you should suspect me of one grain of affectation. The pictures are all in the gallery of the Louvre. There is a [reflection] from the windows on each side of the gallery so that many of the pictures are seen at a disadvantage but the person who has been employed by Bonaparte to arrange them tells us that this is only *un arrangement provisoire*, that they intend to build an additional gallery in which one half of the pictures which are now crowded together are to be placed and as soon as this is accomplished the windows on one side of the present gallery are to be shut up. My aunt Ruxton's favorite Domenichino[1] is not at present *visible*. Several of the finest pictures are (as they say) *sick* and the physicians are busy restoring them to health and beauty. God send they may not mar instead of mending. In one of Raphael's pictures which is just come out of their hospital the eyes are of a very modern odd sort of blue.[2] Raphael's Transfiguration is now in a state of convalescence and has not yet made its appearance in public. We were admitted into the sick room two or three mornings ago and stayed some hours paying our devoirs to it. At first I found the number of pictures fatiguing to my attention. Admiration (No offence to poor human nature) is sometimes very fatiguing. Indeed whatever is felt intensely cannot be felt for a long time together without mixture of pain. I shall not mention the pictures we liked best because I have marked them in a catalogue which I hope soon to look over with you upon Black Castle or Edgeworthstown sofa cushioned up as we were in the happy days when we read Belinda together.

The statues in the Louvre or Musée as they are pleased to rechristen it are much better placed than the pictures—excepting always the Apollo, which although it has the honor of naming an apartment La Salle d'Apollon, is placed in a provoking manner niched up almost close to the wall and railed out as the altar of a church so that nobody can get behind the statue and you have only a three quarter view of it. Even to my ignorant eyes it does indeed appear *admirable*! The Venus de Medicis has not yet arrived at Paris but I hope we shall see her before we go as she has been

[1] Almost certainly the Vatican *Last Communion of St. Jerome*, painted in 1614, in this period one of the most admired pictures in the world.

[2] ME perhaps refers to the *Madonna di Foligno*. There was an account of its extensive restoration in the Louvre catalogue of 1802. Fuseli described it as unrecognizable: Gould, *Trophy of Conquest*, 68, 81.

long upon the road. It is impossible I think that any unprejudiced Englishman or woman can avoid being struck with the liberality with which the French throw open to the public and to foreigners all their treasures of art and science.[1] With such models before them and with such ardor in studying them they must in time improve their national taste—which indeed at present seems much to need improvement. There is but one obstacle to their progress–their preposterous partiality for the works of the French school. Half Paris is at this instant stark mad about a bad picture of Guérins Phaedre et Hippolyte which some of them actually think equal to Raphael's pictures. Every day we see numbers of artists however in the gallery of the Musée copying from the ancient masterpieces. We often meet common market women and persons certainly not above the rank of cobblers admiring the pictures and the pictures of those who are admiring the pictures would be well worth drawing. Whilst Guérin's Phaedre was in L'Exposition Françoise the room was so crowded that it was scarcely possible to wedge in for a sight of it. It has now been purchased by Government. We were informed yesterday from good authority that half a million of money is layed out annually by Government for the encouragement of the arts so that the French are in a fair way to become a nation of painters of some sort or other. I did not intend to have written more than a line and here is a page about pictures. Still as I wrote on I thought my aunt will like to know this or that and I could not stop.

Of the public buildings here the Louvre and L'Hôpital des Invalides appear to me the finest. The Louvre every time we see it strikes us with fresh admiration. In the Invalides all the flags that have been used in battle or that have been won from foreign nations are displayed. A long drawn aisle of glory must create ambition in the rising generation of military in France. We met here a little boy of 9 years old with his tutor looking at Turenne's monument which has been placed here with great taste *alone*—with the one word *Turenne* upon the sarcophagus. My father spoke to the little boy who was looking at the monument and his tutor told him that the child came to look at a picture in the church in

[1] In her Paris Notebook ME writes 'Lucien B proposed that people should pay at Museum &c everybody opposed—for glory of nation—it would disgrace the French nation to shew the spoils of other nations for money.'

which an heroic action of one of his relations is pourtrayed. We went into the library of L'Hôpital des Invalides and found a circle of old soldiers sitting round a stove all reading most comfortably. It was a very pleasing touching sight. One old soldier who had lost both his hands and who had iron hooks at the end of his wrists was sitting at a little table reading Télémaque[1] with great attention. The Hôpital des Invalides is the Greenwich Hospital of France.

L'École Polytechnique which is established in the superb palace of the Prince de Condé is a fine public institution. All the best judges say that it is impossible that anybody should go through the course of education at L'École Polytechnique without being a mathematician and a mechanic. The object of government is to make the cleverest young men in the nation civil and military engineers. The means are admirably adapted to the end but I cannot attempt to detail them in a letter; besides my father will explain all this to you better than I can. He has been chosen honorary member of the society pour des Arts [et Métiers][2] and a splendid letter has been written to him on the occasion [ ] I wish. The director of this establishment shewed us all the various models of machines which are well arranged in a vast apartment. Remember to ask my father about a machine of [ ] for making chains. It is said that the attention of the pupils at L'École Polytechnique has been so exclusively directed to the abstruse sciences that they are shamefully deficient in literature—great mathematicians who do not know how to spell. This was pointed out to Bonaparte and he has taken measures to have it remedied.

The National Institute did not appear so well in reality as in description. My father went to two of their sittings—saw that all the members looked like blackguards.[3] The subject was inviting

[1] Fénelon's romance of 1699.

[2] Otherwise the Société pour l'encouragement de l'industrie nationale.

[3] The Institut National, created in 1795, replaced the pre-Revolutionary learned societies, such as the Académie Française. It was reorganized in 1803 into four classes, Physical and Mathematical Sciences, French Language and Literature, Ancient History and Literature, and Fine Arts. 'Blackguard' at this date merely implies a low fellow, someone without the manners of a gentleman. The Revd. W. Shepherd found the proceedings of the Institut as dull as those of the Royal Society and said that the uniform of the members made them look like 'respectable old English butlers': *Paris in 1802 and 1814*, 102.

to the genius of nonsense—about certain stones which many of the philosophers here firmly believe to have fallen from the moon![1] The Institute is under the direction of Chaptal. He is consulted by Government and has much power. Chaptal you know is minister de L'Intérieur. Berthollet Monge [Hassenfratz] Haüy &c are all under the patronage of Government. The chemists are all very able men but it is said qu'ils ont tous à quoi se reprocher—During the revolution they did many things which must weigh heavy on their consciences. I can say no more here but put me in mind to tell you circumstances relative to the death of Lavoisier! I forget whether I mentioned Mme Lavoisier. She is very obliging to us and we meet excellent company at her house, but I cannot say she quite answers my expectations. However I will see more before I decide. Mme de Staël will be here in a few days. Miss Williams we did not chuse to go to see, though many English do. She is not in any of the societies we are in but sees a vast deal of company. My father I believe will pay her a visit just before we go and he will do the same by Mme de Genlis—for similar reasons.[2]

My aunt asks me what I think of French society. I like all I have seen of it extremely but we hear from all sides that we have seen only the best of Paris—the men of literature and les anciens nobles. Les nouveaux riches are quite a different set who never mix with the others. My father has seen something of them at Mme Tallien's (now Cabarrus) and was much disgusted. Mme Récamier whose name we have been accustomed to see in the newspapers joined with Mme Tallien's as a woman of the first fashion in Paris is quite of an opposite sort—a graceful *decent* beauty of perfectly good character (Put me in mind to tell you an anecdote about her and Lucien B[onaparte]). We were at a very splendid agreeable ball at her house a few days ago. She dances charmingly —The valse especially. God help the heart of the man who ventures to dance it with her! She has all the ambassadors at her house and we are told all that is brilliant and elegant in Paris of decent reputation. In many houses there is a great mixture but of this I speak by report. My father says I must see it though

[1] The stones were meteorites.

[2] The objection to Helen Maria Williams was presumably her connection with John Hurford Stone, who had deserted his wife for her. Mme de Genlis's reputation was tarnished by her association with Philippe Égalité, Duke of Orléans. For the Edgeworths' visit to Mme de Genlis, see below, pp. 96–102.

Charlotte must not. You see I am too bad to be made worse. The dress at Mme Récamier's was decent-ish—gowns not above half way down the back—bosoms not disgustingly naked—Mme R perfectly simple in her dress and manner.

The wife or as I should say the lady of the ambassador of Portugal is a pretty pleasing woman author of Adèle de Senanges[1] which she wrote in England for bread when she was an emigrant. Her friends always proclaim her title as an authoress before her other titles—there is a striking difference in this respect at Paris from what we have been used to. I thought the Portuguese Ambassadress a pleasing woman before I was told that she had one night pronounced at Mme Lavoisiers an eloquent eulogium upon Belinda. She waited till we had left the room before she praised it. For this I am sure you will love her. I have never heard any one person talk of dress or fashions since I came to Paris!—and very little scandal. A scandalmonger would be starved here. Conversation turns upon the new petites pièces and little novels which come out daily and a new novel is talked of for a few days and with as much eagerness as a new fashion in other places.[2] They also talk a vast deal about the little essays of criticism either on men in place or poets which come out in their daily Journals. In their newspapers there are always pieces of literature and criticism and literary disputes run high but though people are warm in conversation they are polite-pungent but not bitter. To give you an idea of the cheek-by-jowl-ism of power and literature in yesterday's Journal des Débats (a newspaper) after a flaming panegyric of Bonaparte the author says 'Et après avoir parlé du maître de L'Univers de qui peut-on parler?—du plus grand des poètes—de Racine—then comes a criticism of Phèdre! The French are certainly mad about their poets as well as about their painters.

[1] Mme de Souza published *Adèle de Senanges* in 1796.

[2] See ME's *Leonora* (1806), Letter xviii: 'Zénobie, which I now send you, is the declared rival of Séraphine. Parties have run high on both sides, and applications were made and innuendoes discovered and wit and sentiment came to close combat, and, as usual, people talked till they did not understand themselves. For a fortnight, wherever one went the first words to be heard on entering every *salon* were Séraphine and Zénobie—Peace or war . . . To say the truth, I am tired of both heroines, for a fortnight is too long to talk or think of any one thing . . .' Zénobie perhaps represents Mme Cottin's *Amélie de Mansfield* (1803) and Séraphine Mme de Staël's *Delphine* of the same year. Cf. Lord Granville Leveson Gower, *Private Correspondence, 1781–1821*, ed. Castalia Countess Granville, 378.

A man of abilities defied my father the other day to point out one single flat line in Racine.

And after Racine of whom can I speak but of le maître de L'univers? I beg pardon for leaving so little room to speak of his grand Review. We saw it the day before yesterday from a window that looked out on the court of the Louvre and Place du Carousel. He rode down the lines on a fine spirited white Spanish horse—took off his hat to salute various generals and gave us a full view of his pale woebegone countenance. He is very little but much at ease on horseback. It is said that he never appears to so much advantage as on horseback. There were about 6000 troops—a fine show—well appointed and some but not all well mounted. On one of those who had distinguished themselves in the battle of Marengo all eyes were fixed. Except for the sight of Bonaparte and his fine horse I would as soon have seen a puppet show for they all looked like pasteboard figures in red coats in the back scenes on the stage.

Whilst I was looking out of the window at the Review a gentleman came in who had passed many years in Spain; he began to talk to me about Madrid and when he heard my name informed me that it was a name not unknown at Madrid. He told me that a Spanish lady is translating Prac Ed from the French. She understands English and he has given me her direction that we may send her the English book. He told me a great many entertaining things about Spain but these I must keep packed up in my head if I can till I see you . . .

Mr. Knox who was presented to Bonaparte and saw all the wonders of the presentation says that it was a huddled business—all the world received in a very small room. B[onaparte] spoke more to officers and generals than to anyone else—affected to be gracious to the English—said 'L'Angleterre est une grande nation aussi bien que la France. Il faut que nous soyons amis!' Great men's words like little men's dreams are sometimes to be interpreted by the rule of contraries.

And now my dear Sophy my father has warned me to go to bed and I must think of obeying him in less than half an hour. It wants quarter of 12—Oh very early for us! This is the 2d. evening since we came to Paris that we have spent at home. I must conclude with a list of things I have forgotten to mention that in case I should not recollect them hereafter you may put me in mind to tell you more about them when we meet . . . I must not tell you everything, else when we meet you will find according to the African proverb (v. Park) that the foolish travellers come home with nothing but the hair on their head[1] . . .

Charlotte Edgeworth to Charlotte Sneyd

Paris, Rue de Lille, 8th December, 1802

My dear Aunt Charlotte, One of the great objects of a visit to Paris you know was to see Bonaparte. The review is over as you have seen in the papers but has my father seen and spoken to the great man? No he did not wish it. All of our distant friends will I am afraid be disappointed but some here are [of] opinion that my fathers refusal to be presented to him shows a proper pride towards inferior virtue. All the reasons for this mode of conduct will serve us perhaps for debate certainly for conversation when we return and if you are not all perfectly content in this particular we will make amends by giving you accounts of those whose good qualities have struck us and whose manners pleased us. Mme Lullin sister of M. Pictet is one of them. She has a sprightly sensible polite countenance and an agreeable figure and manners. Two daughters one of 15 the other 18 are worthy of their mother. The eldest is particularly sensible and charming—added to these excellencies much beauty of face person and expression. We spent two evenings with them. I do not say they were as agreeable as some that we passed at other peoples houses, because here we saw some ladies in particular who were much inferior to Mme Lullin and her daughters and we are much inclined to the opinion of Mme Suard who says that those societies are the most agreeable where there are the fewest women. If all women were not a little inferior to her I should not hesitate to assent to her proposition and I should with pleasure read Madame de Staëls book called Le malheur d'être femme.[2] If on the contrary all

[1] Mungo Park's *Travels* came out in 1799.

[2] *Le Malheur d'être femme* was the title of the French translation of Mary Wollstonecraft Godwin's unfinished novel *The Wrongs of Women or Maria*, first published in *Posthumous Works*, 1798. The translation came out at much the same time as *Delphine*

women were Mme Pastorets or Mme Delesserts or even Mme Gautiers I think I should take up the book with an intention not to be convinced. It is using Mme Suard extremely ill to compare her with those who are allowed on all hands to be the pride of Paris. When we see you we shall have a new object of comparison instead of Miss Pakenham who may condescend to be compared with Mme Pastoret.

Just as I was writing this yesterday evening which by the by was the first that we had spent at home for a fortnight a lady whom we have perhaps not mentioned to you Mme de Prony the wife of a good philosopher and mechanic—No very common thing in this part of the world. Some of the most horrible revolutionists were most skilled in the sciences. Is not that a pity aunt Charlotte? I have never yet heard it said that chemistry and mechanics made men bad tho' many bad men have been chemists and mechanics so I hope you will tell William this. These clever chemists are held in the utmost detestation by numbers of the most sensible men who admire their ingenuity and talents. We saw one who was teacher of some of the sciences at one of the chief academies in France and my father who was standing near him remarked that after having been talking on several amusing and interesting subjects he gave one of the deepest sighs that he ever heard. M. de Prony on the contrary is one that would please William exceedingly. He has a great deal of knowledge, and good nature which makes him ready and willing to communicate it. He is extremely fond of music and plays upon many instruments. His wife has the happiness to possess the same talent. When she was here last night she shewed us that she was not merely one of the most obliging good natured women but also very clever. She spoke among other things of the pleasures she derived from music. She agreed with Mme Chéron niece to the Abbé Morellet an excellent musician who mentioned the same thing about three hours before, that in grief and in solitude music instead of alleviating the pains of

and is advertised at the end of the first edition of the latter. It was a joke that *Le malheur d'être femme* should have been the title of Mme de Staël's book which concerns the misfortunes of a young woman who was always impulsively doing kindnesses of a nature to damage her reputation not only in the eyes of the world but of her lover. The motto of the book is 'Un homme doit savoir braver l'opinion, une femme s'y soumettre'.

solitude always increased them and that she had always been obliged to lay by her instrument while she was in grief so much did it touch her mind or rather awaken her sensibility. She had of late been obliged to give up her harp for that her lungs were very much affected by that instrument. The vibration of the instrument on her breast produced the strongest sensation particularly when she touched some chords that were in unison with her voice. This altogether with the attitude has obliged her to relinquish this amusement.

My father saw Chaptal at the National Institute. He did not appear to be anything very remarkable nor is he much respected here. We hope to go to a chemical lecture at which we shall hear Fourcroy speak—he is the best speaker here among the chemists. The Abbé Delille reads poetry particularly his own verse in a superior manner. We heard him and were extremely pleased. He is very old and is so blind that his wife whom he calls Mon Antigone[1] is obliged to lead him. She is a curious woman who is very docile when he teaches her to read verses, but who beats him when he calls for his chocolate at an unseasonable instant. This is a circumstance told us by an eye witness but I do not know whether these eyes might not be a little tinged with prejudice and whether the tongue did not exaggerate a little. I am inclined to think not because many good people refuse to see her, and the little man who told it to us seems to be good and candid. He has invented a new varnish which he covers silk, paper, leather &c with, of a black shining color on which he can stamp gold and silver ornaments and which may be applied to many purposes and which is better than oil silk because it does not crack . . .

Friday 10th—You see I am very often interrupted. Last night I was very agreeably interrupted by the necessity of dressing myself to go and see our dear Delesserts. I will introduce you to our visit of last night. All soirées here begin at nine o'clock or near it. Mme Edgeworth is announced—room full without being crouded —enough light and warmth—M. Delessert père at a card table with another gentleman who is partner in his bank and an elderly lady not unlike a housekeeper in appearance. There is a warm corner beside the fire which is always large enough to contain Mme Delessert and two or three ladies and gentlemen beside.

[1] In the *Oedipus Coloneus* of Sophocles Antigone leads her blind father Oedipus.

Mme Delessert advances to receive Mme E and invites her to sit beside [her] with many kind words and looks and rather a formal curtsy. With some volubility Mme Gautier expresses her joy at seeing us. Now we are seated. Mme Delessert has an English looking lady neatly dressed in black beside her; this lady is a Mrs. Booker sort of looking woman tho' more genteel looking. Ben Delessert advances to make his bow to the ladies, Mme Gautier my father and Maria get together. M. Pictet nephew to our dear Pictet makes his bow and adds a few words to each. 'Mlle Charlotte I was just speaking of you' says Mme Delessert to me. What she had been saying of me I forget now. I have at present only the agreeable idea that the obliging lady had been speaking of me. Mme Grivel enters. She is a clever good natured little woman and wife to the partner who is playing at cards. Enter François Delessert and another gentleman whose manners are rather forward and disagreeable—Bow to the ladies. How the company divides itself and changes places at present I am not supposed to know for young Pictet has seated himself upon a chair between my mother and me, and has commenced a long conversation with me in which Mme Grivel now and then joins (she is on the other side of me)—Mlle Lullin Pictet our friend and their virtues are discussed. Physics and metaphysics ensue by some of the windings of conversation—Harmony—astonishing power of chords in music—glass broken by the vibration of certain chords—dreams—Spain and its people manners and government. Young Pictet has been there—his books and papers were taken from him by the english in returning to france. People have little to do in Spain because their wants are easily supplied. They have a set of mountains in a part of Spain like Henry's rain gauge which collects the rain when it falls. They have thus a supply against the next dry weather when it is necessary to water their gardens—the contrivance is artificial. Tea cakes sweetmeats grapes cream and all the goods of life and some general conversation. F Delessert repeats some good lines very well—laughing and merriment. When the tea came I forgot to mention that the lady who was playing at cards came and sat beside me and she amused me for a long time with a conversation on what do you think—politics and the state of france. Now we are obliged to go—It is twelve o'clock. With much sorrow we part and all the way home we talk of the delights of the Delesserts.

I hope I have given you some idea of the pleasures of their society which always contains good people. I never was in company with Mme Delessert but what she made some éloge[1] on the character of somebody or other. When the english woman went out of the room she made her éloge. . . .

Charlotte Edgeworth to C. Sneyd Edgeworth

Paris, chez le citoyen Verber, 16th December, 1802

. . . I felt the greatest admiration the other day for little Pastoret who is a boy of ten years old who told us many circumstances in the french history which the best historian amongst us did not know, and the whole history appeared as well fixed in his mind as if the events which he mentioned had happened but a year before. M. Pastoret his father with this little boy went in the coach with us all round Paris shewing us the exact spots where many scenes had happened and many lives spent. He shewed us the house where Molière lived when he was a carpet maker. He shewed us the house where the belle Gabrielle[2] of Henry 4th lived. He shewed us the spot where he was assassinated, told us what sort of a carriage it was that he went in, where his palace was and how far off the carriage was from the Palace. It is remarkable that every house which he pointed out to us except that of Robespierre had a balcony to it. He shewed us the palace of Philippe le bel which is one of the most ordinary looking houses and [in] one of the most crouded streets. He shewed us how Paris had increased in size even since the time of Henry 4th. What are now crouded streets were the fields. He shewed us Sully's house. He told us that the reason why the Louvre has that name is from its being a maison de Chasse where they hunted the wolf from Loup a wolf and Louvrette a little wolf.

We saw where Charles 9th fired upon the people in the massacre of St. Bartholemew. M. Pastoret himself lives in one of the houses near the Hôtel de Courland where we lodged first which is opposite to the place where the king and queen were executed, and where his wife who was imprisoned in her own house was

[1] A somewhat formal discourse in honour of a person.

[2] Gabrielle d'Estrées, mistress of Henri IV.

forced by her guards to view the scene of death which took place there every day, when sixty or seventy people were put to death each day. In the middle of this place which is between the Champs élysées and the Tuileries they erected a statue which they called the statue of liberty. The guillotine was erected opposite to it that it might appear what when the heads of the victims were cut off they bowed to the statue; another refinement was that the back of the statue was turned to the palais des tuileries.

This is one of the most beautiful spots in Paris—we pass over the very spot where the statue was at least twice a day. There is a man who has had the misfortune to have committed several crimes during the revolution who appears exactly as if he was affected by the furies, we have not seen him. There is a woman in the mad house who is well known to have been at the head of one of the troupes of women assassins and revolutionists who begs for money to give to Marat and Robespierre whom she calls braves gens and who repeats the same words that she was employed to cry out in the mobs. We saw Robespierres house which is within a little court with one window in it—to which he went every night alone. His maidservant who was the only being that attended him is now living and perhaps we may see her.

There is an island in Paris the streets of which are very narrow; it carries on little commerce, the inhabitants of which are quite separate from the rest of Paris, they dine at a different hour, their manners are different; and they talk of crossing the bridge as the ancients talking of crossing the Hellespont and they never signalised themselves by any excesses in the revolution[1] . . .

I do not know whether I told you, that one of the greatest pleasures I have received from seeing things here, arises from the very little knowledge which I possess of mechanics (NB Not from the smallness of the quantity). A machine invented by one of the greatest mechanics of France for making a chain which should have each link precisely of equal size—this gave me the greatest pleasure.

We saw the savage of Aveyron. He is very like the print which is at the beginning of Itards report.[2] He has not a savage air. The

[1] Presumably the Île St. Louis.

[2] J. M. C. Itard, *De l'éducation d'un homme sauvage ou des premiers développements physiques et moraux du jeune sauvage de l'Aveyron* (1801). They had read this account of a wild boy found in the woods just before coming to France.

sounds of joy and sorrow which he makes use of have a very savage sound; they appear to be uttered involuntarily, not from any desire to communicate his feelings to others. It must however be remembered that this is a secondary use which we make of language. Our first object is to express our wants. Itard was not with his pupil the day that we saw the savage or else perhaps he would have explained his object in teaching this gentle and docile animal to *bow*. Perhaps with the desire of proving that he was not of such a savage disposition since he could be taught to perform at the will of his teachers one of the ceremonies of civilization. His vocabulary of words has not increased. He keeps his mouth constantly shut. His eyes are placed deep in his head, the light seems to hurt them, at the same time he takes pleasure in looking out of the window, and at the fire. He was the first person in the room that remarked that it was snowing. His eyes are without expression when he is left to himself. That love of order which Itard mentioned is very remarkable in him. His person is clean and his skin remarkably smooth and soft. How do I know this, because he did me as well as Maria and my mother the honour of giving us his face to kiss and this was a voluntary act. He is too much ordered and commanded, it was with difficulty we could persuade them to let him alone. He is most singularly gentle and affectionate in his manner, played very nicely with two little children that were there and who seemed very fond of him . . .

Charlotte Edgeworth to Mrs. King

29 December 1802

It is not very long since Maria wrote to Anna[1] which I hope gave you both some idea of the principal persons and establishments or amusements which we have lately seen. The only addition I think which we have made is a person with whom you are all acquainted and who performed a [ ] of polite address which gained him the hearts of some of his acquaintance. He procured a letter from Mme Lavoisier as a means of admittance to see a picture which he said he was very anxious to see. He resigned however the pleasure for the still greater honor of

[1] Anna Beddoes (née Edgeworth).

possessing the handwriting of Mme Lavoisier. I suppose that Mr. Underwood will shew it to you. He was very much delighted I understand at the philosophic air that surrounds this lady. She is a very shrewd lady I believe very goodnatured but does not in my opinion support precisely the dignified name of Lavoisier. She lives almost quite alone in a house which tho' good and prettily situated is far from the busy hum of men. In short in the room, the house, the society, which she has about her, there is something desolate and melancholy. She is a very clever woman however and has some wit, but she seldom produces either of these, and only utters short sentences to each person in a loud voice and subjoined generally by a still louder laugh. She is a large masculine woman and luckily for the men of science that surround her over twice a week, she possesses a pair of handsome legs which she knows how to betray. She spoke one night exceedingly well on teaching children religion. She said what I am certain is pretty true—If you have a mind to make children believe in your particular dogmas of religion you must teach it before they are well able to speak and if you have a mind that they should possess liberal sentiments attempt this when they are fourteen or fifteen.[1] Do not you think this true—from my experience I find it so. This sentiment was forced from her in the heat of conversation and shew'd that she has thought tho' she does not converse . . .

At present there is a great poverty of discoveries among the chemists. Now is the time for the english to outstrip them. The characters of these men are so bad, their talents at present so much turned merely to teaching what they already know, that the english may take this time to get before them. If they do not now probably for two or three centuries they may not be able to overtake them . . . Our manufactures are superior to theirs; their ideas of the method of gain are much more confined. Their projects for public buildings are much more numerous and magnificent; they are justly celebrated for their love of shew, tho' now they have not the means of producing much of this in their dress because they are poor. They work hard talk much at the same time—are as instantly merry as they had always been represented to be—are

[1] This was not RLE's opinion. Cf. his *Essays on Professional Education*, 78: 'Parents should therefore refrain from all attempts to inculcate dogmas which cannot be comprehended by their young pupils.'

very polite to one another, but I do not perceive that there is such an extraordinary difference between them and the english, in this particular as many travellers remark. All of those who have been acquainted with Paris before and since the revolution, say that the manners and character of the people have not altered. They think their morals have improved. I think that what makes their politeness appear greater than the english civility, is that the french have more action, and that in expressing some of our most ordinary and cool salutations they are accustomed to shew them by certain ceremonies which mean no more nor less than the short and quiet englishman means. The english however when they mean to be uncivil have much less to cut off and therefore the gradation is much smaller . . .

I must tell you my dear how much I am liked here, tho' this appears conceated, yet the effect it has on me is not vanity, because tho' to tell you the truth I sometimes keep it for myself yet in general I refer the praise to you,[1] and for that reason I must tell you what sort of people do me the honor to listen to my conversation in bad french.

Mme Delessert in the first place who is loved by all who hear her takes the greatest pleasure in speaking well of me to all her friends. I am exceedingly proud of this because it is a proof of being good to be liked by her. She is very select in her choice of society which many other good people are not. Now an antidote that you may not be too proud. A man whom I do not much admire and an englishman has given his sanction of my excellence. He is one of those who keep themselves well with everybody, who is admitted into all societies to be sneered at and recieved with much satisfaction and politeness. His name is Sir Charles Blagden a friend of Sir J. Banks—and a rectified[2] pupil of Lord Chesterfield. You will be pleased to hear that he thinks I have the most perfect manners for my age and situation of anybody he ever saw.

M. Pictet good dear man and his charming nieces who are just my age and admired by all, are my particular friends. M. Pastoret an excellent judge whose approbation I am most exceedingly proud of. He is most exceedingly sensible—not at all a man of

[1] Emmeline had had a special responsibility for the education of Charlotte, as had ME for that of Henry, and later, Harriet for that of Pakenham E.

[2] Refined, improved.

science, but knowledge eloquence and sound judgement. He has a most charming wife, who tho' she has manners the most soft and perfect yet I do not entirely approve of her. She is remarkable for her taste (it is for this quality that I admire her the most). She has given her suffrage with respect to my dress and manners . . .

Of late we have stay'd at home more, for there are many people whom we see who have written good books which it is very necessary to read, especially as we prefer the conversation of literary people; it is necessary to have read the fashionable books which all talk about. As one attends much more to books which one hears criticized I chuse those which will be of the greatest service to [ ] . . .

I wish with all my heart that you and King were here. I think if he does not succeed at Bristol he would as a physician here, it is such a rare animal—Brother in law to the famous authoress who is well known by some of the richest at Paris the bankers. Besides poverty is pitied but not despised among the most literary and the most gentlemanlike because the revolution has reduced so many to this situation. Mr. Underwood told us that he has manners that are particularly pleasing among the french, that they are something like Pictets who is much liked here. . . .

R. L. Edgeworth to C. Sneyd Edgeworth

Paris, 3rd January, 1803

. . . I lately undertook to teach a lady to read english. She already understood the language tolerably well but she could not pronounce one word when I began to teach her. With the assistance of my little primer[1] in six or seven lessons I have taught her to pronounce much better than I could have expected and with marks she can read anything *almost* fluently but what surprizes me is the readiness with which she passes from *marked* printing to what is not marked. This I attribute in a great degree to her

[1] *A Rational Primer* (1799). In it RLE proposed that children should be taught to read by means of a phonetic script constructed by means of putting accents and dots &c over or under the vowels. It is an extension of the system outlined in the chapter on Tasks in *Practical Education. A Rational Primer* does not appear to have been published in France nor was there a second English edn., although the Edgeworths' publisher reported enquiries for the book in 1816: R. Hunter to RLE, 3 Feb. 1816.

uncommon memory. By the by this niece about whom your aunts enquire is not Mme Marmontel but Mme Chéron another niece of our dear Abbé Morellet. My success in teaching this lady encourages me to print my primer improved and adapted to french learners and for that purpose I had myself introduced to the famous Didot—the first printer in Europe—author of Stereotype printing.[1] Instead of finding a mere printer I found a sensible ingenious man in an excellent house well furnished a beautiful library &c. He took me into his cabinet which in fact is his workshop and there I saw him actually at work making the steel punches with which he forms the matrices or molds in which his types are cast. So far very well—he entered readily into my plan and has engaged to make me types—but before I took leave he presented me with a copy of his translation from Tyrteus done by himself.[2] What a life of labour this young man for he is not above thirty must have led! to have made himself master of his own language and of latin and greek to such perfection as to have a critical knowledge of both—to have learned the history and practise of his own art to have made the improvements in that art, which have distinguished him so much—to have studied the greek character so carefully in ancient manuscripts and early printing as to enable him to restore many beauties to greek typography which give a new pleasure to the appearance of the pictured language. Examine the work and judge for yourself of the abilities and perseverance of its author.

Yesterday (9th) we went to hear and see the exhibition or lecture of M. Maimieux upon Pasigraphic or pasilatic *Universal language*.[3] The general idea of his art I think you have seen described in Nicholson, the repertory of arts,[4] or some of the monthly journals. I do not see any considerable improvement upon Wilkins except the idea of Greys alphabet to the memoria

[1] Firmin Didot (1764–1836) published his first book printed by stereotype in 1795.

[2] A four-page pamphlet produced in 1800 with on one side the Greek version, for which Didot had designed a new fount, and on the other the French translation.

[3] Pasigraphy, a system of writing for universal use with characters representing ideas instead of words, so as to be intelligible to persons of all languages. Pasilaly, a spoken language for universal use. In her Paris Notebook ME describes Maimieux as 'a self-taught genius—not of clear head or enlarged capacity—but ingenious'.

[4] W. Nicholson, ed. *A Journal of Natural Philosophy, Chemistry and the Arts; Repertory of Arts and Manufactures.*

technica is used for the oral language.[1] I have long thought of forming a language that *might* become universal by means of the Telegraph and the dictionary or vocabulary belonging to the telegraph I proposed to regulate according to a philosophic arrangement of Ideas similar to the tree of knowledge in the novum organum of the great Bacon. Wilkins in his 'real character' follows and improves Bacons plan.[2] M. Maimieux has made improvements on Wilkins and I propose some time or other with your assistance to pursue the subject . . . To save your time and my own I send you the first pages of his book[3] which you must keep as safely as the apple of your eye—as losing it I lose the whole of the book. A mutilated book is like a mutilated creature good for little. Maria has with her accustomed good nature copied for you some verses written by the Abbé Delille very different in value from those of Maimieux which I send. She proposed that you should translate them—I think it would not be worth your while. If you try 8 or 10 [lines] at your leisure from any part of them it will be as much as you can afford to do and will give me a sufficient specimen of how they would appear in English.

Mrs. Edgeworth to C. Sneyd Edgeworth

January 7—1803
[Nivose] 17 11

Having dated my letter learnedly from the double Almanack which all the inhabitants of Paris must keep in their heads at once

[1] John Wilkins published in 1668 *An Essay towards a real Character and a Philosophical Language*, to which was appended *An Alphabetical Dictionary wherein all English words according to their various significations, are either referred to their places in the Philosophical Tables or explained by such words as are in those Tables*. Richard Grey published in 1730 *Memoria Technica, or a new Method of Artificial Memory*. His system 'consisted in changing the last set of syllables of names into letters which represented figures according to an arbitrary table, and in stringing together the new formations in lines with a hexametric beat.' (*DNB*) His book continued to be reprinted until 1861 and was the foundation of other works on mnemonics.

[2] RLE here refers to the numerical code to be used with his telegraphic apparatus. See also p. 26 n. 1. ME's reference should probably be to Bacon's *Advancement of Learning*. The simile of the tree of knowledge is to be found in Bk. i and Bks. ii–ix give the 'Divisions of the Sciences'.

[3] *Pasigraphie ou premiers éléments du nouvel art-science d'écrire et d'imprimer une langue, de manière à être lu et entendu dans toute autre Langue sans traduction, inventés et rédigés par J . . .* de M . . . (Paris, au bureau de Pasigraphie, 1797, 1799).

and having put all obstacles and inconveniences out of my way I sit down to thank you my dear Sneyd for your many kind letters . . . Les Racines grecs you shall have and I hope you will find their food for the mind as wholesome as the root commonly called Potatoe is for the body and something more profitable than Beet-roots—from which it has been proved by innumerable trials that *no sugar* can be made.[1] Syrop like treacle can be produced but it cannot be made to chrystalize. I had a great conversation with M. Lasteyrie the agriculturist upon the subject. He has tried it in large and in small and never could succeed but he has discovered what will be of more use in Ireland—How to preserve the flour of Potatoes for 8 years![2] He has most obligingly written out the whole process for me and I hope to turn it to good account when we return. There never can be a famine in the land of potatoes if the substance of potatoes can be preserved. Last [night] we were at a very pretty—indeed the prettiest and most elegant theatre I ever saw—and we saw the Philoctetes of Sophocles (which is as well translated into French as into English)[3] performed by some young men as a trial of skill. They did perform as well as they could in so difficult a piece where the speeches are so long—the action so simple—and the listening so difficult. The person who played the part of Pyrrhus is a friend of M. Pastorets with whom we went there and after the piece was over washed off the rouge in a very short time and came into our box to look at the farce which was admirably performed by ladies and gentlemen. We all thought of what an excellent Pyrrhus you would have made. Moreover the dress was something like that of Opal[4] as a slave.

[1] Sugar was produced from beetroot as early as 1747 at Berlin, but not in quantities sufficient to make the process economically viable. Benjamin Delessert in 1812 perfected the first satisfactory commercial process: Crosland, *The Society of Arcueil*, 33–6.

[2] Cf. *Ministère de l'Intérieur. Instruction sur la manière de conserver les pommes de terre en les desséchant ou en les réduisant en farine, rédigée par une commission de la Société royale et centrale d'agriculture* [composée par MM Challan, de Lasteyrie, Sageret, Bosc et Sylvestre], 1816. The surviving Edgeworth letters for the period of the Great Famine make no mention of the use of potato flour in their neighbourhood and so far as is known the French technique was not introduced into Ireland. I am indebted for information on this subject to Dr. E. C. Apling and to the Keeper of the Museum of English Rural Life, the University of Reading.

[3] Laharpe's translation of *Philoctetes*, published in 1801. There were two English verse translations, one by T. Francklin (1759) and one by R. Potter (1788).

[4] A character in ME's unpublished play 'Whim for Whim' (Bodl. MS. Eng. misc. d. 648).

The quantity of rouge would have passed all belief from description only but your father was so good as to take me behind the scenes where I saw their daubed faces and was presented to Ulysses with a painted beard and Pyrrhus with his cheeks of scarlet. I saw Philoctetes in ragged trim looking at himself in the glass—the soldiers practising how they should carry him when he faints &c &c and many of the other entertaining items of a green room which you can easily imagine . . .

Adieu my dear Sneyd were I to indulge my fancy I should fill some sheets to you but that would I fear give more pain than pleasure as the ladies here say of dancing. To dance well is so necessary that they devote hours days and months to the mere practising—apropos Charlotte ventured to dance with young de Crillon the other night and if her petticoats had been shorter would have danced well enough for an Englishwoman though not like a Parisian. There is an entertaining Ballet (alias dance) at the Opera called la *dansomanie*[1] in which a gentleman is supposed to love dancing so much that he orders his servants to dance whenever they are in his presence so one man dresses his hair *tout en dansant* and pulls it every minute another brings the breakfast accompanied with the same gambades and spills the coffee &c. . . .

Charlotte Edgeworth to Harriet and Louisa Beaufort

9th January, 1803

. . . What put Mme Pastoret in this place was the word sensibility. If any woman ever was possessed of such a quality she has it—if any woman ever had persuasive words since the time of Pandora[2] she has, if any woman ever had grace in words or manner or mind or person, she has. Whatever she says is sung—in harmonious language, it is above common-place conversation, by one word which her sweet voice and manner sends to your heart or understanding. M. Pastoret in the manner of a man is, can you believe it,

[1] A two-act pantomime by Gardel, first performed in 1800.

[2] According to Hesiod, Pandora was the first woman. She married Epimetheus and persuaded him to open the box given to her by Zeus for her husband. The box contained all the misfortunes of the human race.

more eloquent than she is, but when he speaks of his wife, he becomes more eloquent than himself—but I must reserve a little of my admiration of this couple till I see you . . .

[Mme Chéron] comes and takes her lesson every day about ½ past 11. My father then goes out to order dinner[1] with Mr. Skottowe there they spend an hour. Whilst we stay at home reading or working or drawing, two or three of our acquaintances generally call—So unless we go to the gallery we lead a most domestic life. We have the coach to go out in three times a week. Mrs. E has had two soirées, so you see we are quite respectable inhabitants of Paris . . .

A gentleman—young well dressed—polite and respectful, pays me a visit every other day. I am always ready to recieve him and we have a tête à tête regularly and much to my satisfaction at nine which lasts sometimes till past ten in the morning. Nay he even occupies my thoughts during his absence. I am afraid that I must add something that will take away part of the sympathy which this recital must create in your breasts. This gentleman tho' scarcely grown into a man has been married these five years and his occupation is that of dancing at the opera. Now Louisa respect me and pity the infirmities of my advanced age, to learn to dance at my time of life is a serious thing. Notwithstanding I do not feel very unhappy when I hear my Gentleman enter the room with a genteel bow—Je vous salue Mademoiselle—Bon jour Monsieur—Hum, Il fait beau ce matin Monsieur—Oui mademoiselle—Ployez—c'est ça &c.

Tho' I am writing I am also talking you must know. We are talking over our opinions and notions of the people whom we know when we first saw them. It is singular to look back upon such first impressions—How much effect small circumstances have upon ones opinion at first sight. In deed it is impossible to form a general idea without small facts to indicate character . . .

We have lately become acquainted with a man whose name we all revere and whose extreme simplicity can only be equall'd by the profoundness of his thought and his great invention—Montgolfier. His figure and face are like some ancient painting at the

[1] Dinner was ordered ready cooked from a *traiteur* near by and carried to the lodgings in covered dishes. For Mr. Skottowe, see *An Englishman in Paris: 1803,* ed. J. P. T. Bury and J. C. Barry.

beginning of the sixteenth century but as I have already said he is perfectly simple and lets out his thoughts and inventions to be stolen and admired to all that come to pay their hommage to his talents and to profit by his good nature. That famous pump of Bramah's was his invention, it was twice stolen from Montgolfier.[1] The first and second thief accidentally met and vaunting to each other of their mutual stolen discoveries, betray'd to each other their mutual theft. Montgolfier takes the greatest pleasure in the inventions of his live competitors and his predecessors in fame.

They have a method here of renewing old clothes which makes them look as good as new. The invention is old and has been practiced in an underhand manner to sell off worn-out stuff. Montgolfier went into one of these shops and bargain'd for a coat not knowing of what materials it was made. After some time they asked him whether he was a printer (estes-vous imprimeur?). He replied no and asked what relation there could be between printers and tailors, or why they imagined that he was a printer. They gave no answer but turned the subject to something else. This excited his curiosity and he determined to watch, for he thought there was more in this than met the ear. The question was put to several who entered the shop and many answered in the affirmative. Are you one of those that carry on our business of renewing old cloth was the meaning of the expression, for their manner of performing this operation is by printing a sort of varnish on the cloth and powdering it over with the dust of cloth of the same colour till a new nap is produced.

Montgolfier made a baloon which contains twenty persons ranged round at so great a distance as to have room between each to mend the parts if torn, to guide it &c. He has by him [one] which can carry 1250 men and as many baskets. . . . They have among their numerous public buildings one which contains all the inventions ancient and modern which can be applied or have been or may be applied to arts or manufactures. A large old convent is the receptacle of this valuable depository. M. Montgolfier intends to suspend one of the most improved baloons in a part of the building and along with it my fathers umbrella[2]—Is not this

[1] Bramah patented his hydraulic press and pump in 1795.

[2] The umbrella was to be used to guide the balloon. For a discussion of RLE's interest in balloons, see Schofield, *Lunar Society*, 253–4.

polite? It is rather fatiguing to go down the ranks of machines that are found here, they do not make half the impression that they would if seen at different times and places. It has however this advantage—you can compare the progress of inventions the different powers of each genius and you can judge of what models are likely to succeed when put in practice, by the knowledge of what has been the fate of each machine of which the model is presented to you at the dépôt des arts et métiers at St. Martins.

One feels the same fatigue in going down that immense gallery of pictures and with the same advantages and more disadvantages. Besides this there are certain extraneous circumstances that have much connection with ease of body. At St. Martins it is as cold and damp as mad Pauls palace at Petersburgh which Kotzebue describes.[1] On the other hand in the gallery of pictures there are generally so many people in the room that you cannot be quite at ease and look as long as you please at the same picture. Some times here too the cold makes you walk the gallery and croud round the stove, but here however there are stoves to warm you. It would surprise you to see the sort of people which we sometimes meet there—women with wooden shoes extraordinary caps hoops and coarse gowns and petticoats judging of Raffaelle. Great [beauties] march along the room endeavouring to inspire the admiration which Guido excites. One lady—the princess Galitzíne did succeed with me. I saw her but for a second, just glanced my eye upon her, she was at that instant in the most perfectly graceful attitude and was turning into another when the door was closed. This was not affectation—She could not help being graceful.

I have not been prodigiously struck with the beauty of the ladies—Mme Récamier is the most beautiful—she improves much upon acquaintance. This lady that I mention has the most grace and the finest figure. A young lady that I saw at a bal d'enfans is the next beauty—Mme Pastoret in grace and figure is the next. I forgot my dear Mlle Lullin who has all these qualities joined with sweet manners. I wish we would bring her over for you not only to look at but to converse with for she has most sensible conversation. As her mother leads a very retired life and they are in mourning for the loss of their father we meet this family but seldom

[1] The Michailoff Place: *The Most Remarkable Year in the Life of Augustus von Kotzebue*, trans. B. Beresford (1802), iii. 3–4.

which is much to our regret. I would change our friend Mrs. Skottowe with great pleasure for them but our host only lets his house to strangers. Besides I am not sure that if they could they would.

I believe you have never heard of a person whom we have become acquainted with since we came to Paris and whom we love more and more every day. He is not a Delessert a Gautier a Morellet a Lullin a Pictet or a Pastoret. His surname indeed I have never heard. He is our servant. His name is François—a little confined in understanding, but the warmth of his heart guides his head and supplies often in need, the place of his understanding. He is by no means of the talkative french character, yet not a small number of words supply his tongue when it is set in motion however it may excite your surprise that a man with few words and ideas can talk when set a going. You must take into the account that one idea is not once repeated, the same pitch fork turns the same hay and often even when the sun no longer shines. The corners of Maria's mouth go down when upon giving François a note and a little money he commences his reply by 'd'abords je m'en vais vous dire'—then ensues a list of facts all that he knows on that and indeed often all that he knows on any other subject repeated in various forms and interlaced with d'abords or ensuite &c &c oui oui Monsieur. This habit of repeating the same things in various forms is peculiar I think to the french.

A M. Dupont [de Fougerais] a sensible man who was formerly judge and who now has retired to his family and the country an admirer of Prac Ed told us that when first he retired to the country and attempted the trade of a farmer he looked upon the peasants as a set of beings who lived eat and drank, whose characters and business were all the same like so many sheep who stocked his land. By degrees he began to distinguish between them. He found that there were some who were the oracles of the rest and whom it was necessary to consult before they could give a decided answer upon any subject. Thus he learned to judge of their characters; and their stupidity upon some subjects he says is extreme. However in money matters they act just as the irish do, leave it all to your honour—you know best. Whenever they catch you at a mistake to their advantage they pass it over but take care to make you perfectly sensible whenever they discover one that can hurt them. These facts struck me very much as they prove how cause and effect hang upon each other. M. Dupont a man of knowledge character and benevolence is totally ignorant of the sentiments and feelings of the peasants from whom he draws his wealth. The peasants an ignorant cowardly selfish people whose ignorance cowardice and selfishness arise from the want of freedom in the government. This government is absolute because there are few who feel any inclination to take the part of a peasantry of such a despicable character; thus as long as there is such a love of Paris and society and such a distance between the poor and the gentry so long will there be that servility which the english complain of in the french character.

Maria Edgeworth to Mary Sneyd

Paris, Rue de Lille, 10th January, 1803

... Now to fresh fields—or streets—I will give you a journal of yesterday—I know you love journals. Got up and put on our shoes and stockings and cambric muslin gowns (which are in high esteem here) fur tippets and fur clogs (God bless Aunt Mary and Charlotte for them!) and were in coach by nine o'clock—drove to the excellent Abbé Morellets where we were invited to breakfast to meet Mme D'Houdetot—the lady who inspired Rousseau with the idea of Julie in the nouvelle Heloise.[1] Rousseau's Julie is now 72 years of age—a thin woman in a little black velvet bonnet. At first she appeared to me shockingly ugly—she squints so much that it is impossible to guess who she means to look at. Yet no sooner did I hear her speak than I began to like her, and no sooner was I seated beside her than I began to find in her countenance a most benevolent and agreeable expression. She entered into conversation immediately and her manner invited and could not fail to obtain confidence. She seems as gay and as open hearted as an amiable girl of fifteen. It has been said of her that she not only never did any harm but never suspected any. She is possessed of that art which Lord Kames said he should prefer to the finest gift of the Queen of the fairies—the art of seizing the best side of every

[1] *Julie ou la nouvelle Héloise* came out in 1761.

object.[1] She has had great misfortunes but she has still retained the power of making herself and her friends happy. Even during the horrors of the revolution, if she met with a flower a butterfly an agreeable smell, a pretty color she could turn her attention to these and for the moment suspend the sense of misery. This disposition was not, as you might suspect, connected with want of sensibility or frivolity of character, but arose from real philosophy without any parade. Tho' it is her maxim and her practise to banish as fast as possible from her thoughts every thing that can give her pain and to enjoy every innocent pleasure be it small or great yet she is not in the least selfish. No one, as we have been informed, has exerted themselves with more energy in the service of her friends. She pleased me so much whilst I was with her that I was quite sorry to part with her and long to meet her again. I felt in her company the delightful influence of chearful temper and soft attractive manners and an enthusiasm which age cannot extinguish and which spends, but does not waste itself, on small but not trifling objects. Those objects cannot be trifling which for 72 years have made the happiness of a human being. I wish I could at 72 be such a woman as Mme D'Houdetot but I am sure I shall never either be 72 or such a woman.

She told me a great many anecdotes of Rousseau. She said that he did not steal the ribbon as he declared in his confessions[2]—that whilst he was writing so finely upon Education he left his own children in a foundling hospital and that he defended this with so much eloquence that even those who blamed him in their hearts could not find tongues to answer him.[3] Once at dinner at Mme D'Houdetot's there was a fine pyramid of fruit. Rousseau in helping himself took the peach which formed the base of the pyramid and the rest fell immediately. 'Rousseau!' said she, 'that is what

[1] [Henry Home, Lord Kames], *Loose Nints upon Education* (1781), 43, 46: 'A power to recall at will pleasing objects would be a greater blessing than was ever bestowed in a fairy tale . . . He who constantly beholds the bright side, insensibly meliorates his temper, and in consequence of it, improves his own happiness, and the happiness of all about him.'

[2] *Confessions* (Penguin Classics), Bk. 2, 86–7.

[3] In her Paris Notebook ME writes that this was because he did not want them to know that they were 'the children of a man of genius—else they would not learn trades—be misplaced in society—a rich friend went down on his knees to beg Rousseau would let him take charge of his children—R– refused'. For Rousseau's own, different, account, see *Confessions* (Penguin Classics), Bk. 7, 322, Bk. 8, 333–5.

you always do with all our systems, you pull down with a single touch but who will rebuild what you throw down?' I asked if he was grateful for all the kindness she shewed him. 'No—he was ungrateful. He had a thousand bad qualities, but I turned my attention from them all and thought only of his genius and of the good he had done mankind.'[1]

Mme D'Houdetot from speaking of Rousseau's children in a foundling hospital recollected Virginia and Belinda[2]—spoke very kindly of both. You my dear Aunt Mary who have connected your idea with my Works with so much kindness[3] that I cannot help telling you all the compliments that are paid me and if you think me vain at least believe me grateful. Mme D'Houdetot thought Lady Delacour an original character and Belinda she said she had given as a model to her grand daughter whom she brought with her to introduce to us—a pleasing young woman—but as you do not like to be overpowered with new acquaintance I will say no more of her. I hope you will not be angry with me for introducing Mme D'Houdetot. Pray when I see you put me in mind to tell you a pretty subject for a tale which she told me—about a young Virginia bred up in a wilderness who died for love of her Clarence Hervey[4] without knowing it. The story is too long for a letter and Madame D'Houdetot has taken up too much of mine already . . .

After an excellent breakfast, including tea, chocolate, coffee, buttered cakes and unbuttered cakes, good conversation and good humor we departed casting a longing, lingering look behind. Stay—I must not forget to tell Aunt Charlotte that Mme Chéron and Mme Marmontel are two nieces of the Abbé Morellets. Mme Marmontel we have never had the happiness to see. M. Chéron who is husband to Madame is a clever bald pated friendly man, who is translating Harry and Lucy—has translated Harry and Lucy I mean—since we have been here and is now going on with the remainder of Early Lessons.[5] His translation is excellent.

[1] In her Paris Notebook ME adds that Mme D'Houdetot said Rousseau was 'ungrateful—méfiant . . . in general cold and silent in conversation—but when his imagination was touched—eloquent'.

[2] Virginia in ME's *Belinda* was thought to be a foundling.

[3] Mary Sneyd at this date was helping ME with copying MSS. etc.

[4] The hero of *Belinda*. See p. 25 n. 1.

[5] ME's *Early Lessons* (1801) consisted of three series of stories, 'Harry and Lucy', 'Rosamond', and 'Frank', of three parts each, followed by a tenth part containing three unrelated stories. Chéron published his translation in 1803.

It is to be printed with French on one side and English on the other. . . .

At this lecture [by M. Maimieux, on pasigraphy] we met Mr. Chenevix who is always seen where knowledge of any kind is to be found. He came home with us—dined with us—was more agreeable than I ever saw him—stayed till nine in the evening talking to my father about mechanics &c—Montgolfier's *Belier*[1] and the stones which all the great philosophers here say have fallen from the moon!!! . . .

Did we tell you that we went with Mme Récamier and a Russian Princess Dolgorouky to Laharpe's house to hear him repeat some of his own verses? . . . The Russian princess is a lady who sets up for a wit and talks loud and with a most decided tone and air. She complained the day she was presented to Mme Bonaparte that her neck ached with the weight of her diamond diadem—*Half* a million the diamonds were worth and a *whole* headach! We met at Laharpe's Lady Elizabeth Foster of whom we have heard so much and Lady Bessborough. Lady Elizabeth Foster is very engaging in her manner and was wondrous civil to us—had long wished to see us &c &c.

As I am on the chapter of fine people and fine things I must tell you that we were at a very fine ball a few days ago. We were invited to a *Bal d'enfans*. This you would translate a childrens ball and so did we till we were set right by the learned. At this Bal d'enfans there was not a single child and I believe but half a dozen unmarried ladies. It is a ball given by mothers to their *grown up* children. Charlotte appeared as usual to great advantage and was much admired for her ease and unaffected manners. Many observed 'que mademoiselle avoit l'air très comme il faut'. She danced one English country-dance. The *Walse* and cotillion dancers really danced *too well* as many even of the French spectators observed. I am sure they could gain their bread in England on the stage. I had no idea of such dancing till I came here. Charlotte danced with M. de Crillon, grandson of the Gibraltar Duke—the young man who went to see Anna[2] and Dr. Beddoes and who has now the grace to remember that Anna was very civil to him. When Cha stood up to dance a gentleman came to me and exclaimed 'Ah

[1] Hydraulic pump.
[2] Anna Edgeworth, ME's sister, married Dr. Thomas Beddoes in 1794.

Mademoiselle votre soeur va danser! Nous attendons bien le moment oû elle va *paroître*!' She appeared extremely well from not being anxious to appear at all. . . .

Forgive me my dear indulgent aunt Mary for writing so ill—I am much hurried. Today we stayed at home to gain time but 13 visitors besides the washerwoman have prevented our accomplishing all our great and good purposes. The visitors were all (except the washerwoman) so agreeable that even whilst they interrupted we did not know how to wish them gone. . . .

Maria Edgeworth to Henry Edgeworth, 16 January 1803

Paris, Rue de Lille No. 529
1803 dans *le siècle réparateur* as
Monge has just named this century—16th January

My very dear Henry, . . . It is no easy matter to get into agreeable society at Paris; we hear that many English of rank and fortune far far superior to ours cannot force or win or buy their way into it. They put their trust in chariots and in horses which are of little or no avail here except with *les nouveaux riches*, who are not worth seeing or hearing. The title of philosopher or rather of man of letters or science is the best possible title here. We see the French *sçavans* mixing with most polite and elegant societies of both sexes not only without being considered heterogeneous beings, but as essential to the formation of *good* company. At Laharpe's we met a few days ago—the celebrated French beauty Mme Récamier—the celebrated English wit Lady Elizabeth Foster and a Russian Princess Dolgorouky . . . Would you have expected to meet with such a lady in the study of a philosopher? Nothing but fashion could have brought her there and therefore I mention her as the strongest proof that literature and literary men are in high esteem here. Laharpe lives in a miserable house, in a miserable street, in a miserable room waited upon by a miserable looking old woman, yet he had a levée or rather couchée of fine ladies who all vied with each other in flattery and invitations. Mme Récamier dressed in a robe of white sattin trimmed with fur seated herself upon the arm of Laharpe's elbow chair and hung over the philosopher who was in a dirty night cap and old robe de chambre in the grand costume

2 Mme Récamier and Laharpe, from the drawing by Charlotte Edgeworth

of a literary valetudinarian.[1] He affects to imitate Voltaire but does not do it well. Mme Récamier used all the soft persuasion of the graces to prevail upon him to repeat some verses—he took hold of her arm stroaked the white satin and fur and said 'Ah ma belle Julie que je vous aime aujourd'hui—vous voilà bien habillée.' He is very fond of seeing ladies well dressed. Charlotte has drawn a striking likeness of the beauty and the philosopher. What pleasure we shall have in shewing it to you when we meet my dear Henry! But we must not think of that. Laharpe told us some entertaining anecdotes of Voltaire and repeated some of his poetry which I did not think extraordinary. He is writing a poem on the death of the King of France in which he has introduced the Abbé Edgeworth.[2] He complained that the name Edgeworth was so unmanageable in French verse that he was obliged to modify it and sweeten it to his own taste; Whether or no he has sweetened it to ours we cannot yet tell because he had not time the evening we were there to repeat the lines; he invited us to return to hear them.

I don't know whether we ever mentioned Mme Récamier to you before. We have dined at her house—one room of which is *said* to have cost twenty thousand pounds—with tragic and comic poets, metaphysicians and bankers and the richest man in Paris—beside whom Charlotte had the felicity of sitting at dinner. The gentleman who told me who was who at dinner, after enumerating the titles to consideration of the poets metaphysicians &c simply said 'and there is M. Ouvrard the richest man in Paris—that is all that can be said of him.' That you may know the full extent of our glory and happiness I must further inform you that we have been at the opera with Mme Récamier—that we have been at one of her Balls and might have been at a dozen if we had pleased. She is very

[1] This letter overlaps in its contents with the previous one (10 Jan. to Mary Sneyd). In an omitted portion of the previous letter ME describes Laharpe's *robe de chambre* as reddish and says that the 'very dirty nightcap' was 'bound round the forehead with a dirty chocolat*ish* night ribbon'. In the *Memoir* (i.153) the two letters are conflated. For another description of this occasion, see Lord Granville Leveson Gower, *Private Correspondence, 1781–1821*, 386. Lord Granville describes ME as 'ugly but delightful' and comments on Laharpe's 'insatiable vanity'.

[2] *Le Triomphe de la religion ou le roi martyr* (1814). The Abbé Edgeworth used the name *de Firmont*, from Firmount, a part of his family's property in Ireland, because the French had such difficulties with the name of Edgeworth.

pretty and graceful but nothing marvellous except what is marvellous in a beauty who has been born and bred in flattery and nursed in the lap of luxury she is *good* in every sense of the word. She is obliging in her manners and seems to think of others more than of herself. She lately gave a proof of her goodness of disposition which has made a great impression upon us. M. Degérando (the author of an Essay on the connexion between signs and the art of thinking)[1] an excellent man, married to an amiable woman of whom he is excessively fond, had one child of 14 months old who was taken dangerously ill. The father and mother were almost out of their senses with grief . . . Now Degérando is not rich, nor is he very engaging in his manners and his wife is not a fashionable lady who could do Mme Récamier honor, but during the whole time that the child was ill she constantly went to see them—did not send to enquire, or call and leave a ticket at her door but she got out of her magnificent coach and forced her way up into their poor little room to see them and comfort them. Many people would shower money in charity, who would not do this.[2]

Pray tell Mr. Stewart, that he without knowing it has joined with Mme Récamier in comforting poor Degérando and his wife. A few days after their child died there came from London for Degérando a present of books from Mr. Mackintosh—amongst them Mr. Stewart's Elements of the philosophy of the human mind. A friend of Degérandos said to us 'Je ne sçaurois vous exprimer combien j'en suis aise. Il va le lire tout de suite. C'est là le seul genre de consolation dont il est susceptible dans ce moment.' Ask Mr. Stewart if he has seen Degérando's book on signs as connected with the art of thinking. 4 vols Oct° and ask him if he has seen a little tract of Prevost's on the same subject.[3] Mr. Stewart is frequently quoted in this tract and his writing appears so clear in the midst of the metaphysic fog that it does the benighted readers heart good to see it. Since I wrote the above I have seen Mr.

[1] J. M. Degérando, *Des signes et de l'art de penser considérés dans leur rapport mutuel* (1800).

[2] Mme Récamier, Camille Jordan, and Degérando were great friends; they were all *Lyonnais*.

[3] Dugald Stewart's *Elements of the Philosophy of the Human Mind* came out in 1792. Mackintosh had not a high opinion of Degérando as a metaphysician (*Memoirs of the life of the Rt. Hon Sir J. Mackintosh*, i.177). Prevost's work was *Des signes envisagés relativement à leur influence sur la formation des idées* (1800).

Stewarts 2d Edn in which he mentions Prevost's book. Degérando's Essay was crowned as the French say and as the English would say obtained the prize from the National Institute. He generously says that Prevost deserved the prize which he obtained. For my part both of them appear to me to be 100 years behind Mr. Stewart. They express with prodigious difficulty in obscure inflated language ideas that are and have been long familiar to those who have read the elements of the philosophy of the human mind. I heard one of Degérando's lectures on moral philosophy. Alas! I can never hear one of Mr. Stewart's![1] The French certainly are far behind the Scotch in metaphysics and think they are making great discoveries when they are stumbling in the dark upon things which have been seen by others in broad daylight long ago.

Tell Mr. Stewart that they are going to re-establish the French Academy here—under the general name of The Institute. There are to be four Academies—L'Académie des sciences—L'Académie des inscriptions—and L'Académie des Beaux arts and L'Académie françoise. We are rejoiced because some of our friends here will take their old places and some profit about 80 guineas a year. The good and great Abbé Morellet who is one of our best friends will be the oldest member. My father has been to some of the meetings, or sittings of the Institute and we are to go to a meeting on tuesday. The learned members have of late been entirely full of certain stones that have fallen from the moon. M. de La Place is at the head of these lunar philosophers—did I say lunatics?—and he has proved as clearly as figures can prove it that said stones might could would and should have fallen from the moon. My father and some other sceptics beg leave to doubt a little longer though demonstration stares them in the face!!! You know that your friends Fourcroy and Chaptal are men in power and place as well as great chemists. The chemists at Paris have really found the philosophers stone—that is the art of making money by their science. Fourcroy lectures extremely distinctly and well as my father says. Guyton de Morveau, Chaptal and Vauquelin I know no more, I mean not half so much as you do, but I mention their names to shew you that I do not forget that you might like to hear something. My father knows them all. Mr. Chenevix is here and

[1] Ladies were not admitted to Stewart's lectures at the University of Edinburgh.

spends his life with them; I will collect from him all he knows but experience every day confirms me in Mr. Keir's opinion that the best part of an author is generally his book. I must however make some exceptions—for instance Montgolfier. We saw him yesterday and think him superior to his reputation; he is a dirty unshaved uncombed man, slow of walk motion and speech but his understanding though slow is sure. He will not be put out of his place but then he never stumbles even in the most difficult paths and in the craggy regions of science. He is something like Mr. Watt in the simplicity of his manners and in his patient benevolence. I think it requires a great deal of patient benevolence to explain over and over again what a man knows as well as his alphabet . . . Montgolfier told us that all the theoretic mechanics with whom he had ever been acquainted were prone to make gross mistakes in their machines from omitting to allow sufficiently for friction &c—that he always says to them—try it—try it—try your machine and then you will see your mistake. You who are a practical as well as theoretic mechanic my dear Henry will not be liable to this error . . . It will give you as it gave us pleasure to hear from Montgolfier that he had received from the Marquis de la Poype my fathers letter about the manner of guiding baloons in the air and that he thinks it will succeed . . . It was very pleasing to hear him and my father converse together because they seized each others ideas with such readiness and pleasure. . . . I was surprised to find that Montgolfier had never seen poor Dr. Darwins beautiful lines upon him 'Rise great Montgolfier &c,[1] [ ] M. Deleuze with whom we are acquainted has translated Dr. Darwins Loves of the plants extremely well into harmonious french but it is not liked here and scarcely known.

Whilst all Paris [has] been for a fortnight [Mme] de Staëls Delphine which was to have been called le malheur d'être femme.[2] It is cried down universally. There are fine passages in it but

[1] E. Darwin, *The Botanic Garden*, canto iv, 143–7:

> SYLPHS! your soft voices, whispering from the skies,
> Bade from low earth the bold MONTGOLFIER rise,
> Outstretch'd his buoyant ball with airy spring,
> And bore the Sage on levity of wing . . .

[2] See above, p. 56 n. 2. The book was cried down in public largely because of Napoleon's hostility to the author. The Edgeworths' copy is full of pencil annotations in the hand of RLE which by and large express admiration. The first volume in particular clearly influenced more than one of ME's books.

altogether we are of the general opinion that it is tiresome and immoral or as a gentleman lately said *il manque d'être abrégé—éclairci et épuré.*[1] Innumerable witticisms have been circulated about this novel which with the stones from the moon have filled the conversation of society till every body was heartily tired of both. Mme de Staël it is said is so much displeased by the ill success of her novel at Paris that she will not come to Paris this winter. I am sorry that we shall not see and hear her for one evening—that is all. We have however full as much agreeable society as we can enjoy . . . Mme Lavoisier is very kind to us and we meet some of the best company at Paris in her house. In her sallon are all her husbands philosophical instruments and a picture of Lavoisier seated at a table writing—she leaning over his shoulder. How bitterly the wretches who destroyed or suffered Lavoisier to be destroyed must, now that they have leisure for remorse, repent of their crime.

My dear Henry I have not room to stuff half of what I want to say to you into this letter. There is l'école des ponts et chaussées, l'école polytechnique—La Bibliothèque nationale—the Gallery of pictures—Les Monumens François—La Monnaie—Les Invalides—Les Gobelins &c &c &c of all of which I have not said one word. At the head of l'école des Ponts et chaussées is M. de Prony an excellent mechanic and mathematician. Here we saw two large rooms filled with models of bridges, arches, staircases, and buildings of various shapes and sizes built with little bricks such as my father had made for little William and such as he has recommended in Prac Ed. I am to have a model of a spiral staircase for William . . . At La Bibliothèque nationale we saw a prodigious collection of ancient and modern gems—some the spoils of Italy—many from the King of France's former cabinet—a fine collection of engravings from the first discovery of the art to the present time—curious as it shows how the art sometimes started forward and sometimes fell back. There are also (we hear but have not yet seen) a fine collection of manuscripts. The manuscript of Fénelon's Télémaque with corrections in his own hand I should like to see if I

[1] In her Paris Notebook ME attributes this phrase to Talleyrand. She also quotes 'Elle a plus d'esprit qu'elle ne sçait mener', 'Il n'y a que le bossu qui n'est pas de travers', and 'Il s'y trouve une métaphysique galante', and 'Il y a beaucoup de passion mais point de tendresse'.

had time to examine the corrections but not else.[1] Merely to stare at a great man's handwriting would give me but small satisfaction. The Abbé Millin a great antiquarian and something of a coxcomb (*mum*) is at the head of this Bibliothèque . . .

I am in a great hurry to get to the school of medicine which I kept for a bonne-bouche for you. My father who never neglects any opportunity of seeing what can be useful to his son Henry went to the school of medicine chiefly on your account and whenever you come here you will find the advantage of his having been there before you. He says that there are some excellent preparations in wax of the nerves to teach anatomy without disgust or danger.[2] Here he saw the picture of two sons of Toussaint the negro general—fine young men with open countenances—blacks. They have been inoculated with the cow pox. The appearance on their arms is different from what it is on white arms at the same stage of the disease[3] . . .

Le Jardin des Plantes! I must keep for another letter and the whole museum of natural history and all the beasts in the universe from the shrew mouse to the tall *giraffe*. Of all other animals I had formed some competent idea from picture, print and description —of the giraffe I had no adequate idea and therefore I must despair of giving you any. We are to see a beehive in which I dont know how many men grenadiers can stand. Live in hopes of hearing more of this . . .

Mrs. Edgeworth to Mary Sneyd

Paris, 18th January, 1803

My dear Madam I am almost ashamed to date a letter again from Paris for I am really afraid that you will think that we mean

[1] Cf. MS. Dumont 6: Journal, fo. 2 (Bibl. Univ. et Publique, Geneva): Ce qui m'a le plus intéressé c'est celui de Télémaque . . .' Dumont commented that, magnificent as the collection was, the government did not give a *sou* to keep the library up to date with currently published books.

[2] Anatomical models based on the injection of organs, generally with wax, had been made from the seventeenth century, the best being the work of Italians. According to L. S. Mercier, *Tableau de Paris* (1782 edn.), i. 258–62, ix. 169–9, French teachers of anatomy mostly had recourse to body-snatching, but Mlle Biheron used models she had constructed in wax (op. cit. viii. 123).

[3] Dark-skinned people more frequently form keeled scars.

to spend our lives in this city—but upon the whole I think you will agree with us that it was wiser to stay long enough here to wear out the fancy and de s'ennuyer un peu than to return home with a wish to see more of the society of Paris or to enjoy more of its dissipation. I do not believe that any of us will feel the least wish for any thing but what [we] shall find at our dulce domum whose quiet pleasures when joined to the company of such kind friends as we have there—and to the contented minds which I trust we still retain—will give us many more pleasurable feelings than all the glare of novelty or all the brilliance of flattery among acquaintances whom we can never see without reflecting that we see them only en passant. I am afraid I am hardly intelligible for without affectation I find french words and idioms so jumbled in my head that I can hardly pick out my mother tongue . . .

We have seen once or twice a Scotchman a Mr. Pinkerton who in his Universal geography has given great commendation to Castle Rackrent.[1] Mr. E went to see him and left his name at his lodgings. In a few days Mr. Pinkerton called here and after sitting a few minutes, he said that he came to see young Mr. Edgeworth the author of Castle Rackrent! Mrs. Barbauld it seems had told him that certainly it was written by Lovell. He is a good bookworm and again mentioned the Greek Bulls which Mr. O Beirne had sought for in Dublin.[2]

What sights have we seen since? We have seen a man who teaches children as Mr. E taught little Fanny to pronounce the sounds of the combinations of letters before she could speak plain —who teaches them the names of things they know or see or feel not words merely—and arithmetic as Mr. E taught William—who teaches them at 3 and 4 years old the shape and names of all geometrical figures as you taught Honora and to draw and cut them out by copying by the eye without compasses as you have taught Honora but I hope with better success for it is said that he has only formed clever children but that no man of abilities has appeared in his school. Mr. E and Maria listened to his exposition for two hours in half German and half Swiss French and for two hours more to a commentary and explanation by a Swiss who used twice as many words as were necessary because he thought that twice

[1] J. Pinkerton, *Modern Geography* (1802), i. 222.
[2] ME and RLE's *Essay on Irish Bulls* was published in 1802.

repeating the same thing would explain what wanted no explanation[1] . . .

R. L. Edgeworth to Charlotte Sneyd

Paris, 27th January, 1803

. . . Friday the 21 I lay in bed longer than usual to dissipate in vapour the epidemical cold which had hung upon me for some days. Having just taken another reef into the blanket I heard a strange voice talking to Fanny in the next room. She came and told me that an officer of the Police must speak with me. I desired that he might walk in. He appeared in a blue uniform embroidered with green &c—presented a warrant which he informed me in a manner sufficiently peremptory required my immediate attendance. My being ill was not sufficient excuse. I got up dressed myself slowly to take time for thinking—drank one dish of chocolate—ordered my carriage and with my *exempt*[2] in the carriage to the *palais* de justice. Here I was shewn into a parlor or rather a guard room where a man like an under officer was sitting at a desk. In a few minutes I was desired to walk upstairs into a long low narrow room in different parts of which there were ten or twelve clerks sitting at different tables. One of these tables was pointed out to me and having addressed myself to the clerk he asked my name—wrote it on a printed paper, which he delivered to me and for which he demanded half a crown. I paid the half crown but declined taking the paper, which he told me was a passport. I informed him that I did not want a passport which on the contrary he pressed upon me assuring me that I had urgent necessity for it as I must quit Paris immediately. He then pointed

[1] It is clear from ME's Paris Notebook that the two unnamed people in this paragraph are Pestalozzi and P. A. Stapfer. Pestalozzi was much more interested in abstract political and educational philosophy than the Edgeworths but many of his practical ideas were evolved independently on an empirical basis by the latter and published in *Practical Education* (1798). Some ideas in RLE's later educational writing may have been influenced by Pestalozzi, e.g. on the provision of playgrounds (*Mems. of RLE* (1821 edn.), ii. 430). For RLE's ideas on the teaching of reading and mathematics, see *Practical Education* (1798), chaps. ii ('Tasks'), xv ('Arithmetic'), and xvi ('Geometry'). Pestalozzi was in Paris as a member of a delegation from the Helvetic Republic and Stapfer was at this time Helvetic Ambassador in Paris.

[2] Police officer.

out another table where the clerk placed me in the most advantageous point of view and took my written portrait with great solemnity. This he copied into my passport. I objected to having my nose described as gros as I humbly supposed it was little. He confirmed his former opinion by a second inspection and informed me that my nose was assez gros. I acquiesced and begged to know who was the principal person in the room. To this person I applied to know the cause of this procedure. He coldly said if I wanted to know I must apply to the *grand juge*.[1] To the grand juge I drove and after having waited till the number 93, the number of a ticket which had been given to me at the door, was called. The grand juge most formally told me that he knew nothing of the matter—all that I had to do was to obey. I returned home—breakfasted—looked at my passport and found that I was ordered to quit Paris in 24 hours. I went directly to Lord Whitworth at the extremity of Paris—he was ill. I with difficulty got at Mr. Talbot his secretary. After some conversation in which I distinctly pointed out that I applied to the Ambassador from a sense of duty and politeness—that I had applied to none of my friends previously though I believed I had many &c &c. He then went to Lord Whitworth and in half an hour wrote an official note to Talleyrand to ask the why and wherefore—advised me in the mean time to quit Paris and go to some village near it—some said Passy—some Versailles. All my friends came to see me—advised Passy because Versailles too distant—Passy only a mile and half from Paris.

Before leaving town went with François Delessert to see Grand juge—could not see him or even his secretary for a considerable time—at length obtained a sight of his secretary who said I could not see the grand juge. 'Cannot I write to your grand juge?—hesitating yes. A Huissier[2] took in my note and one (a charming one) from François Delessert. Huissier came out again with my papers held at arms length—'Great Judge knows nothing of the matter'. Returned home—dined—ordered carriage to be ready to take me to Passy—wrote a letter to B—stating my entire ignorance of the cause of my *deportation* and my being unconnected with any political party. François Delessert took care the letter should

[1] The ministry of justice and the ministry of police were temporarily fused under Regnault de St. Jean d'Angely, formerly minister of justice and renamed *grand juge*.

[2] Usher.

be delivered as *directed.* Set off for Passy with Maria. Mrs. E and Charlotte stay at Paris to settle affairs. I forgot to mention that late in the evening F. Delessert as soon as I had determined to take up my abode at Passy set off in his cabriolet and took a lodging for me at an inn there—returned and told me all was as comfortable as he could find in the village. Mme Gautier offered us her country house there but though much pressed we would not accept it lest we should *compromise* our friends. M. Pastoret also offered his country house but for the same reason the offer was declined.

We arrived at Passy about 10 o'clock—small inn—room narrow with a window at each end—scanty curtain—large fireplace—wood fire on hearth just lighted—very cold—small bed in corner close to the window—without curtains—pillow case and sheets damp. Landlord followed into the *apartment* to pronounce its *éloge*. 'Ne craignez rien Monsieur. C'est une chambre parfaitement saine. Il y a une fenêtre à chaque bout et un vent frais jour et nuit.' I begged he would give me an old curtain if one could be rummaged out and a curtain rod, for I told him that we English are not accustomed to sleep in beds without curtains. He laughed like a goose, shewed his white teeth and expostulated 'Mais Monsieur, quel embarras! Il est minuit déjà sonné. On ne peut rien faire ce soir. Demain on enverra chercher quelqu'un, et on arrangera tout ça.' I replied that I wanted no one to help me, my landlord was much astonished to see me begin to work with my own hands and still more surprised was he when he saw my work completed. I built up the chimney board[1] at the foot of my bed and hoisted my old chequered curtain so as to make a tolerable den for the night. Maria and I then overhauled the bedclothes mattrass &c and after two hours drying before a fire such as our landlord said he had never seen in this room except at a wedding they became dry enough to sleep upon and I slept tolerably. Before I was up, about nine o'clock my friend M. Pastoret came to see me—was as usual kind and sensible—breakfasted in a little oven of a parlor heated by a stove—good coffee. Observe our landlord was a pastry-cook and besides an excellent cook—his wife a pretty stirring little body. They were a new married couple—very civil. François Delessert chose well. Before we had finished breakfast he came—spent two hours—conversed most agreeably. When he departed we amused

[1] Used to close a fireplace in summer.

ourselves with reading the French adventurer.[1] Mary may remember that this was the novel full of strange adventures with which I was so much entertained at Ashton.

Interlude of pasting up one of the windows. Whilst I was standing upon the table pasting enter Pictet and Le Breton. My friends said both at once, their faces rayonnant de joie 'You need not give yourself so much trouble. You will not stay here long. We have seen the Great judge and your detention arises from a mistake. We are to deliver a petition from you stating your relationship to the Abbé Edgeworth whose brother they take you to be. This shall be backed by an address signed by all your friends at Paris and you will be then exactly where you were.'[2] I objected to writing any petition. They said a declaration would do. At all events I determined to consult the Ambassador who had conducted himself so well. I therefore wrote to him, stating the facts and declaring that nothing could ever make me deny the glory which I assumed from being related to the Abbé. He advised me to send a declaration that I was not brother to the Abbé. This I did in the form and manner which I will shew you the next evening—for I staid at Passy a second whole day. At seven Pictet and Le Breton took this declaration to the great judge supported by the signature of some of the most respectable people at Paris. The judge acknowledged that it was a mistake and informed my friends that I might return when I pleased. They brought this news immediately to Fanny who set off immediately for Passy whence she conducted me to Paris about eleven o'clock at night.

In my way home I dropped a note at Lord Whitworths to inform him of my arrival. He desired me to walk in. I found him and the Dutchess[3] tête à tête. He informed me that he had just received a note from M. Talleyrand to say that it was a mistake. Thus at length this curious affair ended—which might have been more disagreeable. I believe I need not tell you that any little

[1] The *London Catalogue of Books*, corrected to 1799, lists *The French Adventurer* (anon.), 4 vols. The Edgeworths stayed at Ashton in 1792.

[2] The address was signed by Le Breton, M. A. Pictet, Gallois, Morellet, Pastoret, Suard, Baert, Prony, Degérando, Boissy, Morel Vindé, Bidermann, Lacretelle le jeune, Lacretelle ainé, Tournu Auber, Dupont de Nemours, and Chéron. There are notes at the end by Octave de Ségur and M. Montmorency wishing that they had been asked to sign. Mme de Rémusat told ME that Napoleon knew nothing of the order (Paris Notebook).

[3] Lord Whitworth's wife, the dowager Duchess of Dorset.

inconvenience which I suffered was amply compensated by the kindness of my friends which upon this occasion exceeded any thing which I could have imagined. Since my return my time has been much taken up in receiving and paying compliments and in meeting my friends to rejoice with them . . .

Charlotte Edgeworth to C. S. Edgeworth

Paris, 21st February, 1803

We went yesterday to see the consecration of a Bishop at Notre Dame, and here I endured with satisfaction most intense cold for three hours, and saw a solemn ridiculous ceremony, and heard music that went through me: I could not have believed that sound could have been so fine: the alternate sounds of voices and the organ, or both together, and then the faint, distant murmur of prayers: each peal so much in harmony as to appear like one note beginning softly, rising, rising, rising,—then dying slowly off. There was one man whose voice was so loud, so full and clear, that it was equal to the voices of three men. The church itself is very fine: we were placed so as to see below us the whole ceremony. The solemnity of the manner in which they walked, their all being dressed alike, and differently from the rest of the people, rendered these priests a new set of beings. The ceremony appeared particularly ridiculous, as we could not hear a word that was said, because the church is so large, and we were at too great a distance, and all we could see was a Bishop dressing and undressing, or lying on the ground! The Archbishop of Paris, who performed the chief part of the ceremony, is a man about eighty years of age, yet he had the strength to go through the fatigue which such a ceremony requires for three hours together in very great cold, and every action performed with as much firmness as a man of fifty could do it, and there was but one part which he left out—the walking round along with the other bishops with the cross borne before them. We were told that he has often gone through similar fatigue, and in the evening, or an hour after, amused a company at dinner with cheerful, witty conversation: he is not a man of letters, but he has abilities and knowledge of the world. All these men were remarkably tall and fine-looking, some very venerable:

there were about sixty assembled. It appears extraordinary that there should not be one little or mean-looking among a set of people who are not like soldiers chosen for their height, and they must have come from different parts of France. I think there is a greater variety of sizes among the French than among us: if all the people who stand in the street of Edgeworthstown every Sunday were Frenchmen, you would see ten remarkably little for one that you see there, and ten remarkably tall. I think there are more remarkably tall men in Ireland than in England.

Maria is writing a story,[1] and has a little table by the fire, at which she sits as she used to do at Edgeworthstown, for half an hour together without stirring, with her pen in her hand; then she scribbles on very fast. My father intends to present his lock, with a paper giving some account of it, by way of introduction to the society of which he is a member, La Société pour encourager les arts et métiers.[2]

[MS. missing—printed from *Mem.* i. 154–6]

Mrs. Edgeworth to Mary Sneyd

Paris, 22nd February, 1803

. . . I never mentioned the subject [of RLE's exile from Paris] in any of my letters as I had no notion of the reports having reached Ireland and my cowardly imagination thought of nothing but the danger of relating circumstances that might compromise either our selves or others as I have been frequently told that all our letters are read at Calais. (By the by yours came open yesterday.) Luckily Mr. E. was not so cautious and his full letter saved you all much uneasiness . . . I am sorry that this news was sent over too in that general manner as many people will think that there was something in it, and will always imagine that Mr. E has done, said, or thought something offensive to the government or governors of France. If Mr. E had been presented before, these manoeuvres would never have taken place and I think we should have some more entertaining anecdotes to relate than those that this last

[1] The story was *Madame de Fleury*, published in *Tales of Fashionable Life*, 1st series (1809).

[2] Edelcrantz at the same time presented an improved model of an oil lamp.

month has produced—which truly are not numerous—for though this month has been the Carnival we have seen but little of the dissipation of this joyous season. Except the Masks that have crowded the streets during the last week and which we could not help seeing and the splendid representation of Racine's Esther[1] by the young ladies of Mme Campans school which we saw last thursday, we have not partaken in either the follies or the fancies of this festival. . . .

We leave this town in good earnest *on Wednesday or Thursday next*—that is in a week precisely.[2] We had fixed on next sunday bien positivement and we have been eating our congé these three or four days at the most agreeable dinners breakfasts and suppers where we are overwhelmed with marks of kindness friendship and sympathy besides good eating which will embellish Maria and make me broader than I am long. We are all very sorry that the *grippe* had reached Edgeworthstown for the cold you mention which has been epidemic there seems pretty much the same as the disease which has that curious name here and which has attacked every person—some very violently. We have got rid of *Courbatures—grippes* and all other diseases with or without hard names. The frost and snow are also gone. Sunday the 15th the Thermometer was as low as 9½ in the morning—in the evening it was 36—the next day 40! A very gentle thaw and the most charming weather has succeeded. The streets too have been so well washed and scraped by the rain and snow cleaners that they are actually dry and clean for the first time since October—which is fortunate as they are crowded with people some in Masks only—some disguised as harlequins, old women, apothecaries, and knight errants. These are followed by hundreds and thousands of men, women and children to whom they say what they can—generally nonsense totally devoid of wit—and whom Harlequin disperses every now and then with his wooden sword. Hundreds of hackney

[1] First composed in 1689 for performance by the young ladies being educated at St. Cyr, the school established by Mme de Maintenon.

[2] Because of rumours of impending war the Edgeworths had started to pack. 'M. Le Breton called, and said he was sure of knowing before that evening the truth as to Bonaparte's warlike intentions, and that if Mr. Edgeworth met him at a friend's that night, he would know by his suddenly putting on his hat that war was imminent . . . Mr. Edgeworth went, and saw M. Le Breton, who did suddenly put on his hat . . .' RLE promised his French friends that if there was peace he would return, bringing the rest of his family for a year's stay in France: *Mem.* i. 158–9.

coaches and cabriolets are filled with *masques* five or six within—three or four behind—two or three on the top and as many on the coach box. Two Men clad in complete armour with their horses also clothed in steel as the Chevalier Bayard and his knight and a triumphal car containing 15 or 16 persons all agog were the prettiest exhibitions that appeared. This night which is shrove tuesday the Gallantry ends.

Charlotte has been so unlucky as to miss three balls this week and so contented as not to have sighed once at the loss. One of the days I believe she was full as well entertained at Mme Campans. Last Thursday February 17th *Jeudy gras* we dined at *two* and at a quarter past three having taken up Mme Pastoret we left Paris, and as the weather was fine and the road very good we arrived in due time at a quarter past 6 at St. Germains 4 good leagues. The little Theatre appeared already full when we entered. We had stood only a few seconds near the door below when Mme Campan cried out from above 'Placez Mme Edgeworth—faites monter Madame et sa compagnie.' So we went up to the Gallery where we had very good places next to a Polish princess and half a dozen of her country women who are all polite and well bred. The crowd increased much and many more people came than there was room for—the famous Mme Visconti, Berthiers mistress and Lady Yarmouth sat behind us—Lady Bessborough and Lady E. Foster not far from us—and below there were numbers of English besides the Duchess of Gordon and her beautiful daughter Lady Georgiana. Mme Louis Bonaparte, who had been one of Mme Campans élèves, was among the principal Frenchwomen. The piece was performed admirably—the singing of the Choeur of young girls charming—and the petite pièce, La Rosière de Salency[1] was better still. You know it is a charming thing and was made so touching as to draw tears from every eye. . . . The representation ended at 10 and we got home at two raging with hunger—without cold accident or malheur of any kind. Many of the carriages were broken I understand in the crowd at St. Germains . . .

[1] From *Le Théâtre d'éducation* (1779–80) by Mme de Genlis.

Mrs. Edgeworth to Mrs. Ruxton

Calais, 4th March, 1803

. . . Bonaparte is really a very great man and if a few interested and dissembling courtiers did not misrepresent circumstances and mislead his understanding all Europe would be obliged to acknowledge his powers in peace as well as in war. He has the Manie of doing everything himself. He not only directs the whole but sees to the execution of every part. He thinks that arts as well as arms, manufactures as well as laws—Playhouses, dress, education, everything comes under his [own] immediate control and direction and he composes and writes all the answers that he gives, all the papers that he has published. They say he frequently sits up half the night at this kind of work and Madame Bonaparte by his side. To her it must be poor sport as her early life was somewhat of a gayer nature. Her friends say she is sometimes bien ennuyée with the magnificent monotony of her present situation . . .

We often wished for you at Paris for no one in the world would have such success in their society as you and I cannot help thinking that their manners would please you. Whatever may be the state of their private morals they have great delicacy of sentiment and decency of conversation. And it is now la grande mode to be seen with one's husband and to talk to him in public. The nouveaux riches have succeeded to the crimes and dissipation as well as to the estates of the ancienne Noblesse and without their elegance have twice their luxury. At Cambacérès last public dinner there was a side dish which cost 180 Louis! Apropos of eating—French cookery in every shape is so excellent that I am afraid we shall starve on plain mutton and pine for want of Coffee—Marangles[1]—french Marangles how good they are and how you would like them. I never saw any without thinking of dear Sophys attempts to make them because you wished it . . .

Maria Edgeworth to Mary Sneyd

Calais, Friday, 4th March, 1803

At last my dear Aunt Mary we have actually left Paris and after a

[1] The Edgeworths regularly spell 'meringues' in this way.

very pleasant journey arrived safely at Calais last night; the wind is directly against us, and my father is determined to wait till it is perfectly favorable and the sea calm; because it would be dangerous for Mrs. E at this time to be in a strong gale.[1] Perhaps we may be detained here some days; but we have no reason to lament for we are in Grandsire's excellent house and we have books and *thoughts* enough to entertain us—*Thoughts* of friends from whom we have just parted, and of friends to whom we are soon going. How few people in this world are so rich in friends! When I reflect upon the kindness that has been shewn us abroad and upon the affection that awaits us at home, I feel afraid that I shall never be able to deserve my share of all this happiness—that I shall never be sufficiently grateful. The fine sights we have seen, and the fine speeches we have heard at Paris pass off from the mind like a dream, but the recollection of the real friendship we have received there never I hope will be effaced. The persons we found it most difficult to part with were—You will easily guess—Mme Delessert, Mme Gautier, M. Pictet and the excellent Abbé Morellet, poor old man, it was most painful to part with him because we have no chance of ever seeing him again . . .

Sunday 10 oclock
The wind has changed and I hear my father say in the yard 'Nous serons prêts dans trois minutes!' The carriage is rolling down to the water side and packers and guagers all hurrying scurrying about me. I have only time to tell you that I will carry this letter over with me to Dover and add one line to say what sort of passage we have. You will not be surprised if I leave the rest of the sheet *blank* for you know what the sea is. It does not change one's heart but it changes ones desire to write . . .

Sunday Evening 5 o'clock—Dover
All alive and merry—just landed after a fine passage of 6 hours—poor Mrs. E was very sick—Charlotte tolerable—Father pretty well except for one half hour—Maria perfectly well all the time . . .

[1] Sophy, her third daughter, was born on 27 May 1803.

Mrs. Edgeworth to Charlotte Sneyd

London, 10th March, 1803

. . . On landing in England the appearance of cleanliness and comfort in the middle classes strikes one much more forcibly than the want of them when we landed in France. The women are so much cleaner, fairer, taller, better dressed that one is surprised at perceiving that they are less occupied with themselves and their clothes than their more slatternly neighbors on the other side. As to the men—they are also better dressed and universally fatter with much larger heads, broader faces, and an *air moqueur* that is disagreeable because it seems to be excited by something in the appearance or manner of every person they meet. London is a fine city, though built of brick—though black with coal smoke and tho' all the houses open into the street with[out] the comfortable magnificence of Courtyards before. The streets are large and clean and appear of wonderful breadth—and everything looks rich . . .

Maria Edgeworth to Mary Sneyd

Edinburgh, Dumbrick's Hotel, 19th March, 1803

. . . I believe I got no farther in my account of our visit to Mme de Genlis than saying that we were very eager to see her after having seen her beautiful Rosière de Salency. A few days afterwards we dined with Mr. and Mrs. Scottowe and a rather stupid party of gentlemen and after dinner my father called me out of the room and said 'Now we'll go and pay this visit to Mme de Genlis.' She had previously written to say she would be glad to be personally acquainted with Mr. and Miss Edgeworth. She lives—where do you think? At the place where Sully used to live—in the Arsenal. Bonaparte has given her apartments there. Now I do not know what you imagined in reading Sully's memoirs,[1] but I always imagined that the Arsenal was one large building with the *façade* to it like a very large hôtel or a palace and I fancied that it

[1] *Mémoires des sages et royales oeconomies d'Éstat, domestiques, politiques et militaires de Henri le Grand*, first published in 1638. The Arsenal was originally built as an artillery depot. Sully had been Grand Master of Artillery. The building had been several times reconstructed and now, as well as many private apartments, it housed the Bibliothèque de l'Arsenal.

was somewhere in the middle of Paris. On the contrary it is quite in the suburbs. We drove on and on and at last we came to a heavy archway like what you see at the entrance to a fortified town. We drove under it for the length of 2 or three yards in total darkness, then found ourselves, as well as we could see by the light of some dim lamps, in a large square court surrounded by buildings. Here we thought we were to alight. No such thing—The coach drove under another thick archway lighted at the entrance by a single lamp, we found ourselves in another court and still we went on archway after archway, court after [court] in all which reigned desolate silence. I thought the archways and courts and lamps and silence would never end, but at last the coachman stopped opposite to a gate-way and asked where the lady lived for the tenth time. (It is excessively difficult to find people in Paris.) We thought Mme de Genlis' name and the name of the Arsenal would have been a sufficient direction but Lo the whole of this congregation of courts and gateways and houses is called the Arsenal and hundreds and hundreds of people inhabit it who probably are perfect strangers to Mme de Genlis. At the doors where our coachman enquired some answered that they knew nothing of her—some had heard she lived somewhere in the fauxbourg St. Germains—others believed she might be at Passy—others had heard she had apartments given her by government somewhere in the Arsenal but could not tell where. Whilst the coachman begged in vain from door to door we looking anxiously out at the coachman from the middle of the great square where we were left listened for the answers that were given to him, which often from the distance escaped our ear. At last, a door pretty near to us opened and our coachman's head and hat were illuminated by the candle held by the person who opened the door. As the two figures parlied with each other we could distinctly see the expression of their countenances and their lips move. The result of this parley was successful.

We were directed to the house where Mme de Genlis lived and thought all difficulties ended but no such thing—Her apartment was still to be sought for. We saw before us a large crooked ruinous stone staircase lighted by a single bit of candle hanging in a vile tin lantern in an angle of the bare walls just at the turn of the stairs. There was only just light enough to see that the walls were bare and old and the stairs immoderately dirty. There were no signs of the place being inhabited except this lamp, which could not have been lighted, you know, without hands. I stood still in melancholy astonishment whilst my father groped his way into a kind of porter's lodge or den at the foot of the stairs where we found a man who was porter to various people who inhabited this house. You know the Parisian houses are inhabited by hordes of different people and the stairs and passages are in fact streets and dirty streets to their dwellings. The porter, who was not either obliging or intelligent carelessly said that Mme de Genlis *logeait au second à gauche, qu'il faudroit tirer sa sonnette*—that he believed she was at home—*if she* was not just gone out. Up we went by ourselves for this porter though we were strangers and pleaded that we were so never offered to stir a step to guide or light us. When we got to the second stage we faintly saw, by the light from the first landing place, two dirty large high folding doors, one set on the right and one on the left, and hanging by each a bell no larger than what you see in the small parlor of a small English inn. My father pulled one bell and we waited some minutes for an answer—no answer—pulled the other bell and waited—no answer—thumped at the left door—no answer—pushed and pulled but could not open it—pushed open one of the right hand folding doors—utter darkness—went in (as well as we could feel)—no furniture. After we had been there a few seconds we could discern the bare walls and some strange lumber in one corner. The room was a prodigious height, like an old playhouse. We retreated and in despair went down again to the surly or stupid porter. He came upstairs with us, unwillingly, and pointed to a deep recess between the stairs and the left hand folding doors—'Allez! Voilà la porte et tirez la sonnette.' He and his candle went down and my father had but just time to gain the door and seize the handle of the bell before we were again in darkness.

After ringing this feeble bell we presently heard doors open, and little footsteps approaching nigh. The door was opened by a girl of about Honora's size, holding an ill set up wavering candle in her hand, the light of which fell full upon her face and figure—her face remarkably intelligent—dark sparkling eyes, dark hair, curled in the most fashionable long corkscrew ringlets over her eyes and cheeks; she parted her ringlets to take a full view of us and we were equally impatient to take a full view of her. The dress of her figure by no means suited the head and elegance of attitude. What her 'nether weeds' might be we could not distinctly see, but they seemed to be a coarse shortish petticoat like what Molly Bristow's children would wear (*not* on Sundays)—A woollen grey spencer above—not buttoned, as you have taught them to button theirs, but pinned with a single pin by the lapels tight across the neck under the chin and open all below.[1] After surveying us and hearing that our name was Edgeworth she smiled graciously and bid us follow her. '*Maman est chez elle.*' She led the way, with the grace of a young lady, who has been taught to dance, across two antichambers—miserable looking antichambers—but miserable or not no house in Paris can be without them. The *girl* or *young lady*, for we were still in doubt which to think her, led us into a small room in which the candles were so well skreened by a green tin skreen that we could scarcely distinguish the tall form of a lady in black, who rose from her armchair, by the fire side, as the door opened: a great puff of smoke came from the huge fireplace at the same moment. She came forward, and we made our way towards her as well as we could through a confusion of tables and chairs and work baskets and china and writing desks and ink-stands, and bird cage and harp. [sketch plan of room given] She did not speak and as her back was now turned to both fire and candle I could not see her face or anything but the outline of her form and her attitude. Her form was the remains of a fine form—her attitude that of a woman used to a better drawing room. I being foremost and she silent, was compelled to speak and spoke to the figure in darkness—'*Mme de Genlis nous a fait l'honneur de nous mander qu'elle vouloit bien nous permettre de lui rendre visite et de lui offrir nos respects*'—said I—or words to that effect. To which she replied by taking my hand graciously and saying something in which *charmée* was the most intelligible word—whilst she spoke she looked over my shoulder at my father—whose bow I presume told her he was a gentleman for she spoke to him immediately as if she wished to please—seated us in fauteuils near the fire.

I then had a full view of her face and figure. She looked like the full length picture in black of my great great great grandmother

[1] The girl was Stéphanie Alyon: *Mémoires de Mme de Genlis*, v. 129, 247–8. Molly Bristow was an old servant of the Edgeworths.

Lovell, which you have seen in the garret—very thin and melancholy—but her face not so handsome as my grandmothers—dark eyes—bony—sallow—compressed thin lips—two or three ugly black ringlets on a high forehead—a cap that Mrs. Grier might wear—altogether an appearance of fallen fortunes, worn out health, and excessive, but guarded irritability.[1] To me there was nothing of that engaging captivating manner which I had been taught to expect by many even of her enemies. She seemed to me to be alive only to literary quarrels and jealousies; the muscles of her face as she spoke, or as my father spoke to her, quickly and too easily expressed hatred and anger whenever any not of her own party were mentioned. She is now you know *dévote acharnément* [*sic*]. When I mentioned with some enthusiasm the good Abbé Morellet, who has written so courageously in favor of the French exiled nobility and their children, she answered in a sharp voice 'Oui c'est un homme de beaucoup d'esprit à ce qu'on dit, à ce que je crois même, mais il faut vous apprendre qu'il n'est pas des *notres*.'[2] My father spoke of Pamela—Lady Edward FitzGerald[3]—and explained how he had defended her in the Irish house of Commons. Instead of being pleased or touched, her mind instantly diverged into an elaborate and artificial exculpation of Lady Edward and *herself*—proving or attempting to prove that she never knew any of her husbands plans, that she utterly disapproved of them, or at least of all she suspected of them. This defence was quite lost upon us, who had no thought of attacking but Mme de Genlis seems to have been so much used to be attacked that she has defences and apologies ready prepared as some have books of prayer *suited to all possible occasions*—and capacities. She spoke of literature—of Mme de Staël's Delphine with detestation—of another new and fashionable Parisian novel Amélie[4] with abhorrence—kissed my forehead twice because I had not read it—'Ah,

[1] Mme de Genlis had early lost her beauty. The portrait cannot now be identified but was probably that of ME's great great grandmother, wife of Sir Salathiel Lovell (1619–1713), Recorder of London.

[2] Morellet made no pretence to be devout or particularly royalist.

[3] The wife of the Irish rebel, Lord Edward FitzGerald. She was educated with the children of Philippe Égalité, Duke of Orléans, and reputed, perhaps wrongly, to be the child of the Duke and Mme de Genlis. After Lord Edward's death in prison, she married Pitcairn, the American consul in Hamburg, but very soon separated from him.

[4] Probably Mme Cottin's *Amélie de Mansfield* (1803).

vous autres angloises vous êtes modestes!' Where was Mme de Genlis' delicacy of conscience when she penned and published Les chevaliers du Cygne and the heroine who ran between the two camps *en chemise et chemise bien courte*[1] &c.

Forgive me my dear aunt Mary if, even after you begged me to see her with favorable eyes, and even when I went to see her after seeing her Rosière de Salency with the most favorable dispositions I could not like her. There was something of malignity in her countenance and conversation that repelled love, and of hypocrisy which annihilated esteem. From time to time I saw or thought I saw through the gloom of her countenance a gleam of coquetry *but* my father judges much more favorably of her than I do. She evidently took pains to please him—and he says he is sure she is a person over whose mind he could gain a great ascendancy. He thinks her a woman of violent passions—unbridled imagination—ill tempered but not malevolent—one who has been so torn in pieces that she now turns upon her enemies and longs to tear in her turn. He says that she has certainly great powers of pleasing tho' I neither saw nor felt them. But you know my dear Aunt that I am not famous for judging sanely of strangers in a first visit and I might be prejudiced or mortified by Mme de Genlis' assuring me that she had never seen any thing I had written except Belinda—that she had heard of Practical Education—had seen it mentioned in Miss Hamilton[2] which she was just reading—heard it much praised but had never seen it. She has just published two additional volumes of her petits Romans in which there are some beautiful stories.[3] I will bring them to you—But you must not expect another Mademoiselle de Clermont. One such story in an age is as much as can be reasonably expected.

I had almost forgotten to tell you, that the little girl who shewed us in, is a girl whom she is educating. 'Elle m'appelle Maman mais elle n'est pas ma fille.' The manner in which this girl spoke to Mme de Genlis and looked at her appeared to me more in her

[1] *Les Chevaliers du cygne: contes pour servir de suite aux Veillées du château et dont les traits qui peuvent faire allusion à la Révolution française sont tirés de l'histoire* (1795). The reference is perhaps to an incident where Armosted is wearing a wet and short shift (*Knights of the Swan*, trans. Beresford (1796), iii. 9); she is frequently found scantily clad and in equivocal situations.

[2] Elizabeth Hamilton wrote *Letters on Education* (1801–2).

[3] Two additional volumes were published in 1802–3.

favor than any thing else. She certainly spoke with freedom and fondness and without any affectation. I went to look at what this child was writing—she was translating Darwin's Zoonomia.[1] I read some of her translation: it was excellent. She was (I think she said) 12 years old. It is certain that Mme de Genlis made the present Duke of Orléans[2] such an excellent mathematician that when he was, during his emigration, in distress for bread, he taught mathematics as a professor in one of the German universities. If we could see and converse with one of her pupils and hear what they think of her we should be able to form a better judgment than from all that her books and her [enemies] say for and against her. I say her books and enemies—not her friends and enemies for I fear she has no friends to plead for her, except her books. I never met any one, of any party, who was her friend. This strikes one with real melancholy—To see a woman of the first talents in Europe, who has lived—who has shone in the gay court of the gayest nation in the world, now deserted and forlorn, living in wretched lodgings, with some of the pictures and finery, the wreck of her fortune before her eyes, without society, without a single friend! She is at war with half the literary world, admired and despised, she lives literally in spite and not in pity. Her cruelty in drawing a profligate character of the Queen (soon after the Queen's execution) in the Chevaliers du Cygne, and her taking her pupils at the beginning of the revolution to the revolutionary clubs[3]—and her connexion with the Duke of Orléans, and her hypocrisy about that connexion—and her insisting upon being governess to his children when the Dutchess did not wish it, and its being supposed that it was she instigated the Duke of Orléans in all his horrible conduct, and more than all the rest her own *attacks and apologies* have brought her into this isolated state of reprobation . . .

[1] Erasmus Darwin, *Zoonomia* (1794–6).

[2] Later King Louis Philippe.

[3] Some of the anti-royalist material was eliminated in the second edition (1805). She took her pupils to revolutionary clubs on the instructions of their father, the Duke.

3 Fanny and Harriet Edgeworth, from skiagrams

FRANCE, APRIL–JULY 1820

Harriet Edgeworth to Honora Edgeworth

Calais, 23rd April, 1820

Lost, lost, lost—fairly lost my dear Honora for here we are on French ground—having had a French dinner and slept in a French bed . . . Farewell till Paris . . .

Harriet Edgeworth to Louisa Beaufort

93 Place Bourbon, Faubourg St. Germain,
26th April, 1820

. . . The journey from Calais though generally said to be totally uninteresting was to us perfect strangers very amusing. In the first place the postillions and horses are an endless source of entertainment. The postillions as they are servants of government are almost all dressed in blue jackets turned up with red and ornamented behind with three silver fleur de lis—yellow leather pantaloons and enormous jackboots. Much as I had heard of their size I had no idea of what it was till I had seen them. It is with no small difficulty that they walk at all indeed they do it as seldom as possible. Hanging to their wrists is a whip the handle of which is about 18 inches long and the lash about 2 feet 6. This the postillion whirls round his head whenever he enters a town mounts a hill or wants to warn a carriage of his approach. The crack which is made is really tremendous—exactly like the report of a pocket pistol. Nevertheless it is very entertaining—but the horses seem ill qualified to bear the immense weight of man and boots for they are seldom any of them and never all of them as large as the Spanish mule you had at Collon. As we were three in number we had three horses and for this purpose at Calais our pole[1] was tied under the carriage and a limonière put on instead.

[1] The single shaft fitted to the forepart of a vehicle and to which are attached the yokes or collars of the draught animals.

This limonière is nothing more than two shafts which are fixed to the middle of the splinter bar[1] and on each side of this limonière is tied a little splinter bar. A horse—the largest of the three—is put into the shafts and the two other fastened to the splinter bars. On the horse to the left hand of the limonière the postillion mounts on an immense saddle with his great coat buckled on the pommel before him. Almost all the harness is of ropes and it is miraculous how one goes at all, or how one escapes destruction at every turn. However these little rats do get on sometimes for ten miles but generally about five for a stage. The road is divided into posts and the rate arranged on what is called the tarif but the postillions are paid more than twice what the tarif gives them, which is a great check on them for if they grumble or are impertinent or careless you have only to say the word tarif and it acts like a talisman upon them.

The country from Calais to Samer the place where we slept the first night is frightful—the soil yellow clay, varied only by chalk pits and banks at the road side and fields of corn—hardly a tree and I do not remember one field of grass. At Samer we were much entertained while drinking our coffee by looking through a glass door into the kitchen at the people at supper there. They consisted of an old pensioner in a blue coat and cocked hat a young carter in the light blue embroidered frock which they all wear and two other men. The old man and carter made a most admirable contrast. Both their faces were wholly different from what would have been the faces of people of their rank in England or Ireland—and as different was their food which was soup, fish and salad. They all eat with their hats on and talked incessantly.

The next day the country had a more cultivated appearance. The trees and corn were more advanced and there was an appearance of wood in the distance and now and then we passed through what is called a forest, but which is little better than copsewood. We were detained some time for horses at Abbeville where we dined—so got no further than Poix where we slept at the maison de la poste a wild sort of house where we passed through an open gallery to our bedroom—which was however very comfortable. We got up at a little after five yesterday morning and after having

[1] The crossbar fixed across the head of the shaft and to which the traces are fastened.

divided a dish of coffee between us we set off. The country was almost entirely of yellow clay ploughed or ploughing, with hedge or ditch and studded over with low fruit trees. Near a town called Marseille were two or three châteaux. One of them belongs to a Baron Clermont de Tonnerre who emigrated during the revolution and left his house in care of a 'Brave homme' who took excellent care of it and now lives with the Baron who seems much loved in the country. Another Count spends four months of the year at his house—a vast deal for a Frenchman.

At Beauvais where we had a déjeuner à la fourchette, the hotel was built round a court and the stairs to the bedchambers is out of doors in this court and goes to a gallery which runs round the court outside the rooms and is prettily painted. It is very pretty and odd . . .

Rodolphe our servant is a Vendean and is such a puppy that he left the Countess de Salis because he said her green and yellow livery hurt his complexion! Nevertheless he is an excellent servant. We have a very nice landau and are to have tomorrow a very nice maid—So I think we are very well off . . .

Maria Edgeworth to Mrs. Ruxton

Place du Palais Bourbon, 29th April, 1820

. . . Our apartments here are in the house of a Russian Countess whom I have never yet had time to see notwithstanding a multitude of civil messages (but she has been in the country several days so you need not be angry with me). We have an elegant little salon with two large paned espagnoletted[1] windows—white dimity festooned curtains—handsome chimney piece beautiful pendule—large mirror—sofa—and softly cushioned fauteuils—and plenty of tables rolling and stationary—the room comfortably covered with green cloth. Being at the corner of the Place Bourbon the two windows give varieties of view—it is just opposite the beautiful Palais Bourbon. The Salon opens into a nice little salle à manger—prettily parquetted in oak—an antichambre with good [poële] and then you pass into a very pretty bedchamber with a pretty

[1] See above, p. 31 n. 1.

recessed white canopy bed[1]—mirror—all the elegance and most of the comforts of life including a closet for Fanny's squashings (Sophy will tell you what squashing[2] means). The bedchamber has a green carpet which covers its *tily* floor. You go up stairs that are almost perpendicular and which seem to be leading to a loft but which surprise you by the entrance into a very nice bedchamber—or at least one which Harriet who is not very exigeante says is very nice—Another for the femme de chambre—and the [manservant] sleeps in some hole or loft I know not where. Where the Russian Countess lives I cannot tell but so separated from us by the common stair that we are completely in a house of our own. We have a kitchen of our own and a traiteur opposite to us. So much for our ménage about which your kindness was so minutely interested. I had almost forgot to say we pay only 300 francs—that is 12 guineas a month 3 Gs a week. We have excellent horses and coachman and our carriage is so pretty that Mme de Salis advised us to use it so we do and it costs us [ ][3] . . .

I have been at a splendid dinner at the Countess de Salis where I met Lord Trimleston—2 Barons secretaries of the Austrian embassy and a number of diplomates whose names I have not yet mastered sufficiently to spell correctly. For one I may mention le comte de Semft who was premier ministre du roi de Saxe—a well informed polite frightful looking man with a brilliant star with undiminished rays. We talked much at dinner of Pestalozzi and German literature etc. At the head of the table was General Donnadieu of whom so much has been said in the papers[4]—a black haired uncombed unfashionable looking man—Only 3 ladies present besides Mme de Salis and myself with 10 or 11 gentlemen. Le duc de la Châtre was expected but of him we saw nothing but

[1] Fanny wrote to her mother (26 Apr.): 'Alas what do you think Maria has found—that bugs inhabit the pretty white clean looking bed in her room . . . She and Rodolphe and the Russian Countess's maid have arranged another bed without curtains which can be put in a closet in the day time . . . The Russian Countess's maid is extremely obliging and was quite shocked to hear of des punaises . . .'

[2] Family word for washing.

[3] A coachman cost 20–30 frs. a month and horses 380 frs. (MS. account bk.). Later a carriage was hired as well. The total cost of transport for four months in Paris was 2,220 frs. The whole trip cost not quite £1,000 (MS. summary of accounts).

[4] There had recently been inquiries into his conduct in suppressing Didier's conspiracy in 1816 and he was briefly imprisoned in April. He had also been involved in Ultra plotting against the government.

his chair left empty. The ladies were Mme la comtesse de Podenas—le comte is lieutenant du garde de corps du roi and she is daughter of a duchesse D'Escards. Mme de Podenas is one of the most fashionable belles of Paris. Next but one sat Mme de la Tour du Pin—née Princess de Monaco—and Mme de Martainville an agreeable woman of the world who has been in England much and speaks English well and to whom I had a letter of introduction from Lady Surrey. General Donnadieu forgetting to help her to some ham (which by the by was at the head of the table in one of the removes)[1] she sent it away to the side table bidding her servant help her. At the second course she revenged herself on the general by saying '*Sabrez* dans cette volaille pour moi mon Général.' 'Eh oui Madame la comtesse avec ce bon sabre anglois—c'est ce qu'il vous faut?' All this society at Mme de Salis quite ultra royalists. It is and will be very entertaining to see the different manners and hear the very opposite opinions of the various societies.

I am ashamed of having blotted and interlined and blundered so much but if you knew the hurry scurry in which I write! Fanny and I wrote home an account of a large party at Lady Granards where we were last friday—therefore I will not repeat the names of Counts and Countesses and Russian French and Polish princes and princesses without end to whom we were presented. N B Le Prince Edmond de Beauvau son of the Spanish grandee dances quadrilles and *valses* better than anybody in Europe—Prince Galitzine the Swedish ambassador who looks as if he was rouged and he were dancing à l'envie l'un de l'autre with Lady Adelaide Forbes and Miss Leith and Miss FitzGerald. Among the persons in the magic lantern who caught my eye most was Marmont—duc de Ragusa—but Humboldt held me by the ear and I flatter myself I had hold of a piece of his ear when Lady Granard came up and dragged us asunder to present me to a polish Countess Orlowska, who was full of Early Lessons Frank Rosamond and Practical Education[2] to my great surprise! She won my heart still more by pronouncing Harriet to be charming and Fanny to be bien intéressante. She came to see us the next day and in two hours time I am to go this evening with Fanny and Harriet to see her as she begged

[1] A dish to be changed while the rest of the course remains.

[2] *Early Lessons* (1801) and *Continuation of Early Lessons* (1814) contain the stories of Frank and Rosamond.

to shew her children to us. She is pleasing and *appears amiable* but I am warned that the Polish ladies are in general *not to be depended upon* as to our English notions of *amiable*.

This assembly at Lady Granards was Fanny and Harriet's début. We had all three dined with Mme de Salis where their heads were dressed by *Hippolyte* the first of hairdressers and of coxcombs—Harriets head à la Brutus[1]—Fannys with scarlet pomegranates and small lilies and the hair like the pictures of la belle Hamilton.[2] Their dress was made by the best dressmaker—White lace frocks beauteously and simply trimmed with lace and satin—waists as long as they were before the peace. Fanny and Harriet as far as I could see or hear were much approved . . . They speak bad French without fear and therefore will soon speak well. At all events their belles dispositions pour la conversation make them agreeable to the French . . . Tomorrow we go to Passy to Mme Gautier to dine —Next day we all go to Mme de Pastorets early in the evening to meet Mme de la Briche, Mme la Duchesse de Crillon, the Ségurs, and la Duchesse de Broglie who as Madame assures me is considered the most pleasing and pretty person in Paris (by one party). Of her it was said but not by Talleyrand 'C'est une de ces figures dont le diable se sert quand il veut faire un coup de main.' After having been an hour at Mme de Pastorets we go about eleven to the English Embassadors Sir C. Stuart. The day after I had sent my letter of introduction from Lady Harrowby and my card Madame Maria Edgeworth et Mesdemoiselles ses soeurs (which I was advised was the proper thing) came an invitation to Madame et Mesdemoiselles ses soeurs de leur faire l'honneur de passer la soirée &c *à dix heures*. The hours of the French at Paris I am told are much earlier than in London but the English keep to their late hours in general. It is so very odd to me to be Madame and keep house and go about in this way that I often feel as if I was acting a part in a dream. . . .

Paris is wonderfully embellished since we were here in 1803 . . . I had never seen Paris in summer so I enjoy the novelty. Some of

[1] Cut short, with curls.

[2] Elizabeth Hamilton (1641–1708), wife of Philibert, comte de Grammont. She was very much the fashion at the court of Charles II. She wore her hair long and loosely tied at the back so that it ballooned out by her ears, and with a few ringlets over the forehead and at the sides: *Mémoires du comte de Grammont par Monsieur le comte Antoine Hamilton*, ed. Horace Walpole (1783), pl. facing p. 92.

our happiest time is spent in the carriage driving about in the morning or returning by lamp or moonlight and we enjoy having a chaise much more than a coach because we see out of the windows so much better . . .

Fanny Edgeworth to Elizabeth Waller

Paris, 30th April, 1820

My dear Aunt Bess . . . There was some waltzing at Lady Granard's which I was glad of as Harriet had never seen waltzing. There was certainly some very agreeable conversation but in a large [party] one cannot hope for any continued conversation. Upon the [whole] I was very much amused and particularly happy to see Harriet enjoy every thing so much and be so [much] admired. The Persian ambassador and M. Denon were [to have] been there but failed on the road. There was a fat bon vivant Archbishop of St. Flour who had outlived a long confinement in the Bastille—who had never left France in any of the troubles and is now enjoying himself in a comfortable archbishoprick.

Yesterday we by the indefatigable Countess de Salis's means and by the kindness of M. F. Delessert were able to procure tickets for all of us at the Théâtre François to see Talma and Mlle Duchesnois for the last time they perform this year. The piece was beautiful Marie Stuart translated from Schiller. You remember I am sure the beautiful passages Mme de Staël gives in her Allemagne in prose.[1] The whole play is excessively interesting and every character was so well performed that one really forgot to think how they acted. There are none of the long declamatory speeches of the French tragedy and none of the rant of modern English tragedy. Unfortunately Mlle Paradel who played Elizabeth was beautiful and looked quite the Queen. This rather destroyed the illusion for Mlle Duchesnois is very ugly. She has fine tones of voice and acted so well that one forgot that she was not all that Mary was represented as being. The last scene in taking leave of her woman and of Melville (who was admirably acted) is very fine and touching. There are of course many parts of

[1] Two versions of Schiller's *Maria Stuart* appeared in 1820, the one a translation, the other an adaptation. Mme de Staël's *De l'Allemagne* came out in 1810.

the german play left out—that the blow is struck by Leicester—who—listens—like Rebecca describing the battle to Ivanhoe[1]—and the whole closes with his fainting and sinking into Mortimer's arms. I never saw any play that really interested me before. The dresses were beautiful and the scenery all [especially] Fotheringay Castle—Gothic and very good.

. . . As to news, we know parties run very high about French politics therefore we take care not to meddle on that subject. As to my own country I pine for an English paper. Parliament has been opened for a week and I know nothing of their proceedings!! . . .

We were able to spend only one hour there [at Mme de Pastoret's] and then to go to the English Ambassador's. We there saw the other great object of our curiosity—Talleyrand. Maria and he were introduced and conversed for ten minutes.[2] He did not say anything strikingly witty. He is very ugly but clever looking. All the Ambassadors were there—the Persian amongst others and his nephew. It looked very odd to see coming out of a gown a very very copper colored neck—bare—and a black beard and turbaned head. He took care to pick out one of the prettiest people in the room to talk to—Mrs. Littelton Duke of Wellingtons niece. Mr. Chenevix after much effort on his part and sundry shirkings on Maria's presented his wife.[3] She is certainly handsome and as the French say very well preserved. Mr. Chenevix is so much aged that I did not know him. The mixture of French—English and other foreigners was very amusing . . .

Maria Edgeworth to Mrs. Edgeworth

93 Place Bourbon, Wednesday 3rd May, 1820

Pray don't let any thing we write *penetrate* to Mrs. Tuite because it would go through her to Mr. Chenevix. He is here and agreeable and kind and *malin* as usual and the Comtesse is a fine woman and fine lady—on a large scale—and I don't like her.

. . . I go on to Sunday morning—Sermon—St. Sulpice. We

[1] Scott's *Ivanhoe* (1820), chap. xxix.

[2] Cf. *Letters from England*, 493–4: 'He does not chuse to talk to me or let me hear him talk' (21 Mar. 1831).

[3] Mr. Chenevix's wife, the former Countess de Rouault, had had a dubious reputation before her second marriage. See above, Paris 1802–3, p. 47 n. 1.

went with la comtesse de Salis—le comte and le Baron a batchelor and kind of Cicisbeo man—la Baronne who is also Chanoinesse[1] but goes into the world in roses and pink ribbons nevertheless and is very agreeable. N B le comte de Salis is very heavy and not firm on his legs ever. I am always afraid of pushing him down and he always draws back himself as if he was afraid of it whenever one comes near him. He has one tear always in one eye which is never wiped. I proposed to H and F yesterday that I should wipe it and invented what he would do and say if I made the attempt viz—he would ring and deliberately say 'Emportez-moi je vous prie cette folle Irlandoise.'

But to go on to the sermon at St. Sulpice—Along with us in their own calèche came M. le comte Semft the Saxon minister and the Countess Louisa a sweet pretty creature (about 20) his daughter—Many introductions and compliments on the numerous steps of the church—Then all down upon their knees upon chairs in the church—then up again buzzing like so many bees—and about their worldly affairs—A sea of black heads all looking up to the pulpit for the appearance of the famous Abbé Frayssinous—and when he did appear he was like an Abbé shot up from a snuff box—but old—long white hair with pelerine black with red edges and altogether looking like an actor. He preached in the Kirwan style[2] but with intolerable monotony of thumping eloquence—all against *les libérales*[3] and Rousseau and la nouvelle philosophie. It seemed to me old stuff—ill embroidered—But it was much applauded. Mem^{m}. the *audience* were not half so attentive or silent at St. Sulpice as at le théatre François and the Abbé Frayssinous did not touch nearly so much as the man who played Melville.

After church—morning visit to Mme de Pastoret. Oh my dear mother think of my finding her in that very boudoir! everything the same! But I wont stop to speak of my own feelings. F and H were delighted with the beauty of the house till they saw her and

[1] A cicisbeo was the recognized gallant of a married woman. Houses of noble canonesses often required neither residence, nor the wearing of the habit, nor vows of celibacy.

[2] Probably the Revd. W. B. Kirwan (1754–1805), dean of Killala, a noted Irish preacher.

[3] ME and Harriet E commonly wrote *libérales* for *libéraux*, probably because their society in Paris was so largely feminine.

then nothing could be thought of but her conversation and manners. They are even more charmed with her than I expected. She is but little changed except in being very tidy and clean in the morning.

Sunday night whatever you may think of it we went to a bal d'enfants at the charming Countess Orlowska's (the woman who is diligent in reading early lessons &c). F and H were delighted with the dancing of the children who danced and waltzed like angels—if angels waltz. At this ball were sundry distinguished persons some of whose names (Success to the joint memory of the firm!) I can tell you—Princesse de Beauvau and daughter both beautiful and one well behaved being not yet married—Duchesse de Praslin—fat woman falling to pieces like Mrs. Liddy or Mrs. Sotheby in white satin without corset—Mme de Montjoye and Mme de Dolomieu countesses and Dames d'honneur—the one to young Mme d'Orléans and the other to Mlle Adelaide Mme de Genlis pupil (these dames de [ ] I am told are &c &c—But very good to see and hear). Mme Orlowska's governess Mrs. Ashton beginning in French and ending in English made a panegyric upon Professional Education which she says is most highly esteemed in France and Germany. If this *could* have been heard sooner![1]

After this ball F and H went with me to the comtesse de Salis's and leaving me there went home. I proceeded with Mme de Salis to the Duchesse D'Escards to whom I had been told I must for the first time go without F and H. So Comtesse Baronne Comte and I whirled away to the Tuileries. Duc D'Escards is premier maître d'hôtel du roi and all the expense of their reception days is paid by the king. Mounted a staircase of one hundred or I believe 200 and forty steps. I thought the comte's knees must have failed while I leaned on his arm—my own ached. The long gallery passage lighted well opened into *little low* suites of apartments 4 or five each not larger than the bedchambers at Castle Forbes[2]—most beautifully hung some with silk some with cachemire shawl drapery in *tents* at each end—one end over ottomans—the other over recesses with end ottomans—windows looking out into gardens of Tuileries—moonlight and lamps in profusion—

[1] i.e. before RLE's death. *Essays on Professional Education* came out in 1809.

[2] The home of Lord Forbes in Co. Longford.

beautiful. N B recesses and tents very convenient for les dames de palais &c. In these rooms with busts of king and pictures of princes swarmed dukes and duchesses and old nobility with historic names and stars on their coats and red ribbons with silver bells[1] at their button holes and ladies in little white satin hats and toques with profusion of ostrich feathers or still better because more expensive *marabous* viz *powder puff* feathers. And the roofs were too low for such lofty heads—literally I thought some touched and I am clear that if some of the tallest dukes had looked up and if there had been any cobwebs they must have touched their mouths.

Now for the names of the quality. On the ottoman under the canopy sat la duchesse de la Ferté and the Princesse de Broglie Treveil—the head of the Duchesse de Broglie's family—from difference of politics they never speak to each other. She the princesse is a nice little wizzen simple mannered old lady who took to me directly and when I saw her heart warmed I asked and obtained permission to bring my two sisters to present to her on her next public day. No Englishwoman here ever goes to her except Mme de Salis who is her friend. La Duchesse de la Châtre and Duc were there and invited us—Countess de Clermont Tonnerre—bel esprit—many compliments—will come to see us—and invitation—to sisters and all. I am tired of reciting their names and will only add the brother of Prince [?Koslovsky][2]—not quite so agreeable as he—he thanked us for [?politeness]. Monday—drove about to a million of shops and laid out about 20 guineas a mere trifle Ma'am—met Mrs. Littelton who fell straight in love with Fanny without knowing who she was but for no merit of F's—only on account of a Leghorn hat trimmed French fashion and I had the folly to waste my time writing directions for her by which she could get ditto for 50 francs[3] for which she had been asked 4 guineas. After a most fatiguing morning spent at all the impertinent and pertinent dressmakers and milliners in Paris to whom Mme de Salis had the kindness to accompany us infinitely to the advantage of our *purses*[4] time and reputation for fashion we

[1] A cheap substitute worn temporarily by some émigré noblemen whose Croix de St. Louis had been lost, sold or destroyed during the Revolution.

[2] See *Letters from England*, 66.

[3] Just under £2.

[4] Harriet de Salis kept a very careful eye on expense; this was a joke among the Edgeworths: *Letters from England*, 587–8.

finished by the dear delight of dining at Passy—drive there delicious—found Mme Gautier with her Sophy now a matron mother[1] with her Caroline like what Mme Gautier and Sophy were in that very room 18 years ago—all the Delessert family that remains assembled except Benjamin who was detained by business in Paris. Mme Benjamin is very handsome nearer the style of Mrs. Admiral Pakenham than any body I know—François darling François the same as you saw him with only the crows feet of 18 additional years and sobered into a husband and father—the happiest of the kind I ever saw in France.

Walked before dinner in their beautiful grounds—old M. and Mme Delessert's—Benjamin's and Mme Gautier's. They have three houses on one terrace so that all the hanging gardens from the length of the 3 terraces making one pleasure ground is really charming—trees ash—horse chesnuts—sycamores all in full leaf—and the Judas tree in full pink blow. I never saw it before and it appeared to me to be a Brobdignag almond tree—Lilacs and laburnums in profusion in the fullest blow and there was a variety of lilac—I think Lilas de Varennes—I never saw before nor could they botanically describe it but they told me it was new—between a persian jessamine and lilac—little smell—vast puffs of flowers. The whole hanging shrubbery and grove interspersed with grass and gravelled walks was (tell Honora) more like Dropmore[2] lawn than anything I can suggest. But the air the feeling of domestic happiness was the charm of charms. The little pretty Caroline and a niece or cousin whom Mme Benjamin is educating ran down the walks to take us to their own little gardens and bowers and grottoes under the terrace and above about and underneath and they cropped their prettiest flowers and brought us huge nosegays and Mme Gautier gave me the anemony of the alps with a kind compliment from her countrymen and women expressing an ardent wish that we might see it growing there. She had a letter from Pictet &c. Long hothouses and greenhouses the whole length of the terrace about 150 [feet] have been added. Under the banana tree's broad leaf Harriet looked up with admiration and a coffee tree pleased Fanny.

Dinner in a salon whose large windows look into the gardens—

[1] Sophie Gautier had married her uncle François Delessert.

[2] Lord Grenville's house in Bucks.

Company Gabriel—*Alexander* who takes after the father—very sensible *commercial* conversation—made a panegyric on the jews of Hanover who had received him at their house with the utmost politeness and liberality—all this apropos to Walter Scotts jewess —and vanity must add to my own jew and jewess who came in for more than their due share.[1] Evening happy! happy!—room lighted with *large* globe lamps—large as the globes in the library windows. We sat round little tables looking at prints and talking most agreeably—often of you dearest mother whom François and Mme Gautier love most sincerely. How we did wish you were with us! Forgery of bank notes talked of. François tells me that the forgery of bank notes is almost unknown at Paris. To be sure there is not above 1/20 in circulation here compared with London and they never circulate beyond Paris and they *never* or seldom circulate among the lower classes. The *very best artists* in France are employed to engrave them. This you know was my fathers plan. It takes *a year* to finish a bank note—therefore it is not worth the while of cheats to forge. In fact Paris is as a country bank in England and all the evidence proved that forgeries in those seldom occur. Honora will remember all Watt said about examining officers—checks.[2] Excuse this bit of solid sense. Drive back from Passy by lamplight delicious on green trees—and over the bridges—light in water and on the buildings.

Tuesday went for the first time to the Louvre—Many fine pictures still left but the *finest* gone. Fanny and Harriet were in silent admiration and I let them enjoy it without interruption. That is all *I can* do—dear mother how much you could do for them here—I am *glad* to feel this. We shall go for one hour every morning to the Louvre—this I think better than wearing ourselves out with 2 or 3 hours at a time for *admiration* even is very fatiguing *let alone* the bodily fatigue of standing and walking. . . . Tuesday—dined at home—went to Mme de Pastoret's in the evening to meet la duchesse de Broglie—very handsome little woman—large soft dark eyes—sallow ivory skin—size and shape of Lady Rancliffe when 18—mob gauze cap something like Lady Belgraves—simple dress—winning manner—soft Pastoret conversation—speaks English better than any foreigner I ever heard

[1] Rebecca in Scott's *Ivanhoe* and the Jewish characters in ME's *Harrington* (1817).
[2] Cf. *Letters from England*, 176.

—not only gracious but quite *tendre* for me. Engaged me to dine next day and sisters for evening . . .

Harriet Edgeworth to Harriet Beaufort

98 Place Bourbon, 7th May, 1820

But wherefore all this labor, all this strife?
For Fame, for Riches, for a noble *wife*?[1]
For wife, read husband. No, my dear Harriet it is for nothing at least which at all balances the cost—not but what I have seen more worth seeing and heard more worth hearing than I thought I should but in other respects it is all exactly as I expected and affords me exactly as much pleasure as I had supposed it would. On the whole there have been fewer gauche contretemps than I imagined must have happened to any with whom I was connected in any scheme whether of pleasure or business. There have been also more engagements and more of what is called gaiety but whatever may be the unhappy or adverse feelings of the party we do contrive to laugh more and at less than any three people in the world. Not to disturb ourselves about trifles is our rule, but it is very droll how this rule varies and how the scale which measures trifles varies according to the how the when and still more according to the who of the business. The charm which people find in hearing their friends directly flattered astonishes me, that is having them flattered to oneself. If I heard Fanny admired without my presence being known, I should be pleased but Maria is delighted when the English say lovely and the French say charmante to her face about Fanny—however it makes her happy [ ] so much. Not that I mean to suppose myself or anybody else insensible to flattery but it must be nicely insinuated delicately shaded in—no appearance of hardness no broad splotches of it must be seen or it is revolting—to the last degree revolting where others are concerned but in regard to oneself perfectly overturning to ones whole system. Indeed for a person (always excepting ones friends whose flattery one is content to call Praise) to say [ ] affected admiration straightforward to me—is to make me straightforward detest them all my life . . .

[1] Pope, *Imitations if Horace*, Bk. i, Ep. vi, ll. 38–9.

The buildings here are superb but they are not any one of them Gothic which is the only really imposing style of architecture. We have been three times to the Louvre twice in the picture gallery and once in the statue rooms. In the gallery I do not think there is a single picture equal to some of those at Oxford and Warwick Castle[1]—still it is a most interesting place and we hope to spend much of our time there—that is to say one hour every day if we possibly can—so that we may become thoroughly acquainted with all those worth knowing. There has just been hung up a superb picture by Gérard of Henry 4ths entry into Paris. This of course is the object of all true Frenchmen in entering that room. It is a very fine picture even to English eyes. The first sight of the inside of the gallery disappointed me. It was not so wide nor nearly so high as I expected but when you have walked along it—the length you are well assured of. Altogether the whole Louvre is a splendid sight and even stripped as it has been must delight French hearts . . .

Harriet Edgeworth to Mrs. Edgeworth

93 Place Bourbon, 11th May, 1820

The Rue de Lille is now called Rue Bourbon and it joins this Place. The Hotel de Solms, opposite to which your house was, is now occupied by two or three regiments as a sort of barrack. Near it lives the Duchesse de Broglie and numbers of our acquaintance inhabit that street but I am not yet perfectly certain which is your house.

The house Sir Charles Stuart now lives in was the Ambassadors Hotel in Lord Whitworth's time and it was at that door that you made that famous sitting[2] and which we have looked at and have entered with such different feelings. Fanny and Maria dined there yesterday and I spent the evening with Sneyd and Harriette[3] who were very kind and agreeable. After dinner Sneyd and I walked out down the Boulevards—through the Rue Richelieu, down a

[1] Cf. ME's accounts in *Letters from England*, 219–20, 222. Neither ME nor Harriet E had any understanding of pictures.

[2] At the time when RLE was ordered to leave Paris in 1803.

[3] C. S. Edgeworth and his wife.

dirty flight of steps along a still dirtier lane about a foot wide and entered at once into the gay scene of the Palais Royal which always seems like a sort of enchantment. Several of the shops were lighted but we are to see the Café à mille colonnes by night which is said to be beautiful. It was a heavenly evening—not a breath of wind with an unclouded sky.

After tea à l'anglaise Maria and Fanny came for me and we proceeded to the convent[1] at which Mme Récamier lives. After ascending seventy eight steps all considerably dirtier than the street we came into a room about the size of the Cabinet only much lower. At one end of this was a bed with white curtains and gold ornaments arranged with the most perfect elegance. Opposite to this a fireplace on each side of which were bookcases stuffed as full as they could hold with richly bound books. At one side was a pianoforte and at the other a red sofa on which Mme Récamier seated herself with Maria. She is still very handsome but is grown too fat. She was exceedingly kind received Maria with the utmost friendliness and talked and laughed and seemed as well contented in the little nutshell she was in as if she was performing in the most brilliant salon. She had a long shawl twisted most gracefully round her and a profusion of dark hair uncovered and perfectly unornamented. On another sofa under one of the bookcases sat a long thin woman in white with a bonnet on; this was the widow of Moreau. She does not look as if she could have gone about as much with him as she is said to have done. Maria did not like her much. There were two or three gentlemen in the room and a niece of Mme Récamier who has the nieces face that all French nieces have, with large eyes light hair and pink cheeks. She was very civil to us and is translating some of Marias stories.[2] There was there a man who had made a translation of Homer into French prose and another who had written an epic poem called les Actions d'Amour[3] and whom we are to have the pleasure of hearing read French poetry, I believe his own, next Sunday. There were two young men who were arguing with great vehemence and used such a quantity of action as would have astonished any Englishman.

[1] L'Abbaye aux Bois. Mme Récamier became a boarder there in 1819. She had at first only two smallish rooms on the third floor.

[2] These translations do not seem to have been published.

[3] I cannot identify these writers. The most recent translations of the *Iliad* and the *Odyssey* into French were by Mme Dacier (1818 and 1819).

Besides was a man whose name I never heard—indeed he did not look much worth hearing about for his face looked as if all the parts had been punched and pulled about before it was quite hard and whose legs looked quite uninterested in the fate of his head. After some time came in a little dumpty woman with large eyes and larger mouth in a red hat which she soon threw off and shewed a black head and sallow color. This was no less a person than the Ex-Queen of Sweden who was so wise as to cry one day because she was taken for a governess. She is called Mme le Comtesse de Gergasti. She was followed by Mme de Boigne whom I believe I called Beaumont in a former letter—daughter to the Marquis d'Osmond. She speaks English perfectly—slowly but without the least accent. Maria is considerably in love with her and she is mighty civil. About 11½ Mathieu de Montmorency made his appearance which was very gentlemanlike and looked as if it had been very handsome. He lives with the Ultras and seemed rather puzzled to find out to which party Maria belonged—who relieved him soon from his perplexity by asking most kindly after Camille Jordan who is a complete Oppositionist and by saying she was going to the Duc de la Châtres a thorough Royalist where she hoped to meet him. Camille Jordan is in wretched health and Le Breton I suppose you have heard is dead.

Upon the whole I think it is wonderful that so many of your old friends still exist—and you and Maria seem to exist as fresh in their minds as if eighteen years had not passed away since they had seen you . . .

Maria Edgeworth to Mrs. Edgeworth

11th May, 1820

. . . They [Harriet and Fanny] have an excellent dancing master M. Deschamps—recommended by Lady de Ros who teaches her own daughters and who has made Miss de Ros one of the most *graceful* dancers in Paris. He comes for an hour from 8 till 9 or from 9 till 10 three times a week regularly, but indeed last week he came every day. He is quite satisfied with the attention of his pupils and very zealous. Fanny is now able to dance quite well enough to join in quadrilles with English and French. She danced at Lady de Ros with Prince Edmond de Beauvau last week and looked and performed quite well enough. Said Prince is a very gay little amiable youth who is particularly obliging to me and ended the last time I met him at the ambassador's with saying 'Enfin quand vous voulez que Mesdemoiselles vos soeurs dansent—ou quand vous voulez quelque chose que ce soit dites-le-moi et je suis toujours à vos ordres. Si c'est possible c'est fait—si c'est impossible &c.'[2]

Lady E. Stuart has been most peculiarly civil to us[1]—I suppose in consequence of Lady Harrowby's letter. No one goes to the embassadors parties even in the evening without invitation and these invitations are therefore much *looked after*. She has invited us twice to evening parties in the 10 days we have been here and we have gone and met three large rooms full of all the English and French world. Lady E. Stuart and Sir Charles have also invited Mme Maria E et *Mesdemoiselles* ses soeurs to a dinner but after consulting Mme de Salis I determined that it was best that but one should go—Fanny. Lady E. Stuart reproached me most obligingly with not bringing Harriet but nevertheless I think she liked our discretion for her table was quite full—20. The Hôtel is that which Lord Whitworth formerly had which afterwards belonged to Princesse Borghese—delightful—opening into a *lawn* garden with terraces and conservatories and profusion [of] flowers and shrubs and perfume of orange flowers. The dinner was splendid but not formal and no one can *represent* better than Lady Elizabeth does. She has twice offered us her box at the théatre françois. Once I accepted it but as I could not go myself being engaged to dinner at Mme de Vindés I sent them [Harriet and Fanny] with the Comte and Baronne de Salis who were right glad to go and have the honor of the box.

Yesterday when we dined at the ambassadors there were no other ladies but Mme de Salis—Mrs. Canning wife I believe to the brother of the minister—and Mrs. Burke wife to Dean of Ossory. In the evening when we rose to depart Lady Elizabeth asked us to accompany her to Le Barbier de Séville—au François with Mrs. Canning—but Alas! we were engaged to go to Mme Récamiers and I could not break the engagement more especially as Mme

[1] This phrase derives from a remark made by Calonne to Marie Antoinette.

[2] She was said to be perhaps the most popular ambassadress ever sent to France: A. Hare, *Story of Two Noble Lives*, 36.

Récamier is no longer rich and prosperous. So I refused and Lady Elizabeth ended with 'Ce sera donc je l'espère pour un autre jour'. So much the better because Harriet will then be with me.

We went to Mme Récamier up 78 stairs in a convent—all came up with the asthma—elegant room and she as elegant as ever—Mathieu de Montmorency—Queen of Sweden—Mme de Boigne a charming woman—ready to devour us—Mme la Maréchale Moreau—a battered beauty beautifully dressed—smelling of garlic and screeching (in vain) to pass for a wit. La Duchesse de Clermont Tonnerre has just written to invite us *all* to dinner but I stick to 2 and it is Harriets turn. I hope you admire my discretion . . .

Maria Edgeworth to Mrs. Edgeworth

93 Place Bourbon, Sunday, 14th May, 1820

. . . Yesterday—Saturday—was a remarkably *quiet* day. We got up at ½ past 8—resolving this morning to kill off a number of visits to la Princesse de Broglie Treveil—Duchesse de Broglie—Duchesse D'Escards—Duchesse de Clermont Tonnerre—Princesse de Beauvau &c &c—But the Fates had settled otherwise. ½ after 9—scarcely had we swallowed coffee and bread and butter when in came M. Hummelauer—attached to the Austrian embassy—who sat talking good French and tolerable English an immoderate time. Just departed when Mr. Chenevix and his cane entered and I do believe he would have sat till this instant if we had not told him at last that he must go. He converses delightfully and seems to like us all prodigiously but *then* he never considers that anything is to be thought of but *Talk* and I really sit on thorns sometimes when I know how time is going on and how many things we do *not* do that we ought while this talk is going on—He all the time holding a magnifying glass over every French character shewing us horrible things where we thought all was delightful. Saturday morning he sat *only* two hours. While he was here in came Mme de Villeneuve and Mme de Kergolay—Lovell's friend[1]—great

[1] Mme de Kergolay and Mme de Roquefeuil (below) had befriended Lovell E during his detention in France 1803–13.

screeching of pleasure on all sides—and she spoke with such real affection of Lovell that I quite liked her. Mem^{m}. Mme de Kergolay is a little *jealous* that Lovell has never written one line to her or mentioned her in his letters. Scarcely were Mme de Villeneuve and Mme de Kergolay and Mr. Chenevix gone when I rang to desire Rodolphe would let no other person in as we must put on bonnet and ruffs and get into carriage which had been ordered at 11 and had been waiting till near 2.

'Miladi' cried Rodolphe running up with a card 'Voilà une dame qui me dit de vous faire voir son nom et qu'elle est sure'—'Ah oui. Faites-la entrer.' Enter Mme de Roquefeuil with her bright benevolent eyes—different from what we expected yet very agreeable and we were *friends* in three minutes—Much agreeable conversation about Lovell. By the by it is with some difficulty I could persuade Mme de Kergolay that Lovell is not *married.* I really think she has some private interest about it. I dont think Mme de Kergolay very genteel. Mem^{m}. entre nous—There is a great deal of difference between the manners, *tone*, pronunciation and *quietness of demeanour* of Mme de Pastoret and Mme de Roquefeuil and we perceive strongly the difference between the manners of the old French nobility and others—for instance the little old wizzen Princesse de Broglie and the Duchesse Mme de Staël's daughter quite marked. Mme D'Escards and a little pale *poorish* looking Duchesse de Rohan for instance appear perfectly well bred while others with all the striving and struggling and riches and titles never can attain this indescribable, incommunicable charm. But to go on with Saturdays history—after settling to dine at Versailles with Mme de Roquefeuil saturday next she took leave and we caparisoned ourselves and at last set out . . .

After much time spent in buying necessary nonsense returned home, found cards just left by Sir Humphry and Lady Davy and Prince Galitzine and a note from Lady Elizabeth Stuart enclosing a ticket for her box for the Théâtre François. This is the 3d time she has offered it to us and the second time that we have been obliged to refuse from *prior pre-engagements*—particularly provoking because we should have seen Mlle Duchesnois in her first character Jeanne d'Arc—But it was impossible for we were engaged to *Cuvier* for the evening—Jardin des plantes.

Dined at home—dressed and set off first for M. Jullien's who lives Rue d'Enfer not very far from le jardin des plantes. This M. Jullien is an education man and an amateur worshipper kind of person whom I can't abide—very tiresome and full of his own books apropos to everything—a journalist moreover—but we were obliged to go and to Rue d'enfer we went—thro' strange places which at last through a porte cochère opened most unexpectedly to a fine room, parquet-ed floor large windows looking out on a handsome square and fine large trees. M. Jullien and Count Berthollet have apartments in this hôtel. How Jullien worked himself up to this I don't know but so it is. A company of strange people assembled by degrees—some finely feathered—others wrapped in dowdy shawls and odd men—The ladies the best worth mentioning (especially as I do not know the names of any of the others) were Mme de Villette (Voltaires) and a Madame who 'a beaucoup de talent' and makes a great deal by painting exquisitely on china. I begged that I might be permitted to take my sisters to see her works—settled for next week.

Among the men was one of the most extraordinary of all the extraordinary persons we have seen a Spaniard—squat—black haired black browed and eyed with an infernal countenance, who has written the history of the inquisition and who related to us how he escaped from a monastery to which he had been sent en pénitence by the Inquisition.[1] He got off he told us by presenting a certain number of Kilogrammes of good chocolate to the monks who were to report to the grand Inquisitor that he was very penitent and quite orthodox—and added 'Je faisais l'hypocrite pour un an'. I dare not say more of this man lest I should never get to Cuviers—which in truth I thought we never should accomplish alive. Such streets! such turns!—In the old *old* parts of the city—lamps strung at great distances and a candle or two from high houses now and then making darkness visible—and ruins and opened *sections* of houses seen as we passed—then bawling of fiacres or cart-men at sudden turns 'Ouais! Ouais!'—backing and scolding for no two carriages could by any possibility pass in these

[1] Juan Antonio Llorente, author of *Histoire critique de l'inquisition d'Espagne* (1817). He had been secretary of the Inquisition, but was dismissed for his liberal ideas. A supporter of Joseph Bonaparte, he took refuge in France in 1814, but was expelled at the end of 1820.

narrow allies. My liver was in a very bad way as you may guess but I put down the glasses and sat as still as a frightened mouse—Once diverted Harriet much however by crying 'Ah mon *cher* cocher arrêtez!'—Like Mme Dubarry 'Un moment *Monsieur* le Bourreau'.[1] We all agreed this was very like Lady Granard. It never was so bad with us that we could not laugh you see.

At last—and a long long last it was we turned into a porte cochère under which coachman and Rodolphe bent literally double and in nearly total darkness—but then in a dreamy way suddenly trees and lamps and buildings appeared and one lamp brighter than the rest by the side of an open portal illuminating the large printed letters of

'Collège de France.'

M. Cuvier came down a desperate flight of stairs and to the very carriage door to receive us. Imagine Cramptons[2] face magnified by a Brobdignag magnifier—with keen benevolent full grey eyes—pitted but not deeply with the small pox and the head covered with hair that looks as if it never had been cut and seldom combed but often powdered and the powder half blown half scratched out. This may give you altogether some idea of Cuvier—quite simple in his manners and like Prony often combing his topknot with his fingers and gathering it together in his hand as I would Fosters[3] ears when I am coaxing him (I hope by the by that he is well and good).

We were shewn up narrow stairs where with great difficulty and address I contrived to follow Cuvier's awkward *handing*—into a smallish room where many ladies and gentlemen, of the *most distinguished* names and talents were assembled—M. de Prony as like an honest water dog as ever—Biot ('Et moi aussi mademoiselle') is grown into a fat double volume of himself. I could not see in either his figure or face any hint of the young père de famille—very fat and round faced and bald and then black ringlets on a fine boned skull on which the tortoise might have fallen without cracking it. When he began to converse his superior abilities were immediately apparent—even in the ease frankness and simplicity of his conversation. He began talking of a brother

[1] Mme Dubarry, Louis XV's mistress, was guillotined in 1793.
[2] Philip Crampton, Irish surgeon.
[3] ME's King Charles spaniel.

of mine of whom he had heard much from a lady—could I guess her name? Had I ever heard my brother speak of her? After he had described I recognised and named Mme de Kergolay. He was delighted—Then talked of his journey to England and Scotland and his account of Scotland[1]—Then *Bonaparte*—whether he had protected men of science &c. Biot said of Bonaparte nearly what Mme de Staël says—that he had no *sensibility* and no enthusiasm except for military glory but that he did not chuse to be thought a barbarian and quite ignorant in the present state of the world and that he wished to have the best men of literature and science as he would have desired to have a rhinoceros or a mammoth if he could. While I was very happy listening to Biot Cuvier brought up a blackish grave important looking man with 'Permettez-moi Madame' &c but the name I never compassed hearing. Biot immediately got up and left ⅔ds of the sofa for the newly presented and retired to the end arm of the sofa and standing. I edged after him and went on talking leaving my newcomer at the other end. After a few minutes Biot whispered that he dared not engross Madame any longer and turning I saw my black man had grown blacker and seemed very ill pleased. I edged back to him still not knowing him from Abraham talked him into good humor and in a happy pause found means of asking Mme Biot who in the world he was. '*Put down your ear*' in English 'Prince Czartoryski a pole—formerly minister of the emperor of Russia.' Many compliments passed about works on education and then we went to a table to look at Prince Maximilien de Neufvilles journey to Brazil magnificently printed in Germany.[2] So when we were round the little marble table with a lamp and a book all tongues began to clatter and it became wondrous agreeable and behind me I heard English well spoken and this was by Mr. Trelawney—heard from him a panegyric of the Abbé Edgeworth (he knew him well). Mr. Trelawney was the person who took the first letter and news which the Duchesse d'Angoulême received at Mittau[3] after she quitted France. She came out in the dead of night to receive the letter in her night gown—night shift I believe.

[1] Biot had been in England and Scotland in 1817–18, doing research on the prolongation of the French meridional arc.

[2] Maximilian Alexander, prinz zu Wied-Neuwied, *Reise nach Brasilien* (1815–17).

[3] Louis XVIII and his family established themselves at Mittau in 1798.

Shambling servant—tea and supper altogether odd but very agreeable. Only ⅔ds of the company could sit round the table but all the behind back ranks sitting at every conceivable angle were very happy and wondrous loud and talkative—Science literature politics nonsense in happy proportions. Biot sat behind Fanny's back with his perspiring head at times nearly in her mouth. I like him desperately but the *smell* nearly made me sick while I was talking or listening. I could have wished that every man in the room (Mr. Trelawney and Czartoryski excepted) had been plunged into a bath.[1] F says that Biot talked of the parallax which he thinks is an imagination of Dr. Brinkley's.[2] When he was going on about this not a word he said reached me tho I was within one of him—But that one was Prony who with his hair nearly in my plate was telling me most entertaining anecdotes of Bonaparte and Cuvier's head nearly meeting him across me each talking as hard as he could—but not at all *striving* to shew learning or wit—quite the contrary—boyish Crampton *ish* frankness and open hearted genius delighted to be together at home and at ease. This was the most flattering and agreeable thing to me that could possibly be. Harriet's intelligent animated eyes and bright colored cheek I saw every now and then appearing on the off side of Cuviers shoulder and every now and then he turned to her in the midst of his anecdotes and made her completely one of us. I could have kissed him for [it]—if he had been washed.

There was such a prodigious noise that any body could say anything they pleased in perfect security to their neighbours and the anecdotes of Bonaparte from Cuvier and Prony beginning always with 'Tenez je m'en vais vous dire' or 'Écoutez je vous dirai' in a low voice and snuggled attitude were very curious. Cuvier and P both agreed that he never could endure to have any answer but a *decided* answer—philosophic doubt was his peculiar aversion. One day said Cuvier I nearly ruined myself by an honest doubt or rather by *considering* before I answered. Bonaparte asked me 'Faut-il introduire le sucre de Betterave en France?' 'D'abord sire il faut songer si vos Colonies—' Bonaparte interrupting 'Faut-il avoir le

[1] Personal sloveliness had been a cult in the revolutionary period.

[2] Brinkley believed himself to have discovered relatively large parallaxes for four of the brightest stars; his discovery was illusory: A. M. Clerke, *Astronomy during the 19th century*, 33.

sucre de betterave en France?' 'Mais Sire il faut examiner si—' 'Bah! Je demanderai à Berthollet.'[1]

This despotic laconic mode of insisting on learning everything in two words had its inconveniencies. One day he asked the master of the woods at Fontainebleau 'How many acres of wood here?' The master—an honest man—stopped to recollect and recollect. Bah! The under master came forward and said any number that came into his head. Bonaparte immediately took the mastership from the first and gave it to the second. 'Qu'arrivait-il?' continued Prony 'the rogue who gave the guess answer was soon found cutting down and selling quantities of the trees and Bonaparte took the rangership from him again and reinstated the honest hesitator.'

Prony told me an anecdote of himself in droll half shut eyed way which made me roll with laughing and there was such a noise that I could laugh *out* quite at my ease without attracting anybody's attention. You know Prony is one of the most absent men alive next to Farcy? 'Once' said he 'I was in a carriage with Bonaparte and Gen. Caffarelli. It was at a time when Bonaparte was full of going to Egypt. He asked me to go. I said I *could* not—that is I would not—and when I had said those words I fell into a reverie collecting in my own head all the reasons I could for my not going to Egypt.[2] All this time Bonaparte was going on with some confidential communication to me of his *secret* intentions and views and when it was ended le seul mot *Arabie* m'avoit frappé l'oreille. Alors je voudrais m'avoir arraché les cheveux [*sic*] (making the motion so to do) pour pouvoir me rappeler ce qu'il venoit de me dire. I never could recollect a single word or idea I had been so absent.' 'But why did you not ask Caffarelli afterwards?' 'I dared not because I should have betrayed myself to him.' Prony says that Bonaparte was not obstinate in his own opinion with men of science about those things of which he was ignorant but would bear no contradiction in tactics or politics. Cuvier and Prony both agreed that the whole face of Europe was changed and Bonaparte's

[1] After the Egyptian expedition Napoleon referred to Berthollet as 'my chemist' and if a chemical question arose would say 'I must ask Berthollet': Crosland, *Society of Arcueil*, 61.

[2] Prony's refusal to go to Egypt cost him Napoleon's favour, although his wife was a friend of Josephine: Crosland, op. cit. 58, 60.

fate decided by his neglecting to look at the thermometer when he was at Moscow.

I forgot another Russian Prince Podorowski or something like it but while Cuvier and Prony were so entertaining it was very little matter to me who or what he was. In Admiral Pakenham's language I might observe that these Russian princes *never make small beer of themselves*. They seem to have a high and mighty opinion of themselves and of all the Russias and all therein contained. My dear little pocket Prince de Beauvau for me!—worth all the Russian bears and giants put together.

At twelve o clock I began to think of returning from between my most agreeable and *hot headed*, companions. Returned from the Jardin des plantes through all the crooked narrow darkling dim-lamped streets in marvellous safety, jabbering to one another all the way—sent Josephine and Rodolphe to bed (separately)—found a note from Countess de Salis with a ticket of two places for the kings chapel mass next morning—procured for us by Duc de Luxembourg—a favor. Slept—*Dressed*—and this included some difficulties—gowns not sent home—and it is necessary to be very nice—*white gloves specified*—So you may guess the style. At last all equipped—But the carriage ordered at eleven (*Precise* as Rodolphe always roars out for his parting sound) did not come till past twelve and we walked ¾ of a mile and were late and could not go at last.

Note—Prince Czartoryski—It is always my misfortune to find out too late the history of the celebrated people I meet. This prince was passionately in love with the present Empress of Russia and she with him. The emperor as proof of his esteem made him his prime minister and to shew his confidence in his wife's virtue placed her lover as near her as possible. I remarked to the Countess Razumowska who told me this story that in most cases especially in Zadigs[1] this receipt for curing love had not succeeded. 'Mais je vous en réponds dans ce cas &c.' Well—be that as it may. Bonaparte came to be Emperor and disliking Czartoryski he was displaced and returned to Poland where he has magnificent establishment and does all manner of good as the Comtesse R assures me. Cuvier is said to have no force de caractère as this Countess ex-

[1] *Zadig*, chap. viii. The queen and Zadig did not however fall in love until after his appointment.

pressed it doubling up her pocket handkerchief and [bending] it to this side and that [ ]. 'Cuvier a beaucoup d'esprit [et de savoir] mais pour le caractère il est comme ça—bien en contraste avec le duc de Richelieu qui comme on sait n'a pas trop d'esprit mais il a un caractère. Il est ferme c'est pourquoi il est fort considéré.'

Fanny Edgeworth to Honora Edgeworth

Place Bourbon, 21st May, 1820

I do believe that I have been more than three weeks at Paris and have never written to you. I have often wished for you but I think never more than yesterday when I was with Mme de Roquefeuil and her poor old mother. I am not disappointed in Lovells friend. She has more mind than he ascribed to her. Her conduct since the return of the Bourbons has been very noble and I should think very uncommon among the royalists. They have been very kind to her in words—the Duc de Berry particularly. He had been formerly the intimate friend of M. de Roquefeuil. The King was particularly struck with her petition. She merely stated the infirm state of her mothers health and what M. de Roquefeuil had been—never said anything of what she had sacrificed or what she had perhaps a right to demand. The whole was contained in four or five lines. The King answered it himself in the handsomest manner. From the state of her mother's health and her own philosophy she thinks herself happier than if she possessed her former fortune. This and a noble species of pride has prevented her from reminding the King of his good intentions. Her manners are very charming and very dignified—her conversation agreeable and *sisterly* affection for Lovell quite delightful . . .

I must go back to tell you the great enjoyment I had in the hour at Bréguets. I felt the advantage of all the attention I gave with you to the explanations of the different suspensions and Escapements in Rees.[1] To see these beautiful contrivances in motion—performing every second without difficulty the complicated motions which cost so much thought and time to invent and

[1] Bréguet was the great watchmaker. Fanny E refers to Rees's *Cyclopaedia* (1802–19).

execute—inspired me with a degree of wonder and satisfaction which I have scarcely enjoyed since the beginning of 1817.[1]

The day we wrote last we dined with Mme Rilliet who is always souffrante et mon mari aussi—and we were nearly an hour too late and they had half done dinner when we arrived. They are really domestic people. She has only one daughter who is married and lives in the house with her not very unlike Fanny Browne. Her husband and she are as fond of and intimate with one another as any English people could be. There were but few people there but all of them the most dreadful ultra royalists—by far the most violent we have seen. One of them declared she was of no party because all that were not royalists should cease to exist &c &c. Poor Mme Rilliet said she was very near unpacking her things (they are just going into the country) to give us a ball!! The only place at which I thought Maria's company totally undervalued and where we lost two hours was at Mrs. Howse's vulgar friend la Vicomtesse de Riolz marked all over with the small pox and raddled either by nature or herself—who brought Maria to her house for no purpose that I can understand but to hear a child play on the pianoforte . . .

We went with Mr. Hummelauer who is a very well informed man, particularly modest—to the Comte de Lasteyrie's where I saw all the process of the stone engraving which has been brought by him to great perfection. He is at present making engravings for a work on natural history which [he] understands very well which are extremely good.[2] Lovell might with great ease and very little expense have a press made for taking off the impressions—the only difficulty. He might find it very useful in the Lessons for his school[3] if he would wish it as I am going to learn the method of drawing on the stone. I can make notes of the frame and of the whole process and if he will be at the expense of bringing over stones and ink from France all the rest can be easily done at home. He can have a cheap and commodious method of immortalising

[1] RLE died in June, 1817.

[2] Lasteyrie went to Munich in 1812 to learn about lithography and on his return to Paris in 1815 established a lithographic workshop there. The book referred to is possibly *Histoire naturelle et économique du chien, du cheval &c*, 6 vols. (1834).

[3] Lovell Edgeworth had established at Edgeworthstown a school at which pupils were accepted regardless of class and religious affiliation. It had for a brief period considerable success.

his admirable method of teaching if he wishes for it and undertakes what I have stated . . .

On Friday we went to Mme de Rohan's. She had a very nice set of people at her house and she herself did the honors particularly well. The name of the Abbé Edgeworth is held in veneration by that set. There was a grand person with a broad red ribbon who did not know well what was saying but when his daughter called to him and told him that Miss E. was cousin to the Abbé he went [and] listened with great attention to what she was saying. At one moment one admires their attachment to the Bourbons and one is obliged to respect them for all they have sacrificed to their loyalty but the next instant the excessive nonsense they talk places them below contempt. They are always telling some dream of the royal family. The Duchesse d'Angoulême I think it was dreamt just before the assassination of the poor Duc that he would meet with some violent death[1]—the Duchesse de Berry is certain of having a son because she has so often dreamt it—and all the horrors and exaggerations which they are eternally repeating about the *libéraux*. Mme de Staël did not succeed in conciliating the Royalists by her last work.[2] They were disgusted with her compliments to the Bourbons which they do not believe to have been sincere. Various facts they say are falsely stated or rather falsely colored. In their anger against her they are forced to sympathise with Bonaparte and to say that he did quite right in not allowing a person of such revolutionary principles to remain in Paris!! In this world it is curious how from some cause extremes always meet. We live too much with these *wrong thinking* people but their manners are decidedly superior to any of the other party that we have seen.

The Duchesse de Broglie has an affectation of ease that makes her sometimes awkward and always not exactly what one would wish oneself to be. We have just paid a visit to her and found her at home—alone with her little girl running about the room. She was talking of her little brother Rocca[3] and wishing for a good tutor for him. She spoke very sensibly about education. We shall

[1] The Duc de Berry was assassinated in February, 1820.

[2] *Considérations sur les principaux événements de la Révolution française* (1818).

[3] Louis Alphonse Rocca (1813–38) was Mme de Staël's son by her second husband.

see her at Coppet—indeed she seems very anxious not merely to see Maria but to know her. She has come here twice in the morning, we were unfortunately out—but that was a great exertion for her. I have never seen the Duc de Broglie. She is said to behave perfectly well—I hope it will continue. It is very good of the Duc to let Miss Randall (the person who attended Mme de Staël during her illness and supplied a daughters place when the Duchesse during her confinement was unable to be with her mother)—the Baron de Staël and Schlegel[1] all live in his house.

Mr. Chenevix and M. Buchon came here this morning and the agreement is I believe concluded about the translation.[2] He is not to add either notes or preface. He will mark whatever passages he does not approve or that he thinks will not interest the French reader but all is to be submitted to Maria's approbation. Whatever intro he thinks necessary to explain certain passages to French understandings Maria undertakes to write. If the book does not sell she agrees to indemnify M.B. for any loss he may incur—so the matter rests. On Thursday he is to bring the Memoirs—marked according to his wishes . . .

Maria returned in great spirits last night from Châtenay Mme d'Osmonds. She went with Mme Récamier. Old Mme D'Osmond and her husband were at one time ambassador and ress in England. He is a gentlemanlike yellowskinned old man and she something of the sort of Mrs. Moutray—Very good natured and well mannered but not much more. They married—or rather sold their daughter to General de Boigne when in England. This old Genl. who is immensely rich fell desperately in love with Mlle d'Osmond and declared he would marry her on any terms. The father immediately made his own terms—securing to himself an annuity of £1500 and a large dower for Mme de Boigne. Soon very soon after their marriage the young wife found her husband insupportable and plainly said she preferred living with her father and mother which she has done ever since—excepting when in want of money and then she goes for a fortnight or a week or whatever length of time is necessary to wheedle some more money from him—for she is not able to keep within the large income

[1] A. W. Schlegel had been tutor to Mme de Staël's children and a regular member of her circle. The Baron was her eldest son Auguste.

[2] Of the *Memoirs of* R. L. *Edgeworth* (1820).

which he settled upon her. She is however a very agreeable little, pretty spoilt child. As she sacrificed herself to her father and mother they are obliged to humor her in everything. Their house in the country delightful—elegant without any of the faste de la richesse—beautiful flowers—hot house plants ranged in gradation round the house—beautiful avenue meeting at top of tall horse chesnuts &c.

Amongst the company was M. and Mme Dillon and their daughter—a M. Karoly his tutor and friend M. Walstein—but not like the hero.[1] In this case M. Karoly is the hero—and as much in love as he could be in a romance. When M. Dillon was Ambassador at Florence, he admired his daughter and courted her very openly but made no further advances. This went on for a year and then the Dillons thought it time to draw in. This soon forced a proposal—he went to Hungary where he lives to complete the settlements which are too magnificent for me to write. This was done in the shortest possible time and he travelled night and day for 7 days and nights till he reached his beloved!! Is not this something fine? It is very droll how people love telling all their affairs to Maria—she had not been an hour there before Mme de Boigne told all this history of her cousin Mlle Dillon to her and in the evening after they were gone they sat round the fire and began criticising the young lady's appearance and saying that there never were two people more totally occupied with one another. It was rather contre gré as you may imagine that Maria went without us but she found it turned out very well and she is to take us some morning to breakfast . . .

Harriet Edgeworth to Louisa Beaufort

Paris, 93 Place Bourbon, 21st May, 1820

. . . I think my letter from Paris was written the day after our arrival, while the buildings, people and whole appearance of the town was fresh and new. The buildings have lost nothing by being better known. I see the view from the Pont de Louis 16, which we pass over every day with every day equal admiration, whether it is in the brilliant sun and under the unclouded sky of the day time or in

[1] In Mme de Montolieu's *Caroline de Lichtfield* (1786).

the delightful nights with the soft light of the moon which is so clear that it seems cut out from the sky and surrounded with stars which are as bright without being as cold looking as our finest frosty nights. I could not have believed that there was so much difference between the nights here and those in Ireland for the days are less fine, less hot and less constantly dry that I expected. The heat is not so great now as I have sometimes felt it in Ireland at this time of year—67 is the greatest height I have seen the thermometer before 12 in the shade, and 70 the highest afterwards. We have had some beautiful lightning which really made the sky seem on fire while it shone. It was followed by magnificent thunder and straight heavy drenching rain which refreshed the air and made the trees and flowers start forward. The lilacs are past—the laburnums are still beautiful and contrast admirably with the Judas trees which are to be seen with their thick flowers in every garden here . . . The horse chesnut flowers are now gone but while they lasted were most beautiful covering the trees, so that only a spot of green here and there was to be seen, on the majestic trees in the Jardins des Tuileries—the only places where there are any trees at all to be compared with those in England—and even there their stems are but small but the shade they gave is so thick as to be impervious even to the summer sun. Their dark shade might give the idea of gloomy sadness or soft retirement both of which you may have in as much perfection as is possible among the multitude of readers talkers and walkers; the talkers is a name that may be applied to all but the readers for the talking is incessant to everybody, about everything whether the multitude consists of the old sick and idle of the poorer class in the morning —or of the young fashionable and brilliant assemblage of the afternoon, or of the fat brown handkerchief-headed citizens with their beautiful eyes and bad countenances who walk there in the evening and always stay to the last moment of the drum beating at which the gend'armes shut the gates and all who loiter too long are enclosed till the next morning. The lower classes of women are very ugly though they have the most wonderfully black and sparkling eyes. Their skins are too dark and too coarse and they have a total absence of all modesty of countenance. There are some few exceptions of course, but this is perfectly true with regard to all the fishwomen, criers and shopgirls whose manners to customers are in general a curious mixture of the affected indifference which makes them treat you with the most provoking inattention and of the real anxiety for your custom which prompts the millions of lies which they pour forth upon every yard of ribbon. They are as provoking in their interest as in their carelessness because they insist upon being your intimate companion and not only knowing and interfering in all your history and affairs but telling all they did and knew or know about everybody else. They are a very strange but entertaining people.

The violence of party governs everything here except dress which is an affair of too much consequence to be altered to suit the opinions of liberales, Bonapartists, Ultras or Royalists. So all are equally drest in long waists, trailingly long petticoats very high up necks for all ages and for those past the bloom of youth gauze bonnets or hats with a profusion of soft feathers called Marabous. These hats are made of chip[1] or gauze and put crooked on the side of the head. I think the Ultras or Royalists (for there is some difference even in loyalty) are generally to be distinguished by light blue which usually appears in some part of their dress and which I do not recollect to have seen worn by any of the libérales. Those men attached to Bonaparte are known from others by a moustache on their under lip which is not worn by the loyal lips of the rest of the army but such flourishing whiskers and moustaches I never saw on any English face, as appear on almost all officers here. They never wear their uniforms except on a Sunday but almost everybody has a red ribbon to mark their belonging to the Legion of Honor and some have little gold crosses one of which denotes Chevalier of the Legion of Honor the other Chevalier de St. Louis—and some few appear with the grand cross of St. Louis and its broad red ribbon.

We have the advantage of seeing three or four regiments pass through this Place every day. The men are in general fine and stout looking but the horses are mere rats and in general their music [is] frightful. Except one march played by the corps of sappers and miners we have heard nothing to compare to English martial music. This corps of sappers and miners are curious looking men with long beards and white leather aprons who always carry axes on their shoulders and are constantly attended by a band. Besides

[1] Wood or woody fibre split into thin strips for making hats or bonnets.

these military we have the advantage of the constant passing and repassing of the Duc de Bourbons carriages and horses as his palace is directly opposite to us and beyond it the Chamber of Deputies. The palace is not a strictly beautiful building but the two wings are joined by Corinthian pillars, which have a fine effect as they are of dark stone contrasted with the light color of the chambre des Députés behind and by moonlight it is beautiful. The front of the Chambre is a very handsome building looking upon the Pont Louis 16 with corinthian pillars and a long flight of steps with figures of Sully and other renowned Frenchmen in front. The place de Louis 15 is very fine and so is the Place Vendôme which is a Quadrangle built round the beautiful pillar of Trajan in bronze—the whole Place faced with stone and opening at opposite sides into the Rue de la [Paix] and the Rue Castiglione, most magnificent it is. The Rue de Rivoli which was begun by Bonaparte and was intended to have reached from one end of Paris to the other, that part which is finished is on one side the Jardin des Tuileries and on the other is an arcaded footpath. The whole front is stone of a grey color and prodigiously handsome. The Rue Faubourg St. Honoré is the Grosvenor Square of Paris and filled with English and the Rue St. Honoré is the Oxford Street and filled with shops. The Palais Royal is a sort of large Bazar. That is to say there is a covered and flagged way which goes round a square and which has pillars on one side and the most glittering shops on the other. The most numerous are those of Jewellers, horlogers, and glass shops, besides quantities of Cafés and Cafés au Billard which are very entertaining to see as one passes for there are always numbers of people sitting at little tables or playing at chess for five francs a game, an excellent receipt for learning to play.

The great advantage which Paris possesses over English towns is the buildings being all stuccoed or of stone, which prevents the glaring red of brick—and from burning wood and from the natural clearness of the air the whole town when seen at a distance is free from that dull and black cloud which envelopes London when seen from a distance.

I have seen none of the environs of Paris but Versailles where I have been twice and where I had yesterday at the house of Mme de Roquefeuil the honor of drinking some Bourdeaux given to her by *the* Mme de la Rochejacquelein who lives at Versailles and whom we are to see in September, when we intend to return from Geneva whither we go at the end of July. I have also seen the Marquise d'A[ntichamp][1] the woman mentioned in Mme de la Rochejacquelein who lived for several years disguised as a shepherdess. Her husband is now Governor of the Louvre and she is a little crumpled old woman with a long nose and nice old dried face. We met her at the house of the Princesse de Broglie Treveil where we saw four of the prettiest people I ever beheld. Indeed the higher ranks of French are upon the whole much handsomer than I expected—many very fine looking and some very pleasing. Besides these people there is a certain little old Duchesse de Rohan who walked to Versailles and back in one day at the time of the Revolution!—and wears Louis 16ths hair in a ring with 'Fils de Louis montez au ciel' written at the inside.[2] She is a very great Ultra but she is exceedingly well informed and perfectly acquainted with Marias works, which she reads in English. She is very agreeable and very much attached to us. At Versailles I saw the regiment of Vendeans commanded by the last of the Rochejacqueleins. They are very fine soldierly men wearing very high furry caps and dark blue uniforms . . .

Upon the whole French tragedy acting has appeared to me better and French comedy acting worse than I expected but I cannot justly compare them for I have seen their best tragedy actors—Talma, Mlle Duchesnois and La Font. Their incomparable comic actress Mlle Mars has had the impertinence to lose her daughter and fears are expressed that she will not act this season—perhaps never—but this is too heartrending an idea to be endured. When I say that the comic acting was not as good as I expected I mean that it was more farcical but all the actors are more equal and some of them excellent altogether far superior to any comic acting I ever saw in Ireland. A little after piece Le confident

[1] See *Mémoires de Mme la marquise de la Rochejacquelein*, ed. Vitracet Galopin (n.d.), 308.

[2] These are the words reputed to have been said by the Abbé Edgeworth at the execution of Louis XVI. The Abbé himself did not remember saying them. This is not conclusive because of the stress of the moment, but as the drums were ordered to beat to drown the king's last words it would have been difficult for an onlooker to have heard anything said by the Abbé. Lacretelle half confessed to inventing the story for a newspaper. It came into currency immediately after the king's death.

par hazard[1] was incomparably played in every part but L'Avare I thought might have been more really well and less farcically played . . . She [Mlle Duchesnois] acts still better in Jeanne d'Arc[2] [than in Marie Stuart] but she is so awkward that one is at a loss to discover the secret of her acting. I believe it is her voice which interests one so completely in all she says that one forgets to observe her ugly face and ill shaped person. Louis 9[3] was the most complete French tragedy and French Tragedy acting that I have seen—consequently the least interesting but I have not yet seen any of Racine or Corneille or any of the 2 page long speech plays.

We have seen almost all of the old French friends who seem to have preserved my mother and Maria as fresh in their heads as if they had parted from them yesterday. Mme Pastoret was very different in appearance from what I had expected but very much the same in manner and conversation—very soft—elegant and agreeable. Mme Gautier was exactly what I thought she was, only younger and not so prim—her daughter less pretty and older looking. François Delessert is delightful but blacker and taller than I thought he would have been. Mme de Vindé is next in affection to the Delesserts. Indeed she doats upon Maria so much that she takes her in her arms whenever she sees her. She is quite an old shawled woman with three very nice grand daughters. Mme Récamier is still lovely, though she is grown very fat but she has charming, though not very *good* eyes—large dark and with long black eyelashes. She lives in a little elegant room about 16 feet square at the top of a convent—where we went last night to hear a man bawl out a poem, in the most barbarous manner. The verses were beautiful in themselves but he would have ruined any party —but he was a good study of the true French screeching manner. We gave our knees good exercise that night for after mounting seventy eight convent stairs we climbed a hundred and four at the Tuileries to the Duchesse D'Escards . . . On Monday Fanny and I spent the evening with the Comtesse de Salis while Maria paid an evening viz to the Princesse de Beauvau who is a very amiable woman living with all her family, drawing reading and [?working] together. The Prince is a Spanish Grandee and is in

[1] A one-act comedy by L. F. Faur, first acted in 1801.
[2] Schiller's *Die Jungfrau von Orleans*. A translation by Kramer was published in 1802.
[3] A tragedy in verse by Ancelot, first acted in 1801.

disgrace because he carried Napoleons chair during the hundred days and said the Bourbons were down for ever. These evening viz's are very odd but are on the whole more agreeable than our morning vizes. It is the fashion for gentlemen to endeavor to get away with the least possible observation from the lady of the house.[1] For this purpose he always looks round till he sees she is engaged in interesting conversations and then out he slides and happy he who gets the door shut without any remarks from Madame whose business it is to catch and regret him before he escapes.

Tuesday Maria dined at Mr. Chenevixs. Fanny and I went to the play and we all soiréed at Mr. Creeds and then at the Ambassadors whose evenings are always pleasant from the entertainment of watching or talking to those we do know and diverting ourselves with the faces of those we do not. The greatest lions are the Persian Ambassador and the Popes Nuncio who both always select the handsomest young ladies to talk to. These are among the English Miss FitzGerald daughter to Lord Robert, Lady Adelaide Forbes, Miss Leath, Mrs. Cadogan, Lady Hemlock [*sic*][2] who is beautiful. Among the French or other foreigners there are few young ladies ever to be seen, but the handsomest people we know are the Princesse Gabriel de Beauvau and her sister Comtesse de la Grange—the Duchesse de Castries Mme de Podenas—the Princesse Octave de Revel and a nameless woman in black . . .

Fanny Edgeworth to Mrs. Edgeworth

Paris, 31st May, 1820

. . . I must abandon the triste subject of the toilet to tell you something of ourselves. Maria seemed a little hurried and tired last week but she is now herself again. She went to the Chambre des Députés yesterday with Harriet and was not tired. On Monday we went to the little theatre of Pont St. Martin where we were much amused. We went with the Creeds. In the morning we had such a

[1] Cf. Mme de Genlis, *Mémoires*, v. 107. The object was to avoid '*l'importunité réciproque des compliments et des reconduites*'. The custom belonged to the *ancien régime* and had been dropped during the Revolution, but was later resumed.

[2] ? Lady Hunloke.

sitting—the translator brought an author lady who was très spirituelle et charmante. She has the remains of great beauty and is very entertaining. She told us that Mme de Staël took it into her head to die in Mme Gay's bed! When Mme Gay after a little persuasion left her apartment to her she remained in the house and heard from the Duc de Broglie everything that passed.[1] Mme de Staël was excessively afraid during her whole illness that nobody would receive her last breath. Her friend Miss Randall had never left her and for days and nights together neither she nor Mme de Broglie had a moments sleep. If Mme de Staël saw them close their eyes she immediately called to them. The last night Mme de Broglie completely worn out threw herself on a sofa and was soon asleep. Miss Randall saw her and likewise lay down. They had scarcely been two minutes asleep when they were wakened just in time to see her die!! Mme Gay is one of those people who are really clever but she talks too much and too loud. She was most pleasingly succeeded by [ ][2] and Mrs. Graham. The former is a most friendly woman so quiet and so plain—An American by education but a niece of Wilkes. She is aunt to Mrs. Jeffrey. It was with her that the match was formed but that is too long and too pretty a live story of the loves of a satirical reviewer and an ugly American. Mrs. Graham is delightful . . .

Yesterday we breakfasted with Cuvier he again dull—wrapped up in politics. After breakfast we went to the Museum. There was an American and a friend of Mr. Hutton's—a German Count Brunner—very agreeable . . .

Maria Edgeworth to Mrs. Edgeworth

4th June, 1820, *La Celle*[3]—M. and Mme de Vindé's country house

. . . Just as we received your letter in which you say that we never speak of Mme de Vindé we were at her country-house. In coming

[1] The object of the move was to be in a house with a garden into which Mme de Staël could be wheeled.

[2] Probably Mme Louis Simond, wife of the author of *Journal of a Tour and Residence in Great Britain in 1810 and 1811* (1815). Mrs. Jeffrey was the second wife of Francis Jeffrey, editor of the *Edinburgh Review*.

[3] La Celle St. Cloud.

here we breakfasted at Passy with dear Mme Gautier and Mme François Delessert and their little Caroline who has quite recovered from the measles. Mme François who is like Sally Brinkley translated into French took us up to her own and her mothers apartments—delightful *comfortable* rooms with beautiful views of Paris and its environs from all the balconied windows. She shewed us the little bed and little room next Mme Gautiers in which she had slept always before she was married—in which Mme Gautier also had slept always before she was married and in which little Caroline now sleeps. There is something in the duration and uniformity of these family habits and attachments which pleases and touches the mind especially in these revolutionary and changeable times and countries. After eating sweetmeats and cakes and cutlets and drinking wine and coffee &c for breakfast and after having walked through honeysuckles and roses and beautiful hothouse plants (including the most magnificent Cactus my eyes ever beheld of which you are to have a cutting—yes a cutting) we came on to dinner at La Celle—Arrived in good dinner time. La Celle is as old as Clotwold the son of Clovis who first came here to make a hermitage for himself—then it was called La cell*ule*. Then wonderfully enlarging and changing by the way it came in the course of some centuries to be the residence of Mme de Pompadour, and I now write to you in her very apartments in which Lewis the 15th and she revelled and probably helped to prepare the way for the French revolution—with their motto 'Après nous le déluge'.

The suite of apartments which we have now the honor to occupy consist of a *high* comfortable but not large bedchamber about 20 feet square exactly resembling one of the prints of sallons in Gil Blas[1] or Molière—with three very large mirrors forming each a pannel from ceiling to surbase—the room wainscotted and painted white—small daubs of landscapes over the double doors—Two large windows for that time *very* large croisées, opening within a foot of the ground into a large and beautiful old fashioned shrubbery garden with low rose acacias and rhododendrons in profuse flower—the garden surrounded with lime trees thick

[1] Le Sage, *Gil Blas de Santillane* (1715–35). Harriet E later possessed a probably inherited edition printed in Amsterdam in 1747; it has appropriate plates.

and high and cut like the beech walk at Collon[1]—but at the bottom arches are cut through the foliage and the stems left so as to form rows of pillars through which you see on one side fine views of lawn and distant country and on the other the lime grove is continued in arcades 8 or 9 trees deep—well gravelled underneath—a miniature champs élysées. The folding doors opposite to the folding doors of entrance into this bedchamber lead into a pretty little dressing room and that into a pretty little cabinet about the size of that in which Lucy[2] now sleeps—low sofas in tent stitch—painted wainscotting—in flowers and fruits and odd devices—large window and glass door opening to garden—To each room boudoir dressing room and bedchamber especially there are exquisitely contrived private exits and little dens of closets and antichambres which must have seen many strange exits and entrances in their day—and in their nights. In one of these small rooms our Rodolphe now sleeps. Another which is our washing closet about 10 feet by 6 was I am sure Mme de Pompadours favorite retreat. The white wainscot now very yellow is painted with grey imitation of Indian ink pictures of monkeys in mens and womens clothes in groups in compartments[3]—The most grotesque figures you can imagine. I have traced for Lucy's diversion two of the best. (Private) Many of them are not only grotesque but dirty—for instance monkeys in old men and old womens clothes administering and receiving clysters. This favorite subject with the French is here represented à plusieurs reprises. I have some notion of having somewhere read of this cabinet of monkeys and of having heard that the principal monkey who figures in it was some real person.

The house which has been built as you understand at many different periods is very large built round a square—not unlike an old English house of Elizabeth's time—One front a range of apartments opening into one another [ ] entering from the lawn—Mme de Vindés beautiful boudoir hung in drapery with English calico like the curtains of your dressing room bed—then a gallery sort of passage, like Sonna, opening to a large dining room then a *very large* billiard room then antichamber the

[1] At the vicarage of the Revd. D. A. Beaufort.

[2] At Edgeworthstown.

[3] Mme de Pompadour also had *singeries* in her rooms at the Château de Champs.

whole depth of the house like (but very unlike) that of Ardbraccan[1]—then a very large drawing room—antichambre—and then the apartments of Mme de Pompadour which I have described. These apartments are exceedingly *comfortable*—window shutters ugly—plaid green silk curtains—*yellow white* silk curtains to the high canopy beds—mattrasses excellent—An immense speckled reddish marble slab dressing table with two deep deep drawers deep as in Honoras wardrobe. This old meuble I sketch because it was Mme de Pompadours best chest of drawers. It is painted in blue or grey birds and gilt ornaments tarnished as you may guess [sketch[2] follows]—plenty of towels oval basons and brown cruches for water—no damp in the beds. NB—There is in this house an admirable water closet which I am sure Prony constructed. The rest of the house I must take leave to take its chance in your imaginations as I have not time to describe it. I can only say in Mme de Vindé's words as she took us through the galleries of each side of the square 'Il y a ici quinze lits de maîtres et je ne vous dirai pas combien de lits de domestiques.' The situation of La Celle and the country about it beautiful! The grounds—terraces—orchard—farm yard—dairy &c &c would lead me too far so I shall only note that to preserve the hay rick from the incursion of rats the feet of the *Stand* which is higher than that in our back yard is not only slated at the bottom but has panes of *glass* instead of slates next the hay—the glass defying climbing reptiles.

So much for our lodging here. The kindness of our host and hostess I can only describe by saying that they are to us exactly what you remember them to have been 20 years ago and their *Beatrice*[3] the little girl you remember is as kind to F and H as if she was their sister. She looks very like their sister by the by with light ringletty hair fair complexion blue eyes and gentle modest English appearance and dress. As you are curious on these points I may mention that F and H wear in the mornings their chintz gowns made with long waists but not frightfully long—pelerines of the same trimmed with frills of same which have just the effect of a high up gown with trimming round the bosom—three little

[1] Sonna was the home of the Tuite family in C. Westmeath and Ardbraccan House the official residence of the Bishop of Meath.

[2] The sketch shows a large *bombé* commode.

[3] Beatrice Terray, a granddaughter.

flounces round the petticoat—much admired—Beatrice in English buff spotted callico very like that which Fanny bought and made like F's and H's. The distinguishing characteristic is a silk organza handkerchief which she almost always wears crossed tight across the breast—Old womanish! . . .

This is our way of life.[1] We sleep well in two beds in the same room. Harriet of course gets up first—wakens me at ½ after seven —dressed by 8 or ½ after (I have corrected before breakfast all of the 2d vol of Rosamond[2] which accompanies this letter). Coffee is brought to us in our bedchamber at 8 o clock—family assemble to breakfast in the dining room about ten. This breakfast has consisted of mackarel stewed in oil—cutlets—mutton or veal—eggs—boiled and poached au jus—peas stewed—lettuce stewed and rolled up looking like sausages—raddishes and salad of lettuce—stewed prunes—preserved gooseberries—chocolate biscuits—apricot biscuits that is a kind of flat tartlets—sweetmeats between paste—The breakfast finishing with coffee—a servant placing a cup before you and pouring coffee and *cream* boiled or milk as you please. As a remarkable circumstance I may mention that there are tea tongs in this house an appurtenance to the sugar basin which I have seen nowhere but here and at Mme Gautiers—Salt spoons never to be seen—So do not be surprised at seeing me take salt and sugar in the *natural way* when I come back.

Breakfast being finished we wash paws as we rise from breakfast table and order carriages for about 12 o clock for driving out to see places in the neighborhood—go to our own rooms or stay in the salon or play at billiards or chess—in short do as we like till then—Then stay out till near dinner time—dinner at ½ past five—no luncheons—no dressing for dinner. If gown be changed still it must be for another morning gown and bonnet or cap—no dressing in the country. I give you one dinner by which you may judge all the rest—Bouilli de boeuf—large piece in the middle—all the other dishes round it and they were rôti de mouton or de boeuf—ris de veau piqué—maquereau—pâtés de cervelle—salade—2d service—oeufs au jus—petits pois (stewed)—lettuce (ditto)—gâteaux de confitures—prunes—dessert—gâteaux—cerises—con-

[1] Cf. the description of the meals and way of life in an English country house (Bowood): *Letters from England*, 92–4. 60a.

[2] See below, p. 164

fitures d'abricot—de groseille—Wash at side table—Coffee in the salon—men and women all gathering round the little table as of yore. But I should observe that in general a great change has taken place and the men huddle together now in France as they used to do in England talking politics with their backs to the women in a corner or even in the middle of the room without minding them in the least and the ladies complain and look very disconsolate and many ask themselves if this be Paris and others scream *ultra* nonsense or *libérale* nonsense to make themselves of consequence and to attract the attention of gentlemen . . .

But to go on with the history of our day—after coffee Mme de Vindé sits down at a round table in the middle of the salon and out of a work basket which is just the shape of an antediluvian work basket of mine of orange paper and pasteboard which lived long in the garret she takes her tapestry work chair-cover of which she works the little blue flowers and M. Morel de Vindé pair de France ancien conseiller de Parlement &c does the ground work. M. de Vindé has had a cold and dresses himself in all sorts of odd huddles a black silk handkerchief sometimes tied tight round his head and a hat over it in the house and a silk handkerchief of many colors round his neck with ends stuffed or being continually stuffed into his waistcoat and coming out again. He wears 3 waistcoats one of blue silk two of English callicoes—he wears two coats —viz a coat and a great coat—Then over his blue great coat which is buttoned down carefully a blue spencer thrown on his back with sleeves hanging down and the whole holding on Thady[1] fashion by one button round the neck. I know few creatures more good natured than M. de Vindé and no one human being who can speak faster or more indistinctly. He speaks as if the roof of his mouth was made of water but F and H either understand or make believe to understand him in a wonderful manner and he likes them and all goes well. While Mme de Vindé works and while I talk the young people play at billiards in the billiard room—folding doors open. Beatrice plays about as well as Fanny.

When it grows darkish we all migrate at a signal from Mme de Vindé—'Allons nous passerons chez M. de Vindé.' So we all cross the billiard room and dining room and strike off by an odd passage

[1] The old steward who is the narrator in ME's *Castle Rackrent*. He was based on the Edgeworths' steward John Langan.

into M. de Vindé's study, where almost in the fire we sit round a small table playing a game called *Loto*[1]—with different colored pegs and collars for pegs—and those who have ever seen or heard of Loto will understand what it is and those who have never heard of it must wait till I come home to make them understand it. At ½ ten to bed to bed—a dozen of small round silver hand candlesticks *Bougeoirs* with wax candles. Who dares to say all French country houses have no comforts? Let all henceforward *except* La Celle.

The three first days we were here M. de Prony and Count Brennar were the only guests the count only for one day. M. de Prony is enough without any other person to keep the most active mind in conversation of all sorts scientific literary—and humorous! He is less changed during these 20 years than any of our friends. Indeed I see no difference except that some grey hairs have mixed with his brown, that his whole mop of hair is cut much shorter and though it looks all blown from the crown over his forehead as heretofore it does not hang into his eyes. It now seems clear that his *good humored frown* is quite independent of the hair which no longer overhangs the brows—the eyebrows are quite grey—the handcuff wristbands are gone and I must do him the justice to say he is as clean as any Englishman *ever you see*! His humor and good humor are really delightful—he is as Mme de Vindé says 'the most harmless benevolent good creature that exists'—*and* he has had sense enough to stick to science and keep clear of politics—always pleading *qu'il n'étoit bon qu'à cela* even when they wanted to make him a minister. He has been very kind to Fanny and Harriet whom he seems to like very much. He accompanied us on our morning excursions to Malmaison and St. Germains. We all went in 2 carriages—Mme de Vindés large berlin and a berlin landau (which I have taken for the ensuing 6 weeks finding that the wheels of our carriage would be unfit for future journeys if I run them longer at Paris).

Malmaison, which did belong to Josephine and afterwards to Beauharnais is still his property; but is now occupied only by his stewards. The place is *very* pretty. Tell Honora that it is like Dropmore in the style in which the grounds are laid out.[2] There

[1] A sort of Bingo.

[2] In the picturesque style. Lord Grenville made large plantings of trees and later had a well-known pinetum.

are the greatest profusion of rhododendrons as underwood in the groves—on the grass—beside the rivers—everywhere and in the most luxuriant flower. Poor Josephine! Do you remember Dr. Marcets telling us that when he breakfasted with her she said pointing to her flowers 'Here are my subjects. I try to make them happy.' They do credit to her care. Here were many trees and shrubs that were new to me and nobody who could give me English names and in the hothouses several plants and beauteous flowers that must forever remain without names in my imagination. As we walked through the grounds all that Josephine had *intended* to do in enlarging the park &c was pointed out to us. The grounds are admirably well taken care of, the solitude and silence of the place and the continual reference to the dead and the absent possessors were striking and melancholy even in the midst of sunshine and flowers and the song of nightingales which was heard. In one pool we saw swimming in graceful desolate dignity two black swans which as rare birds were once great favorites. Now they curve their necks of ebony in vain and in vain sail towards the shore and stretch their red beaks. There is a little pretty temple in another part of the grounds with a white marble statue of Cupid with the motto 'Qui que tu sois voici ton mâitre'[1] &c. On the arms legs bosom of this statue were many inscriptions written in pencil avowing Cupids mastery over many French princes and subjects.

The grounds are altogether very small. The house is small too but fitted up with exquisite taste—the perfection of French decoration. In the salon is the most elegant white marble chimney my eyes ever did or ever will behold. It was a present from the Pope to Beauharnais. Fanny has taken for me a sketch of the mosaics in the tablets and I have made a scrawl for you of the design of the whole. From the gallery of pictures the finest pictures have been taken—all sold or taken or given up to the Emperor of Russia—king of Prussia &c. The gallery itself is exquisitely beautiful and some good pictures still remain—The places of others left blank or filled up with French daubs. One of the most striking of the French pictures was a picture of Genl. Desaix reading a letter with a calm countenance and an air of absorbed attention while two mamelukes are eagerly bending forward to read his looks and wait his orders. In the finely polished

[1] From a verse by Voltaire inscribed on a statue at Cirey.

parquetted floor there are two or three places where great holes appear. These were the places from which fine statues of Canova &c were dragged up as Beauharnais' steward told us for the Emperor of Russia and this he told under his breath speaking of his master and of the armies without distinctly naming persons as J. Langan used to talk of the *rubbels*.[1] You may imagine the thoughts and feelings that crowded on the mind and made us walk in absolute silence through the library which formerly was Napoleons—The gilt Ns and Js still in the arches of the ceilings. The library appeared to be full of useful books—the busts and portraits of great men all round and the bust of Josephine admirable!—and all gone! This *all gone* feeling recurred continually. This sense of the mutability of all human things is I think a much stronger source of the sublime than Mr. Stewarts favorite *depth* or *height*.[2] Then added to this came the reflexion 'How soon may all who are now in power at Paris be driven from their palaces and be even as these that are gone!'

After Malmaison we next saw St. Germains—That immense palace which has been a barrack for the English army of late and which Francis the first Henry the 4th and Lewis the 14th inhabited in its days of splendour. While we walked through the apartments of Henry the 4th we were told that these very rooms had afterwards been inhabited by our James the 2d. in his exile and at this moment the pannels from which looking glasses and pictures were taken are hung with fresh green paper put up to make the place *convenable* for the temporary lodging of an English general by whom it was inhabited as our female guide expressed it *des tems de l'invasion*—when the English and Cossack troops were here. Our female guide, by the by, was an exceedingly clever well informed [woman] who talked fluently and in good language of Francis the 1st and Henry the 4th and Mary de Médicis and Lewis the 14th and Mme de la Vallière—seemed to have been her very intimate acquaintance. She was in all their secrets. She took us to see the little private staircase by which Lewis went up to the leads when he came to visit La Vallière and shewed us the passage in the leads and the window where he got in and then shewed us Mme de la

[1] The Irish rebels in 1798.

[2] See D. Stewart, *Philosophical Essays* (1810), Pt. ii, Essay ii, 'On the Sublime', esp. chap. i.

Vallières room—poor soul—all gilt—the gilding of her woe!—and this gilding by accident all escaped the revolutionary destruction. In the high gilt dome of this little room the guide shewed us the trap door through which Lewis the 14th used to come down. How they managed it I don't well understand for it must have been a perilous operation the room is so high—but my guide who I am clear saw him do it assured me his Majesty came down very easily let down in his armchair—And as she had great keys in her hand and is as large nearly as Mrs. Liddy I did not hazard contradiction or doubt. So after having further seen the passage to the old Duchesses bedchambers and the places where the chinks were through which they saw what they had no business to see we went to another side of the palace to see the immense salle des gardes built by Francis the first his F still in stone over the chimney piece. In this hall the duc de Berry on their return to France gave a splendid ball to the officers of the regiment of the guards—and the hall was hung with *superbe* drapery &c. What changes! If these walls could speak! . . .

Next day sunday we went to mass early in the morning in the chapel belonging to this house—and such mummery! F and H were very glad to have this opportunity of seeing it. Then dear Prony took us to see a belier hydraulique[1] which he has made for M. de Vindé which supplies the house with water. He explained it admirably much to Fannys satisfaction. The day was wet we stayed at home and had delightful music and singing. The preceding day a crowd of men and boys black and grey headed men and boys had arrived—An uncle of Mme de Vindé mon oncle François et puis a monstrous paunched homme de confiance with him—3 nephews Édouard—Amadée and René who are at a school in Paris—whom she good creature has with her every saturday and sunday. Then there were various men not worth naming, besides I can't remember their names—so very like different kinds of monkeys that I am sure if they were put into Cuviers glass cases with the monkeys[2] they would not know them from their brothers nor would the spectators if the monkeys were dressed in coats and waistcoats like those in our cabinet.

But there was one man M. Gibbert [?Guibert] more like a

[1] A hydraulic ram or pump.
[2] At the Jardin des Plantes.

Calendar[1] than a monkey he having but one eye and looking much as if he had a history belonging to him. His history he has not yet told me. All I know is that he sings delightfully and has been teaching Fanny to sing and he and Prony who is madly fond of music have been at it all day with Beatrice who accompanies them very well I *hear* I mean I am *told*[2]—Billiards—Backgammon—and a huge cup and ball as large as a ninepin ball—besides *ivory* tiring-*irons*[3] supplied for men women and boys amusement this sunday and at night Loto in M. de Vindé's room. Poor man he has taken it into his hypochondriacal pate that there is a smell of paint in the salon which was painted 3 months ago and in which there is no more smell than in my aunts dressing room but he dare not enter it except with a handkerchief stuffed into his mouth in which plight and with his black silk cap on his head he comes to hand me to dinner every day and he is in such a hurry to get in and out that I wonder we have not both come down on the slippery parquetted floors. By the by I forgot to note the remains of grandeur in the handsome oak parquetted floors of the whole house... F met Mme la Comtesse d'Haussonville at the Duchesse de Clermont Tonnerre where I went to a *secret* reading party—of Mme Cottin's letters.[4] Oh such a scene! I will tell it to you some time dearest mother but not now for I must go to breakfast having been called three times. I have been up since quarter past seven have packed all our things and have written 3 sheets of this. Dont pity me—rejoice that my eyes are so good—not in the least tired—and I have been fed literally with apricots. Good Mme de Vindé sent a tray of bread and preserved apricots to our room at 8 o'clock... After breakfast Monday the 5th

We took leave of dear Mme de Vindé engaging to return to la Celle to see a fête de Village about a fortnight hence. Beatrice followed us actually into the carriage to kiss us at parting. Prony accompanied us and we had a delightful drive home—first through the Bois de la Celle a fine wood chiefly of Spanish chesnuts which Prony says are vieux autant que la monarchie. We owe to Mme de Pompadours intrigues a well paved excellent road all the way from Paris to La Celle. So it is that private vices are public bene-

[1] A Persian or Turkish mendicant dervish.

[2] ME was not musical. [3] Ring puzzles.

[4] The letters of the authoress Mme Cottin were not published until 1914.

fits. Prony was very entertaining all the way from La Celle to Paris —told us the history of Talleyrand whom he has known from the time he was Évêque d'Autun—told us many anecdotes of his own life. Did you know that it was Prony who built le pont de Louis seize? Perronet was at that time 84 and almost bedridden. Prony worked under him and as a young engineer did the whole. He had a tent pitched in the champs élysées or on the place de Louis XV—slept at Mme de Vindés who lived near and so their friendship began. During the time when the building of the bridge was going on people used to come at night and throw themselves into the Seine. One night about 11 o clock when Prony had supped at Mme de Vindés he went out to give a look at the bridge and he saw—

But I have not time to tell you that story—au revoir

During Bonapartes years of Spanish war Prony was employed to make tables of logarithms and different astronomical and nautical tables on a magnificent scale. When the business was first put into his hands he found that to execute what was required would take him and all the philosophers in France 150 years work. He was very unhappy having to do with a despot who *would* have his will executed. While he was meditating on this difficulty the first vol of Smiths Wealth of nations fell by accident into his hands —he opened on the chapter on the division of labor.[1] He read our favorite passage on pin making. 'Ah Ha! voilà mon affaire. Je ferai faire mes calculs comme on fait faire des épingles.' He determined to divide the labor among a vast number of men who without knowing more than the simple operations of division, subtraction multiplication and addition each took their part under his direction. He assembled in one large building above 200 men clerks and common apprentices even of traiteurs and confectioners and shop men. During the time of various political troubles these arithmetical men-machines worked on and as Prony observed with him all these people found a place of security and were lodged and happy. The tables are now complete. Only 2 manuscript copies of this immense work exist but the English Government or Royal Society I am not sure which through Sir C. Blagden have made proposals to the French Government to defray half the expense of engraving them and whether it is to be or not non so.[2]

[1] Adam Smith, *Wealth of Nations*, Bk I, chaps. i–iii.

[2] 'I do not know.'

During the time when the English and foreign armies were here they destroyed poor Pronys country house and all the machines which we saw and several others since erected especially a windmill which I cannot stop to describe to you but which went with the slightest breath of air—so much to the surprise of the neighboring millers that they used to assemble in the road to stare at it astonished to see it going when theirs all stood still and they used to agree qu'il faudroit bien que le diable s'y mêloit. The demon of war meddled with it at last and it was destroyed merely to get the wood and iron of which it was made. Poor Prony however takes it all philosophically and amuses himself with music and philosophy[1] and keeps clear of ambition and of avarice and of all the malevolent passions.

93 Place Bourbon

. . . My dearest mother just when I was going to fold up this letter I hear there have been during our 3 days absence in the country some little disturbances at Paris—and very near us at the Place du Carousel &c. As things of this sort are often magnified and misrepresented in the papers I add this postscript to prevent your being alarmed and to tell you the simple truth. As the deputies came out of the Chamber of deputies on saturday after a warm debate on the election laws some of them cried out violently 'Vive Chauvelin!' and followed him as he was carried across le pont de Louis seize. They went to the Tuileries gardens and wanted to force their way into the Tuileries to see the king. They overturned a centinel who then killed the man who attacked him. This is the sum of the mischief done. Troops arrived and dispersed the mob who had followed M. Chauvelin. It is said that *the people* took no part in this disturbance and that it is only a party affair—'des jeunes gens ma foi qui ne sçavent pas ce qu'ils veulent'. All is quiet and what I hear from the best informed is that if government use well the power they have in their hands there can be no danger of disturbance. Be assured my dear mother that if I see any danger I shall decamp for Geneva[2] . . .

[1] Science.

[2] The new law on elections was a compromise which pleased neither left nor right. The ministry was unreasonably alarmed by student demonstrations and overreacted.

Harriet Edgeworth to Harriet Beaufort

La Celle, 4th June, 1820

. . . We arrived at Paris too late—the gaiety was past but I think upon the whole it was better. It is provoking to hear everybody say you have come too late you should have been here a month sooner; yet as I could not at all and Fanny not very well have danced their numerous figures and their pretty quadrilles and as the chief regret of everybody for us is that we have missed the balls I think it is as well we were not in time for them—even if I liked that wonderful science but finding myself fail in it every day would not have decreased my abhorrence for it.

Many of Marias friends have left Paris but we have seen all that are now living except Degérando and Mme Rumford[1] who is in Italy. We have made many new French acquaintance and have been more in French company than almost any other English. We have been admitted into their small private parties where English are seldom or never received. All this is owing to Marias fame and the Abbé Edgeworths name. Indeed Maria is treated by foreigners of all nations in the most distinguished and at the same time gratifying manner, not as an odious author but as a delightful gentlewoman—not as one who must be received because she has written but as one whom everybody is glad to know because they have when unknown given them pleasure, and whom everybody is glad to be intimate with because when known she is seen to be all that is most agreeable in her most agreeable books. Indeed she well deserves all the attention she receives for well as I knew her I did not know the extent of all her talents—the extent of her modesty I was well acquainted with—but the best idea I can give you of her is to say that after displaying all that is most brilliant to Princesses and Peers, or after the deepest arguments with the most celebrated and the most scientific she goes to order our gowns, or to continue a new habit shirt or to talk nonsense or sense with us. How astonished some of her solemn admirers would be if they were to see her rolling with laughter at some egregious folly and still more would some of the brilliant wits be [surprised] at the quantity of fancy and talent she wastes on us. My dear Harriet this is no burst of enthusiasm but the settled conviction of

[1] Formerly Mme Lavoisier.

my mind, and in telling you my feelings I only do justice to the extreme kindness with which she has treated me.

After all, these poor Frenchwomen gain as little as possible by all they do.[1] They are with a few exceptions all declared to be or to have been good for nothing. In former times gentlemen were always at their feet—at least were always about them in every direction—but now—the gentlemen retire to a corner to talk politics—the ladies form a circle near them and talk of dress. If there is another corner the gentlemen retire to that. If a lady appears, they take flight and settle in some other spot. All places are alike to them so that they are apart from all things female. At dinner at least here, all gentlemen are put together at one side, and all the women at the other side of the table. The Conversation has lost much by what the french have gained in liberty. During Napoleons time none dared to whisper of politics—now, none can speak of anything else. The Ultras are the most furious because the weakest—the Libérales the most noisy, because they have much appearance and little reality of object or of sense. The Bonapartists are the most silent because the most afraid, and the Royalists quietly hold their tongues and the reins of power. How they will use their power is a doubtful question but that they have it is clear from their having conquered in the chamber of deputies . . .

Fanny Edgeworth to the Revd. D. A. Beaufort

7th June, Paris

. . . The present discussion of the law of elections is one which will in a great measure decide what portion of liberty the people will obtain and what degree of strength the Royalists have. The minds of the young students of the different colleges have been heated by an idea of liberty and they have ever since Saturday assembled in numbers outside the Chambre des Députés and cried Vive la Charte independently of Vive le Roi—cheering M. Chauvelin the casting voice against ministers in one question. He was carried from the house as in triumph in his litter (he is too ill to come any

[1] This follows on from a not very original discussion at the beginning of the letter on the sharp change in behaviour which occurred after marriage.

other way). . . . From what we hear the military have been in some degree foolishly severe and in consequence several people have been wounded.

The violence with which they all speak the women particularly is dreadful. Those Ultras who have really suffered and sacrificed everything to their devotion to the royal cause one cannot but pity and sympathise with—at first—but after I have pitied them my sympathy was prevented by the violence and foolish security of their present power. We have been mostly with these, their manners and rank and agreeability are superior to the libéraux and as strangers we can be received equally well by either set and may be silent about their politics. At first it was amusing to hear them talk and screech but now it becomes melancholy—now when something *real* is to be or about to be done. The de Beauvaus and the Duchesse de Broglie and her brother are our principal acquaintance amongst the libéraux. It was with Prince Edmond de Beauvau that Maria and I went one day to the Chambre. We both saw and heard Lafayette. He is very honest and has an excellent private character, but for public life he has always been deficient in talents and steadiness. It shews a want of both his again attempting to be the head of a party when he was placed or rather placed himself in so doubtful a situation at Versailles at the beginning of the revolution. Maria went another day with Harriet. The discussion was still the same subject on the amendments proposed by different members of each side to the law of elections of 1817—very interesting and very violent on each side—but this you have seen in the papers . . .

Malmaison is close to La Celle. It was excessively interesting to see the retreat of poor Josephine—the study in which Napoleon had sat and thought—the table at which he wrote—the maps which cost Europe so much in war and blood!—the gallery where the J's and N's still mark to whom all had belonged . . . During the cent jours Napoleon went to Malmaison accompanied by but one person. He had not been there since Josephine's death—he went up to the room where she died. Everything had been preserved as she left them. He took the corner of the Quilt knelt down and kissed it in silence and left the room! This was not told by the person who keeps the house but by a gentleman who heard it from the person with Napoleon . . .

Another day we went with the engineer Prony to Marly to see the machinery once the wonder of the wonder making mechanics of Louis the fourteenth's court. It has been much simplified lately by Prony and two wheels made to perform the work of fourteen and three stages of machinery. By these two wheels Versailles is supplied with water at a wonderfully small expense. Thursday . . . on tuesday we went to the first representation of a new [play]. I was excessively entertained, the acting [was] admirable and the piece something [? in the old] style—evidently an imitation of Voltaire a satire upon the newspaper writers—the story much the same as the Journaliste[1] of Mme de Genlis. The editor of the Drapeau Blanc was in the Balcon and contradicted some assertion which gave much amusement to the audience.

Lady Morgan[2] passed a week in Paris on her way back from Italy. We did not meet fortunately. I suppose her *Italy* will soon appear. The French are all very angry at her France and she was not received by those who had before really treated her with distinction. The French Ambassador at Naples would not receive her though the Duchess of Devonshire (who took it into her head to take her up) did everything she could to persuade him to do so. At last she sent word that she would not go without Lady Morgan and the Ambassador answered 'She may let it alone then for receive the woman who wrote that book on my country I never will.'

I have just returned from seeing the manufactory of a species of carpets like what we call Turkey carpets—all worked by hand. This magnificent manufactory has lasted since Henry the 4th's time —he established it. One of the workmen was a Lieutenant under Napoleon—was with him in Egypt and Italy!! Whan a triste change for him to be confined to the house working fleur de lys!! . . .

[1] Published in 1802.

[2] Lady Morgan's *France* was published in 1817 and translated the same year. It was particularly unpopular among royalists. Her *Italy* appeared in 1821. For ME's unfavourable attitude to her, see *Letters from England*, 166–7.

Harriet Edgeworth to [?] Honora Edgeworth

[n.d. June, 1820]

. . . The French journals dare say but little and indeed it is very difficult to give an exactly just idea of the state of things as to the degree of alarm which ought to be felt . . . On Monday when Maria wrote just after we had returned from the country everything was perfectly quiet. When we set out to go [to] dine at Mme Suards the Pont Louis 16 was lined with Gens d'armes and though there all was quiet a great crowd was assembled which delayed us some time. When we got to Mme Suards we sat for some time very placidly talking of her life of her husband till in came a woman in a blue cloth pelisse and straw bonnet all lame with the rheumatism with large eyes and a face that had been handsome a little while ago. She was followed by a man whose face was like a scull whose underjaw had been pushed out as if the teeth had been much broken in this pushing out and as if the jaw was opened always by a machine. His cheeks were only bones with a thin parchment cover and his hair was either a wig or so like one that it did him no credit as his own. This strange creature was M. Stapfer who was once ambassador from Switzerland and whom Maria knew with Pestalozzi in olden times.[1] Mme Stapfer immediately began in great agitation telling of the crowd that she had passed, of their horrid revolutionary cries and of the still greater horror of the manner in which the Gardes du corps had without [ ] beaten down the young students with their iron headed sticks. This account did not please Mme Suard and she began arguing the point with Mme Stapfer and they grew so furious that I thought if they did not come to blows Mme Suards tremendous eyes would start fairly out of her head. M. Stapfer gave us a rational account of the thing which was what I have told you and that they were now in great crowds calling out vive la Charte and told by the soldiers to cry vive le Roi. There was nothing really very shocking in this but Mme Stapfer has two sons students at the École des Médecins and as they were the people most in fault she was most alarmed for them and most enraged against the Garde du corps who had however behaved rather brutally. Her chin trembled with terror and her eyes flashed with

[1] See above, p. 86 n. 1.

rage and both she and Mme Suard were complete pictures of what all Frenchwomen bring themselves to by meddling with what they don't understand.

After they had talked and battled till they nearly overturned the little table which formed a barrier between them a little man in brown with a powdered head and red face came in. Whether fright or fury predominated in him is still a disputed point between Maria and Fanny but whatever he felt he poured forth a torrent of words wiping his forehead and taking snuff alternately and finishing most of his sentences with a violent pook which he seemed to think added to a side wag of his head gave more idea than any words could. This M. Pariati was a furious Ultra and was bent chiefly upon proving it to be all the fault of the feebleness of government and the irresolution of the King. Mme Suard despairing of two deputies whom she expected now ordered dinner and Maria and M. Stapfer succeeded in bringing the conversation into a very composed train till the door opened and in walked M. Maine de Biran who was fresh from the Chamber and had to tell all that had passed there and all that was passing in the town and of all the détours he had had to make. He brought fresh fuel and all voices and most hands and arms rose to agree or disagree prove or disprove what he said. M. Pariati, with his usual pook, got out a quantity of Ultra nonsense between the lumps of paste which he was tearing off a fish pye and ramming into his mouth. M. Maine de Biran (who once wrote a book on Les Habitudes [ ][1] had hardly finished his story, and not nearly his dinner, when a young man M. Boisson came in. He was a tall, plump, open fiery clever looking man, and when he had seized upon a sufficient portion of chicken he fastened upon M. Maine de Biran who is a hollow cheeked lank meek hypocritical looking sentimental man with two red spots on his cheek bones, who agreed with a sort of shrugging bow to all that Maria said about moderation &c and a moment afterwards began with a sort of calm ferocity to fight it out with M. Boisson. Then the ladies raised their voices and a bawling and screeching began which lasted the whole of dinner and which no efforts could divert though Maria made two or three vain attempts, but at one, that it was beginning

[1] *L'Influence de l'habitude sur la faculté de penser* (1803).

to rain, M. Pariati turned round and gave as furious a pook to it as he had done before to the Garde du Corps.

At last we went into the drawing room and the ladies were quieted by Marias [ ]. M. Boisson spoke of M. Maine de Biran when he was gone as of his best friend, though while they were disputing it seemed that they could never speak to each other again—if they did not kill each other on the spot. They were very much calmed by the time the young Duc de Crillon came in. He is rather little very black looking with very prominent eyes a sticking out nose and a mouth which opens square so as to shew his very white teeth. He recognised Maria and spoke of having met her and then went on to tell his story which was that of Louvels trial.[1] He was fresh from the Chamber of Peers. All this he told very quietly and distinctly and all parties were silent for all agree in condemning Louvel. M. Pariati gave a few [pooks] but we soon left them and came home not quite sure whether we were most diverted or tired with the scene we had just passed . . .

Maria Edgeworth to Mrs. Edgeworth

Paris, 8th June, 1820

Answers to questions—Fanny secretary[2]

My dear Mother you ask how we get dressed when we trudge the streets one minute and are in fine company the next—answer—We never do trudge the streets. Once when our carriage was late I attempted to walk to the Countess de Salis's and was so tired that it has never been done again. Once Fanny and Harriet walked home through the Tuileries and once from Mme de Broglie's—a very short distance. These three times excepted we have been constantly in a carriage which we have used almost from morning till night. We have an excellent coach or berlin and Mme de Salis's coachman—with Rodolphe the best servant I think I ever saw. As to dress F H and M wear in the morning petites robes de

[1] Louvel was the murderer of the Duc de Berry. He was tried on 5 June and executed two days later.

[2] This letter is partly in the hand of Fanny E and partly in that of Harriet E.

gingham—or calico[1] bought here—which all the ladies here wear at home. These are made plain to button up about the throat like Lucy's, except two inches longer in the waist. When we go out in the mornings to breakfasts à la fourchette, or to visits without fourchette, cambrick muslin gowns trimmed to the tune of from two to three guineas worth of embroidery. Striped muslin gowns trimmed with flounces of themselves, made halfway up to the throat, serve either for dressed morning, or undressed evening visits. Fannys plum colored and Harriets lilac tabbinets are the French say two of the prettiest gowns they ever saw—they serve morning and can serve some evening. My two tabbinets,[2] sage and fawn ditto have done excellent service, new furbished. Fannys blue and Harriets lilac silk gowns well stood the first three weeks of morning necessities. A broad belt let in and very broad sash over covered all deficiencies.

Now for evening, Ma'am, we have each the lace gowns over white sattin very elegant—then muslin gowns each trimmed with rouleaux of sattin—a degree less elegant but more useful—and for figuring at the finest places such as the Duchesse D'Escards &c Fanny and Harriet have two white gauze[3] gowns trimmed with flounces of gauze like blonde.[4] To the beauty of the tout ensemble of this dress, nothing but French exclamations and superlatives can do justice. Two jaconette muslin[5] gowns I omitted to mention with embroidery and bouffants—très distingué.

The gowns are made much higher up than English and all bare necks appear absolutely indecent, or what is much worse, bien Anglaise. I have never seen a slipped-off shoulder since I came to France.

Harriet has a beautiful watered pink spencer and a new kind of hat recommended by the Countess de Salis, riding hat shape turned up at side, and made of peacocks quills, like white baskets you and I have seen—lined with pink and with a pink ribbon tied round it—altogether very becoming. She also has a white Lyons

[1] An Indian cotton material. Gingham, also a cotton material, was not necessarily checked. ME reckoned her own expenditure on dress during the whole expedition at £100 (Irish). This probably includes some clothes for Fanny and Harriet.

[2] A watered fabric of silk and wool, resembling poplin.

[3] A thin silk organza with a twisted thread giving a shimmering effect.

[4] Straw-coloured silk lace.

[5] There were innumerable kinds of muslin. Jaconet was a very soft material.

Cashmere shawl for wearing at night. Fanny has a beautiful Leghorn bonnet which struck Mrs. Littelton so that she begged to have ditto. She also has an immense scarlet shawl with a broad border—Superbe! I have been obliged to get one DO. as a large square shawl is an absolute necessary and decency of life at Paris, no scarfs worn except by the notorious English. I have a pretty white silk bonnet trimmed with blonde, not immoderately large, and a little riding-hat-shaped hat, made of silk, I dont know how, to look like Leghorn or like straw. We have all 3 large white bonnets, something like Celbridge hats, very cheap and pretty. Of the quantities of frills, chemisettes, and canezous[1] of various shapes which we have been obliged to buy, I can give no description, but I know they have cost many guineas.

For my own unfortunate head I have been obliged to buy a front of Parisian hair 2 caps for morning (1 of lace, 1 of [linon][2] worked which said [linon] worked and unworked makes a great figure in Parisian dress)—2 small sattin and crape hats, distinguished by different white feathers—one set 5 or 6 white ostrich put in by the literally inimitatable Mme Guérin said to be the only woman in Paris who can put in feathers with true taste. The other hat is adorned with what are called Maraboos in great profusion. These are the soft powder-puff feathers. Besides these I have a turban made by Mme Guérin, of *Gauze* trimmed with silver, very neat and handsome.

Now I hope you are satisfied. I forgot to mention that I have got a new pelisse,[3] not quite so bright a color as Harriets tabbinet of a silk nearly the same as one belonging to the Comtesse de Salis which she will shew you. The alarm about waist long peaked before was groundless. I have seen such among Ultra dressers but they are by no means usual or necessary. Oh! dear I beg your pardon—I forgot two sets of gowns, one a morning, one an evening set—the chintz[4] which trimmed with themselves and made up

[1] Celbridge hats were chip hats made at Celbridge, co. Kildare. The manufacture there dates from the late eighteenth century. A chemisette was a bodice, like the upper part of a chemise, to fill in the neck of a low dress. A canezou was a blouse-like garment of silk or cotton.

[2] Lawn.

[3] A mantle.

[4] Figured and glazed Indian cotton.

half way to the throat, with pelerines[1] to wear occasionally—said pelerines trimmed with frills of the same. These form beauteous dress or undress morning gowns—So beauteous that a monstrously fat confectioner woman, very like the Persian Ambassador in petticoats, fell so distractedly in love with them, that she literally could not serve out the bonbons for Fanny. She stopped short in the middle of what she was doing to exclaim 'Pardon, mesdames, mais vos robes m'enchantent tellement! Les avez-vous achetées a Londres?' And then at once giving a fall to our vanity she added 'Ah j'en ai acheté de pareille pour ma nièce.' And some time afterwards she took an opportunity of edging herself out from behind the counter, and opening the parlour called to her niece to look at the gowns. This was very satisfactory.

The other gowns of which I was going to speak (before this confectioners wife came across me and spoiled my style) are the canvas[2] gowns. Harriets well known fawn colored is new made up with sattin trimmings and satin-puff-short sleeves with hanging figured blonde round the bosom worn over white satin—it looks beautiful. The peak that you see added to the waist is a flap of the same canvas edged with narrow blonde and whatever you may think it is very pretty and is worn by the French to make themselves strikingly like Mary Queen of Scots. N.B. a whole set of caps bonnets and hats are poked down in the middle and curved at the sides to be like Mary Queen of Scots, which worn by Frenchwomen and loaded with flowers certainly do look very droll. But to go on with Fanny and my canvas gowns they are trimmed round with brown satin ribbon and brown cord with hanging blonde round the bosom, and are pronounced to be beautiful and very rare. They are very good for dinners and parties.

At the English Ambassadors the Duchesse D'Escards the Duc de la Châtre—the Duchesse d'Orléans and two or three places, white dresses of lace or muslin over satin are necessary—at all other places, striped muslin, tabbinet, canvas, cambric muslin or even morning gowns are more genteel in these summer parties than fuller dress. Of course tabbinets are not worn in this weather but we have lately had very cold. To all *French* dinners we might

[1] Short capes.

[2] Almost certainly linen.

go in morning dresses even in cambric muslin, with large, not very large, white crape or silk bonnets. There is a great difference between the dress for French dinners and English evening parties . . . You may go to the play and just as you would go drest for breakfast and much dirtier if you like . . .

You will perhaps imagine that we have spent little money. But in this you or at least we shall find ourselves confoundedly mistaken for trimmings cost a mint of money and without trimmings it is impossible to live—that is to appear. I forgot to mention little square pink white or lilac silk net handkerchiefs, which are worn morning noon and night tied round or hanging over the neck.[1] Net silk are now giving way to gauze of many colors. You think, perhaps, that French couturiers and milliners get their work done in the twinkling of an eye but they are the slowest workers I ever knew. I have had the hardest work you can conceive to get the gowns I have mentioned out of their hands and some of them are but just finished by this time. It was impossible to get the 3 corsets finished in less than three weeks and six cambric muslin gowns with two different mantua makers took a month. This does not arise so much from their having a vast deal to do, as from their having a vast love of pleasure. In London anything can be done for money, not so in Paris. The love of pleasure is stronger than the love of money and every couturière mantua maker and milliner and all their apprentices must keep their jours de fêtes and have time to dress themselves. These jours de fêtes continually recur. Josephine's answer of 'Ah! madame c'est jour de fête demain' is as unanswerable as John Langans 'Its a holiday sure on Monday'. Said Josephine saves us a great deal of trouble in putting by clothes, and works well but slowly. It was a visionary idea of mine that she could make dresses for 3 people—she has however made 6 or 7 gowns and done jobbing to the amount of some guineas . . . We should have been ruined if we had not brought a stock of muslins &c from England—N B the word mousseline is at Paris applied only to India muslin and all British muslin is called organdie . . .

[1] Neck implies shoulders and bosom. I am indebted to the Museum of Costume at Bath for most of the information on fashion.

Harriet Edgeworth to Honora Edgeworth

Paris, 15th June, 1820

Maria desires me to say that if you and Hunter find that you have not enough or if without Hunters remarking upon it you think so—tell him with the next packet that there is a little play which can in any emergency be added and she gives you her permission to add it if you think it necessary putting before it 'This is the tiny play acted by Mrs. Hartes pupils'. She wishes it should conclude the 2d volume. She sends you two chapters and hopes you will approve. She recollected that dear Aunt Mary had expressed a wish that some [? thing] more should be made of the palanquin so she has added 2 or 3 pages which Fanny and I are delighted with. I hope Aunt Mary will like them and the little Palanquin which she recommended and to which that chapter is now entitled. Will you put it rightly who it was who sent to the generous Hotem for his horse. I think it was a Pacha—Fanny that it was the Grand Seignior and Maria the Emperor of Constantinople. The chapter containing Hotem would have been too long as part of the Palanquin and I have named it the Forest Drive. Pray alter if you dont approve. It ends at 'repeated the poem' and the next chapter is that containing Louise Dudley. Those chapters which have been sent are as follows Petty Scandal, Airs and Graces, The 9 days wonder, Egerton Abbey, The Black Land, The Palanquin, An Evening Drive[1] . . .

Maria Edgeworth to Mrs. Edgeworth

93 Place Bourbon, 15th June, 1820

The law of election which has either caused or been the pretence for so much violence and disturbance here has at length past. It is certainly a shameless infringement on the part of government on the liberty of the people but it is not, as I am assured by those who have read the *charte* absolutely contrary to the letter however it

[1] The play was The Dame School Holiday, published in 1827 in *Little Plays*. The references to it are in *Rosamond. A Sequel* (1821), The Palanquin, ii. 58–76, and The Forest Drive, ii. 77–98. The Emperor of Constantinople sent for Hatem (or Hatim)'s horse. Hatem was a Bedouin chief famed for his generosity and 'generous as Hatem' was a proverbial Arab expression.

may be to the spirit of the constitution—and from all I can observe, or hear of the conduct of the *libérales* they in general care very little about liberté and la nation except as pretences and party cries to raise their own price. Some young men, about 800, of l'école de Médicine and de loi are I believe enthusiastically in earnest in their patriotism and these were worked up by the orators to parade about the streets and make disturbances. They at first assembled at the Chambre des députés and afterwards in different streets in hopes of being joined by the people—but the *people* having no votes at elections had nothing to gain or to give up and took no or very little part in the quarrel. The number of the whole body of troops that paraded Paris during 3 or 4 days and nights was about forty thousand. The usual number in Paris is 26,000 . . . Great cry and little wool is the motto of all their operations. I do not think there is much real love of liberty or any principle of political virtue yet in France. To speak more philosophically it will take another generation or 2—another century at least to educate them to value or enjoy or understand that English constitution about which they jabber so much. I send you a paper which contains the new law of elections. All is now perfectly quiet in Paris and will I think continue so till the death of the king and then! Heaven knows what will happen—*the duc d'Orléans—Prince of Orange* or *little Napoleon*[1] with Beauharnais.

I send you two papers containing notes of what Louvel said on his trial before the peers and what he said in private after the trial was over and at the place of execution . . . Louvel throughout his whole trial shewed wonderful calmness and courage. It appears that he was an ignorant enfant de la révolution—absolutely without moral or religious instruction, or principles—with wrongheaded notions of love of his country—not a madman—except you admit the definition of a madman which someone gave viz 'A man who is very firmly of his own opinion while all the rest of the world are of another opinion'. He would have made a fine Roman citizen—he had the soul of a hero in him as appears by his last words about the kings pardon. It seems clear to all but the Ultras (to whom the power of being convinced by reason or demonstration is denied) that Louvel had no accomplice. Denon who was

[1] Napoleon's son, the King of Rome, with Eugène Beauharnais, the son of Josephine.

present at his trial has taken his portrait and will have it *lithographed*. He has promised me a copy and you shall have it . . .

Fanny Edgeworth to Mrs. Edgeworth

Paris, 19th June, 1820

. . . On Thursday evening we went to Neuilly and were presented by the Dame d'honneur Maria's devoted admirer Mme Dolomieu to S A S le Duc d'Orléans[1]—and much was I disappointed with his appearance—rather English in his manner but not high bred or the least dignified—short and fat. The Duchesse daughter to the King of Sicily thin and pulled looking just got out something about 'vos ouvrages et le plaisir de vous voir &c' when Mme Montjoye Mme Dolomieu's sister took us round the outside of the circle to Mademoiselle her particular charge. She found three chairs for us and there we sat—talked a little to Mme d'Orglandes—and one of the two sisters kept continually talking to Maria and the rest of the circle of ladies looked critically at each other and dolefully at themselves except the immediate neighbours of the Princesse and Mademoiselle.[2] At 10 o clock everybody seemed struck with panick and took leave. Mademoiselle came and said some words to Maria. They look as if they had suffered much and in private I doubt not very agreeable but such a circle prevents all rational conversation. We took our leave. We have since had the diversion of hearing our visit round through M. Degérando. They were pleased with Maria and I hope sufficiently so to make them ask us to dinner or breakfast . . .

Mme la Duchesse de Duras whom we have been aching to see as everybody told us she is charming and who had been dying to know Maria we have at last seen. We went with Lady de Ros. She is a striking looking person fine figure tall and thin—beautiful black eyes and the remains of much beauty. Her conversation was perfectly natural and rather uncommon—about the Russian character. Amongst the most polished Russians she said exactly like Mrs. D. Stewart that she always perceived the savage. She is much devoted to Maria and hoped to see a great deal more of her.

[1] Later King Louis Philippe.

[2] Adelaide d'Orléans, sister of Louis Philippe.

They say she is very violent about politics—till quite out of her senses. I can well imagine it from her appearance and the softness of her manners. Fernand [Marchang]y was sitting by her—I thought them like the hero and heroine of a political romance. . . .

Everything is perfectly quiet now—the law of elections is going on in the Chambre des Pairs—the budget (which the French maintain is an old French word[1]) is being discussed by the Députés and every body is now really leaving Paris—and our time now appears very short not quite a month. It is astonishing how rapidly the time appears to go now that we have got into a routine of amusement &c. I must tell you of Mme de Châtenay's saying of us 'Voilà les pauvres petites qui suivent leur guide!' which enraged Maria very much.

Yesterday we paid a visit to Mme de Pomaret—a very clever woman who writes. She and her daughter are this moment translating Miss Aikin's Queen Elizabeth.[2] She is going to translate letters for literary ladies. Have we mentioned how much Patronage and Leonora are admired [? by those] who have read them.[3] Hers and Walter Scotts works are read and talked of with the greatest interest by almost everybody.

Judge of the melancholy of hearing that there is a degree of romance in Mme de la Rochejacquelein's book.[4] That is to say that she places M. de Lescure in a situation in which he was not etc. This was said by the General who commanded the avant garde in La Vendée but I never could hear his name. M. de Boullé who is now blind commanded in La Vendée for a long time.

Mme Gallatin is talking very fast and I have not much sense left. She says the Dowager Queen of Würtemburg is very clever reads much is very amiable and her senses are as good as anybody's can be. Mme Degérando was here this morning very entertaining. Degérando was pressed to become the secretary of Alexander[5] in

[1] From *bougette*, diminutive of *bouge*, a leather bag.

[2] Lucy Aikin, *Memoirs of the Court of Queen Elizabeth* (1818). A translation by Alexandrine Aragon came out in 1827.

[3] *Letters for Literary Ladies* (1795), *Patronage* (1814) and *Leonora* (1806), all by ME. Translations of *Leonora* and *Patronage* had come out in 1807 and 1816, respectively. No full translation of *Letters for Literary Ladies* was published in France, although there had been excerpts in *La Bibliothèque Britannique*.

[4] The *Mémoires* of Mme de la Rochejacquelein were edited by Prosper de Barante, who was responsible for some of the material in the book.

[5] The Czar.

1815 but he refused though much solicited and well for him for he has preserved a noble independence of character which he said in refusing he felt that he must lose in becoming the servant of a foreign sovereign . . .

Maria Edgeworth to Mrs. Edgeworth

93 Place Bourbon, 22nd June, 1820

. . . We have spent a day and a half delightfully with M. and Mme Molé at their beautiful country place Champlâtreux. (Lady E. Stuart who is going to England was expected to dine en passant at Champlâtreux but did not arrive while we were there.) He is very sensible and she very obliging. Mme de Vintimille there and very agreeable and kind—Mme de Nansouty—a widow fattened and très coquette—the granddaughter of Mme d'Houdetot now Mme Bazancourt a mother of 3 or 4 children of whom she takes great care *and* who reads Early lessons.[1] All remember you most kindly. Mme de Vintimille is very good to Mme Chéron whose son is Préfet I think of Toulouse or some Provincial town. He is an excellent jeune homme très distingué and he makes the happiness of her life. She is as happy in short as a Frenchwoman can be out of Paris. Mme de Vintimille goes to see her and had her for some time before we arrived at her house at Paris! You see these court ladies can shew friendship. At Champlâtreux there was an Italian gentleman Triori passionately fond of music and of flirting with Mme de Nansouty and a M. Fleury whom we formerly saw at Mme de Vindés . . .

We went last night to Lady Granards where there was a crowd of company—dancing—and Fanny danced—was asked by le Comte Édouard de la Grange to waltz but declined[1]—danced a quadrille with a gentleman attached to the portuguese embassy whose name I cant write. He wore spectacles and smelt—not of perfumes. The people who formed this quadrille were Lord Bristols daughters The Lady Georgiana and Augusta Hervey The two comtes de Polignac Miss de Ros Miss Rumbold and the beautiful Miss Locke Baron Dellengen other gentlemen very grand but names unknown . . .

[1] See p. 76 n. 5.

[2] Waltzing was still considered 'fast'.

Maria Edgeworth to Mrs. Edgeworth

24th June, 1820

. . . You ask for Dupont de Fougerais. Alas he has been dead some years and when I asked Mme Rilliet for him I wakened that sorrow. I went to see Camille Jordan and he is I think less altered than you could have imagined. I had heard he was very ill and expected to see a skeleton. Quite the contrary he is fatter and better looking than when we knew him with his sentimental [   ]. There is no alteration but for the better. He has got rid of all that might be thought a little affected and the vivacity is elevated into energy and the politeness into benevolence. We found him lying on a sofa and his pretty little good wife beside him. He wore upon his head a blue or black cap like Pakenhams. His illness is not *la poitrine* as I had been told by his friends but '*des obstructions*' (as I was told by himself) which did not permit him to leave his sofa except pour se traîner à la chambre des députés.[1] He is much respected for his public and private conduct *and* I have not seen any *man* here except François and Benjamin Delessert who were so glad to see us as Camille. He thinks Fanny like Charlotte and he spoke of her and you in the most affectionate terms . . .

Harriet Edgeworth to Honora Edgeworth

Paris, 29th June, 1820

. . . Tell my mother that I shewed her message to Mme Gautier, who read it out in the droll way she does read English but exceedingly well, and was very much pleased at it. We had a very pleasant dinner there on Saturday—our Sundays adventures I believe Fanny described to you; on Monday we had a large assembly at home in the morning—first Mr. Chenevix and after we had talked over his last review with him Mr. Creed came in and then Mr. and Mrs. Malthus. To Mr. Malthus Maria appealed to convince Mr. Chenevix that it was beneath a philosopher and man of Genius to spend his abilities in raking up all the dirt he could find in every part of a foreign country and instead of trying

[1] He had taken a prominent part in the debate on the new electoral law.

to unite in science two contending nations to take every possible opportunity of inflaming every cause of discord between them. After much warm argument against the French from Mr. Creed and Mr. Chenevix who have been several years here and some softening replies from Mr. Malthus who has been here only a few days Maria was brought nearly to own that she had thought less well of the French the more she had seen of them. It was a very interesting 2 hours conversation, during which Mrs. Malthus informed me that she had known Lovell in former times before the detention in France so she cannot be very young—but I daresay a long time ago she was not very ugly. After these people had all gone various events occupied us till Fanny went to ride. While she was there, Maria and I went to tell Mme Suard that we could take her to the French Opera as we had doubtfully told her we would. When we went in Mme Suard, in a white dimity petticoat and jacket without any stays, came running out saying 'Suis-je heureuse?' 'Oui' said Maria. 'Ah Dieu comme vous me faites heureuse' and throwing herself into Marias arms she embraced her as if she had just saved her life and having left her in a state of extasy we returned home, drest and dined at Lady de Ros's . . .

We were soon however obliged to leave them and set off with Major de Ros. We called on Mme Suard who in transports got into the carriage and never ceased talking till we got to the Theatre. There she skipped upstairs a great deal faster than either Fanny or I did—ran along the doors reading the numbers of the boxes and when there was some difficulty about the ticket no power could keep her quiet. Instead of sitting down along with us she flew from door to door poking in through the little windows, resolved to lose nothing that could be got out of this days pleasuring and when we did get in, over the benches she hopped sat herself down in the front row and was at last silent. She only spoke to express her enchantment at a frightful opera of Oedipe which was going on and which touched her so much that she was all in tears though even the French allow the music to be detestable. When the opera was over a fancy seized her that she would go out and walk in the passage and great fears were entertained that nothing could quiet her. Poor Mr. de Ros was horrified at the idea of being found stroaming about with this wild old Frenchwoman and at last Maria told [her] it could not be and that sit still.

4 Mme Suard and her husband, from a drawing by Charlotte Edgeworth

she must. She submitted like a naughty girl and only stood up moving about so incessantly that there was some danger that she would have fallen backwards into the pit. The beginning of the ballet Clari silenced her and most beautiful it was. Mlle Bigottini acts beautifully and actually touches simply by her extreme grace for it is a pantomime and Mme Suard was charmed though the whole time she did not know one of the actresses from the other and was not always quite clear that they were not real people.[1] A delightful drive home and turn in the Champs Élysées by the most lovely moonlight and without a breath of wind completed this evening and brought us home about 12½ . . .

Maria Edgeworth to Francis Beaufort

1st July, 1820

. . . To go no farther back than the two or 3 last days—Thursday—We went to the national or as it is now the fashion to call it the royal library—where M Langlès devoted two hours of his time to shewing us the manuscript letters of Henry the 4th Francis 1st Lewis 14th and various celebrated people and from the 500,000 volumes of which it is said this magnificent library consists directed our attention to what was best worth our seeing. Through the whole changes of the revolution Langlès has kept his place as librarian but once was very near losing it when upon Bonaparte's sending him some books and mss pillaged from Spain and Italy he observed that it would be a great deal of waste trouble to put them into the catalogue for that he was sure they would be afterwards restored to their own countries In fact 8000 volumes were restored at the peace of the Allies.

After seeing the library we dined with an amiable agreeable family of *Creeds* (Scotch). He is here employed to arrange if possible the national debt between France and England. We dined with his family under the trees in their garden and between 9 and 10 went to see Camille Jordan and took with us Mr. Creed and Mal-

[1] In a letter of 18 Dec. 1875 to her brother M. Pakenham E, Harriet wrote; 'When we went with Mme Suard to the Français where Oedipus was acting she rushed to the front exclaiming "Je suis folle d'Oedipe"—and Major de Ros who was our cavalier said afterwards "How the old lady *took* the 3 benches"!'

thus who is now at Paris. Both had much wished to be made acquainted with Camille whose talents and honorable conduct entitle him to the large share of public esteem he enjoys. He is now so much out of health that he is obliged to lie on a sofa most of the day in the intervals of public exertion. At his house we saw assembled almost all the distinguished people of the moderate libérales—and there was Mme Récamier—a much happier woman now she has lost her fortune and has a few real friends attached to her own good qualities than she was in the blaze of her wealth and beauty. Malthus enjoyed himself much. One of the greatest pleasures which I have had at Paris has been in introducing some of our friends to each other who had long desired to meet. After Camille Jordan's we ended the evening at the Duchesse de Clermont Tonnerres—all her society Ultras—very entertaining contrasts—N B French fashionable nonsense—delightful ice—and fine music here.

Another day—Morning between 11 and 1—Mr. Malthus—Mr. Creed and Bréguet. Bréguet explains on mechanical subjects as well as all those do and only those who perfectly understand them—talked with Fanny of Brown's iron chain bridge[1]—went to meet us at the Observatory, to introduce us to *Arago* the astronomer. Arago has something in the simplicity and cordiality of his manner and in his way of going straight forward to the business of science like our own dear Dr. Brinkley. He spoke of Dr. Brinkley with the highest esteem—thinks him far superior to Pond in abilities and science—yet on the question of the parallax[2] thinks Brinkley wrong and Pond right and admires the ingenious mode of proof Pond has devised. It was great pleasure to me to see Fanny enjoy all that she saw and heard at this Observatory and to perceive that she was appreciated—But poor W[3]—could not but be present to our minds—with deep regret. Bréguet has all the simplicity of a man of great talents. . . .

After returning from the Observatory we dined at Ivry a few miles from Paris where the Duchess Dowager of Orléans lives (she whom Mme de Genlis plagued). She is a benevolent dignified

[1] Samuel Brown (1776–1852), engineer, designed in 1819 the first large suspension bridge, the Union Bridge at Berwick-on-Tweed.

[2] See p. 126 n. 2.

[3] ME's engineer brother William, suffering at the time from a mental breakdown. He had a special interest in astronomy and a small observatory at Edgeworthstown.

old lady. Her countenance is said to resemble Lewis 14th. Her dame d'honneur Mme de Casteras a Spanish lady who followed her in all her misfortunes and who is a person of strong character and warm indignation interested us much by the originality of her observations and the force of her expressions. While an Archbishop of Rheims &c &c played at Whist after dinner this lady conversed delightfully and a French officer (name unknown) gave us an account of the Russian campaign and of his own sufferings. I asked whether La Baume's[1] is an exaggerated account—Not at all. After returning from the Duchesse d'Orleans went to Mme d'Haussonville and enjoyed the cool breeze in the gardens at the back of her beautiful house till between eleven and 12—Agreeable conversation—except from a woman who has written 4 quartos on 'The happiness of Nations' and who was conceited and tiresome.

The next day we went to Champlâtreux—the country house of Comte Molé the descendant of President Molé. His father was guillotined. Their very large property and magnificent château seized as national property and for some time the present Count Molé was in prison and afterward supported his mother and sister as he told me by the hard work of his hands. He cooked for them the very little they had to eat and often went to bed so hungry himself that he could not sleep. This was when he was about 15. His property was restored by a decree of the convention after Robespierres death as was the property of almost all those who had not emigrated. His house however he found only bare walls—the magnificent tapestry—glasses—*books*—all destroyed. To speak according to their mode of describing the house had formerly forty *lits de maîtres*. He has restored 15 excellent bedchambers. The principal sitting room about 40 feet long is fitted up with every English comfort and luxury—a round library table in the centre—plenty of tables with books inkstands &c a pianoforte—and all things well arranged in every part of the house so as to unite French taste and English comfort. We have spent 4 days at two different visits in this house. We were very glad to see the style of a French country house and the mode of living. They all breakfast together as we do and their children breakfasted and dined with them. When I said that I had heard that French families usually took coffee in their own room instead of

[1] Eugène La Baume, *Relation circonstanciée de la campagne de Russie* (1814).

breakfasting en famille Mme de Vintimille a lady between 50 and 60 assured me that from her childhood in all the houses where she had been intimate the custom had always been to breakfast together—Excepting at the Duc de Choiseul's. When he was in the country and in his famous banishment the crouds of people at his *court* used to order breakfasts and dinners in their own apartments or in public as they pleased. N B in the palace was a milliners shop from which the ladies might send for whatever they liked—letters—washing—horses—servants—all paid for. This lasted 44 years. Every person who went there inscribed their names on marble tables in a temple—which were turned inside out afterwards in the time of the republic . . .

Paris appears perfectly quiet since the law of elections is past but the causes of discontent remaining I would no more trust [ ] than the interval of silence of a Volcano. The alternating of the spirit of insurrection and frivolity is striking. One moment we hear a Frenchman expressing his regret that his country cannot be as free as England is. The next moment we hear him say he is au désespoir because he cannot make his neckcloth sit like an Englishman's—without inserting some stiffening collar which I am told spoils the effect and is considered a misfortune.

I begged my mother to transmit to you Louvel's last words and what he said at his trial. As well as I recollect one remarkable expression was omitted He said the night before his execution 'People may think it is an easy matter to poignard a man but I can tell them that between the drawing the dagger and plunging it in is an *hour* of horror and *difficulty* that no man can conceive beforehand.' How near this comes to Shakespear's Macbeth 'between the thinking and the acting of a dreadful deed'[1] &c . . .

Harriet Edgeworth to Mrs. Edgeworth

Paris, 2nd July, 1820

. . . We have never been in company with Benjamin Constant but we have heard and seen him at the Chambre des Députés. He is tall awkward and ungainly with whitish grey hair—but we are not

[1] ME's inaccurate quotation is from *Julius Caesar*, Act II, Sc. i, ll. 63–4.

so much Ultras as not to have been in company last Thursday with M. Kératry—M. Casimir Périer—M. Rollin and M. Ville L'Évêque four of the most decided côté gauche. We have seen Mme de Coigny. She is little rouged as red as fire with a very dirty yellow looking neck barer than any other in Paris. She is a dashing looking and talking person. We were all presented to her and have called on her but have never seen or heard more of her.

Mme de Vindé's son in law[1] the Bonaparte Domestique keeps his children in the most profound subjection. Beatrice is allowed to live a good deal with her grandmother but a Bonne (a vulgar Englishwoman) is sent down from time to time to watch over her and see that she is not allowed too much liberty and made to keep the fasts duly. Her two sisters Christine and Elizabeth live always with their father who has a fine Château in Champagne and they will have good fortunes. You are right in supposing Beatrice had a brother. He is 18 and is never allowed to go down from his Pension at Paris to La Celle without this Bonne.

Odelebens campaign[2] is accounted good and true. Chateaubriands book is exactly fit for the Society. Louis Bonapartes account of his family[3] I know nothing of. Mme Suards life of her husband[4] is not published but given as a great favor to everybody in Paris. We have sent it to you by Willy Foster and if you wish to have it translated you have it there to yourself—it is not to be bought. Another life of him by Garat is published but Mme Suard won't read it because he is of an opposite party . . .

Maria Edgeworth to Mary and Charlotte Sneyd

93 Place Bourbon, 7th July, 1820, before breakfast

It is a great refreshment to me to have a quiet half hour in which I can write to you while Fanny and Harriet are dancing with M.

[1] Hippolyte Terray.

[2] Baron d'Odeleben, *Relation circonstanciée de la campagne de 1813 en Saxe*, traduit de l'Allemand (1817). The Society was a book club in the Edgeworthstown neighbourhood It is not clear which of Chateaubriand's works is intended.

[3] Editions of Louis Bonaparte's *Documents historiques et réflexions sur le gouvernement d'Hollande* were published in Brussels, Paris, and London in 1820. Their titles varied slightly.

[4] Amélie Suard, *Essais de mémoires sur M. Suard* (privately printed 1820); D. J. Garat, *Mémoires historiques sur la vie de M. Suard* (1820).

Deschamps in the next room. 'Allons! Faites la révérence Mlle Henriette—*douce*ment—bien doucement—Regardez-moi—baissez la tête et les yeux. Allons Mademoiselle (F)—la troisième figure—Éloignez vos bras—chaîne angloise—chassé en avant—allons—glissade &c . . .

A few days ago we had a delightful breakfast at Degérandos. Tell my mother that he is now well lodged and we breakfasted in a room hung round with pictures—some of them very valuable—One in particular, which was sent to Degérando by the town of Pescia as a proof of their gratitude for his conduct at the time when he was sent into Italy in Bonapartes time to assist in establishing his government and to improve the education of the people. To the honor of Degérando and of the Italians it should be mentioned that this picture was sent two years after Degérando had left Italy and when he was no longer in place or power. We had a delightful breakfast. An Italian Marquis Ridolfi who has large fortune and a benevolent mind and who is intent upon improving the education of the people about him was one of the guests. He has given us pressing invitations if ever we go to Milan and his family he says knows us well already.

Another of the breakfasters at Degérandos was the Marquise de Villette—Voltaire's Belle et Bonne. She has still some remains of beauty and great appearance of goodness and chearfulness of temper. It was delightful to hear her speak of Voltaire with all the enthusiasm of affection and with tears in her eyes beseeching us not to believe a hundred misrepresentations we had heard but to trust to the person who had lived with him long and late and who knew him best and to the last. She said he was passionate but the moment it was over he would turn about and say 'Qu'est-ce que je viens de dire?' and that he never rested till he had made reparation if he had hurt any of his inferiors. His servants doated upon him and so did the peasants in his neighborhood. After breakfast Mme de Villette took us to her house where Voltaire had lived with her. She shewed us his salon—a very handsome large salon where he received *all Paris* on his last visit to the Capital—and we saw the laced waistcoat and fine robe de chambre in which he appeared for the last time. Some people like to see these above all things but we were rather more interested by his chair and writing desk turning on a pivot on the arm of the chair. In one corner of the room was a smiling keen eyed emaciated statue of Voltaire said to be a perfect resemblance and on one of its plaster hands hung the crown of bays, the brown withered leaves of that crown of bays which was placed on his head when he appeared for the last time at the Théatre François.

Mme de Villette shewed us some of Voltaire's letters—The last note he ever wrote with his own hand 4 or 5 days before his death was as follows—It seemed to be an answer to a friends invitation:

'Je sais ce que je veux mais je ne sais pas ce que je ferai. Je suis malade partout. Je souffre depuis la tête jusqu'aux pieds. Il n'y a de sain que mon coeur et cela ne vaut rien—Tout à vous.'

This was written in as small a handwriting as that which I now write and full as steady and distinct.[1] Another letter of Voltaire's which interested me still more than this—for a reason which you will immediately understand—It was to his steward with directions about sheep and various common business concluding with 'Let there be no drinking, no rioting and above all *no beating of your wife*'. The most precious relic in this room of Voltaire's is a little piece carved in wood by some untaught genius and sent to him by some peasants as a proof of gratitude. It represents him sitting listening to a family of poor peasants who are pleading their cause or thanking him for having assisted them. It is excellent. I have begged Fanny to try to take a sketch of it when we return in October—In which month of October more is to be done seen and heard than ever was done seen or heard in any October since the beginning of time . . .

We took Miss Lawrence to one of the great schools here established on the Lancaster principles[2] and we also took her to hear a man lecture upon the mode of teaching arithmetic and geometry which my father has recommended in Pracl' Ed.[3] The sight of little cubes &c was at once gratifying and painful. The man never mentioned him but plumed himself much on his new

[1] This undated letter of May 1778, was addressed to Mme de St. Julien. I have not identified the second letter. RLE had directed that at his funeral his coffin should be carried by his own tenants, wife beaters excluded.

[2] On Joseph Lancaster's system, broadly speaking, by teaching with the help of monitors. Bell and Lancaster's ideas were taken up with great enthusiasm in France after 1815, fostered by the *Société pour l'instruction élémentaire*, whose secretary was Degérando. The lecturer may have been Martin, master of the first *école d'enseignement mutuel* set up in Paris.

[3] See *Practical Education* (1798), chaps. xv and xvi.

discoveries and great improvement in the art of education. In paying my compliment to him at last, I said I particularly approved his method because I had seen it practised so long and with such success by my father. The man did not relish this I believe—but Malthus whom we had taken with us approved of it much and so did Miss Lawrence—whom I liked much for the warmth with which she spoke of the service these parts of Practical Education had been to her. She knew them perfectly—and Professional Education[2] too. Oh my dear Aunt how many things would have gratified him! But I am grateful and well I may be for all I have left me.

Harriet has written to Lovell an account of this man's methods. Degérando to whom I spoke of him will go and see him and in an account which he is now drawing up of the state of Education in Paris[1] will do my father justice. Tell Lovell that the school of enseignement mutuel which I have seen is not in any respect equal to his—Indeed I did not like what I saw. There was much noise and little attention. Two Indian children, two little Madagascar princes of 9 and 10 years old were produced to us, to shew how much had been taught in a few months and it is true they had learned to write and read and to parse what they read—but by no means to understand it. This I found by cross questioning them after they had fluently read a very simple story which I am certain a child of five or 6 years old in Lovell's school would comprehend. The fault I found was not that these children had been taught too little but too much. They were jabbering on with *parsing* sentences without having the smallest conception of the meaning of what they read. I thought [of] Lovell's pupils and of Honora's stories[3] and of the manner in which those had been read and written. I send Lovell specimens of the handwriting of some of the pupils—good enough. The little sketches of vignettes were drawn by the children for their amusement. The sentences they write do not appear to me to be adapted to their comprehension.

I have just heard from Hunter that he is printing Rosamond and

[1] RLE's *Essays on Professional Education* (1809).

[2] Perhaps *Compte rendu des travaux du Conseil d'administration de la Société pour l'instruction élémentaire à l'assemblée générale* (1826).

[3] A reference to stories written by Honora E (1776–90, only daughter of RLE's second marriage), e.g. 'Rivuletta', written in 1786 and published in *Practical Education* (2nd edn. 1801) and in ME's *Early Lessons* (1801).

that my dear friends at home will correct the proofs for me. God bless them! I will send a little preface of a page or two before the publishing time comes.

We dined and spent the day last monday with dear Mme de Roquefeuil and we were delighted to be able to sacrifice to her an offered dinner of the Duchess of Orléans; and an invitation to Mme de la Briche's fine place near Paris. Both these were for monday last. We determine that is better to put off going to Mme de la Briche's till October. We are now so much hurried that we could not manage a visit there except for a day and the distance (36 miles) is too much—le jeu ne vaut pas les chandelles. We do not regret a certain Comtesse Charles de Damas a very fine bel esprit whom we were to have met at Mme de La Briche's—But I own I a little regret missing Mme de Boufflers who went to the Duchess of Orléans on purpose to make our acquaintance as we hear and who as we hear is an uncommonly agreeable woman—but all this is to be repaired in *October*!

Meantime we had a day worth a hundred at Mme de Roquefeuil's. When we arrived she opened her dining room herself, hearing somebody coming upstairs. At first she looked in dismay at the appearance of company but the instant she saw who we were her countenance lightened and she ran forward and embraced me till she almost flattened me against her warm heart. 'Mais ma chère amie vous me trouvez dans un embarras!' 'What is the matter?' 'Two bishops who have just sent me word they will come from Paris to dine with me today—One an old man of 87 whose whole soul and body now are in his dinner—Tous les deux, gourmands on ne peut plus—Mangeant comme des ogres tous les deux—L'un comme un ogre, mais vraiment!—L'autre comme quatre ogres—and I have receved their note by this vile petite poste but this moment and I have nothing—nothing but the stomach ache—which I have had all night and all day.'

She sent however to a traiteur—that last and best resource!—and much of our morning was spent in guessing whether these bishops would or would not come and 4 o clock came—and it was settled they would never come—then a rattling carriage—Here they are! No—rattle passed. At last however when we had just given them up rattle rattle—dash and stop—Here they are! And a more curious, entertaining, tiresome, comic—melancholy scene than the whole dinner and whole appearance and conversation of these two old bishops I never saw or heard. The first—the 75 [year old] Bishop of Agen, grand aumônier du Roi—was a little hunchy backed decrepid man—with a face of a monkey with eyes that had been acute but were now almost meaningless—a head close shaved in a little white wig made to imitate grey hair as well as it could (viz very ill)—and this wig was quite crooked on the unconscious prelates head. No collar to his black coat left his little shrunk neck more conspicuous. Still and through all this he looked like a gentleman—at least like a gentlemanlike baboon. The other of larger stature and more erect mien—might be about 60—a jovial Mr. Butler kind of bishop—The bishop of Carcassonne.

Dinner—dinner—dinner!—was the grand sole object of both for the first two hours—the first hour in expectation—the second in enjoyment—Yes in real enjoyment—for in spite of all obstacles Mme de Roquefeuil had a good dinner for them—not such a dinner as would have contented two English bishops—Because their souls would have been set on far different and more substantial and more grandly served and in different [forms]. But the substance of good eating no matter for the form was here and much it was enjoyed with napkin under chin and chicken legs gnawing and dragging from side to side of the mouth. I beg your pardon my dear Aunt Mary I know how it disgusts you but upon my word it is true. It was amusing to me to observe the different manner of doing the honors—and where to put the wines &c. The ease and good breeding of Mme de Roquefeuil were charming. No one who saw her could have doubted that she had been used to live in the very best company—tho not of this day or this day's fashion. The *talk* was now and then of the great and the princes of other times and often of the court of this day—often with bitterness and indiscretion on the part of *Carcassonne*. Poor Agen was dead and gone almost to all things but his dinner—and of this he could not eat as much as could be wished. In the middle of dinner he turned to Fanny and said pathetically 'On dit que je suis gourmand mais vraiment je ne le suis pas. Je ne mange *que* mon diner—point de déjeuner—*que mon diner*!' And indeed Fanny who pitied him much avers he eat but little after all. These two bishops came 12 miles to this dinner and returned that night . . .

When we returned from [Versailles] we stopped on the road to the Champs Élysées to pay a *latish* visit to the Princess Potemkin. What a contrast was her graceful, youthful figure to those of the two bishops! What a contrast her conversation and the whole of the two societies! Certainly no people can have seen more of the world than we have done in the last 3 months. By seeing the world I mean seeing varieties of characters and manners and being behind the scenes of life in many different societies and families—so as to be able to form strong and large comparisons and to decide upon what happiness depends. The constant chorus of our moral as we drive home together at night is 'How happy we are to be so fond of each other! How happy we are to be independant of all that we see here! How happy to have our own dear home to return to at last!'

To return to the Princess Potemkin we went yesterday to see her again. She is Russian but she has all the grace and softness and winning manner of the Polish ladies. [ ]—her face oval pale with the finest softest most expressive *chesnut* dark eyes I ever beheld. When animated and when looking at a person she likes her eyes and the whole expression of her countenance reminded me of what Honora's mother[1] was when *I first saw her at Northchurch*. The Princess Potemkin has a sort of politeness which pleases peculiarly—mixture of the ease of high rank and early habit with something that is sentimental without affectation. In short you see she has won Rosamond's[2] heart . . .

Mme Lebrun is painting a beautiful picture of the Princess Potemkin and she was so good as to come from the country and to stay a day in Paris on purpose to shew it to us and to shew us her other pictures. Fanny was exceedingly pleased with them especially with one of Lady Hamilton[3] as a bacchante and with a portrait of Grassini which might represent F observed Corinne at the Capitol.[4] Mme Lebrun a woman of[5] great vivacity as well as great genius is I think better worth seeing than any of her

[1] RLE's third wife, Elizabeth Sneyd, whom he married in 1780. She had a daughter Honora (1791–1858). Northchurch was a house RLE rented in Herts.

[2] Rosamond in ME's stories is often to be identified with herself. 'Sentimental without affectation' is a reference to the chapter called 'Airs and Graces' in *Rosamond. A Sequel* (1821), i. 74–126.

[3] Nelson's Lady Hamilton.

[4] Corinne, the heroine of Mme de Staël's novel of that name, was an *improvisatrice* and on her first appearance in the book is reciting at the Capitol in Rome.

[5] '66' is here inserted above the line with an omission mark below.

pictures because though they are speak*ing* she speaks and speaks uncommonly well.

The dame d'honneur or companion of Mme Potemkin Mme la Comtesse de Noisseville educated her and her sisters and followed her to England on her marriage—her health being delicate. The friendship of the pupil and preceptress for each other does honor to both and gives great security for the sincerity and steadiness of the young princess's character. Mme de Noisseville in figure and face something like my aunt Fox is a well bred woman of very decided character and superior understanding who is very entertaining and exceedingly agreeable to those she likes but would I dare say be very disagreeable to those she did not like—for she would not think it worth her while to speak. N B—She likes us very much. She is one of the people who would make a good figure in le palais de la verité[1]—Very extraordinary for one who has lived so much in other palaces—But she seems to have seen and felt so much and to have so made up her mind as to all human affairs as not to think it the least worth while to dissemble or deceive—à quoi bon?

I mentioned I believe having been struck with the sight of Rostopchin when I first met him at la Duchesse D'Escards. The Princess Potemkin and Mme de Noisseville repeated some of his bons mots which appear to me in a *higher* style of wit than even Talleyrands—more general and national—less satirical and personal. For instance—some Russians at court were boasting of the perfection to which certain articles of luxury had attained in Russia—'We have such fine carriages and mirrors &c.' 'Yes' said Rostopchin 'Russia may be represented by a naked man in a coach with a mirror in one hand.' Speaking of the Parisians Rostopchin said 'Il y a trois choses sur lesquelles les parisiens se font illusion. Ils croient qu'ils ont un beau climat. Ils croient qu'ils ont un gouvernement représentatif et ils croient que le bois de Boulogne est un bois.' The emperor of Russia gave the government of Siberia to Prince X suppose for I cannot recollect his name—But take it so—Prince X governed Siberia living always at Petersburg. One day at the court of Petersburg the courtiers were talking of

[1] See Mme de Genlis, *Veillées du château.* Everyone who entered the palace of the geni Phanor was obliged to declare their secret thoughts, to speak what was in their mind even though they thought they were saying something different.

short sighted people. The Emperor is long sighted and was boasting of it. 'But commend me' said Rostopchin 'To Prince X who sees from here to Siberia!'

I have not time to do justice to these *traits*. Wit taken out of its place in conversation and huddled together bons mots always spoil and kill each other but from what I have said you may have some idea of Rostopchin's style. The Princess had invited him to meet us but his daughter was ill and he could not come. This daughter you know is married to *young* Ségur (our translators son)[1] . . .

I have just had a long and interesting and therefore fatiguing conversation with M. Buchon[2] our translator. What he has translated is admirably well done but I find there are great doubts among the booksellers whether this work would succeed here. In fact nothing but politics or novels are read at this moment at Paris. One of the principal booksellers was at me to engage to write a novel and let him have the translation of this novel upon condition of his undertaking the risk of the publication of the Memoirs. I flatly refused. I think the translator will go on without my interference. He behaved perfectly well but I have a notion that the booksellers are——. I cannot know the ultimatum before this post goes out but in my next you shall know how it is settled. If the translation appears it will M. Buchon says be published about the end of October . . .

Fanny Edgeworth to Harriet Beaufort

Monday [10th July, 1820]

. . . I wish to make you acquainted with the amiable manner in which the Duc and Duchesse d'Orléans and his sister live—quite free from politics and court intrigues—putting aside all form and ceremony enjoying the society of literary and scientific people and anxious about the education of their children. They have several very fine intelligent looking boys and girls—quite intimate with their father and mother sitting on their chairs running of messages

[1] Octave de Ségur, translator of ME's *Belinda*. His eldest son married in 1819 Sophie Rostopchin.

[2] See above, p. 132.

for them and joining in all that is going on. Mlle d'Orléans not only overlooks their progress but herself teaches the girls to play on the harp—the eldest boy goes to a public school every day like any other boy . . .

Mme Lebrun is well worth seeing . . . She seems to enjoy all she does with enthusiasm and not as a triste devoir. Some weeks ago we saw the picture of the death of the Abbé Edgeworth—pale and almost extinct supported by a venerable priest on one side—on the other is the Duchesse d'Angoulême preparing some medicine—bending over him in all the freshness of youth and beauty.[1]

We dined one day with M. Bréguet whose simple manners and benevolent indulgence to ignorance must endear him. M. Monti M. de Prony and M. Bréguet's son and Mr. Chenevix were the company. Bréguet has made a new thermometer[2] for delicate experiments which will please Mr. Robinson but delight Mr. John Brinkley—a lamina composed of platina gold and silver of imperceptible thickness about 1/10th of an inch in width and about six french feet long coiled in a small spiral—suspended at top—at bottom bearing an index pointing to the degrees marked on a dial at the bottom of the machine. The extreme sensibility of the coil of metal shows every slight variation in the temperature of the surrounding air *immediately*. I saw the common mercury thermometer and this compared under the [receiver] of an air pump. It shews the rapid change in the temperature in vacuo—before unknown or at least not known to their full extent. His beautifully adjusted clocks and the clear and quick mind of his son engaged all my attention but also filled my mind with melancholy. The object that made me understand and love these works and the mind which afterwards sympathised with me are alike gone—and I selfishly enjoy these beautiful inventions without a hope of being of use to others. He Bréguet I mean in the kindest manner gave us each a platina pen.[3] Maria had mentioned with gratitude those which he had formerly given to Maria and Mamma . . .

[1] The Abbé died in 1807 at Mittau, where he had been living with the exiled royal family.

[2] This thermometer was made for sale. An example purchased by Professor Daubeny is now in the Museum of the History of Science at Oxford. It operated by the differential expansion of metals.

[3] Platinum was a recently discovered metal in whose use the French had been particularly interested.

Fanny Edgeworth to Louisa Beaufort

[fragment, n.d.]

. . . At dinner at Ivry—the dowager Duchesse d'Orléans—I sat beside a moustached officer who had seen hard service—been in Spain and Portugal and afterwards in Russia—spoke of the despair when they found Moscow on fire. All their hopes of existence were rested on what they should find there. Of his regiment a thousand strong but sixty horses and a hundred and seventy men returned . . .

I have now seen the miserable gouty King who is very like the little portraits you used to draw of him on your skreens. Monsieur is gentlemanlike and princely looking. Le Duc d'Angoulême looks as weak and mean as I believe he is. He in his late tour has been caught hold of by the libéraux and is now more inclined to favour that party than the King ever was. Not such does the Duchesse appear—she is a fine dignified woman, with a very disagreeable countenance. In the late disturbances I hear that but for Macdonalds steadiness (he fortunately happened to be the Marshal then commanding) the King would have committed the same fault that was the beginning of Louis XVI misfortunes. Macdonald at last said to the King 'If you dont allow me to have troops sufficient and permission to fire upon the people if necessary—I will—I must give up my command.' . . .

Harriet Edgeworth to Mrs. Edgeworth

Paris, 17th July, 1820

. . . most undoubtedly I can say that the quantity of pleasure has far and far surpassed my expectations. Indeed I should be the most insensible and ungrateful of mortals if I did not think so—received as we have been by all the best as to fortune, rank talents or character that are to be found in this wonderful city. This appears like the very perfection of vanity but I know no other way of expressing to you the astonishing kindness with which Maria has been received here and the immense advantages we have enjoyed as belonging to her . . . Marias health is my chief reason for being glad to quit Paris. She has been on the whole wonderfully well but she suffers so much from the heat, and the quantity of anxiety of mind and exertion of body necessary for existence in the life we have led would soon have undone her I think . . .

We dined with Lord Carrington on Thursday last. As he was in a disagreeable hotel we dined at a café on the Rue St. Honoré in which the only disagreeable thing was the extreme lowness and great heat of the room. When we came in we were received by Lady Stanhope who is tall rather handsome looking speaking french very well. With her was Mrs. Heneage a rather little woman with very black hair and not pretty (she is a daughter of Lord Yarborough's). She sat down at Lord Carrington's right hand Lord Paulet next—Lady Stanhope—M. Chavral—myself—next to Mr. Heneage a gentlemanlike man who never said one word to me the whole of dinner which lasted 2 hours except 'I can't conceive how they can get their turbot so fresh at Paris.' I dont think his observations to Fanny were more brilliant and he said nothing to anyone else but to ask for champagne or tell the names of the dishes. Next to him sat Fanny and between her and Maria a gentleman who after talking some time about different countries at last said speaking of France '*We* think so and so'. 'Is it possible' said Maria 'that I am speaking to a Frenchman?' And so it was that this man Count de Noé did speak English so well that till I saw the red ribbon of the legion of honour in his button hole I could hardly believe that he was not English born. He was however English bred for he had been 30 years in England and is now the only one of his name left in France. He is very entertaining but very ugly . . .

Maria Edgeworth to Mrs. Ruxton

Paris [n.d. July, 1820]

. . . From what I have seen of the Parisians, I am convinced that they require, if not a despot, at least an absolute monarch to reign over them; but, leaving national character to shift for itself, I will go on with what will interest you more—our own history. We have been much pleased, interested, and instructed at Paris by all that we have seen of the arts, have heard of science, and have enjoyed of society. The most beautiful work of art I have seen at

Paris, next to the façade of the Louvre, is Canova's Magdalene. The prettiest things I have seen are Mme Jacotot's miniatures, enamelled on porcelain—La Vallière, Mme de Maintenon, Molière, all the celebrated people of that time; next to these, which are exquisite, I should name a porcelain table, with medallions all round of the marshals of France, by Isabey, surrounding a full-length of Napoleon in the centre. This table is generally supposed to have been broken to pieces, but by the favour of a friend we saw in its place of concealment . . .

Yesterday William Everard went with us to the Chapelle Royale, where we saw Monsieur, the Duchesse d'Angoulême, and all the Court. In the evening we were at a *fête de village* at La Celle, to which Mme de Vindé had invited us, as like an Irish *pattern*[1] as possible, allowing for the difference of dress and manner. The scene was in a beautiful grove on each side of a romantic road leading through a valley. High wooded banks: groups of gaily-dressed village belles and beaux seen through the trees, in a quarry, in the sand-holes, everywhere where there was space enough to form a quadrille. This grove was planted by Gabrielle d'Estrées for whom Henry IV built a lodge near it. Fanny and Harriet danced with two gentlemen who were of our party, and they all danced on till dew-fall, when the lamps, little glasses full of oil and a wick suspended to the branches of the trees were lighted, and we returned to La Celle, where we ate ice and sat in a circle, playing *trouvez mon ami*—mighty like 'why, when, and where'—and then played loto till twelve. Rose at six, had coffee, and drove back to Paris in the cool of the delicious morning. Today we are going to dine again at Neuilly with the other Duchess of Orléans, daughter-in-law of the good old Duchess, who by-the-bye spoke of Mme de Genlis in a true Christian spirit of forgiveness, but in a whisper, and with a shake of her head, allowed 'qu'elle m'avait causée bien des chagrins.'

Among some of the most agreeable people we have met are some Russians and Poles. Mme Swetchine, a Russian, is one of the cleverest women I ever heard converse. At a dinner at the young and pretty Princess Potemkin's, on entering the dining-room, we

[1] Saint's day festivities, from patron. Mme de Genlis (*Mémoires*, v. 108–9) speaks of the post-Revolution changes in *fêtes champêtres*; the gentry no longer danced with the lower classes and their gardens were opened to *cabaretiers* and *traiteurs* etc.

saw only a round table covered with fruit and sweetmeats, as if we had come in at the dessert; and so it remained while first soup, then cutlets, then fish, one dish at a time, ten or twelve one after another, were handed round, ending with game, sweet things, and ice.

A few days ago I saw, at the Duchesse D'Escards' Prince Rostopchin, the man who burned Moscow, first setting fire to his own house. I never saw a more striking Calmuck countenance. From his conversation as well as from his actions, I should think him a man of great strength of character. This *soirée* at Mme D'Escards' was not on a public night, when she receives for the King, but one of those *petits comités*, as they call their private parties, which I am told the English seldom see. The conversation turned, of course, first on the Queen of England, then on Lady Hester Stanhope,[1] then on English *dandies*. It was excessively entertaining to hear half-a-dozen Parisians all speaking at once, giving their opinions of the English *dandies* who have appeared at Paris, describing their manners and imitating their gestures, and sometimes by a single gesture giving an idea of the whole man; then discussing the difference between the *petit marquis* of the old French comedy and the present dandy. After many attempts at definition, and calling in Mme d'Arblay's Meadows,[2] with whom they are perfectly acquainted, they came to 'd'ailleurs c'est inconcevable ça.' And Mme D'Escards, herself the cleverest person in the room, summed it up: L'essentiel c'est que notre dandy veut plaire aux femmes s'il le peut; mais votre dandy Anglais ne le voudrait, même s'il le pourrait!' . . .

[MS missing—printed from *Mem.*ii.73–6]

[1] First-hand news of the eccentric Lady Hester and her settlement on the slopes of Mount Lebanon had been brought back to England in 1819 by her physician, Dr. Meryon.

[2] The coxcomb in Fanny Burney's *Cecilia* (1782), which was first translated into French in 1783. The *petit marquis* in seventeenth-century French comedy was a nobleman who gave himself ridiculous airs. 'Dandy' is a word of uncertain origin; *c.* 1813–19 it was in vogue in London for the 'exquisite' or beau. Cf. Thomas Moore, *The Fudge Family in Paris* (1818), i. 48: 'They've made him a Dandy. A thing you know, whiskered, great-coated, and laced like an hour-glass, exceedingly small in the waist.'

Maria Edgeworth to Sophy Ruxton

Passy, 19th July, 1820

Most comfortably, most happily seated at a little table in dear Mme Gautier's cabinet, with a view of soft acacias seen through half-open Venetian blinds, with a cool breeze waving the trees of this hanging garden, and the song of birds and the cheerful voices of little Caroline Delessert and her brother playing with bricks in the next room to me, I write to you, my beloved friend. I must give you the history of one of our last days at Paris—

Here entered Mme Gautier with a sweet rose and a sprig of verbena and mignonette—so like one of the nosegays I have so often received from dear Aunt Ruxton, and bringing gales of Black Castle to my heart. But to go on with my last days at Paris.

Friday, July 14—Dancing master nine to ten; and while Fanny and Harriet were dancing, I paid bills, saw tradespeople, and cleared away some of that necessary business of life which must be done behind the scenes. Breakfasted at Camille Jordan's: it was half-past twelve before the company assembled, and we had an hour's delightful conversation with Camille Jordan and his wife in her spotless white muslin and little cap, sitting at her husband's feet as he lay on the sofa, as clean, as nice, as fresh, and as thoughtless of herself as any mother. At this breakfast we saw three of the most distinguished of that party who call themselves *Les Doctrinaires*[1]—and say they are more attached to measures than to men. Camille Jordan has just been deprived of his place as Conseiller d'État and one thousand five hundred francs per annum, because he opposed government in the law of elections. These three Doctrinaires were Casimir Périer, Royer Collard, and Benjamin Constant, who is I believe, of a more violent party. I do not like him at all: his countenance, voice, manner, and conversation are all disagreeable to me. He is a fair, *whithky*-looking man, very near-sighted, with spectacles which seem to pinch his nose. He pokes out his chin to keep the spectacles on, and yet looks over the top of his spectacles, *squinching* up his eyes so that you cannot see your way into his mind. Then he speaks through his nose, and with a lisp, strangely contrasting with the vehemence of his emphasis. He does not give me any confidence in the sincerity of his

[1] Moderate constitutional monarchists.

patriotism, nor any high idea of his talents, though he seems to have a mighty high idea of them himself. He has been well called le *héro* des Brochures. We sat beside one another, and I think felt a mutual antipathy. On the other side of me was Royer Collard, suffering with tooth ache and swelled face; but, notwithstanding the distortion of the swelling, the natural expression of his countenance, and the strength and sincerity of his soul made their way, and the frankness of his character and plain superiority of his talents were manifest in five minutes' conversation.

Excellent Degérando gave me an account of all he had done in one district of Spain, where he succeeded in employing the poor and inspiring them with a desire to receive the wages of industry, instead of alms from hospitals, &c. At Rome he employed the poor in clearing away many feet of earth withinside the Colosseum, and discovered beneath a beautiful pavement; but when the Pope returned the superstition of the people took a sudden turn, and conceiving that this earth had been consecrated, and ought not to have been removed, they set to work and filled in all the rubbish again over the pavement![1]

After this breakfast we went to the Duchesse d'Uzès—little, shrivelled, thin, high-born, high-bred old lady, who knew and admired the Abbé Edgeworth, and received us with distinction as his relations. Her great-grandfather was the Duc de Châtillon, and she is great-granddaughter, or something that way, of Mme de Montespan, and her husband grand-nephew straight to Mme de la Vallière: their superb hotel is filled with pictures of all sizes, from miniatures by Petitot to full-lengths by Mignard, of illustrious and interesting family pictures—in particular, Mignard's La Vallière en Madeleine; we returned to it again and again, as though we could never see it enough: a full-length of Mme de Montespan, prettier than I wished. After a view of these pictures and of the garden, in which there was a catalpa in splendid flower, we departed.

This day we dined with Lord Carrington, and his daughter, Lady Stanhope: the Count de Noé, beside whom I sat, was an agreeable talker. In the evening we received a note from Mme Lavoisier—Mme de Rumford, I mean, telling me that she had just arrived at Paris, and warmly begging to see us. Rejoiced was I

[1] Degérando had been one of Napoleon's chief administrators in the Papal States.

that my sisters should have this glimpse of her, and off we drove to her; but I must own that we were disappointed in this visit, for there was a sort of *chuffiness*, and a sawdust kind of unconnected cutshortness in her manner, which we could not like. She was almost in the dark, with one ballooned lamp and semicircle of black men round her sofa, on which she sat cushioned up, giving the word for conversation—and a very odd course she gave to it—on some wife's separation from her husband; and she took the wife's part, and went on for a long time in a shrill voice, proving that, where a husband and wife detested each other, they should separate, and asserting that it must always be the man's fault when it comes to this pass![1] She ordered another lamp, that the gentlemen might, as she said, see my sisters' pretty faces; and the light came in time to see the smiles of the gentlemen at her matrimonial maxims. Several of the gentlemen were unknown to me. Old Gallois sat next to her, dried, and in good preservation, tell my mother; M. Garnier ('Richesse des Nations'[2]), and Cuvier, with whom I had a comfortable dose of good conversation. Just as we left the room Humboldt and the Prince de Beauvau arrived, but we were engaged to Mme Récamier.

15th—We breakfasted with Mme de L'Aigle, sister to the Duc de Broglie. (Now Mme Gautier is putting on her bonnet, to take us to La Bagatelle.) I forgot to tell you that Prince Potemkin is nephew to *the* famous Potemkin. He has just returned from England, particularly pleased with Mr. Coke, of Norfolk, and struck by the noble and useful manner in which he spends his large fortune. This young Russian appears very desirous to apply all he has seen in foreign countries to the advantage of his own.

After our breakfast at Mme de l'Aigle's, we went home, and met Prince Edmond de Beauvau by appointment, and went with him to the Invalides: saw the library, and plans and models of fortifications, for which the Duc de Coigny, unasked, sent us tickets, and there we met his secretary, a warm Bonapartist, whom we honoured for his gratitude and attachment to his old master.

[1] Mme Lavoisier's relations with her second husband, Benjamin Thompson, Count Rumford, were notoriously bad and they had separated.

[2] Germain Garnier, *Recherches sur la nature et les causes de la richesse des nations par Adam Smith, Traduction nouvelle* (1802).

Dined at Passy, and met Mrs. Malthus, M. Garnier, and M. Chaptal—the great Chaptal—very interesting man. In the evening at the Princesse de Beauvau's and Lady Granard's.

Sunday with the Miss Byrnes to Notre Dame, and went with them to introduce them to Lady (Sidney) Smith: charming house, gardens, and pictures. To Mme de Rumford's, and she was very agreeable this morning. Dined at Mr. Creed's, under the trees in their garden, with Mr. and Mrs. Malthus, and Mrs. and Miss Eyre, friends of Anna's,[1] fresh from Italy—very agreeable.

Now we have returned from a very pleasant visit to La Bagatelle. What struck me most there was the bust of the Duc d'Angoulême, with an inscription from his own letter during the Cent Jours, when he was detained by the enemy: 'J'espère—j'exige même que le Roi ne fera point de sacrifice pour me ravoir; je crains ni la prison ni la mort.'

Yesterday we went to Sèvres—beautiful manufacture of china, especially a table, with view of all the royal palaces, and a vase six feet and a half high, painted with natural flowers.

Louis XV was told that there was a man who had never been out of Paris; he gave him a pension, provided he never went out of town: he quitted Paris the year after! I have not time to make either prefaces or moral. We breakfast at Mr. Chenevix's on Monday, and propose to be at Geneva on Saturday.

[MS. missing—printed from *Mem.* ii. 81–6]

Maria Edgeworth to Lucy Edgeworth

Passy, 23rd July, 1820

. . . Yesterday we dined—for the last time, alas! this season—with excellent Benjamin Delessert. The red book which you will receive with this letter was among the many other pretty books lying on the table before dinner, and I was so much delighted with it, and wished so much that Pakenham was looking at it with me, that dear François Delessert procured a copy of 'Les Animaux savants'[2] for me the next morning. We never saw Les Cerfs at

[1] ME's sister, the widow of Dr. Thomas Beddoes.

[2] Perhaps G. Casti, *Les Animaux parlans, trad. de l'italien en vers français par L. Mareschal* (1819).

Tivoli,[1] but we saw a woman walk down a rope in the midst of the fireworks, and I could not help shutting my eyes. As I was looking at the picture of the stag-rope-dancer in this book, and talking of the wonderful intelligence and feeling of animals, an old lady who was beside me told me that some Spanish horses she had seen were uncommonly proud-spirited, resenting always an insult more than an injury. One of these, who had been used to be much caressed by his master, saw him in a field one day talking to a friend, and came up, according to his custom, to be caressed. The horse put his head in between the master and his friend, to whom he was talking; the master, eager in conversation, gave him a box on the ear: the horse withdrew his head instantly, took it for an affront, and never more would he permit his master to caress or mount him again . . .

Mme Gautier, in a most eloquent manner, described the character of each of her brothers, ending with speaking of Benjamin. 'Men have often two kinds of consideration in society; one derived from their public conduct, the other enjoyed in their private capacity. My brother Benjamin has equal influence in both. We all look up to him; we all apply to him as to our guardian friend. Besides the advantage of having such a friend, it gives us a pleaure which no money can purchase—the pleasure of feeling the mind elevated by looking up to a character we perfectly esteem, and that repose which results from perfect confidence.'

I find always, when I come to the end of my paper, that I have not told you several entertaining things I had treasured up for you. I had a history of a man and woman from Cochin China, which must now be squeezed almost to death. Just before the French Revolution a French military man went out to India, was wrecked, and with two or three companions made his way, LORD knows how, to Cochin China. It happened that the King of Cochin China was at war, and was glad of some hints from the French officer, who was encouraged to settle in Cochin China, married a Cochin Chinese lady, rose to power and credit, became a mandarin of the first class, and within the last month has arrived in France with his daughter. When his relations offered to embrace her, she drew back with horror. She is completely Chinese, and her idea of happiness is to sit still and do nothing, not even to blow

[1] A French version of Vauxhall pleasure gardens.

her nose. I hope she will not half change her views and opinions while she is in France, or she would become wholly unhappy on her return to China. Her father is on his word of honour to return in two years . . .

[MS. missing—printed from *Mem.* ii. 86–9]

SWITZERLAND, AUGUST–OCTOBER 1820

Maria Edgeworth to Mrs. Ruxton

Pregny,[1] 5th August, 1820

. . . I did not conceive it possible that I should feel so much pleasure from the sight of the beauties of nature as I have done since I came to this country. The first moment when I saw Mont Blanc will I think remain long an era in my life—a new idea—a new feeling standing alone and above others in my mind . . . On the third or 4th day after our arrival we set out on our excursion into Savoy to Chamouny. Notwithstanding all the sublime and beautiful the sun was almost intolerably hot and by dinner time we were fairly tired out with heat and *admiration* (which by the by is very fatiguing). The inns on the Chamouny[2] road are admirable—much better than on the Paris road. This road is now so much frequented that it is worth while to have good inns and the innkeepers are most simple hearted, active, obliging people. At Chamouny especially we grew quite fond of the honest family of the house. The family affection among these Swiss or rather these Savoyards is quite delightful. It suits with the romantic country and adds infinitely to the pleasure of travelling through it. It was impossible to see this country to more advantage than with Pictet and impossible to see him to more advantage than on this journey. He knows all the people and wherever we stopped they flocked round him with such joy and cordial gratitude in their faces! From the little children up to the greyheaded old men and women all seemed to know and love him. We were for his sake received by these good people as if we had been *Swiss*. The great difficulty was to make them take payment from us.

My dear Sophy do try to make out that pencil scrawl. *If you can*

[1] Swiss home of J. L. Moilliet, formerly belonging to the Empress Josephine.

[2] The valley of Chamouny first became a resort for travellers after 1741 when it was visited by Pocock. It was not accessible for *chars* or carriages until 1778.

it will save the trouble of going up La Flégère again.[1] In coming down the nine miles descent we were to walk as the mules could not we were told safely carry us down—so each with a guide and a long pole armed with an iron spike such as my uncle described to me ages ago and such as I never expected to wield we set out. The guides especially one Pierre Balmat and his son are some of the best informed most agreeable young and old men I ever conversed with. Indeed for six months of the year they keep company with the most distinguished travellers in Europe and the effect of this on their language and manners mixed with their natural honesty and strong sense and the habitual simplicity of their lives render them a most interesting and extraordinary people. In talking to an old woman who had brought us strawberries and who sat down to rest beside me as we were descending the mountain I was surprised to hear her pronounce an Italian proverb Poco a poco fa lontano nel giorno.[2] I thought then that she had crossed the Alps. No—she had never been beyond the range of her own mountains. She and several others I met seemed surprised at our admiration of their country and said that for their parts they would rather see a *plain* if they could if it were only for the curiosity.

After having safely descended the nine mile wonder we went in the evening to a nearer view of the mer de glace. The fear of the winter torrents and of the avalanches is in truth more than enough to balance the love of the picturesque—Very different for those who see the country as visitors and those who live there. The *mer de glace* is continually advancing. The whole mass is in motion though not perceptibly to the eye in motion, yet certainly advancing every hour—many feet this year. Our evening walk was in the valley under the glacier to the mouth of an arch or cavern of ice through which a rapid torrent of water poured. This is the source of the Arveyron. Part of the arch had given way a few days before our arrival and vast blocks of ice lay unheeded by the torrent before its entrance. Tremendous cracks appeared in the mountain of ice over the arch, threatening almost immediate destruction to two peasants chalets which were within a few yards of the spot and

[1] The pencilled 'scrawl' which accompanied this letter does not survive. La Flégère is a buttress of the Aiguille de la Floriaz.

[2] Literally, 'little by little makes a long way in the day'. Cf. 'Many a pickle (or little) makes a mickle', but there is no exact English equivalent.

in the very path of the avalanche. An old woman the owner of one of the Chalets stood trembling near us. I asked why she did not remove whatever could be carried away of her habitation instead of leaving it to be destroyed. She answered 'Land is so dear here. We could not get another spot to stand upon and we must stick by the only bit we have on earth.'

The whole world seems to be overpeopled—even in this remote valley our Pierre Balmat told us that there would soon be no living. 'And why do you not emigrate?' 'Ah ça il faudrait prendre avec soi toute sa famille et puis ses amis—cela ne se peut pas vous voyez—faut rester comme ça—puis j'ai beaucoup questionné ceux qui ont émigré et je n'ai pas trouvé qu'ils se sont mieux trouvés pour ça—puis on aime ses petites terres des l'enfance—c'est ça.' The patois of these people is very agreeable—a mixture of the Italian fond diminutives formed by accents on the last syllable for instance speaking of the time of year when their cows are brought home—'Nous gardons nos petites vach*ées* jusqu'à Septembré—peutêtre Octobré—comme ça.'

Late on this day on which so much was seen we went in the dusk of the evening to see a *manufactory* of cloth—Made by a single individual peasant—The machine for spinning—carding—weaving all made by his own hands every part woodwork ironwork all —and from his own memory aided by his own invention. He had in his youth worked in some manufactory in Dauphiné. The machinery and workmanship was astonishing and the modesty of the maker and his good sense and sound philosophy still more astonishing! When I said 'I hope all this succeeds in making money for you and your family', he answered 'Money was not my object. I make just money enough for myself and my family to live by it and that is all I want. It was for employment chiefly for myself and my family that I made all this. In the long winter evenings we had no work and then if it lasts and lives after me and if my family use it it may be of some service to them perhaps when I am gone—but I do not much look to that even. Often it happens the sons are of different ways of thinking from the father and mine maybe may think little of these things and if so—why no harm—and if otherwise so much the better. All this may serve them.'

This man was to me one of the most striking and touching

sights I ever behold and you know my dear aunt the associations that made him such.[1] But independently of these he was wonderful. I forgot to tell you a *hundred* things! I forgot to tell you that we dined at a table d'hôte with 30 people at Chamouny and I forgot to tell you that at Chamouny we met a M. and Mme Arago who were most agreeable additions to the pleasure of our stay. M. Arago's name Sophy must have seen in scientific journals. He is the Astronomer who is at the head of the Observatory at Paris—was very civil to us at Paris and glad to meet us again here. As we were walking together to see a cascade he told me a most romantic history of his adventures in Spain and Algiers; having been taken prisoner by the Algerines and set at liberty and retaken all which with an episode about a lion and a lie I will tell you by the fireside hereafter. But I must tell you now a curious circumstance of Bonaparte. After the defeat at Waterloo when he had abdicated he sent to Arago to offer him a considerable sum of money if he would accompany him to America. Bonaparte had formed the project of establishing himself in America and carrying there in his train several men of science! Mme Bertrand was the person Arago says who persuaded him to go to England. Arago was so angry with him for deserting his troops he said that he would have nothing more to do with him . . .

We left our carriage *long ago* at St. Martin and travelled in char-à-bancs with which you are well acquainted and with which you and Sophy made me intimate. They are cousin germans to an Irish jaunting car,[2] but they have this advantage that it is scarcely possible to overturn them and they go down and up and into places that appear absolutely impracticable. We were once well drenched in the rain and having imprudently lined our great straw hats with green and tied them with green ribbons, when the rain came through the roof of the charabanc we were in due time dyed green—green shoulders green chins. We arrived at St. Gervais looking like the daughters of Blue Beard. I forgot to mention that M. Gontard the master of the baths came to meet us in a fine new car in which he drove us himself the last two miles. The Hôtel at St. Gervais is the most singular looking house I ever saw. You drive

[1] A reference to RLE.

[2] A two-wheeled vehicle carrying a driver and four passengers, the latter either back to back or facing each other.

thro' a valley between high pine covered mountains that seem remote from human habitation and suddenly in a scoop-out in the valley you see a large low strange wooden house built round 3 sides of a square half chinese-looking half American, with galleries and pigeon holes and domes and stories beneath and above and shed half Swiss half *Chester* fashion[1]—The whole unpainted—the wood freshly planed as if the edifice had been but lately framed and stuck together for the day and in the gallery that surrounded this house under the projecting roof that almost touched their heads stood a lady fair in a purple silk gown plaiting straw with a ridicule on her arm and a child beside her and various other figures French figures in shawls and caps and flowered bonnets—some looking mighty fine and others deadly sick, all curious to see the newcomers. And the daughters of bluebeard were ushered into the house by the master M. Gontard—himself better worth seeing than his house. I could represent him at once to my mother and my aunts M and C by saying that he is a French Samuel Essington but I am afraid you dont remember that butler of ours, who afterwards set up the Essington Hotel at Malvern.[2]

Pictet had discovered the spring of these Baths[3] for M. Gontard and he was full of gratitude and joy at seeing him again—shining round face perspiring gratitude—eager to say a hundred things at a time, but with a great difficulty of utterance, his tongue somewhat too large and a goitre besides impeding his pronunciation—but his very confusion and eagerness said more than words could have said. He whisked about and ran with us here and there and everywhere with keys in his hand and wrong keys and right keys—but all in vain. A room, even a wooden room could not be made on the spot and he was obliged to wipe his forehead and jam us under a kind of a shed in a passage where the rafters were so low that even my little head could not stand upright—but here nevertheless we refitted to the best of our abilities and in five minutes were summoned to dinner at a table d'hôte in a narrow low wooden room between fifty and sixty feet long—a company of about 50 people—two or three of them tolerably genteel—all the rest semi-genteel, semi-shabby—one and all very hungry and intent upon

[1] A reference to the arcaded *Rows* at Chester.

[2] See *Letters from England*, 72–3.

[3] These were sulphur baths.

the main chance. M. Gontard himself sat at the head of the table and thinking poor goodnatured grateful creature that he never could do enough for the guests his benefactor and friend Pictet had brought to St. Gervais plied us with good dishes and good wines—and that no one might be affronted when he brought out his best wines for us gave the same to all the table—so it was a jour de fête.

Benevolent Pictet went with him after dinner to see all his baths and *douches* and contrivances many of them very ingenious—spits turned by water &c—various things that put me in mind of Mr. Corry.[1] After dinner having a little recovered his head which his heart had previously taken off his shoulders he recollected a nice little wooden room belonging to an Italian Marquis who was absent on a party of pleasure—and having found the key we were ushered into this to take coffee—white callico curtains and all very smart—a *select* party let in—Many very unexpected compliments on Patronage[2] from a marquise from Dijon who was at the baths to get rid of a little red nose. Enter from some receptacle from which she had never before been seen to step a sick but very gentlewomanlike Prussian countess in a close cap large bonnet and pale lead coloured pelisse like one of yours and M. Gontard introduced her to me—I should say introduced me to her—Patronage again—which has found much more favor abroad than at home—Walter Scotts novels—as well known as in England—Ondine[3]—admirably criticised . . .

M. Gontard absolutely refused to receive any payment from us and at last seemed so much hurt by the offer that Mr. Moilliet after following him all about the house was obliged to put his purse in his pocket. I do believe M. Gontard would have built another wooden room for us that night if we could have staid. He did find a bedchamber about the size of our carriage in which we took our seats on four chairs which just fitted into it—But we were expected at Chamouny and away we drove—fine evening—fine rocks—fine trees—fine cascades—Mont Blanc in all his glory—and Pierre Balmat for the pure love of Pictet would go with him all the

[1] Mrs. Ruxton's over-ingenious brother-in-law, James Corry of Shantonagh, Co. Monaghan, from whom was taken the idea of King Corney in ME's *Ormond*.

[2] ME's novel, published in 1814.

[3] The fairy romance by Baron Friedrich de la Motte Fouqué, translated into French in 1819 by Mme de Montolieu.

way sitting on the jolting front of the charabanc—heaven knows how.

At Chamouny there is a little museum of stones and chrystals &c where Pictet and Mr. Moilliet contrived to treat their geological souls to 7 napoleons *worth* of specimens and where an English ladies maid treated herself to a chrystal necklace. An English lady was buying some baubles of this sort when her husband followed her and exclaimed on seeing her purchase in a strongly accented manner 'God bless my soul and body *another* napoleon gone!' My dearest aunt the amusement of telling you all the nonsense that comes into my head carries me away so that I shall never get back to Geneva . . . While we were standing at the window of this inn some boys in the street threw up a sparrow they had tamed and on whose head they had fastened a bit of scarlet cloth, like a cockscomb. Pictet caught the bird and declared he would carry it home for his little grandson—*So* he put it into his hat tied a handkerchief over it and hatless in the burning sun drove off. Chirping at the bird and feeding it with biscuit crumbs half the day he brought it home to Geneva.

6th August, 1820

This day, the day after our return from the excursion to Chamouny we dined at Mrs. Marcets, met M. Dumont, Mr. and Mrs. Prevost, M. de Candolle M. de la Rive and M. Pictet and young Prevost Mrs. Marcets nephew and M. Bonstetten—a very agreeable dinner with variety of literary conversation. M. de Candolle the botanist is a particularly agreeable well informed man. Among other things he told me that they are now trying experiments upon the mode of curing the disease of the goitres. They attribute it to stagnant *air* and stagnant water. Iodine powdered has been tried with some success but sufficient experimets have not yet been tried to confirm it as a specific. Coffee has had more success than any other medicine. It was given de Candolle said as a stimulant—as a tonic—upon the principle that the goitre and the scrophula are of the same nature of disease and may be assisted by more generous diet. In proportion as the lands here have been cultivated in certain districts the goitres have disappeared. One man lately had the resolution to cut off his own goitre while one of his family held his head. When he had finished the operation he fainted. M. Bonstetten told me a curious fact of some Cretins whom he knew. The Cretins[1] you know are almost ideots—the lowest in the scale of beings yet they are the most fond of laughing at others. 8 or 9 of these Cretins used to assemble regularly every day in the sunshine before a barbers shop. The barber used to hear them laughing continually and attending to them he discovered that they had a language of signs by which they imitated for each other all who came to the shop—ridiculing all their persons and gestures.

But to return to a more agreeable subject M. de Candolle has you know lately given a delightful course of lectures on Botany at Geneva and has become extremely popular especially among the ladies who attended these lectures. They have shewn their gratitude in a most distinguished and meritorious manner. A friend of M. de Candolles had lent him a valuable manuscript volume of curious plants with a thousand paintings of all the plants. The book was given or lent upon condition that if the [owner of] the original was ever appointed professor of Botany in a certain Town it should be returned. This happened and to M. de Candolle's sorrow the book was to be returned. The ladies of Geneva in the course of a fortnight copied the MS for him each taking a certain number of pages and in 8 days another set of his pupils copied for him the thousand painted flowers! Mme de Candolle was all day long employed in giving out and receiving and comparing pages of MSS and drawings and messengers came for them and returned them without M. de Candolle ever knowing to what individuals he was obliged for each. It was said that during those 8 days anyone who passed through the streets of Geneva might at every window have seen the prettiest hands at work against the panes tracing flowers[2] . . .

[1] Both goites and cretinism are caused by lack of iodine. The stagnant air theory was De Saussure's.

[2] De Candolle wrote 'Lorsque je montrai cette collection à Miss Edgeworth elle fit une réflexion bien digne de la grâce et la bonté qui la distinguaient. Par un mouvement assez naturel je cherchais à lui montrer surtout les desseins les mieux exécutés: 'Non, me disait-elle, montrez-moi les moins bons, ce sont ceux qui prouvent que ces résultats sont dus à l'esprit public et non à l'amour-propre': *Mémoires*, 290. For more details about the 'Flora', see op. cit. 219–21, 288–91.

Harriet Edgeworth to Louisa Beaufort

Pregny, près de Genève, 8th August, 1820

I suppose you know that we performed our journey from Paris with safety ease and expedition and established ourselves very happily at this pretty place but we did not remain more than four days here and those four were engaged from morning to night—Our first day writing letters and unpacking and arranging all our goods—and in the evening we went a beautiful drive under the shade of Walnut trees along the very banks of the lake to Mrs. Marcets country house,[1] who was not at home but we were very warmly received by Dr. Marcet who speaks a kind of language which he calls English but who has no small difficulty in speaking any language. The next day we spent the morning in Geneva at the Exhibition and the Museum. At the Exhibition we met Pictet and a certain M. Arago, belonging to the Observatory at Paris, whom we had known there and had met again at Dijon on our way here—so that most of our time in the picture room was spent talking to those whom we met there. Pictet dined here with M. Dumont, who I also now saw for the first time. He was as fat red and ugly as I expected but much gayer and more entertaining. Then in the evening came a certain Mme Pigott who has in her own opinion many perfections, but in Maria's had but one, that of possessing two very pretty English spaniels, almost as pretty as Foster . . .

The next day Tuesday our morning was spent at the Library where there is nothing very remarkable except the numbers of the commonest people who were coming in and going out with books in their hands. All the citizens of Geneva down to the very lowest are allowed upon writing their name to borrow any book they please and hardly any are ever lost. The Bibliothèque Britannique is the most popular of any and as any Genevese may send his son to the college, all classes are to a certain degree well informed. The distinctions of rank are so little regarded here that at what is called The Promotions or distributions of prizes once a year, the poorest Genevese, with hardly a coat to cover him receives his medal along with the sons of some of the first English and German families. These prizes are all given in the great church of St. Peters by the first magistrate the whole town almost

[1] Malagny.

assembled with all the judges clergy and council in full dress—so that the anxiety and stimulus given by these rewards is very great —particularly as all their parents relations and friends are present and so great is the enthusiasm felt by the boys themselves that when any of their companions, at the last Promotions, received two medals they all burst forth in a shout of congratulation, forgetting all the awe their judges usually inspired.

Dr. and Mrs. Marcet, his sister Mme Prevost her husband and her son and M. de Candolle a famous botanist dined here; Mrs. Marcet I had heard so much of that I was very curious to see her. She was much younger than I expected, so young as to wear her hair without cap or turban. She was altogether better looking than I expected, much gayer and less elegant.

After many doubts because of the illness of Mrs. Moilliets youngest daughter, we fixed a party for the valley of Chamouny and agreed to be all ready by four o'clock the next morning. The next morning we were all drest by ¼ before 4. The heat was very great, the thermometer being then before the sun was risen 72—but the cloudy appearance of the sky instead of being dispersed by the bright sun fell in thick torrents of rain which added to no carriages arriving made us all look not a little doleful. After many hesitations we set off in Mr. Moilliets large landau instead of in two calèches[1] which we were to have had and having taken up M. Pictet we six consisting of Mr. Moilliet, his daughter Emily, Pictet and we three settled ourselves as well as we could for a five hours drive in pouring rain. At a small town called Bonneville we stopped at last to dine. The whole appearance of the inn was most truly Irish a glass door into our salon, every pane of which door was broken completely out, and in some places ill mended with paper, gave not only light but air to a long dark passage, leading from a staircase without any roof which led to all the bedchambers and was ranged with bottle racks. On each side of this passage were doors leading into receptacles into which no prudent eye would look, particularly one, at the door of which appeared a creature called a cook who Maria said looked, not as if she had been steeped in, but as if her whole body was made of butter, a sight which added to the various exhalations with which we were greeted from this apartment, had rather an unfortunate influence

[1] See below, p. 213.

upon Marias appetite—which had originally met with a severe check from the appearance of the innkeeper who in a waistcoat which had once been white just meeting over his immense stomach looked like a tallow candle much marked with smallpox and then covered with brown ochre. Having however contrived, as we had nothing else for it, to dine mighty comfortably we remounted our carriage and drove on . . .

We arrived at St. Martin . . . Here we were most comfortable and the next morning had the pleasure of the company of M. and Mme Arago who were making the same tour. We had a very pleasant walk at 6 o'clock in the morning along the banks of the Arve under the shade of oaks, till we were joined by the Char à bancs which are exactly like half a jaunting car with iron pillars at each corner supporting a flat tarpolin cover and little leather curtains which are in general rolled up except in very bright or very wet weather. These are drawn by two mules driven by a postillion—the guide sitting in the front just at the horses tails. The part on which your feet rest is about 16 inches from the ground and but just keeps ones feet out of the water in passing the numerous streams, through which and over whose rocky sides and stony beds the char à bancs go without the slightest regard for wheels mules or passengers and indeed nothing can be pleasanter for the country than these machines because they go everywhere and mind no more going right over a block of granite 2 feet high than we should walking over a pebble . . .

The next morning Friday the 4th we mounted at 6 o'clock upon mules forming a long cavalcade each mule attended by a guide and mounted slowly but most agreeably up one of a chain of mountains opposite to that of which Mont Blanc forms a part and called the Chaîne Rouge . . . Our interest this day in looking at it was much encreased by observing the ascent of a Dr. Hamel, a co-partner, a friend of Pictets who was climbing up it by a new path[1] . . .

[1] On his first and unsuccessful attempt Hamel took the same route as De Saussure had used, also without success, in 1785. Ten days later he tried again and the three front guides, among them Pierre Balmat, were lost in a crevasse. The expedition was then abandoned.

Fanny Edgeworth to C. Sneyd Edgeworth

Pregny, 9th August, 1820

. . . We came back on Sunday evening. On Monday we dined at Mrs. Marcet's, a pretty campagne at this side of the lake. The company were Prof. Prevost a benevolent old philosopher and his wife (Dr. Marcets sister) and son—M. Bonstetten a chearful old bachelor who has been a hero. He was one of the noblemen of very antient family and fortune in the canton I believe of Berne. He thought in a republic like Switzerland that it would be better to become a private citizen of Geneva—which he now is having relinquished all his titles—M. de la Rive who knew Lovell at Edinburgh—M. Pictet M. Dumont and M. de Candolle the botanist. Several people came in the evening—some very agreeable Italians who comfort us for not going to Italy by saying that we should be disappointed with it after the beauty of Switzerland. They prefer the Lake of Geneva to their own. We sat out under the trees with two or three moonlamps placed on tables round us. Do you remember M. and Mme Constant Mme Achards daughter?[1] They asked most kindly after you and their two daughters now both married and mothers said they remembered you and your playing with them and their throwing you down.

Yesterday Prof. Pictet dined here and we spent the evening at Prof. Prevosts which was still more agreeable. We saw and heard the Pictet who translated Practical Education[2]—a very sick ghost who is very agreeable . . .

Fanny Edgeworth to Mrs. Edgeworth

fragment n.d. [August, 1820]

. . . We have returned from our little excursion quite delighted with the mountains and vallies—the bright sun and the masses of snow and ice . . . At dinner we compared notes with M. and Mme Arago who had returned from their expedition to the Montagne Viste. We each thought we had done the best and were satisfied. M. Arago is delightfully enthusiastic and at present indignant with

[1] M. and Mme Charles de Constant.

[2] Charles Pictet de Rochemont.

Mr. Chenevix and going to answer his review where he says both the facts and the calculations are inexact. He and Pictet had a quarrel arising from Pictet having said that a young man whom Arago had recommended received a large sum of money to try some experiments on galvanism which he never tried. This was not correct but Arago attacked him unhandsomely and they had ceased to have any intercourse.[1] This we fancied would prove very inconvenient to us as we overtook the Aragos the first night. However M. Arago went up to Pictet acknowledged that he had been in the wrong and they mutually agreed to forget the past and be friends. We were consequently much together and as Maria says one cannot be a quarter of an hour in M. Arago's company without learning something we had advantage as well as pleasure in his society and that of his pretty lively wife . . .

Maria Edgeworth to Mrs. Edgeworth

Pregny, 10th August, 1820

. . . So now to something new. It is not new to tell you that Pictet is the kindest of friends to us . . . Yesterday we dined with him and his 3 daughters and 3 sons in law Mme Prevost Pictet and M. Prevost Mme Vernet and M. Vernet Mme Rilliet Pictet. Mem^{m}. The families of Geneva seems to me to have but five or six family names among them and of these 3 seem to be Pictets Prevosts and Rilliets. They distinguish them by adding the *wife's* name to the husbands.

Mme Prevost-Pictet and Mme Vernet are both very agreeable and sensible and have the remains of great beauty. Mme Prevost-Pictet is of the Mme Gautier style and character—with easier manners and less vivacity. Besides the 3 husbands and 3 wives at dinner were a grandson and granddaughter Prevost and Rilliet and in the evening [shoals] of Pictets and Rilliets and Prevosts—*great* fish and *pretty* fish and *odd* fish and little fry. Mme Lullin was

[1] Fanny E's account of this quarrel is not accurate. In 1816 the *Bibliothèque Universelle* had published a critical report on the lack of first-rate work in France on electrochemistry, despite government subventions. Arago in patriotic resentment then attacked the editors of the *Bibliothèque Universelle* in the new French periodical *Annales de chimie et de physique* (ii (1816), 210). The 'young man' (men) concerned were Gay-Lussac and Thénard. I am indebted to Professor Crosland for this information.

there and two of the three daughters whom you may remember to have seen. *Amélie, Mme Beaumont*, luckily I had guessed the moment I saw her. Time, without doing her much damage, has turned her into a matronly happy looking mother. *Her* daughter was talked of but did not appear. Caroline Lullin has married a M. Budé[1] and both these daughters have country houses and carriages and children and all that is good. But the grandest of all the married daughters of Pictet is the youngest who was a child when we were in Paris in 1803. She is now the wife of M. Eynard who is building a magnificent house, the admiration, envy and *scandal* of Geneva. We have called it '*le palais de la république*'. As he has no children he had better leave it to the republick for a palais de justice. He has also a very handsome landau-calèche just arrived from Munich which has an *excellent contrivance in the forepart* which supplies the place of a crane neck[2] and of a vast deal of heavy work. Fanny has drawn it and will shew this hereafter to Mr. Hutton. This carriage which would I am sure cost at least 300 guineas in England cost only 130 napoleons here including 20 for bringing it from Munich. Pictet took us a drive this evening after coffee time in this carriage and delightfully easy it was.

On our return we found a crowd of people assembled for the evening party. The first thing I disliked at Geneva was the Genevese pronunciation of french—very disagreeable—with the broad *r* s. The chief differences I observe between the Parisian and Genevese *society* is the stiffness and uniformity of the manners. If you except half a dozen distinguished persons such as Pictet, Dumont, De Candolle, Prevost &c the men are all mere *husbands*. The women are far superior to the men in appearance information and conversation. They have all accomplishments many in a high degree especially music and drawing but they have a something prim and stiff and *apprêté*[3] in their manners which I cannot bear. They all hold themselves well but they stand in a room like dolls with their legs tied. Their backs are *too flat*—their bodies look as if they were made of wood or as if they had taken an eternal *sit* from the stiff square stays of former day. Their hair is all nicely curled and plaited and shining, but it has all

[1] Amélie married M. Budé and Caroline, M. Beaumont.

[2] A bent iron bar uniting the back and front timbers of a carriage.

[3] Unnatural, affected.

precisely the same look, opened at the same angle on the forehead and as if the wind of heaven *could* never visit it too roughly. Harriets and Fannys heads refresh my eye in a room full of this Swiss uniformity. They have almost all the same large dark eyes—very fine, yet tiresome—But they are all very good and kind and I am ashamed of feeling that *manner* influences me so much. To do them justice they do not roar all at once about politics as the Parisians do. The conversation of such men as the 4 or 5 I have named must be always sufficient to please and instruct and this would be delightful if we could have it without *the others* but every instant we feel the weight and the insipid interruption of *the others*, N B amazing good cakes—piled in profusion. Enter 3 English ladies overdressed in silks blonde and flowers! 'Ah c'est ainsi que les Anglaises tuent nos petites réunions.' Enter a man in a sword and bag looking very fond of his sword but not much used to it nor to its jangling chain—not at all military—rather like Mr. Gregg at five and twenty—in a yellowish coat moreover. I asked Dumont who he was? Dumont with his satirical-joyous smile, answered '*One of our kings*, one of our Syndics, M. Turrettin.' This Turrettin is brother to the old [ ] Mlle or Mme Turrettin whom you may remember scolding me for never being able to swallow.

They have now at Geneva a representative government but have retained no created a state council of 20 counsellors who call themselves *noble* and wear and *love* swords—a chamber of 200 deputies when *formed* exactly like our house of commons but the elections not exactly the same. About half a napoleon enables a man, if he pleases, to be an elector of the *candidates*; from the number of which at a second election the deputies are chosen. They have gone through all the same discussions about the law of election which we have seen at Paris and Dumont and the representative government party has triumphed. There is another and I think a much greater good he [ ] for his countrymen. He has prevailed upon them to have their courts of justice *open courts*—not secret tribunals. Numbers of the old politicians opposed this; especially old Prevost (Stewarts[1] friend and rather dull and dry). Dumont after much debate obtained permission to try the open courts as 'arrangement provisoire' for 2 years. At the

[1] Professor Dugald Stewart.

end of the 2 years, on the day when the discussion was to be resumed and a great battle expected Prevost came into the assembly and declared that after having attended the courts during these 2 years he had been completely convinced that all his former objections to the practice were groundless and he therefore withdrew his opposition. Others less courageous in their candor contented themselves with silently withdrawing their opposition and the open-court system was established unanimously. Both for Dumonts sake and for the sake of human nature you will forgive me for filling a quarter of a page (most unusually for me) with politics . . .

Pray tell Honora that Dumont is much more agreeable and less cold and *stickish* than he was at Bowood[1]—very kind and cordial. He seems to enjoy his universal *consideration* here exceedingly—and he loves Mont-Blanc next to Bentham above all created things. I had no idea till I saw him here how much he loved the beauties of nature and the fresh air. This comes of his Swiss original nature. Will you believe it? He said last night that he would rather dine on mutton broth or eat the worst dinner in the worst cottage than eat the best dinner in the best company in any town in this hot weather. He added that he had dined 3 days in Geneva and felt rejoiced when he could breathe freely again at his own little cottage —which cottage we have not yet seen (something about a man servant who is gone and is to come).

Among the many delightful conversations of Dumont's, I particularly wished you to have heard one about Mme Necker de Saussure's life of Mme de Staël[2] and Garat's life of Suard. Dumont quite agrees in our opinion that there are too many words and too few anecdotes in Mme Necker's life of Mme de Staël. He says the few instances of her conversation or of her wit that appear are spoiled in the telling especially that of the coachman and the overturn and her father. He gave us one instance of a charming answer of Mme de Staëls when she was very young. One day M. Suard went to pay a visit at l'hôtel de Necker. When he entered the salon no company had arrived; he saw Mme Necker going out of

[1] For ME's visit to Bowood, see *Letters from England*, 82–104. Dumont translated much of the work of Jeremy Bentham into French and was a convinced Utilitarian.

[2] Mme Necker de Saussure, *Sketch of the life, character and writings of the Baroness de Staël-Holstein*, trans. from the French (1820), 223. For Garat's book, see Introduction, p. ix n. 2.

the room at the opposite door and Mlle Necker then a girl of 15 standing in a melancholy attitude with tears in her eyes. Guessing that Mme Necker had been lecturing her Suard went towards her to comfort her and whispered '*une caresse du Papa vous dédommagera bien de tout ça*.' She immediately wiping the tears from her eyes answered 'Eh oui monsieur. Mon père soigne mon bonheur à present et ma mère songe à mon avenir.' There was more than wit and presence of mind heart and *soul* and greatness of mind in this answer and her biographer's full dressed head ought to be knocked against the wall for omitting it . . .

But to return to Geneva. Gibbon's one word that describes Geneva, the word borné,[1] I own occurs to me when I hear them speaking of the affairs of their own little world with exclusive interest but then we must consider that Attica was only the size of one Riding of Yorkshire. The great present object of conversation and interest at Geneva is a new *catholic* bishop. Part of the territory now annexed to Geneva did belong to Savoy and was under the jurisdiction of the king of Sardinia and is catholic. It hurt the pride or independance of the Genevese that this should continue to have only part of a foreign Savoyard bishop—So they fumed and fumed and worked and worked at the Pope till he granted and sent them a whole catholic bishop of their own. All dinner time yesterday M. Vernet (Pictet's grey-headed son-in-law) was going on at every pause talking of this new bishop who was at the moment at a grand dinner with the Syndics. 'And why' quoth Pictet, 'were you not at this dinner my dear Vernet? Since your head is so full of the bishop why did you not dine with him?' 'In the first place' replied Vernet 'because I was not asked. I might have begun with *Because I preferred dining with these ladies and you*—but the truth came first.' This made us all laugh and may serve as a specimen of the difference between Genevese and French habits and manners. Vernet mentioned a compliment of a protestant curé to the new catholic bishop which French politeness might envy and which I wish that Party spirit in Ireland and all over the world could hear and imitate 'Monseigneur, Vous êtes dans un pays où la moitié du peuple vous ouvre leurs coeurs; *l'autre moitié*

[1] Gibbon (*Letters*, ed. J. Norton, iii, no. 800) said that the manners and style of life at Geneva were on the whole less easy and pleasant than at Lausanne, but I have not located *borné*. ME may have misremembered her source.

vous tend leurs bras.' Pray my dear mother tell this to your father—it is very like him.[1] Dumont says it is worthy of Lewis the 18th who never says a foolish thing.[2]

I believe I have not yet mentioned poor Mme Achard who by the by is *rich* Mme Achard; and lives in a handsome, *very handsome* house with a salon hung with pictures, and large windows down to the ground opening to a terrace rich with pomegranates oleanders orange flowers &c and below the terrace is a real English park. Fanny and Harriet declare we have slandered her voice and that it is not as disagreeable as—*many others.* I will allow it—for instance, not so horrible as her sister's—Mme Pigott's. A blind beggarman after having heard Mme speak to him and having received alms from her went away saying 'mille bénédictions, *mon Général*'. F and H think Mme Achard very clever and so do I. I stick to it you see. She has left off the rigmarole compliments; and is rather plainspoken and blunt than otherwise, when you come to the real natural woman. She adores us all 3 and thinks Harriet very like you and she has a proper sense of what you are. Her very odd daughter (whom you could never bear) is so odd now that she keeps many of her mother's friends away from the house. She has taken such an inveterate dislike to Dumont that he often cannot go there. Poor creature! There is in this some touch of insanity—like Miss Malone. There is something very odd in the whole family. I will not undertake to tell you the names of three generations I saw there—Grandmother daughters and grandchildren. Suffice it to say that we have seen Mme A's famous handsome charming daughter Mme Constant of whom Lord Lansdowne and half the world used to talk to us. We think she has been *very* handsome *perhaps* and *perhaps* is very handsome still—but there is always a *perhaps.* It is impossible to determine whether to like her or not. There is something one minute handsome, intelligent, charming; and the next cross, crabbish American in her look, manner and words—something like a Swiss Mrs. Jephson yet with great differences. I think there is a twist in all the family. Heaven be praised we dont *live* with them . . .

I forgot to mention that we met M. and Mme Sismondi at Mrs. Marcets. I don't like Sismondi much at first sight, or first hearing

[1] The Revd. D. A. Beaufort.

[2] ME omits 'and never does a wise one' (Rochester's epitaph on Charles II).

but you know all *that* changes with me; Observe I don't *decide*. I like Madame very well but not so well as our dear Mrs. Jos,[1] your likeness. George Knox is here and as white and silent and helpless looking as ever and as droll *within*.

Mr. and Mrs. Moilliet Emily and Susan travel in their own spacious landau and with their own horses. *Note it well! In this Alpine country a pair of horses never think of refusing to draw a heavy landau with six people in it.* We have taken a very pretty and comfortable calèche. I presume that you and yees have a correct idea of a calèche; and that you do not represent to yourself Gil Blas and his secretary in a two wheeled chaise[2] but rather a landau with half a head and in rain a hood or veil of leather with windows in the lower part of the veil and air holes of sliding blinds between the windows; and two side pieces that fold and unfold in fairy-board-way when the whole hood is let down or thrown back. Add to this a leather apron which from the top of the back of the seat next the horses draws over your knees and you are as snug as a bird in a cage. This cage holds 3 birds of our size perfectly on the seat farthest from the horses and in fine weather two more can sit on the seat *next the horses*. I dare not call it the *front* or the *back* seat—'Car on dit tous les deux'. We pay for our carriage, not quite a pound a day coachman included. We must often however take mules and charabancs and send the carriage round by carriage roads. This journey will I should guess cost about forty pounds—our excursion to Chamouny which took 5 days cost (our share) about eleven pounds but then under Pictets guardianship we paid only as Swiss. This new tour will take up about 3 weeks . . .

But now to go to our visit to M. and Mme de Candolle. We went to them purposely to see some volumes of drawings of flowers which had been made for him by the ladies of Geneva . . . When the copied work was completed De Candolle went himself with his Spanish friend's original Flora, to see it forwarded to Spain. He was to send it through Lyons. Now the custom house officers between the Genevese territory and France are the most strict and troublesome in France and that is saying much. When

[1] Mrs. Josiah Wedgwood II (née Allen) was sister to Mme Sismondi.

[2] Perhaps as illustrated in the Amsterdam edition of 1747 (once belonging to Harriet E), iv. 8. This represents a two-wheeled vehicle with a closed back and a roof shaped like a canopy, but completely open in front.

De Candolle produced his book and they saw 1500 paintings they exclaimed 'You will have a duty of 1500 francs to pay for this Sir' but when they had heard De Candolle's story and saw this work of the citizens and the ladies of Geneva they caught the enthusiasm. The Chief Custom House officer albeit unused to the melting mood is said to have had something like a tear in his eye and he whispered to his companions 'We must let the book pass—I hazard my place Sir—but let it pass—say nothing about it.' When I expressed to M. De Candolle a hope that this story would be published he said 'No. It might injure my Spanish friend. This Government is very jealous and might be displeased by his having lent his book to me.' . . . Since that time M. de Candolle having expressed a wish that the plants in the botanic garden here should be drawn to make a national botanical work the ladies of Geneva have begun it for him and we saw today two folio volumes beautifully finished since April. Goodbye I must now go and drink tea at Mrs. Marcets to meet M. De Candolle and some Italians.

[At] night—spent a delightful evening—No Italians but M. De Candolle and Mrs. Marcet conversed the more agreeably. [ ] M. De Candolle entertained me with the account of various journies he took in diligences in France in the beginning of the revolution when often Dukes and duchesses and all the grand people of France used to travel in them *incognito* and he used to find them out by their physiognomy or conversation. This put me in mind of my father's paper in the farmers journal.[1] De Candolle once travelled with a man and woman who at different periods had been cook and chambermaid and prince and princess. The man talked by turns of his feelings and adventures in both conditions. The lady was enraged with him and in agonies whenever he alluded to his cook side of her femme de chambre [ ] . . .

Maria Edgeworth to Francis Beaufort

17th August, 1820

. . . Before I met or at least before I knew who Captn. Hillyar was, I had just determined to write to your brother William about an

[1] *Irish Farmers' Journal*, iv. 117–18 (9 Dec. 1815), signed 'P.Q.'.

establishment for the deaf and dumb which I went to see here.[1] I have not time to write two letters; will you be so kind to tell him that I have been much pleased with what I have seen of M. Naef whose prospectus I enclose. I went into his house quite unexpectedly and saw about 9 of his pupils from 8 to 14. Their countenances shewed that they were kindly treated. In eight months one of them a boy of eleven years old has learned to speak *intelligibly*—I do not mean fluently. His voice and the voices of all whom I heard speak were less harsh and disagreeable than any I ever heard from the pupils of other masters who profess to teach the deaf and dumb to speak. I may say more—their voices were agreeable. They read aloud quite intelligibly. Most of them are Germans—a few French—no English. M. Naef does not understand English but by the same methods by which he teaches one language the pupil of course could learn any other. I saw one cast up this sum with ease 4764 x 3460 x 2179. He made 2 mistakes and corrected them when pointed out. The bedrooms are good—each child a separate bed—large garden and various means of amusement and bodily exercise under the head *Gymnastics* . . . The expense in the whole—instruction boarding and lodging—is 50 Guineas a year. The food is good and sufficient as the health of the boys shews but it is not luxurious—breakfast—soup—plain meat and vegetables at dinner. The religion in Yverdun is protestant and Mr. Naef is a protestant . . .

[ ] to Pestalozzi.[2] He is almost past mental labor but others are carrying on his plans at his establishment. Mr. Schmidt one of his pupils teaches mathematics well—exceedingly well as far as we can judge by the clearness and intelligence of his pupils. Mr. Greaves a gentleman who has been here 2 years for no purpose but to learn the system of teaching German and English. Of German he knew nothing. He teaches language by shewing the external objects first and annexing the names at the moment—then their qualities and then their actions. He tries to make the children invent the rules of grammar from shewing their use. The revd. Mr. Mayo from Oxford teaches Latin and Greek and

[1] H. C. Naef (1789–1832) taught deaf mutes at Pestalozzi's school from 1810 to 1817. In the latter year he set up an independent school near by. The Revd. William Beaufort, brother to Mrs. E and to Francis Beaufort, had a deaf and dumb son.

[2] See above pp. 85–6. Cf. *Diary of Frances, Lady Shelley*, ed. R. Edgcumbe, i. 225.

English for Pestalozzi on this plan. He is rather too full of words . . . I need say no more to *you*. There seems to me a great inconvenience in the variety of tongues spoken at Pestalozzi's. The English is a barbarous jargon—the French bad and the children and their masters mix French English and German together so that they will I fear speak none correctly. But what is worse their ideas seem confused by this inaccuracy of language—Sum total—I would not for any consideration that Francis or one of your boys were at Pestalozzi's for their education but I should be glad that they could learn mathematics from Mr. Schmidt—provided they could not learn them as well elsewhere—which is the thing to be proved . . .

Maria Edgeworth to Honora Edgeworth

Berne, 19th August, 1820

. . . I left off in our history with our breakfast at Coppet of which I proposed you some details. The château is not so large or *handsome* as I expected. It has neither the external beauties of age or youth. It is old without being picturesque or venerable. This is the style of the front [sketch given]. It is like old fashioned English houses—The inside, the hall and library lyeing lengthways at the back of the hall and opening from glass doors upon a broad terrace. The broad low-staired staircase on the right as you enter the hall altogether reminded me, tell my aunts of my early recollections of the palace at Lichfield.[1] The inside of the house is much better than the out. The library a very large good room had been in Mme de Staëls time a theatre but M. de Staël said he could not bear that it should ever in future be used for that purpose. The Duchesse de Broglie is at Les Eaux[2] and the Duc with her.

From some misapprehension of our note they had not expected us and had breakfasted; but M. de Staël is remarkably well-bred, easy and obliging in his manners and this did not *put him out* at all. While breakfast à la fourchette was preparing he took us to see

[1] In ME's childhood the handsome seventeenth-century bishop's palace at Lichfield had been the home of Canon Seward and his daughter Anna. Mrs. Honora Edgeworth had been brought up there.

[2] A watering place.

some pictures and busts of Mme de Staël and M. Necker. These were in M. de Staëls apartment and in going to it we saw almost all the house—All the rooms which she had inhabited and of which we could not think as of common rooms. They have a classical power over the mind and this was much heightened by the strong attachment and respect for her memory shewn in every word and look—and silence by her son and the friend Miss Randall who walked with us through these rooms. Miss Randall I believe I told you was the person who attended her in her last illness. She is a fat coarsish-looking woman but with a delicate tenderness of mind and strong feeling. The statue bust and picture of M. Necker I should be sorry to shew if I were his descendant. They do not give the idea of any mental superiority. There is an expression of great benevolence but of a heavy sleepy yet *prominent* eyed fat lipped thick necked man—of feeble character and self important habits. The pictures of Mme de Staël it was evident were *flattering* as to beauty; but the superior mind was visible in all, at every age. M. de Staël has promised me one of the best engravings of his mother that can be had.

Breakfast and an excellent breakfast or rather dinner was ready in less time than anyone but a french cook could have even supposed to be possible. After breakfast we took a very agreeable walk in the grounds which the Baron de Staël is improving with good judgment and taste after the English fashion. There is one fine broad avenue of lofty trees which he has had sense enough to leave an avenue. As I walked down it I thought 'How much eloquence and such as can never more be heard has been heard here!' I like M. de Staël much for the manner in which he speaks of everything his mother did and for his feeling so strongly the change that there must be at Coppet. I walked on with him and he walked always with encreased celerity when he talked of his mother. He is correcting for the press a manuscript of hers—*Dix ans d'exil*[1] which Dumont says is full of curious anecdotes and contains an excellent description of all she saw in Russia. M. de Staël told me that she never gave any work to the public in the form in which she had originally composed it—that she *changed* the arrangement and expression of her thoughts with such facility and was so little attached to her own first views of the subject that

[1] Written in 1810–13, but not published until 1821.

often a work was completely remodelled by her as it was passing through the press. Her father had disliked to see her make any formal preparation for writing when she was young, so that she used to write on any corner of a table, often on a corner of a chimney piece or on a pasteboard held in her hand and always in the room with others for her father would not bear that she should be out of the room where he was.[1] She preserved this habit of writing without preparation ever afterwards. M. de Staël told me that whether at Coppet or at Paris during the time when she was most eager in writing any of her works she never shut her doors—Visitors came to her as usual! Some hours of the morning were of course excepted. Indeed all the mornings I suppose were her own because the French are not in the habit of morning visits.

M. de Staël gave me an account of a remarkable interview he had with Bonaparte at the time when Bonaparte was enraged with his mother and with M. Necker who had published Remarks on government and on the constitution fit for France.[2] B spoke in a low and gentle tone of voice at first and then with violence but the whole of the conversation which is too long to detail tended to prove the Baron's belief that Bonaparte has perfect command of temper and that the violence and intemperate language which seem to prove the contrary were only affected to gain his point where he thought he could intimidate. Like a true Irish referee I decide that half and half is true—that he sometimes affected to be angry—for his interests—but often was really carried away contrary to his interests by bursts of passion. His conclusion to M. de S. was 'Eh bien vous avez raison aussi. Je conçois qu'un fils doit toujours faire la défense de sa mère. Mais enfin si Monsieur veut ecrire des libelles c'est en Angleterre qu'il faut aller—Ou bien s'il cherche la gloire. Encore *c'est l'Angleterre ou la France. Il n'y a que ces deux pays en Europe—dans le monde*.'[3] In this abrupt way scarcely using the necessary connecting words to make French or sense he bolted out his thoughts.

Miss Randall told me that Mme de Staël admired the writing

[1] ME also had always written in the family sitting-room, with other people round her.

[2] *Dernières vues de politique et de finance offertes à la nation française* (1802).

[3] Lord Granville Leveson Gower attributes a similar remark to Berthier: *Private Correspondence*, 383.

of 'Manuscrit d'un inconnu de St. Hélène'.[1] Before any other copy was to be had of it the Duke of Wellington had one which he lent to Mme de Staël who was very anxious to see it. She began to read it eagerly but when she had read about half stopped and exclaimed 'Where is Benjamin Constant? We will wait for him.' As soon as he came in she began to give him an account of what they had been reading. He listened with the indifference of a person who had read the book; and when Mme de Staël urged him to read up to them, he said he would go on with them and read the previous part at leisure but Miss Randall observed that he never did read it. When Mme de S criticised it, he defended it and when silent writhed under the attacks as if they were personal. When accused of being the author he denied it with vehemence. Miss R said to him 'If you had simply denied it I might have believed you—perhaps—but now you come to swearing I am sure you are the author.' She thinks so but so do not I. I do not think M. Constant has ability enough to write it or sufficient force of mind to invent the thoughts. On the other hand Constant had great means of knowing Bonaparte and had noted down many conversations of his. I forget whether I confessed to you not my love but my antipathy to B. Constant. I like Miss Randall for having the same aversion to him that we have. She expressed the same feelings that we had when we breakfasted with him. 'I always felt when he was beside me as if I had a toad or some cold blooded venemous animal. There is not a creature I ever disliked so much. As I never heard him speak truth when he swore he was not the author I believed he was.' I suppose the foundation of her dislike was in her having seen duplicity in his conduct to Mme de Staël . . .

M. de Staël called young Alphonse Rocca to introduce him to us. He is a pleasing gentle looking ivory-pale boy with dark blue eyes like Mme de Broglie; not in the least like Mme de Staël—intelligent enough but not any appearance of genius or of a bold enthusiastic character. M. de S told me that he is as prudent as an old man and careful of his property. When I asked whether he was generous he said 'No—good natured but not generous'. By the way I never heard any Englishman speak English so well as M. de Staël—a carefully studied but perfectly acquired English tone and manner—the manner of a perfectly well-bred English man of

[1] [Lullin de Châteauvieux], *Manuscrit venu de St. Hélène d'une manière inconnue* (1817).

fashion—like some of the *exquisites*—not Frank Standish[1]—not humor enough—but like Mr. Ellis—in voice—not conceit.

After our walk M. de S proposed our going on the lake. I suppose you know (by instinct) that Coppet is on the banks of the Lake of Geneva. When we had seated ourselves in the boat seeing that little Rocca was not there I asked M. de Staël if he might come and immediately he sent for him. I liked the manner in which he spoke to the boy and in which the boy spoke to him and looked at him. It shewed they were on right terms together. The boy evidently felt both love and respect for him. He asked him questions about everything he wanted to know about the management of the sails &c. He asked why some sails are called voiles aux scisseaux.[2] M. de S shewed him the sails and explained why they are so called. When the boy saw him use the rudder, he wanted to try to use it and M. de S let him and shewed him the use of it. In short all he said to the boy was sensible and F H and I were much pleased with his kindness to this little brother. It is the best proof of his respect for his mothers memory. We rowed for about an hour on this beautiful part of the lake of Geneva. The deep deep blue of the water and the varying colors as the sun shone and the shadows of clouds appeared on it were beautiful beyond description—The colors of a peacocks or a pigeons neck one minute—Then in others streams of light resembling the soft green and pink and orient varying colors you see in mother of pearl and shells.

When we returned from this boating on the lake we went in to rest in M. de Staëls cabinet and Dumont having while we were on the lake quoted some lines of Voltaires from an *ode on the lake of Geneva* we asked him to read it—and exceedingly well he did read it. Pray look for it and tell me where *you* think it ought to begin. Before we went away M. de S made me promise which I did most willingly to return to Coppet to spend some days there when the duchesse de Broglie arrives. That will be about the 15th of September.

Our whole days journey and a quarter of the next days continued to be on the road by the banks of the lake of Geneva—

[1] Frank Hall Standish, connoisseur and author (1799–1840). Mr. Ellis is George James Welbore Agar Ellis, M.P.: *Letters from England*, 187, 193.

[2] *Voiles latines*, 'lateen sails', triangular sails suspended from a long yard at an angle of 45°.

beautiful—Tuesday slept at Morges. Early in the morning while I was dressing Fanny and H read and re-read to me Voltaires Ode to Geneva and a dialogue between un Russe et un François—proceeded to Cossonay near which place Mme Benjamin Delessert lives but she was gone to les Eaux so we went on to Yverdun—arrived late and tired. We were glad to find an excellent clean well regulated well attended inn as any in England allowing for the difference of fashion. The object at Yverdun was next morning to see Pestalozzi's establishment in [ ]. As I intend to write to Lovell[1] all my thoughts about Pestalozzi—Père Girard—Fellenberg and Wehrli—I will not trouble you with my wisdom—especially as I opine that you round the breakfast table or round Lucy's sofa or Lucy's tree would all prefer my nonsense.

One indisputably good thing Pestalozzi has done but without intending it. He has made an excellent inn at Yverdun and procured us as good a breakfast as well served by as obliging intelligent people as ever were seen on the Bath road, with much better honey preserved apricots and preserved plums than any lady or gentleman *called to the Bar*[2] on that road could produce. Pestalozzis establishment has drawn and draws such a concourse of visitors of all nations to Yverdun that it has become worth while to supply the demand for a right good inn.

A broad faced simple looking *sort* of a gentleman in a thick grey frieze coat pantaloons and all (the thermometer at 80) presented himself to breakfast with us; he being a sort of Cicerone of Pestalozzi's establishment—and moreover having come from England, from Liverpool to volunteer his services as English master—as far as I could understand for the pure love of humanity —and of teaching English which he certainly has nearly forgotten. He spoke a barbarous jargon with great affluence of words and poverty of ideas, having first learned the cant of his master without having his sense. This Pestalozzian Cicerone's name was Greaves—from Liverpool . . . He stuck to us till he had us fairly in the classroom.

Pestalozzi recognised me and I him.[3] Tell my mother that

[1] ME's letters to Lovell E. have not survived.

[2] Fielding, *Journal of a voyage to Lisbon* (1892 edn.), 208; cf. *Tom Jones*, bk. x, on the inn at Ufton.

[3] See above, pp. 85–6.

except the change of 18 additional years and a black and grey beard of half an inch's growth may have made in him he is the same wild-looking black monkey sort of german whom we saw at Mme Gautier's. His gibberish appeared to Fanny and Harriet even more strange and unintelligible than our description had led them to expect. But poor man he is grown old and tame. He does not gesticulate now or struggle to explain with arms, legs, chin, jaws and eyebrows as he used to do. He leaves it all to others. The whole establishment is now conducted by his masters, but all under his name and nominal superintendance. He meets strangers in the outer room and shews them into the school and walks about a little and walks out and reappears when you are going away with a look that pleads irresistibly for an obole[1] of praise . . .

I do not recollect anything that particularly struck me at Yverdun except that the women and children were ugly as far as I saw in driving through it. From Yverdun—look at the map—the beginning of our evening drive by the lake of Neufchâtel was beautiful—and then the road turning off we mounted continually but gradually till we came late at night to Paienne where we supped in a *church* which has been annexed to the inn and been turned into a dining room for the civil and military table d'hôtes &c. The last time Mr. Moilliet was here he slept in this monstrous room alone. They were bountiful in candles—12 I think; while we drank tea at one end and could hardly see what was at the other. Next day a beautiful journey from 4 in the morning to 9 to Freyburg a curious strange old town as I believe I told you in my last—and the dirtiest of Irish straggling inns—kept by *chance* as it seemed that last day and with such horrid mixtures of onion grease, dirt—fat—putrefaction—bad air and dunghill smells as I think have scarcely yet quitted the nose of my imagination. But never mind it—I would bear all and more to see père Girard and ten times more to read his little book[2]—but all this I must reserve for Lovell. You shall not even know who Père Girard is.

So we go on from Freyburg to Berne. The moment we entered

[1] An *obole* was an old French coin of low value and the word is used figuratively to express the smallest possible sum. An obol was also the Greek coin placed in the mouth of a corpse to pay the ferryman for passage across the rivers of the underworld.

[2] Grégoire Girard, *Bericht über die pestalozzische Erziehungs Anstalt zu Yverdun*. ME must have had a translation; she did not read German.

the canton of Berne, we perceived the superior cultivation of the land, the comfort of the cottages, the Irish colored honest jolly independant hard working yet independant appearance of the lower class of the people. The stoutness of the horses in all the carts we met and plenty of them we did meet trotting uphill and downhill in their nets and bells and leather hoods the men and women sitting in their carts with more than the air of lords. Trees of superb growth—beech and firs on the sides of mountains mix beautifully contrasting in color and shape—fine chesnuts walnuts and a kind of Sycamore of much smaller leaf and lighter more picturesque branches than ours—The hedges rich in acacias and barberries. The road from Freyburg to Berne is delightful. We had the finest lightning I ever saw flashing from the horizon. Arrived late. Town stands upon a hill and the streets slope much in many directions. Town is built chiefly of a white stone resembling Bath stone cut. Before the houses in the grande rue are arches on which are flagged walks covered overhead like the rows in Chester but the cover here is a projecting wooden roof two stories above your head and you walk on smooth flags not dirty wood. In the middle of the street runs not a mere gutter but really a clear rivulet in its cut stone channel broad enough to hold the wheels of a small cart. I saw a cart lying in it to have its wheels washed as the stream ran past. Into this noble gutter all that ought to be swept from the houses is swept every morning. Those who are to be punished for breach of the laws are employed in this as scavengers and the whole of this work must be performed before 8 every morning on pain of a 5 sh. fine. I never saw so clean a town. The street on *each* side of this gutter is broad enough for two carriages to pass. The street slopes from the houses to the gutter—but Enough and too much about gutters. Berne I think unites the beauties of Bath Oxford and Chester—Bath for its stone and general beauty of the outside of the houses—Oxford for the width and winding beauty of its streets and Chester for the convenience of its rows and odd variety of some of its buildings. I might add the beauty peculiar to Edinburgh—the sudden sight at every turn of rock, wood and water.

Besides all this there are delightful public walks and private walks I am told round the Town and add to these the charm of the novelty of the appearance of persons and dress and the new ways of carrying on their occupations as foreign climate directs. You know the prints of the Berne Costume. Pray look at the *butterfly wing* caps—Brobdignag butterflies. They are made of black woven (not *air*) but horse hair which to the eye has all the appearance of stiff black gauze or lace—the hair combed tight back pendant in a queue behind and black streaming ribbons. This is worn by all ages from 3 to threescore. It has a very odd effect to see grey hair and wrinkled peachstone tanned leather faces in this picturesque Psyche costume.

When you have the Swiss costume before you look at a Freybourg woman and take my word for it that the *wad* of plaited hair and ribbon round their heads is frightful except for the very young when only their natural hair is used but imagine thick yellow Irish hair with plaits of black hair or black ribbon intermixed and fastened on the top like a pad for carrying a pail—straw hats painted or plaistered over with sulphur—quite stiff—no crowns or only ½ inch turned up at sides. A pretty face *may* bear it. The women seem to have their bodies framed in a frame of black velvet. It binds their boddice and neck and seems to hold on the petticoat behind the back [sketch]. One sunday we saw the peasants in their holiday clothes—very pretty—The men and women with flowers in their hats—the mens particularly pretty I presume because chosen by the women . . .

Harriet Edgeworth to Harriet Beaufort

Grindelwald, 21st August, 1820

I am sitting in a blockhouse, every part of which stairs roof floor and walls are of wood. I am writing at a table made of a single plank of walnut 2 feet wide. Before me rises a dark mountain covered with gigantic pines—at my left a green cultivated sloping ground clothed with trees and cottages. Behind me rise the Grand Nègre nearly white with snow and at its foot the Glacier de Grindelwald out of which proceeds the source of the Lutzen which river runs through the whole valley and then down the neighbouring Valley of Lauterbrunnen.

Unterseen, 22nd August—Before I began my letter to you yesterday we had a most delightful drive through the aforesaid valley of Grindelwald . . . The road was about 3 feet wide, just cut out in the side of the rocks—with innumerable little streams tumbling over stone and bank and crossed by rough bridges of trees and branches and stones or conducted by aqueducts formed by trees just hollowed out in the form of troughs and supported upon y shaped poles placed just high enough to permit the driver of a char à banc head to pass. These simple machines carry the water across to a considerable distance whether to one of the numerous fountains which are to be seen at every little knot of houses—or else to turn the wheel of one of their saw mills. These necessary articles of life in a country where everything is made of wood, are to be found at every town and village in these valleys. They are very simple consisting of two smaller wheels turned by the larger water wheel. One of these moves a crank which draws the saw down and lets it up at each turn of one wheel. The other draws on a frame on which the wood is laid so as to keep it constantly close up against the saw—so that it goes on laboring by itself and seems like a machine endued with life and with the power of moving for ever, so that frequently in some of these wild spots, these mills are the only moving things to be seen . . . The people here are in general tall and very handsome. They have a much happier and healthier appearance than in the valley of Chamouny . . .

Stein, 29th August . . . I believe she [Maria] said nothing of the Pestalozzi school. I had not expected much but the lamentable want of attention in the first room we went into at once settled our opinions. The children were very young and of all nations. A boy of about 8 years old was teaching them fractions, he was Swiss and had to translate his questions backwards and forwards from French to English—the boys began to write what they could—not one wrote the same thing and none could give the answer or explain the question. In the next room the boys sat more still and when the master was near them were rather more attentive. With great difficulty on their part in speaking a foreign language and with as much on ours in understanding what they meant through the mass of useless phrases, 2 English boys explained a difficult sum in fractions—but they did it better than any of the others. It was done without energy and the appearance of all of them was so loitering unanimated and indifferent that it surprised me less that they knew but little, and that little but ill but that they knew anything at all.

While they were singing we walked down to a teacher of dumb children[1] . . . We then returned to the château where the great school is kept where they were just finishing their music lesson . . . The children then returned to business—to mathematics and certainly this they are admirably taught and explain perfectly. This branch is taught by M. Schmidt a very sensible man—but the instant the problem was over the same lounging and talking recommenced and how they ever arrive at this state of perfection I cannot understand because in the first room nothing could equal the absurdity of the scribble little boys were making by way of describing a certain number of angles. The worst symptom of the success of the establishment was that the boys seemed to take no interest in their occupations to have no pride in appearing well to strangers and no enthusiasm for the system they were taught by. Pestalozzi himself is now nearly doating—really and literally unable to say two words together of any European language . . .

After breakfast in this town [Freybourg] the capital of the Canton [bearing this name] we went to see a fine old Cathedral with a pretty tower the highest in Switzerland. We then went to a school which is really a phenomenon. It is on the Bell and Lancasterian system—established and conducted by a Jesuit priest.[2] He is a very simple benevolent and clever person. His school consists of about 400 boys. The little children look miserably unhealthy but those older seemed happy and tolerably attentive. One of them knew perfectly what he was reading and all understood and attended well to the Geography they were learning. They sing a hymn in the morning when they come—when they leave off for dinner and when they return and when they go away at night. They are all catholics but seem very well taken care of by their interesting priest. Here the children seemed gay and interested in their business. No bodily punishments are inflicted so that it is hardly possible that rewards which are distributed once a year can have sufficient power to rouse their attention to the degree necessary. We saw translations of Mrs. C. Smiths rural

[1] Naef.

[2] Père Girard. Bell and Lancaster's schools both used the method of teaching through monitors.

walks[1] as one of the prizes. Parents assistant is among the books translated and sold here.

The town of Freybourg is old dirty and ruinous but very picturesque and curious. It is divided by the river Saune. All the inhabitants on one side speak French and on the other German so that having crossed the bridge we found ourselves in a country where all spoke a language which not one of our party could understand. Mr. Moilliet possessed a few phrases and with these we were to make our way as well as we could. A beautiful drive through a haymaking orchardy country with the snowy Alps rising to our view between every interval of trees, and a splendid storm of thunder and lightning brought us to Berne. The next day was spent in walking about the town and seeing the Museum . . . The people sit in long rows with their baskets of fruit and vegetables fresh at the pillars of the arcades and the shops behind with their goods spread out so that the whole has a most singular and lively appearance.

In the evening we drove to Hofwyl.[2] M. Fellenberg received us very civilly but none of the scholars were at home. Having promised to return and see the children we went back to Berne slept and the next morning drove to Thun. It was Sunday. The people in their pretty dresses all as clean as possible were pouring out of every house to church on the road as we came along and heaps of children in little sociables about 2 feet from the ground drawn along by the brothers and sisters. Thun is a pretty little town filled with people in all dresses—soldiers and officers the day we were there. Having breakfasted and packed up for 3 days we took leave of the carriages and all our baggage except a bag and dressing box we embarked on the Lac de Thun—with wooded grassy banks with here and there a bare rocky and wild spot down to the waters edge—and after a two hours voyage a superb view of snowy mountains half covered with clouds . . . At Lauterbrunn we slept and the next morning proceeded to Grindelwald . . . All these places are still in the Canton de Berne so that the dress is nearly the same. The people here are the handsomest I have seen,

[1] Mrs. C. Smith's *Rural Walks* came out in 1795 (translation not located). Harriet E probably refers to *L'Ami des parens*, an undated translation of *The Parents' Assistant* by C. Pictet.

[2] Fellenberg's agricultural school.

the men tall, the women fair and fresh. Their goiters are not so much seen as loose handkerchiefs are tied round their necks and this terrible drawback to the healthy and happy appearance of the people in these lovely valleys is here concealed . . .

The next day we had the pleasure of seeing all the people going to church [at Zug], the women wear their heads bare and their hair fastened in a knob behind with a long pin very different from the Luzernois who wear it in 2 long pigtails behind and from the Schwyz people (a canton on the border of the Lac de Lucerne where we had dined two days before) who wear a white frill like a cocks combs fastened in their hair behind. The men wear mostly long dark cloaks and the cocked hats. We proceeded in our carriage which met us here through heavy rain to Zurich where a M. Escher to whom we had a letter shewed us all that the town contains of wonderful. It is large, the university is the rival of Geneva. The houses are very high and being whitewashed look less foreign than the other Swiss towns. Having spent an evening and a morning here we went on to Baden and thence to this place Basle . . .

Maria Edgeworth to Honora Edgeworth

Soleure, 30th August, 1820

. . . F H and I have this evening walked about the town and public walks and have seen the church—a very handsome church—the finest I have seen since I left Paris. Soleure is a very *genteel* town seemingly inhabited by rich people with good houses and gardens —the people in the street well dressed in the French fashion which they much affected in all things till the Austrians came into play and power and then turn again gentleman and turn again gentlewoman[1] . . .

[1] German-speaking Soleure had not in fact submitted tamely to the French in 1798. In 1815 the liberal party there had been completely extinguished.

Harriet Edgeworth to Mrs. Edgeworth

Berne, 1st September, 1820

. . . She [Maria] has really enjoyed this tour much more than I thought she could[1] and her greatest pleasure is giving the account of it to you at home. She has walked ridden [ ] surprisingly—one walk of nine mile added to the next of three was of sovereign use to her, she was amazingly little tired and has been stronger ever since. Her eyes are on the whole very well. She has often read to herself and aloud in the carriage without much fatiguing them and can write a length of time, before her eyes hurt her. In short I think I may presume that she has not only borne this long travelling well but that it has been of real use to her. Her spirits are in general admirable and [she] can always make laugh and can sometimes make speak fast the four Moilliets even when the soup is full of soot, the room full of geese and the fish swimming in oil and with herself and her own two companions never fails, even when the smell of the dunghill enters at every window and fleas at every fold of the blanket—Not that you are from this to imagine that the Moilliets are nice about their dinners or we about our beds. I merely put the worst state of things we meet to shew you how good humored we are and how good spirited she is—she is indeed a wonderful creature and though I talk of peace at Geneva I never saw her so surrounded or so adoringly attended to. Rows of four deep encircled her chair and Fanny and I are scolded from her orbit—which is very fair but very hard because the best conversation and cleverest people are always talking to her without considering what she says herself . . .

Maria Edgeworth to Elizabeth Waller

Coppet, 1st September, 1820

I am sure that you have heard of us, and of all we have done and seen from Edgeworthstown as far as Berne: from thence we went to Thun: there we took char-à-bancs, little low carriages, like half an Irish jaunting car, with four wheels, and a square tarpaulin

[1] Her health had not been good during the hot weather.

awning over our heads. . . . The valley of Lauterbrunn is beautiful; a clear, rushing cascady stream rushes through it: fine chestnuts, walnuts and sycamores scattered through, the verdure on the mountains between the woods fresh and bright. Pointed mountains covered with snow in the midst of every sign of flowery summer strike us with a sense of the sublime which never grows familiar. The height of the Staubbach waterfall, which we saw early in the morning, astonished my mind, I think, more than my eyes, looking more like thin vapour than water—more like *strings* of water; and I own I was disappointed, after all I had heard of it

We went to the valley of Grindelwald, where we saw as we thought two fields off, a glacier to which we wished to go; accordingly we left the char-à-bancs, and walked down the sloping field expecting to reach it in a few minutes, but we found it a long walk—about two miles. To this sort of deception about distances we are continually subject, from the clearness of the air, and from the unusual size of the objects, for which we have no points of comparison, and no previous habits of estimating. We were repaid for our walk, however, when we came to the source of the Lutschine, which springs under an arch of ice in the glacier. The river runs clear and sparkling through the valley, while over the arch rests a mountain of ice, and beside it a valley of ice; not smooth and uniform, but in pyramids, and arches, and blocks of immense size, and between them clefts and ravines. The sight and the sound of the waters rushing, and the solemn immovability of the ice, formed a sublime contrast.

On the grass at the very foot of this glacier were some of the most delicious wood-strawberries I ever tasted.

At Interlaken we met Sneyd and Henrica in a very pleasant situation in that most beautiful country. We parted on the banks of the lake of Brienz. On this lake we had an hour's delightful sailing, and *put into* a little bay, and climbed up a mountain to see the cascade of the Giesbach, by far the most beautiful I ever beheld, and beyond all of which painting or poetry had ever given me any idea. Indeed it is particularly difficult if not absolutely impossible, to give a representation of cascades which depend for effect upon the height from which they fall, the rush of motion, the sparkling and foam of the water in motion, and the magnitude of the surrounding objects.

After passing the lake of Brienz, we came to the farfamed valley of Meyringen, which had been much cried up to us; but, whether from the usual perverseness of human nature, or from being spoiled by the luxury of cascades, valleys, and Alps we had previously seen, we were disappointed in it, though to do it justice, it has nine cascades.

We slept at a wooden inn, and rose at three; and, before four, mounted our horses, set off for the Brünig; and after having gone up La Flégère at Chamouny, the crossing the Brünig was a small consideration. Brava! Brava!

But—something happened to me and my horse; the result being that I went up the Brünig and down the Brünig on my two legs instead of on the horse's four, and was not the least tired with my three hours' scramble up and scramble down. At the little town of Sarnin we ate eggs and drank sour wine, and Mr. Moilliet, Fanny, and Harriet remounted their horses; Mrs. Moilliet, Emily, Susan, and I went in a char-à-banc of a different construction; not sitting sideways, but two phaeton seats, one behind the other, facing the horses. Such jolting, such *trimming* from side to side; but we were not overturned, and got out at the town of Stanzstadt, where after seeing in the dirtiest inn's dirtiest room a girl with a tremendous black eye, beside the two with which nature had favoured her, we took boat again about sunset, and had a two hours' delicious rowing across the lake of Lucerne, which I prefer to every other I have seen. The moon full and placid on the waters, the stars bright in the deep blue sky, the town of Lucerne shadowed before us with lights here and there in the windows. The air became still, and the sky suddenly clouded over; thunder was heard; bright flashes of lightning darted from behind the mountains and across the town, making it at intervals distinctly visible for a moment. It was dark when we landed, and we had to pass through two or three streets, servants, guides, bag, and baggage, groping our way; and oh, wretched mortals, went to the wrong place, and before we could reach the right one, down poured a waterspout of a shower on our devoted heads and backs. In five minutes, running as hard as we could, we were wet through and Fanny, in crossing the street and plucking at the guide's bundle for a cloak for me, was nearly run over, but stood it; and, all dripping, we reached our inn, Le Cheval Blanc. An hour spent in throwing off wet clothes, and putting on dry—tea, coffee—bed —bugs, and sleep, nevertheless.

We rejoined our landau and calèche at Lucerne, and proceeded in them to Zug, where there is a famous convent or frauenkloster, which escaped being destroyed during the Revolution, because the abbess and nuns established a school for the female children of the neighbourhood, where they still continue to teach them to read and work: Mme Gautier had desired us to go and see it, and to it we walked: rang at the bell, were told that the nuns were all in the refectory, and were asked to wait. The nuns' repast was soon finished, and one came with a very agreeable, open countenance and fresh, brown complexion, well fed and happy-looking, becomingly dressed in snow-white hood and pelerine and brown gown. Bowing courteously, she by signs—for she could speak neither French nor English—invited us to follow her, and led us through cloister and passage to the room of the boarders; not nuns, only there for their education. A pretty Italian girl, with corkscrew ringlets of dark hair, rose from her pianoforte to receive us, and spoke with much grace and self-complacency Italian French, and accompanied by way of interpreter our own conductress, who *motioned* us to the sitting-room, where nuns and pensioners were embroidering, with silk, cotton, chenille, and beads, various pretty, ugly, and fantastical, useless things. Luckily, none were finished at that moment, and their empty basket saved our taste from danger or disgrace.

I had spied in the corner of the Italian interpreter's apartment a daub of a print of the King and Queen of France taking leave of their family, with a German inscription; and thinking the Abbé Edgeworth had a good right to be in it, and as a kind of German notion of an Abbé appeared in the print, and something like Edgewatz in the German words, I put my finger on the spot, and bade the interpreter tell the nuns and the abbess, who now appeared, that we were nearly related to the Abbé Edgeworth, Louis XVI's confessor. This with some difficulty was put into the Italian's head, and through her into the nuns', and through them, in German, into the abbess' superior head. I heard a mistake in the first repetition, which ran, no doubt, through all the editions, viz., that we were *proche parens*, not to the King's confessor, but to the King! The nuns opened the whites of their eyes, and smiled regularly in succession as the bright idea reached them and the abbess—a good-looking soul, evidently of superior birth and breeding to the rest, all gracious and courteous in demeanour to the strangers.

A thought struck me—or, as Mr. Barrett, of Navan, expressed it, 'I took a notion, ma'am'—that Fanny would look well in a nun's dress; and boldly I went to work with my interpreter, who thought the request at first too bold to make; but I forced it through to nun the first, who backed and consulted nun the second, who at my instigation referred in the last appeal to the abbess, who, in her supreme good-nature, smiled and pointed upstairs; and straight our two nuns carried Fanny and me off with them up stairs and stairs, and through passages and passages, to a little nun's room—I mean a nun's little room—nice with flowers and scraps of relics and religious prints. The nuns ran to a press in the wall, and took out ever so many plaited coifs and bands, and examined them all carefully as birthnight beauty[1] would have done, to fix upon one which was most becoming. Nun the second ran for the rest of the habiliments, and I the while disrobed Fanny of her worldly sprigged cambric muslin and straw hat, which by the bye, nun the second eyed with a fond admiration which proved she had not quite forgotten this world's conveniences. The eagerness with which they dressed Fanny, the care with which they adjusted the frontlet, and tucked in the ringlets, and placed the coif on her head, and pulled it down to exactly the right becoming sit, was exceedingly amusing. No coquette dressing for Almack's[2] could have shewn more fastidious nicety, or expressed more joy and delight at the toilette's triumphant success. They exclaimed in German, and lifted up hands and eyes in admiration of Fanny's beautiful appearance in nun's attire. The universal language of action and the no less universal language of flattery was not lost upon me: I really loved these nuns, and thought of my Aunt Ruxton's nuns, who were so good to her. Down corridors and stairs we now led our novice, and the nuns showed her how to hold her hands tucked into her sleeves, and asked her name; and having learned it was Fanny, Frances, Sister Frances, were again overjoyed, because one of them was named Frances, the other was

[1] A beauty dressed to go to Court on the King's birthday.
[2] The fashionable London Assembly Rooms.

Agnes. When, between Sister Agnes and Sister Frances the first, Sister Frances the second entered the room, where we had left the abbess, Mrs. Moilliet, Emily, and Susan, they did not know Fanny in the least, and Harriet declared that, at the first moment, even she did not know her. Mrs. Moilliet told me she said to herself, 'What a very graceful nun is coming now!'

After all had gathered round, and laughed, and admired, the abbess signified to me, through our interpreter, that we could do no less than leave her in the convent with them, and grew so mighty fond of Fanny, that I was in as great a hurry to get her nun's dress off as I had been to get it on; and when I had disrobed her, I could not think of a single thing to give the poor nuns, having no pockets, and my bag left in the carriage! At last, feeling all over myself, I twitched my little gold earrings out of my ears, and gave one, and Fanny gave the other, to the two nuns; and Sister Frances and Sister Agnes fell on their knees to pray for and thank us.

[MS. missing—printed from *Mem.* ii. 105–11]

Maria Edgeworth to Mrs. Edgeworth

Pregny, Wednesday, 6th September, 1820

. . . I wish Mr. Chenevix had been writing another bad tragedy[1] instead of troubling himself to write accounts to alarm you about our wheels and passports at the very time when God knows you had enough to worry you without unnecessary fears. The wheels I must in justice to myself assure you were examined by no less than 3 competent judges Mr. Sismondi a noted traveller—Mr. François Delessert and Mr. Creed and the result of their separate and conjoint opinions coinciding with that of Mr. Tremblay Mr. Chenevix own coachmaker was that they would carry us in perfect safety to Geneva—that possibly a spoke might start in consequence of the heat of the weather in the most infirm of the wheels but that if it did only a clip would be necessary. In going from Paris to Mr. Chenevix (where I am sure I wish I never had gone and never will go again) the spoke did start for the weather was excessively hot. The wheel was mended with a clip at the next inn at Fontaine-

[1] R. Chenevix, *Two Plays: Mantuan Revels, a comedy in five acts; Henry VII, a tragedy, in five acts* (1812).

bleau. It never stirred afterwards. The wheels were examined by Pictet and Mr. Moilliets coachman the day after we came to Geneva—I proposing to get a new wheel if necessary—but I am assured that it is not necessary—that the wheels will carry us in perfect safety back to Paris and to London. All that is wanting Mr. Moilliets excellent steward has done—viz he has kept the wood wet which had shrunk with the heat. From what I have stated you may judge how ill Mr. C judged or how much he exaggerated for the dear pleasure of producing effect . . . If he had any good report to make of us I am sure he would not have troubled himself to write in such a hurry . . .

Maria Edgeworth to Mrs. Edgeworth, Honora Edgeworth and Mary Sneyd

Pregny, 7th September, 1820

With respect to Rosamond let me assure you that whatever you have done I shall like and I am convinced the public will like her the better for all you have added and taken away. You have my cordial thanks.

I now send a letter to Hunter and a tiny address to the reader. If you approve forward to Hunter to alter to your taste. My dear aunt Mary I think Hunter is right in numbering this book vol 1 and 2 because it may be sold as a separate work and the purchaser will not be compelled to purchase the 4 previous volumes of Early Lessons.[1] If he like to buy them I have no objection and these being numbered 1 and 2 makes no difficulty. It is a book that joins with Early Lessons but need not be purchased all together as parents might not find that it would suit their purses or wants or wishes for their children of such different ages as the two works comprehend.

I should further observe that the word Sequel does not exclusively mean *end*. It means also *Continuation* or *what follows* vide Johnson[2]—Therefore the title *Sequel to Early Lessons* does not

[1] *Early Lessons* was first published in 1801 in ten paper-covered parts. An edition in two volumes was not published until 1813. The *Continuation of Early Lessons* in two volumes came out in 1814. It contains continuations of the Rosamond, Frank, and Harry and Lucy sections of the original *Early Lessons*.

[2] Johnson's *Dictionary*.

preclude my hereafter publishing 'Frank Sequel to Early Lessons' and 'Harry and Lucy Sequel to Early Lessons'. If you my dear Triumvirate Council of critics and friends should nevertheless not be convinced by my fine reasoning I leave you to decide according to your better judgment. The only thing upon which I positively insist is—that you believe me to be your grateful and affec
Maria Edgeworth
Letter to Hunter—to be copied for me and signed and sent by Ho . . .

Maria Edgeworth to Mrs. Ruxton

Lausanne, Thursday, 14th September, 1820

. . . Yesterday we began our tour round the lake of Geneva, our third excursion in Swisserland. Mr. and Mrs. Moilliet and their two daughters were to have accompanied us as well as M. Dumont but Mrs. Moilliet was taken ill the day before we set out, and it was agreed that the Moilliets should meet us at Martigny or St. Maurice.

Dumont Fanny Harriet and I set out this fine day in one of the calèches of this country—a mixture of sociable and Irish jingle,[1] with some resemblance to a hearse but withal extremely comfortable and the fashion of the place—The hearse-like, flat wooden top protects from the burning sun which we had felt too powerful in chaise and landau. Here is our route—Lausanne—Vevay—Bex—St. Maurice—Martigny (if the Moilliets meet us there) and retracing a bit of the road, back to St. Maurice again—thence to St. Gingouph—Thanon—Évian—Geneva—Pregny.

After a delightful drive on the banks of the lake of Geneva of which I am grown exceedingly fond and after enjoying alternately all the variety of beautiful views—and the variety of M. Dumonts conversation, the sun set, for the sun will set, whatever is going on in the world—and it grew cold and late and dark before we arrived at Lausanne so that we could scarcely see by the few lamps strung across the streets here and there, the forms of the great black horses, scrambling and struggling up the almost perpendicular streets. How could you my dear Aunt ever bear it?

[1] A jingle is a covered two-wheeled carriage used in Ireland, a sociable a four-wheeled carriage with two seats facing one another and a box for the driver. In chaises and landaus the roof, which could be folded back, had sides to it.

We thought of you, when we heard the sound of the horses feet, slipping on the horrible pavement, and wondered how you had ever borne to live at Lausanne where you must have been put and kept in perpetual fear of your life. Lord Bellamonts famous description of the County of Cavan may well be applied to Lausanne—'Acclivity and declivity without any intervention of horizontality'. How the horses did manage to scramble up and down, without breaking our necks, I do not know. How horses must hate Lausanne! I am sure that when the travelled horses from different parts meet in their stable, the first thing they say one to the other is '*Were you ever at Lausanne! Don't you hate Lausanne? How could men build a town in such a place? What asses!* And how provoking all the time we are almost breaking our backs straining up those slippery places, to hear them talking all through the windows of picturesque beauty. If we were not the best creatures in the world, we should break their necks. I should like, brother, to see how they would look in their picturesque situations if I were to back or slip and let them roll down hill.'

Lausanne is so full of travellers nevertheless that we could scarcely find a night's lodging and after waiting at the top of the accursed slippery hill in the street where *all* the inns are placed M. Dumont and his servant hunting backwards and forwards to Faucon—Lion d'or &c which were all full to the garrets, we were humbled down to be mighty thankful at finding ourselves in the worst inns worst room. But indeed the beds were clean and good, and we are not grumblers. We were all very happy—drank coffee —and while bed chambers were preparing Dumont read us a pretty french piece *Le faux savant*.[1] He has been so good to bring with him four darling little volumes of French plays and will, we hope, read one to us every evening.

15th September—Our first object this morning was to see Mme de Montolieu, the author of Caroline de Lichtfield[2] for whom I had a

[1] The plays read during this tour were probably taken from *Théatre des auteurs du second ordre* (Paris, 1816–19, 40 vols.). *Le Faux Savant* (vol. 34) is there given as by Du Vaure. It was first performed in 1728. I am indebted to Dr. R. Shackleton for the identification of this work.

[2] *Caroline de Lichfield* (1786), 'publié par le traducteur de Werther', G. Deyverdun. Gibbon (*Letters*, ed. Norton, iii. no. 642) says 'Deyverdun and myself were patrons and judges of the manuscript.' New editions continued to appear in France till after the middle of the nineteenth century. Mme de Montolieu was also translator and part author of the expanded, French, version of Wyss's *Swiss Family Robinson*.

letter of introduction. She was not in her house at Lausanne, but we were told that we should find her at her house at Bussigny, a village about a league and a half from the town. After breakfast we set out for Bussigny. I pass over a long half hour's episode about Dumonts gold snuff box and his Henri's forgets and mistakes. We had a delicious fine morning and through romantic lanes and up and down hill and valley—bye-roads. We at last found ourselves in the middle of a ploughed field where road there was none—nor trace of any. The voiturier-coachman's pride of ignorance was at last obliged to give up, and to ask and beg our way to Bussigny a village of scattered Swiss cottages and houses, all irregularly built high upon rock, with far spreading prospects below. In the court before the door of a house which we were told was that of Mme de Montolieu we saw a lady of a tall upright fine, active looking figure with much the appearance of a gentlewoman but we could not think that this was Mme de Montolieu, because for the last half hour Dumont, when he grew impatient at losing our way had been saying that Mme de Montolieu must be almost too old to receive us—that she was very old 20–30 years ago—that she must be now *quatre vingts* at least and at last it came to *quatre-vingt-dix*! But the lady *in my eye* did not look above fifty and as flat backed as Mrs. O Beirne (my dear Mrs. O Beirne give my love to her)—asked what or who we wished to see. The moment I saw her eyes, I knew it was Mme de Montolieu and stretching down from the open carriage put the note of introduction into her hand, and upon it our card. She never opened the note but [the] instant her eye had glanced upon the card, she repeated the name with a voice of joyful welcome and opening her arms to receive me I jumped out of the carriage. She embraced me so cordially, received my sisters so kindly and M. Dumont so politely that we were all at ease; and acquainted and delighted with her before we were half way upstairs. While she went into an antichamber for a basket of peaches I had time to look at a set of prints which hung up in her little drawing room. They had struck me the moment we came in as scenes from Caroline de Lichtfield—Indifferent, old fashioned, provoking figures—of Count de Walstein and Caroline in the fashion of 30 years ago—with a large black hat and feathers, bouffant white handkerchief and black silk cloak dragged sideways for drapery's sake. While I was doing my best to turn this figure into my notion of Caroline de Lichtfield Mme de Montolieu returned and bid me not look at it. 'But' said she 'I will tell you how these prints came to be here where they ought not to be.' She then told us that they were English and had been given to her by Gibbon. He was the person who *published* Caroline de Lichtfield. She wrote it, without the least thought of publishing it, for the entertainment of an Aunt who was ill. During this Aunt's illness she happened to meet with the German story from which she took the first idea of the story. This was in three or four pages. 'I never,' said she, 'could invent an original story—but give me the first hint and I *can go on* and supply all the details and characters and feelings.' She went on to some purpose, and just when Caroline de Lichtfield was finished, Gibbon who was then residing at Lausanne became acquainted with her Aunt who shewed it to him. He seized upon the manuscript, said it must be published and published it without a name. She threatened him she said, that she would put his name to it and it would have done him honor. It ran in a few months through several editions. While it was in the first vogue, Gibbon went to London and saw these prints, which had then just come out. On his return to Lausanne he told Mme de Montolieu, that he had brought her a present of some prints from London but that he would give them to her only upon one condition that she would promise to hang them up and let them always hang up in her drawing room. After many vain efforts to find out what manner of things they might be, Gibbon and curiosity prevailed and the Comte de Walstein and Caroline de Lichtfield, in half a dozen scenes have been hanging up ever since as *per promise*.

N.B. It is said that Gibbon was in love with Mme de Montolieu, and that the story of his falling on his knees, to make his declaration, and not being able to get up again till the servant was rung for, to help him up belongs of right to Mme de Montolieu instead of to Mme Necker.[1] Far be it from me to decide on such a delicate point—I can only state the 'on dits' and this was averred to me by Mme de Montolieu's sister in law. At all events I am sure that Mme de Montolieu is a woman with whom he or any man of taste

[1] The tale is probably apocryphal. It may originate in the occasion in 1792 when the Duchess of Devonshire in mock show dubbed Gibbon 'chevalier': *Letters*, ed. Norton, iii, no. 813, n. 2.

might easily have fallen most comfortably and desperately in love. She must have been a beautiful woman with that kind of beauty which depends upon mind and expression, more than upon features and which therefore lasts in age. She told me that she is 70 —but she does not look above 50. She has fine dark, enthusiastic eyes, a quickly varying countenance, no affected enthusiasm, no practised manner either in sentiment or politeness but well bred and naturally *feeling* and *eager* in conversation—full of life—and with all the warmth of heart and imagination, which is thought to belong only to early youth. She often put me in mind of my dear Aunt in this respect. She is quite free from authorship vanity, and from affected humility—so much so that she speaks of herself with a freedom and simplicity which a fool might mistake for vanity. But she really has not *time* to be vain, even if she had inclination. Thoughts and feelings pour on so rapidly in her mind that they cannot stop, as with egotists, always at self. She thinks and feels so much for other people and about such a variety of entertaining things, that she has not leisure to think even of *not appearing to think of herself*.

You know there are persons with whom every subject of conversation you can start, falls soon and flat or trails on without leading to anything—and others with whom the slightest word wakens ideas, and starts fresh game for the mind. Mme de Montolieu is one of the fresh-game people and besides she is one of those lucky romantic persons, to whom adventures happen wherever they go . . .

Meantime, leaving these episodes, and going on with our own affairs, we went all over Mme de Montolieu's nice Swiss cottage house, and from every trellice window saw the beautiful views of lake wood and mountain and we went into a wooden balcony gallery reaching from one side of the house to the other. At one end of this was a seat and the table at which she had been writing when we arrived—at the other end of the gallery was a sort of bower of trellice work, raised up a few steps, with a window from which the distant road, and distant country could be seen. This, as we all exclaimed, must have been Caroline de Lichtfields pavillon . . . At parting I had the assurance to ask Mme de Montolieu to give me a book, as a keepsake. She instantly ran upstairs, bidding me follow, and choose from her library any book I liked.

I pounced upon Caroline de Lichtfield—But this was the only one she could not give me, she confessed—and I suspect this copy was given to her by Gibbon. She gave me another work of hers which was new to me, and I hope will be to you 'Les Chateaux Suisses'.[1]

At parting, I said, but no such thing—we often took leave, but were loath to depart. M. Dumont luckily asked if she could direct us to the road to a fine old château in her neighborhood, which we had been told was particularly well worth seeing—*Viernon*. It was her brothers she said, and if we pleased she would go with us herself and introduce us. She was sure he would be &c. The walk was through a wood and it was about a mile. The carriage was sent round by the high road to meet us, at the house, and we set out. Mme de Montolieu walks with the activity of Mrs. O Beirne. Far before the rest of the party she walked on and I kept up with her, listening with delight to the history she gave me of her youth. Her brothers place is indeed romantically beautiful . . . Just as we came within sight of a cascade, and a wooden bridge, which crossed the stream, a little pug dog came running down the hill at a turn of the walk, betraying that some one was near—then running back, as if afraid he should be seen by strangers. Mme de Montolieu immediately pursued the dog and called to her brother for it was the Baron de Polier and Mme de Polier. She ran on, explained who we were, and they came forward, receiving us graciously—The Baron a thin tall, gentlemanlike, German, pale and insipid looking as a turnep—Madame, nothing remarkable except an air of languid, affected ill health and sentimentality. She was an Englishwoman and to my surprise I found that she was niece to an old schoolfellow and friend of my fathers Mr. Mundy of Markeaton. Her mother Mrs. Nicholson, I well remember to have seen in 1813 at Mr. Mundy's. She was a woman of charming manners. It is a pity her daughter did not inherit them. Dumont after hearing two or three phrases, and seeing two or three languishments took such an aversion to her that he came sidling over the bridge to me, to whisper that we should be late, that we had better not go any further &c. But kind Mme de Montolieu was so eager that we should go on to the house with her brother

[1] *Les Châteaux suisses* (1816), a sort of romantic guidebook with a story (generally fictitious) about each château.

that on I went—leaving the insipid Baron (an *ultra* moreover) on Dumont's hands, in a remorseless manner . . .

The only rooms in the house we saw were the hall, an antichambre and salon . . . Eat peaches and grapes—and fine wines were poured out for Dumont but not even these could avail. He was never happy till he saw me get up to go away . . . No sooner were we seated in the carriage than Dumont vented his long suppressed indignation against Madame's affectation—mimicking in the drollest manner her *conjuring me by all the affection I bore her*!—the affection of five minutes growth—and then he told us the reason of his dislike. She is said to behave very ill to M. de Polier's daughter by a former marriage—to this Mme de Blonay and her sister. 'Ah cette *sensibilité* qui rend malheureux tout ce qui l'environne—toute une famille! Comme je la déteste!' said he. The Baron had wearied Dumont with a history of—but I will not weary you with it. Nothing more happened this day, except that we had a very bad dinner, at our bad inn at Lausanne, which was by no means a matter of indifference to poor Dumont. But he was very good humored about it and it did not prevent him from reading to us this evening another petite pièce Le Somnambule,[1] very laughable when well read.

Next morning at 7—breakfast and then a beautiful drive from Lausanne to Vevay . . . Horses like this town much better than Lausanne but I do not—excellent inn however and very good table d'hôte. It is very much the custom for travellers to dine at table d'hôte now, and it is very entertaining. This day besides several Genevese there was a party of Irish—a clergyman his wife son and a young lady. Such a vulgarian as the son I think I never did meet with at any table, or table d'hôte. Some time you shall *hear* and *see* them all to the life but I must tell you a little bit, by way of memorandum for the rest.

The father hearing me say that I thought that a Mr. Mulock, who has been giving lectures lately on English literature at Geneva was an Irishman fell into such a rage, that he was as white as paper and trembling all over. Mistaking me for an Englishwoman who despised and wanted to attack the Irish, he asked if I

[1] In *Théâtre des auteurs du second ordre* (vol. 36) *Le Somnambule* is attributed to Pont de Veyle. The Comédie Française records suggest that the comte de Caylus and M. Salle were the authors. The play was first performed in 1739.

was one of *them* that supposed nobody could write well in Ireland —If I was one of them English, that thought there was no good writers in Ireland. I protested that I should be very sorry to hold such an opinion but on he and his wife went. The lady said she was 'sure we were some of those English who fancied the Irish had wings on their shoulders'. They had not the least guess who I was, and we had excellent diversion. M. Dumont and Mr. and Mrs. Roche friends of his from Geneva were all so amused at the scene. I mentioned *Burke* for instance, as a writer that did honor to Ireland but the man would have nothing to do with Burke or *Bourke*, as he called him. 'Ma'am Mr. Burke was no writer, he writ very little.' 'Only five quarto volumes Sir.' 'Not at all Ma'am them are *speeches* and whats the name, the sublime and Beautiful. Dumont mentioned Burke's Essay on the French Revolution.[1] 'Oh! that indeed—But still he wrote but little.' And when I suggested that some of his speeches were written orations, he flew into another rage—'As if I did not know—how the members of parliaments speeches were taken down.' He was asked what Mr. Mulock had said in his lectures of the modern writers on Education and then he repeated and rejudged all he had said of Miss Edgeworth &c. He never found out who we were. We found out that his name was [Barton].

The master of the Inn afterwards told us, that these people had behaved so ill at the table d'hôte the preceding day, putting their forks and their fingers into the dishes, that two French ladies had been obliged to leave the table—and when they asked the master of the inn the next day at what hour the table d'hôte would be he answered 'There will be none at any hour for you Sir at this house unless you can behave at it more politely.' This I believe was addressed to the son. We were ashamed of our countrymen—but they seemed to belong to 60 years ago . . .

[1] *The Cambridge Bibliography of English Literature* lists sixty items published separately, nine being speeches. *A Philosophical Enquiry into the Origin of our Ideas of the Sublime and the Beautiful* was first published in 1756 and *Reflections on the Revolution in France* in 1790.

Harriet Edgeworth to the Revd. D. A. Beaufort

Pregny, près de Genève, 19th September, 1820

[Sketches and description of types of char à bancs]

. . . The common carts used to convey manure are very low—long and narrow exactly like ammunition carriages and in these the manure is beautifully packed so as to contain a great quantity. These are at present to be met in great numbers preparing the ground for the autumn crops. Besides these they have large barrels filled with all the washing of their cowhouses stables and kitchens and these barrels are carried out to the fields very easily in the morning and spread over the meadows, or upon the fallow ground just before the corn is sown—All of which arrangements are exceedingly gratifying to the eyes but not at all to the nose. The smell of their beautifully packed dunghills pursues one in every house belonging to every rank in Switzerland—Very differently from a common Irish dunghill a heap just thrown together like a haycock. These are made flat in long laires beat down tight together and kept perfectly smooth and level. Besides the ever varying beauties of the country the observing the variety of their instruments and employments in the different cantons is very entertaining.

Near here in the cantons of Berne Unterwalden Freybourg and Lucerne they use immense fat bullocks to plough and draw but the traces are fastened to their horns and their heads are forced down and pushed together by a flat board placed across their necks. In the cantons of Argovie Basle and Soleure they draw with yokes and their heads are not so painfully fastened down together, but they more generally make use of cows which it always seems a waste to use in carriages. They are more respected here. The farmer who holds Mr. Moilliets land has 21 cows. Their house is nicely paved—deep channel passes just behind the cows, through which a rapid stream runs, which when stopped overflows the whole house and carries off all the dirt. It then runs off through the yard into various channels as the different parts of the field want it and the richness of the grass along its edge sufficiently shews how efficaceous it is. The cows are kept in the whole year except one summer month which they are allowed to spend in the country. They are brought out every morning to drink at the fountain close to their house and are immediately put back into their stalls where they are fastened by chains loosely round the neck.

The butter they produce is very good but very different from Irish butter. The cream is very much like milk but is always sweet. These cows are fed on lucerne, the 6th crop of which since May is now mowing. They also have a variety of red clover which grows almost as abundantly. Indeed the fertility all over the country is wonderful and the prodigious cultivation which is carried on up to the very tops of the highest and steepest mountains is astonishing. Corn of all sorts is not much to be seen but we have had a constant hay harvest for no sooner had we seen it finished in the open plains than we had it in the shaded valleys and it is not yet ended on the rocky mountains where there are to be seen little green islands among the masses of grey stone covered with men in their various shaped dresses and women in their many colored costumes looking Maria says like little bits of Arcadia which have been kept since the golden age—and so they appear at a distance and so you think as long as you look at their picturesque occupations, their romantic cottages and brilliant sky—but when you look nearer and see the darkness, the dirt and the poverty of these cottages, when you perceive their countenances sallow with ill health their figures disgusting with immense goitres and their whole appearance odious from the long pipe which hangs eternally from their mouths, when you perceive how different the winter of the year must be, when you know that often seven months of that year must be spent almost under ground barricaded by the snow from all light air and occupation, one ceases to envy their lot.

But of course there are exceptions to this—I have seen men at work without a pipe. I have seen many young people fresh colored and without goitres and I have been in two clean houses. And they have many advantages over the poor in our countries—particularly in the vineyard parts—for they have constant occupation and an almost certainty of gain from their labor for it rarely happens that a whole wine harvest fails . . . They have hardly any employment which machinery can rob them of and they have plenty of hemp for the women to work during the winter. I have hardly seen any flax but this hemp is dried very much like it and then very nicely hackled by a little frame into which is fastened either by a hinge or on a pin a moveable piece which is cut into three sharpish edges like a gauffring stick[1] only flat—on the top of the frame is the same. This hemp is laid on that and is thus hackled less laboriously than with us. Where their thread when spun is woven into linen I do not know for I have never seen more than two looms in all my travels. They have also the advantages of having hardly any manufactures which would rise or fall in value by every change of the surrounding countries, while they were destroying the health and happiness of all employed in them—All the materials of comfort in abundance—profusion of stone and wood—Fruit trees broken down by the weight of fruit—potatoes and vegetables of all sorts in quantities . . .

Fanny Edgeworth to Honora Edgeworth

Chateau de Pregny près de Genève, 21st September, 1820,
Thermometer Far.t 52 Cent. 12 Reau.r 9

. . . M. Dumont in buoyant spirits kept us in an almost uninterrupted laugh the whole way to Rolle where he preferred dining at the table d'hôte . . . Now Honora I expect that you should begin with surprise and a little incredulity at all I have said of the delight of this journey, but that you should end by no small degree of envy. Never from early morning till late in the evening—eating or fasting was M. Dumont out of humor or the silent stupid person you described him at Bowood—The gayest of the party and making amusement of all the little nonsenses we observed. Could anything be more constantly amusing to Harriet and me—we were completely audience and Maria and he exactly like people on the stage . . .

. . . Politics are not at all the fashion in this house and it is only by little hearsay driblets that I have heard that there is a revolution in Portugal and that Austria detestable government which has always been cursed with power and desire to oppress all neighbouring nations—is now sending 40,000 men into Italy.[2] This

[1] An implement for making starched, crimped frills.

[2] Fanny E refers to an army-based revolt which started in Oporto. The rebels demanded a free constitution. A revolt with a similar aim took place in Naples and the dispatch of Imperial troops followed.

alarms the English who are there. Many are returning and many have stopped half way here. Geneva is overflowing with them.

Harriet and I have read with great pleasure and less difficulty than we expected Alfieris tragedy of Maria Stuarda. It is beautiful. Did you read it? The following lines I must copy for you as being so applicable to our Queen—addressed to Mary speaking of her life—

obbrobriosi giorni
Quivi favola al mondo onta dal trono,
Scherni di tutti, orribilmente vivi[1]—

We began today Mme de Souza's new novel[2] and thought it pretty.

During the French Revolution the Marquis de Pastoret hid himself. He told Benjamin Constant 'I could think of no place but in the narrow angle under the stairs among the brushes &c. There I remained two days and half bent double trying every posture to ease myself.' 'Qu'un homme a peu d'esprit,' said B. Constant, 'de se donner tant de peine pour sauver la vie de M. de Pastoret.'

. . . Tell Mamma that since we have seen M. Sismondi and twice without liking him. His countenance is very disagreeable and what I have heard of his character rather contemptible. Notwithstanding all he has written about liberty he went in the most servile manner cringing to Napoleon.[3] M. Dumont says there are very good things in Les Républiques Italiennes[4] which when he shews them to us I will mark for you . . .

Maria Edgeworth to Sophy Ruxton

Malagny—Mrs. Marcet's country house, 26th September, 1820

. . . We visited the château de Chillon and the dungeon of Bonnivard—which in summer time is after all very comfortable. If I

[1] *Maria Stuarda*, Act v, Sc. i. The words are from the prophetic speech by Lamorre (Murray) to Mary:

. . . there drag along,
The throne's disgrace, the laughing stock of men,
Scorned e'en in wretchedness, opprobrious days . . .

The Tragedies of Alfieri, trans. E. A. Bowring (1876), i. 575.

[2] *Mademoiselle de Tournon* (1820).

[3] Sismondi was disgusted at the ineptitude of the royalist government in 1814, and wrote in favour of Napoleon after the return from Elba.

[4] *Histoire des républiques italiennes* (16 vols., 1809–18).

were to take lodgings in a dungeon I should prefer this to any I have ever seen because it is high and dry and with beautiful groined arches and no bad smells and there is ample room and verge enough—and there is light enough through the loop holes to read by. I read with ease after I had been a few moments accustomed to the dimness of the place a manuscript page which is fastened up against one of the pillars and which gives the melancholy history of Bonnivard. Lord Byrons name and *coat of arms* are cut in the pillar over this page and the guide remembers well his coming here and asking a number of questions and taking notes of dates and places &c.[1] The two brothers of Bonnivard however whose deaths are so pathetically described in the poem are poetical not historical persons. In the true story no mention is made of any brothers. After reading the Château de Chillon again with all the impression of the scenery fresh in my mind I think it most pathetic and sublime! How can that man have perverted so much feeling as was originally given to him . . .

I hope my aunt and you have been at St. Maurice? If you have not I cannot give you an idea of the surprise and delight we felt at the first sight of the view going down through the archway. On comparing our tastes and opinions we settled this night at St. Maurice that the first view of Mont Blanc was the most sublime we ever saw and the first view of the valley of St. Maurice the most beautiful. But what a miserable, dirty, melancholy deserted looking town!—with the houses half roofed—windows broken—walls cracked—habitations, if habitations they may be called, half sticking in and half out of the rock, like the caves of the Troglodytes—only these are 5 or six stories high. The inhabitants of this place are a mixture of the most frightful, withered, blackened, ragged goitred, depressed, ill looking creatures I ever beheld and some of the freshest prettiest women of the finest most active figures. These come down I am told from the mountains and when they remain long in the valley they lose their beauty. This place with all its picturesque beauty appears to be a sacrifice to disease and ignorance and superstition . . .

After Fanny had sketched from the window of our inn at St. Maurice a group of children who were amusing themselves with

[1] Byron's *Prisoner of Chillon* describes the long imprisonment by the Duke of Savoy of the Genevan patriot François de Bonnivard (d. *c.* 1570).

sweeping the street with a broom much larger than themselves, and after wise reflections on seeing a child learning the balance of its own body sitting on a window in such perilous situation as would have made a fine nursemaid scream and a fond mother faint, we finished our evening by hearing one of the delightful little French plays which Dumont read incomparably well—*Les Châteaux en Espagne*[1] . . .

Upon the whole this last tour, taking in the pleasure of the French plays every evening and Dumonts agreeable conversation in the carriage, besides all the beauties of the views, was the pleasantest of all our excursions—No accident, no difficulty—nothing of any kind to complain of except that screaming woman.[2] We had settled that Dumont would be a helpless traveller and perhaps also nice and cross about his dinners—But far from it he was very helpful and his man Henri was so attentive that we had no manner of trouble. As to the dinners some were baddish and Dumont certainly did not relish that but he was not cross and he recovered his spirits always time enough to read the French play. I forgot to mention the name of the last he read 'La Pupille'[3]—which was the least entertaining. It is either taken from 'The Guardian' or '*The Guardian*[4]' is stolen from it. It is insipid and not comic.

We dined two days after our return *home* at Coppet with the duke and Duchess de Broglie M. de Staël Miss Randall (the English lady who always lives with them) M. de Stein who was the Austrian minister for many years—a great diplomatist—very able in that line I am told—but too much of a diplomatist to be entertaining in ordinary conversation—a black-wooden heavy face. His daughters were wonderfully handsome considering they were his. A M. Pictet Diodati was also at this dinner—a very sensible man, but who speaks so indistinctly that half he says is unintelligible. Mme de Staël said of him. 'If one could take hold of Pictet Diodati's neckcloth and give it a good shaking what a

[1] A play by Colin d'Harleville, first performed in 1789 (*Théâtre des auteurs du second ordre*, vol. 22).

[2] A drunken woman who kept them awake at night.

[3] A play by Fagan, first performed in 1734 (*Théâtre des auteurs du second ordre*, vol. 34).

[4] *The Guardian* was translated and adapted by Garrick from *La Pupille*. It was acted in 1759.

number of good things would come out.' A Mlle Pictet Diodati of whom you would not and need not care to hear and Dumont and a brother of Rocca's (an inferior person) were all the company. The Duc de Broglie who had never talked to me before was very agreeable and the Duchess is always agreeable. So in *my* opinion is the Baron de Staël who is in general undervalued. He has promised to shew me Gibbon's love letters to his grandmother Mme Necker[1] before she was married. They regularly ended with this phrase 'Je suis Mademoiselle avec les sentimens qui font le désespoir de ma vie' &c.

We came to Mrs. Marcets last Friday and have spent our time most happily with this most excellent friend. I never saw any authoress so free from vanity and so good for all the common affairs of this life—especially in making her house a comfortable home for her friends as well as delightful for acquaintance strangers and foreigners who continually are passing to and from Geneva into Italy. Dr. Marcet has gained much upon our affections during these last days spent in the house with him. We see that his children are all exceedingly fond of him and that he is quite their companion and friend. They go laughing and skipping to meet him the moment he comes in and we perceive that he has a degree of simplicity of character and good nature which we never till now rightly understood. How many forms mauvaise honte takes!—*conceit* among the rest.

The children have all been happily busy in making with their father a large paper fire balloon[2] 16 feet diameter by 20 feet high. A large company were invited a few evenings ago to see it mount. It was a fine evening. The balloon was filled on the green before the door of the house—The lawn slopes down to the lake and opposite to it magnificent Mont Blanc the setting sun shining on its summit. After some heart-beating about a hole in the top of the balloon through which the smoke was seen to issue—an evil omen!—[it] went up successfully and the little firework which it carried suspended to it went off when it was high overhead—the

[1] Suzanne Curchod who became Mme Necker and the mother Mme of de Staël had been engaged to Gibbon, who threw her over on the orders of his father. For the letters, see *Letters of Gibbon*, ed. Norton, i, app. ii. A letter of 24 Aug. 1758 ends 'avec les sentiments qui font le tourment de ma vie'.

[2] For ME's use of the fire balloon incident, see her *Harry and Lucy Concluded* (1824), iv. 82–115.

falling sparks of the rocket looking like falling stars. The balloon mounted exactly to the height of a mile. I say *exactly* because Pictet had an instrument of a new invention with which he measured the distance exactly.[1] This instrument I name to you for future fireside explanation. The air is so clear that at a height of a mile we saw the balloon most clearly. One circumstance was new —The sun had set but we saw the reflection of the sun beautifully on one side of the balloon so that it looked like a globe half ice half fire half moon half sun self suspended in mid air. There was no ray of sun at this time on Mont Blanc and yet Mont Blanc you know is much more than a mile high and we were sure (by the instruments measurement) that the balloon was only a mile high. Then how came it that we saw no ray on Mont Blanc? Because the balloon was much nearer the sun than was Mont Blanc. Perhaps this will instantly occur to you but it cost Pictet at least 3 minutes thought.

My dear Sophy you will feel without my saying it how much this balloon—and the children and the father must have recalled past happiness.

I have not yet mentioned I believe M. Pictet de Rochemont who wrote the latter to my father about Prac Ed[2]—brother to our friend the Professor. By the way I have always in writing and speaking applied the title of Professor wrong between these brothers. Our old friend is Professor P—and his brother is not a professor. He has been of late years much employed in diplomacy. He has a high character for integrity, patriotism and talents. He is

[1] This may have been one of the devices in David Brewster's *Treatise on New Philosophical Instruments for various purposes in the Arts and Sciences* (Edinburgh, 1813), bk. iii, 'On Instruments for Measuring Distances'. Chap. 1 describes a telescope for measuring distances: the action depends on achieving a clear focus of a distant object by manipulating three lenses. The focal position varying according to distance, it is possible to work out a figure from a scale engraved along the sides of the telescope tubes. Another device involves measuring the angles attained by an object, so that if its actual diameter is known the distance can be worked out from the angle. Brewster was a friend of Pictet. ME describes instruments for measuring height in *Harry and Lucy Concluded* (1825), i. 23—a portable barometer, which is impossible in this context—and in *Frank. A Sequel* (1822), i. 190. The latter reference deals with a theodolite with a telescopic attachment, and it is perhaps of an improved form of theodolite that she speaks in this letter.

[2] Charles Pictet de Rochemont translated *Practical Education* into French, first for *La Bibliothèque Britannique* (1798–9, vols. ix–xii) and then as a separate book published at Geneva in 1800.

indeed a man of superior abilities and you will not wonder that I think highly of him and feel gratefully towards him when I tell you that he has taken most kind pains to translate and select the best passages from my fathers Memoirs for the Bibliothèque Universelle which he conducts. Yesterday evening we spent at his house where there was a large party—and where for the first time we met Mme Necker de Saussure—The lady who wrote Mme de Staëls Life[1] and of whom Mme de Staël said 'Elle a tous les talens qu'on me suppose et toutes les vertues qui me manquent'. She is much more agreeable than her book. Her conversation and manners are quite free from the pomposity and *preparation* which appear in the style of that book. In manner, figure, countenance she reminded me of our beloved Mrs. Moutray—Mme Necker too is deaf and she has something of the same resignation free from suspicion in her expression of countenance when she is not spoken to and the same gracious attention to the person who speaks to her. She heard us when close to her ear without my raising my voice and as I sat on the sofa beside her and M. Pictet de Rochemont on the other side leaned back behind her, close to her ear. Also she heard what we said to each other as well as what we said to her. What was said by the crowd of other people in the room never interrupted us for a moment . . .

Château de Coppet—Thursday 28th September
8 oclock A. B. Ante Breakfast—I should have said A D
*A*nte *D*éjeuner—but I thought it might be wrong

We came here yesterday to spend 4 days. Here we are in the very apartments in which M. Necker slept—opening into what is now a library but what was once a theatre in which Mme de Staël used to act like her own Corinne.[2] Yesterday evening as I was sitting in the arm chair on the right hand of the fire where the Duchesse de Broglie had placed me, one of the oldest friends of the family M. de Bonstetten taking his chair beside me, whispered 'You are now in the exact spot in the very chair in which Mme de Staël used to sit!' He gave me an account of his last interview with her. I dare not begin to tell you any of his anecdotes of her—this would lead me too far—I must reserve them for fireside converse. Her friends were excessively attached to her. This old man of seventy talked of

[1] See above, p. 181 n. 4.

[2] Heroine of her novel of that name.

her with tears in his eyes and with all the sudden change of countenance and twitchings of the muscles which mark strong uncontrollable feeling. There is something inexpressibly melancholy!—awful! in this house in these rooms where the thought continually recurs '*Here genius was*! Here *was* Ambition! Love! All the struggles of the fury passions! Here *was* Mme de Staël!

The respect paid to her memory by her son and daughter and by the duc de Broglie is touching. The little Rocca 7 years old is an odd, cold, prudent old-man sort of child—most unlike the son you would have expected from such parents—yet one little circumstance makes me think he has more sensibility and less selfishness than his manner indicates. Mme de Broglie finding him crying by himself the first day he came from some other place to Coppet asked him why he cried. 'I don't know—I am always so—when I change place—when I go from an old place to a new.' 'Then you will be unhappy when I take you to Paris with us next week?' 'No—I shall not.' 'Why?' 'Because though I change place I shall be with the *same persons*.' He speaks with the caution and exactness of a grown up man but with a mumbling indistinct full-tongued watery pronunciation as Tom Knox used to do when I first saw him at Black Castle and when I used to turn to you to explain what he meant to utter. Genius may come out of him yet! But it will be hard to get it out.

M. Sismondi spent the whole of yesterday and his wife dined here. He is black and ugly and heavy in conversation but touch on certain historical subjects and he will talk like a book—like his own book. We all agree that *we* should be very sorry to be his wife. I know I should go to sleep some day when he was talking or waken some morning tired to death of him. But whoever likes his 'Italian republics' might like him. The company here yesterday were—a Judge whose name I forget and of whose conversation I heard O—M. Rocca brother to the Rocca—handsome—but I know no more and doubt whether more is to be known—a tutor—and M. Dumont—and M. *Bonstetten*—very entertaining with anecdotes of all the last century. At his house at Geneva all strangers of note are seen—gratis. Three Saladins, father—mother—daughter, awkward spent 2 hours of the evening here and it was a relief to see their vacant chairs when they went away—and a delight to see these pushed away and to see the closing circle round the sofa and round the fire, when Mme de Broglie, the duke, M. de Staël, Miss Randall, Dumont and Bonstetten all joining comfortably told witty or comic or interesting anecdotes and talked on till eleven o clock all manner of good nonsense.

But I ought to tell you something *sensible*. The Emperor of Austria has been such a fool as to put a stop to the improvements in education in all the parts of Italy submitted to the Austrians. They had established an *École d'enseignement mutuel*[1] at Naples but he has destroyed and forbidden it.

At Berne you know there used to be an excommunication of Caterpillars—and a regular advocate du diable to plead for the caterpillars before sentence was passed. This year at Pescia[2] there was a bull published against the caterpillars there and they were formally excommunicated. The Excommunicators wisely waited till the caterpillars had eaten everything they could eat—pretty sure that they would then march off—as they did as soon as the sentence of excommunication was pronounced—much to the edification of the people. When the king of Sardinia was re-established and returned to his palace and when his gardener first went into his garden he ran up to the plants which the French had planted and plucking them up by the roots he threw them indignantly from him exclaiming '*Va t'en Jacobin!*' And he stamped all over the beds. Better still the Prince of fools, the king of Naples—he met some of his own troops one day when he was out hunting and not knowing who they were, much less to whom they belonged he stopped to ask what and who they were. 'Your Majesty's own troops.' 'Well, what are you going to do?' 'Please your Majesty, to fight your Majesty's enemies—the French.' 'Ah oui allez! allez! Vous serez joliment 'rangés (arrangés)'—*You will be well settled*—or *you'll be well drubbed* . . .

Your descriptions of the winter gardens in Swisserland made me anxious to see one—and so I did at Mrs. Marcets but hers disappointed me—for hers is only a great house with an earth floor in which cauliflowers &c &c are planted in rows for winter . . . N B I have been up three hours—Coffee, Thank heaven! is brought to us in our bedchambers—breakfast—déjeuner à la fourchette does not come till between 11 and 12.

[1] A school established on the monitorial system of Bell and Lancaster.

[2] Sismondi's mother lived near Pescia and the story is probably his.

Maria Edgeworth to Honora Edgeworth

Château de Pregny, 1st October, 1820

I received your letter about Rosamond late last night and I answer it early this morning. How could it happen that we could *all* be mistaken in counting off the pages I do not know and I was a little provoked with Hunter for not having counted it himself and for not letting you sooner know the result and the whole of his wants and wishes. But this feeling of vexation or disappointment believe me lasted but a moment and my mind fixes on *what is to be done*? and *how can it be best done*? Impertinent my dear Honora! How could I think you impertinent for giving me fresh proof by the eagerness and truth of your counsels of your anxiety for my best interests?

In the first place I agree with Hunter that it would be better to omit the play and to supply its place with narrative. If I recollect rightly it was about fifty pages of printing. I have never yet learnt what proportion my present MS page bears to the printed page of the present book. Will you let me know this as you have now I believe the means in your hands. Mr. Hunter says that this 'Rosamond' including the play will contain only 504 pages that is 250 pages each volume. I have looked at several volumes here of about the size of the Continuation of Early Lessons and find that some contain 220 some 250 and as to mere size and look of the book I see no inconvenience.

Having completed to the best of my abilities the plan for Rosamond and according to the material made it *in good proportion* I am unwilling to add 150 pages which would put the whole plan out of proportion and instead of the gradual improvement and progress which appear in Rosamond's character there would be *a going backwards and forwards* or a repetition of examples of faults and follies which would tire the reader. There should not I think be more of these volumes. Books at this age should not be detailed. As far as this Rosamond goes the subjects are new but I have worked up my materials and my plan and for the utility of the book the amusement of the public and my own reputation it is of consequence that no make-weight pages should be added; no interloping subjects foisted in to break the unity of design. Suppose the public have 25 pages less in each of these volumes than in the Continuation of Early Lessons? What then? Who cares? But if there were 25 pages in each volume that broke the interest it would lower the value of the whole. Were I at home and quite at leisure to add 200 pages to Rosamond I would not do it. I think it would be spoiling the work. Hunter says that he could not charge 3 shillings per volume for volumes that contained only 250 pages each—That he could charge only 5 shillings for the book and that he should not be able to reimburse himself for the large price which he is to give me of 500 Gs. When you have read the copy of my letter to Hunter you will see how I propose to obviate this difficulty. I would infinitely rather give up a hundred pounds than run the hazard of hurting the whole plan and effect of Rosamond by lengthening it 200 pages . . .

The public who have seen *Rosamond* advertised I am told are impatient for it and for so small a work I do not think it would be prudent to let hope be long deferred—for you know the consequence and the feeling of 'After all the delay is *this all*?' It is by no means necessary for me to be *at home* or in any particular place to invent, or *write*. You were satisfied as you all assured me with the *little palanquin addition*[1] I sent you and I trust that I shall be able to please you my dear friends with what I shall write to supply the place of the play. This must come after the Polignac story. I will make use of the traveller to tell about Bautte's wonders and Chamouny and will introduce some useful deductions about indulgence in taste for ingenious trinkets—the application of talents, knowledge necessary for enjoying travelling etc.

I need not further explain my plan only mark to you where the addition must come in. This will be entirely in the second volume. Therefore the first will end exactly where you have decided that it *should* end and Hunter may at his leisure go on printing and send you the proof sheets up to the Polignac chapter. I desire him to send the remainder of the Mss. back to you that you may see that my intended insertion and the end shall hang properly together. Be under no apprehension my dear friend that I should hurt my

[1] *Rosamond. A Sequel*, ii. 58–76. The Polignac story can be found on pp. 6–9. Lady de Ros told her the story of the escape of the Polignac brothers from Vincennes after they were imprisoned for their share in the conspiracy of Georges to assassinate Napoleon in 1804. Chamouny was not used but Bautte's toys are described in The Bracelet of Memory, op. cit. ii. 130. Jean François Bautte (1772–1837) was a well-known Genevan watch-maker.

health or hurry myself by writing this addition to supply the place of the play. It would hurt my spirits much more to feel that I had left undone any part of what I ought to do to fulfill my original engagement or intention. I must only deny myself the pleasure of writing letters home and I gain by this abstinence all the time necessary for my purpose—and you will lose nothing for F and H will write constantly.

Maria Edgeworth to Honora Edgeworth

Château de Pregny, 18th October, 1820

Here are 50 pages to supply the place of the little play—I shall be very happy if you and my mother and my dear Aunt Mary and all my dear home critics approve of them. You will put it in its right place. Take care the traveller is not *gone*.[1] I trust that the quantity is sufficient to fill the place of the play—if not let me know exactly what is wanting and I will *fall to*—having another sketch in reserve in my head and I can if required fill it up during the time when my sisters take their dancing lessons at Paris. We have resolved never to let in any mortal before breakfast.—We were worried before 10 o clock last summer. We will never open doors till eleven . . .

Tell Lovell I am very much obliged to him for sending money for me—he is the most punctual and kind of brothers. His friend M. de la Rive who is a merry mortal is to dine here today. He speaks of him as every body who knew him does with the greatest regard. M. Maunoir asked me for him with expressions of great kindness. I reproach myself for never having gone to see some booksellers wife at Geneva who is aching and has been 3 months aching to see the sister of M. Lovell Edgewartz. M. de la Rive made a good distinction the other day between *Charmante* and *intéressante* applied to a woman. He says charmante always looks to the future—intéressante to the past. A femme charmante—may charm you—Look forward to that—a femme intéressante—is to him only interesting by the loves adventures and misfortunes she may have had. He says he never likes a femme *intéressante* unless she has a story to make up for the depredations of time.

[1] i.e. gone away from the house where Rosamond was staying.

She is only a *has been* charming. There is little or nothing in all this but it will amuse Lovell by recalling M. de la Rive's stile of conversation . . .

That I may not end without once having made you smile however I must tell you a bit of French English which made me very near disgrace myself by laughing in the wrong place the other day. M. Maunoir who by the by I have consulted about my eyes and who assures me that nothing is wanted for them but rest was giving me an account of a journey he took to England to see his daughter—'My daughter Ma'am took a fancy to have me over for she thought no one else could attend her so well *when she was in a child*.' . . .

You cannot conceive how captivating-looking *all* these Duvals are! Dumont with secure pride of family said of his youngest nephew (Harriets prey) 'Ah celui-la au moins n'est pas *détestable* il me semble'. Dumont was excessively kind to us and at parting gave Fanny and H La Fontaine and Gresset[1]—and to me presented a little map of the lake of Geneva and of the tour we took together round that beauteous lake. Adieu in scribble haste—going out to breakfast with the little sliding précieuse.

Pleasant breakfast—daughter pretty—little less than nothing—less than me—Sung played on harp and pianoforte—taught Fanny a French song—sang English songs Moores[2] wonderfully—begged the music of some pretty French songs for Sophy—One in particular for which Fanny had been looking a year and a half—I have it! . . .

Harriet Edgeworth to Mrs. Ruxton

Lyons, 21st October, 1820

. . . The visit to Coppet was most interesting, both from its present inhabitants and the recollections of those who formerly collected strangers from all parts of Europe by their celebrity . . . The extreme blank left in the minds of all those accustomed to live with her [Mme de Staël] is easily seen and easily conceived by

[1] The poems of J. B. L. Gresset, author of *Ververt, a tale of a parrot.*

[2] Songs by Thomas Moore.

those who know what it is to live with and to lose the stimulus of great abilities—But the extreme kindness which Mme de Staël shewed to all who were her inferiors in talents much enhanced all the splendour of her talents—her conversation upon trifles was said to be a poussière d'or and when Benjamin Constant, as it was his delight to do at her house, used to attack some unhappy wight on some subject on which he was wholly ignorant and force him to make himself perfectly ridiculous, she used to come forward—bring forth a blaze of eloquence in support of the attacked and overwhelm Benjamin by the power of her words and the animation of her arguments. M. Schlegel she used to treat in much the same way—but he was much more difficult to manage, for he had little esprit, an immense quantity of learning and a most superabundantly good opinion of himself—and when once set off—on he would go from the creation to the present hour, giving an unlimited account of all that had ever happened in any country in the universe. One night some subject of history was started and Mme de Staël desired Schlegel to decide it. He began as usual soon after the Deluge and had gone on very satisfactorily to himself till Mr. Brougham suddenly exclaimed 'Voilà Monsieur Dumont qui s'est endormi pendant deux siècles'. Dumont however having the faculty of hearing in his sleep, was able to give an account clear enough to satisfy German slowness and Schlegel's vanity.

How she could bear such prosing people I cannot conceive, but Sismondi has the same manner exactly. If you ask him any question he tells you everything about it, every date, every name and every collateral circumstance with the most undaunted perseverance. She however always required someone whose facts she could make use of, without the trouble of searching for them, and what charmed her in Benjamin Constant was his power of throwing out paradoxical assertions upon which she could display her eloquence and to which he could reply by the peculiar conversational finesse which he possesses. It is curious that he should have been brought up much as she was with the idea that succès de société was the first thing in nature—for he was brought to Paris at 16 and put under the care of Suard, who was so delighted with his abilities and his quickness in learning that he brought him into society, gave him full liberty and at 18 he was a complete metaphysic petit-maître.[1] He has been all his life imagining himself in love, and constantly carries a bottle of poison to put an end to himself in case a good opportunity should occur . . .

We were introduced to Mme Rilliet Huber at Geneva, who was one of Mme de Staëls most intimate and early friends. Her name was the last Mme de Staël ever pronounced. She lent us a MS collection of anecdotes of their childhood, which are interesting from their truth and from shewing the steps which led to forming her character. These anecdotes are most of them given and spoilt in Mme Necker's book. She, by the bye, is much simpler and more agreeable than her book but she is so deaf as to make it tiresome to converse with her.

Another intimate friend of the Neckers is M. Bonstetten a Bernois gentleman, a most entertaining butterfly of 72. He never sticks to any one subject for above five minutes, but if you can get him to speak for those five minutes, he can tell you of the most celebrated people for the last fifty years. He was intimate with Gray, and has several most interesting letters of his[2]. . . . He had previously been married in rather a provoking manner. He was exceedingly fond of dancing and there was one young lady with whom he danced every night till he left Berne to travel in England. His friends wrote him word that the young lady refused everybody and that it was a great pity he did not come back to her. To this M. Bonstetten did not agree, for he thought her a great fool and did not care for her, but in process of time he returned and the very evening of his return he went to a ball and the first person he saw was this young lady as pale as death and looking very unhappy. This he interpreted as love for him—proposed for her, in a waltz, and in a few days married her—but talking one day of how much her melancholy appearance had interested him at that ball she exclaimed, 'Oh yes indeed, I did suffer terribly that night, I had eaten too much pâté, and I did not recover it all evening.' Luckily M. Bonstetten was not a person inclined to concern him-

[1] A coxcomb. Constant's father sent him to lodge with Suard in 1785. They did not get on together. He made a dramatic gesture of taking poison in 1794 at the beginning of his love affair with Mme de Staël.

[2] Three letters from Gray to Bonstetten are printed in the collected edition of his correspondence edited by Paget Toynbee and W. Whibley (nos. 515, 520, 523). They were first published in 1799 in *Letters written from various parts of the Continent between the years 1785 and 1794*, ed. Anne Plumptre.

self much for the want of his wife's affection and he never saw much of her afterwards. He has been now many years a widower and his house is the resort of all strangers who come to Geneva. He has a constant panorama passing before him of English, Germans Italians and Russians.

He took a journey once to Rousseaus famous house on the Isle of St. Pierre. The house was occupied by farmers but M. Bonstetten observed a heap of papers on the top of an old press. These he took down and found they were the original copies of all Rousseaus published works—and some things he had never heard of. Having no means of carrying them away, as he was on horseback, he begged the farmer to send them to him instead of burning them as he intended. The man promised—but a few days after a letter arrived saying that the papers had been left there with an injunction to use them for lighting the stove, and that he thought it was his duty to do so, and so ended the brilliant hopes of stores of unknown eloquence left by Rousseau and to be published by M. Bonstetten.

Among others whom we saw, while with Mme Achard, was M. Huber, the blind discoverer of the characters and manners of the bee nation.[1] He was when young very much attached to a young lady who thinking his character too superficial and his principles too unsteady refused him, tho' his manners and conversation had much attached her. He left Geneva fell extremely ill and returned blind. Upon this, the young lady, struck with the resignation with which he bore this calamity and the resolution with which he turned his mind to literature and science, begged of her father to allow her to retract her refusal. He did so—they were married and she has ever since continued, thirty years of most unvaried kindness and attention to him.

Harriet Edgeworth to Elizabeth Waller

Lyons, 22nd October, 1820

. . . We left Pregny at 9 o'clock on thursday the 19th and after travelling six hours in uninterrupted rain, through a wild and singular country, we came to the frontier town, Bellegarde, where

[1] *Nouvelles observations sur les abeilles* (1792).

is the custom House. A little black eyed man in a furry cap appeared at the carriage door and two tall men in cocked hats began undoing the imperials from the top of the carriage—while at the other door appeared a swarm of goitred women begging us to go and see the Perte du Rhône, that is to say the place where the Rhône is lost underground—which may be beautiful when it is not raining cats and dogs but Maria preferred looking after her clothes, and first having declared herself incapable of smuggling, and finding that the Imperials were nevertheless fast descending, she took a much surer means, and asked the black eyed furry cap what she was to pay the men for their trouble in undoing her baggage. 10 francs seemed to please him very much and he did no more than make a sort of mock search all over the carriage, touching everything and then declaring everything right. He just looked over the clothes in the imperials—cut open a bundle which contained our habits, and then gave us leave to depart. Before our horses were put to however we saw the difference which 10 francs had made for we saw our friend ramming and poking with a long kind of dagger into every bundle contained in a carriage which arrived after us—and dire havoc he must have made if any forbidden goods were there hidden. This absurd operation over we proceeded through an extraordinary marshy, hilly country till we got, just in the dark, to a little town called Nantua (not Mantua) where we slept very happily and setting out early the next morning we went along through a frightful country where nothing was to be seen but clayey hills and marshy rivers—the fields brown with buckwheat and dried grass. We stopped some time waiting for horses at a lone house called Pont d'Ain where we amused ourselves looking at a large dinner cooking by an elegant little brown coated, grey headed man, with a long pigtail, going about making fricandeaus and dabbing little spoonfuls of things from divers saucepans upon every dish, and explaining the mysteries of his art with as much solemnity as Dr. Brinkley could have done the parallax[1] . . .

[1] See above, p. 126 n. 2.

Maria Edgeworth to Mrs. Edgeworth

Lyons—Hôtel du Nord, 22nd October, 1820

Lyons![1] Is it possible that I am really at Lyons—Lyons of which I have heard him speak so much—Lyons where his active spirit once reigned and where now scarce a trace scarce a memory of him remains. The Perraches are all gone—Charpentiers[2] no more to be heard of—Bono—a name unknown—De la Verpillière—Yes—one descendant has a fine house here—But he is in the country. Almost all the principal proprietors, the court end of the Town of Lyons are at their country houses—the city people all confined minds as well as bodies to their counting houses know nothing care nothing for anything but their correspondents and Exchange. The two letters which dear Camille Jordan gave us to the Maire of Lyons and to one of his relations were of little use because we unluckily arrived on Saturday when both gentlemen were setting off for their country houses like our London citizens to take a mouthful of fresh air on the day that comes between saturday and monday—au désespoir de manquer cette occasion de faire la connaissance d'une dame &c &c.

But off they went—one of the head clerks of M. Caesar Jordan however trudged for me indefatigably half the day yesterday umbrella in hand for to mend the matter it drizzled or poured all day—and he at last scented out for me M. de Fleurieu who was of my father's society. But M. de Fleurieu was at one c'clock in his bed confined by a violent cold! He sent word that he should have the honor of waiting up on us at one today. Mme de Pomaret one of our Parisian bel-esprits gave us a letter to a Mme de Fontebrune and she came with her two daughters in hats crowned with roses a little creature less than I am très maniérée making hundreds of curtsies and slidings and '*Ah Madames*' at every going in and out of a room at the head of the stairs at the carriage door walking like a paper woman blown across the table or like Mrs. Godley on the edges of her gown. Nothing could appear to us more tiresome, more desolate more melancholy than the day we spent here

[1] RLE had lived for a year at Lyons in 1772–3. His experiences there are told in his *Memoirs*, chaps. x–xii.

[2] RLE had lodged with the Charpentiers, whose daughter Charlotte became the wife of Walter Scott.

yesterday. The look of the town and the fine façades of the principal buildings and the place de Bellecour are just like the prints in the great portfolio and even this strict resemblance makes them melancholy to me for I used to see their pictures with such notions of happiness! Such a radiance was thrown over them by his descriptions. I hear his voice saying *La place de Bellecour—l'hôtel de Ville*—and we passed it yesterday and saw the steps on which he told us the city guard insulted the English and where he made the man beg pardon for it afterwards at the playhouse the night afterwards.[1] *Hôtel de Ville—Steps—Playhouse—square* all remain—even thro the horrors of the Revolution but human creatures, the best the ablest, the most full of life and gaiety and feeling all passed away!—and forgotten. Only his three children here know anything of him . . .

Harriet Edgeworth to Elizabeth Waller

Hotel Vauban, 366 Rue St. Honoré, Paris, 28th October, 1820

The rest of our stay at Lyons corresponded with the beginning. It was melancholy and unsatisfactory and we left it at 3½ on Sunday evening the 23rd and arrived that night at a comfortable little inn at a place called Arnas where the people were very civil, but all their civility and all the charmante which they lavished upon us were of no avail against the gusts of wind which blew through the windows and kept the curtains in constant motion, our only refuge was bed—which was perfectly comfortable, and we proceeded the next morning to a little place called St Symphonien where the people came into the room always with one half of a potato in their mouths and the other in their hands, and were so delighted with a shawl which Fanny wore, that they took hold of it—asked her where it came from—how much it cost—if the border was woven with it—or sewed on, and she seemed so much interested in it, and as if she knew as much about it as the finest

[1] RLE had betrayed slight amusement at the elaborate formalities at the installation of the Mayor of Lyons. On leaving the Hôtel de Ville he was very roughly stopped by the sentry whose action was supported by his superior officer. The latter was obliged by the commandant and his colonel to apologize.

fine lady in London could, tho she was tumbling about, for it can hardly be called walking, in vile wooden sabots and almost all her dress in rags. Having left these pleasing people we travelled on rapidly the whole day till about 8 in the evening, when at a wretched lone looking house St. Imbert we asked if we could have good rooms. 'Oh oui Madame des grandes salles—des apartements superbes.' Maria went up to look at these superb apartments up a crooked tumbledown old staircase, into dirty little holes, with carters beds in them, and a riff raff set of postillions and carmen in the house. Maria thought we were better without these magnificent rooms and we went on to another place, not better looking at the outside, however the sight of roast turkey, just taken off the spit in the kitchen, gave us hopes—and we did find a room in which the bolster was very agreeable put against the window. A blazing fire and part of the newly roasted turkey made us most comfortable. No further adventure than that of breaking an egg-cup happened here.

After a long days journey, disappointed at our first attempt for a sleeping place, we arrived at 11 at night at Briare. No light was seen, and no sound was heard in the house. The postillion alighted knocked, and after some time, the door was opened by a tall man in a blue frock, naked legs and night cap. His bed was in the kitchen, where the few embers of fire which remained were soon stirred up into a blaze. A fat, red faced old man, also in a night cap now came down and began grumblingly to give out sheets to two half dressed girls, shuffling in sabots. The man whom we had first wakened leaned his back against the chimney piece—the postillion in his red embroidered frock stood opposite to us, completing an admirable group round the fire, the room barely lighted by one dim candle. Maria observing some fleur de Lis on the iron back of the grate asked the man how old they were. Oh said he very very old, they have been there a length of time. What said Maria since before the revolution. Yes said the man—but there is another side can be turned, whenever it is necessary. Oh yes—said the master, those are the Royal arms but here in this very room sat the Emperor when he was going to Elba. There, where you have your feet, his cook burned the floor, in cooking the supper and here in this corner sat Napoleon himself. And said Maria, was he in good humor, when he was here? Oh admirable, he was as gay as I, and not in the least like a man who had lost his crown the day before.

Unfortunately our beds being ready and the master being very impatient to get to bed, the servant having already composedly settled himself in his—we heard no more of the fallen Emperor. We left the place next morning very early, and reached Fontainebleau that night and at four yesterday this town which whether spring summer or winter is always gay.

Our apartments here are very comfortable. You come in to a little antichambre—then into our very small dining room—which just holds us and would scarcely contain a fourth however dear to us that fourth might be. It is heated by a stove and opens into a very comfortable drawing room, with white and green silk curtains, elegantly draped—a very pretty carpet plenty of tables and green covered chairs. The walls are painted grey and white—an *iligant* pendule and mirror are over the chimney piece and two pretty bouquets of artificial flowers in purple vases upon it. This room opens into Fanny's and Maria's bedchamber, hung with yellow silk and with yellow paper a very nice carpet—comfortable escritoire—nice chest of drawers &c. This bedchamber, which is so nice as to be a second sitting room, as a bed is in France so elegant an affair as to be rather ornamental than otherwise—this room opens into a very small one, where are washing affairs and then into another of the same size where I sleep, a little closet for our maid, a passage and backstairs complete our suite of apartments.

Maria is pretty well but is not today quite recovered from the fatigue of our long journey. By the by you must not imagine from what I have said that French Inns are bad, or that we were in any difficulties or dangers from damp or wind, no such thing I assure you. You would be astonished at how comfortable all these little places are. The apartments we occupy here were Benjamin Constants for two years!—so you see it is a classical place.

FRANCE, OCTOBER–DECEMBER 1820

Maria Edgeworth to Mrs. Edgeworth

Paris, Hôtel Vauban, 366 Rue St. Honoré, 28th October, 1820
. . . We arrived here yesterday evening . . . I must now tell you of our household concerns and our *establishment* here. Good Mrs. Creed whom I troubled to look out for apartments for us after looking above about and underneath found these at the Hôtel Vauban the best for our short stay. We have one floor of a comfortable side of the square of this hotel completely to ourselves. It is within a porte cochère—no noises but of carriages belonging to the house that come into the yard . . . The misfortune of the house is that there are no waterclosets. Oh how my poor aunt Mary will sigh for us! We pay only 300 francs the same price we paid in Place Bourbon. Our apartments here are much better and more conveniently situated. They are the apartments which Benjamin Constant occupied for two years and which Mr. and Mrs. Malthus had when they were lately at Paris.

The woman of the house is respectable and civil. To our great satisfaction we have Rodolphe again who seems to be as glad to come to us as we are to have him again . . . Miss Creeds have engaged for us a femme de chambre called Marianne who seems a steady respectable willing plain person. I like her better at first sight and first hearing than Josephine. She speaks in a natural voice—has no airs—is active and underjawed . . . We are to have a very handsome carriage, superbe as Rodolphe pronounces it to be—for 500 francs per month—same price as before. It belongs to the mistress of this hotel and therefore putting up in the remise here is always at hand—an advantage which has decided me to prefer it to Beauvallets carriage which we formerly had . . .

Maria Edgeworth to Mrs. Ruxton

Paris, [n.d. November, 1820]

Never lose another night's sleep or another moment's thought on the Quarterly Review[1]—I have never read and never will read it.

I write this merely to tell you that I have at last had the pleasure of seeing Mme la Comtesse de Vaudreuil, the daughter of your friend; she is an exceedingly pleasing woman, of high fashion, with the remains of great beauty, courteous and kind to us beyond all expectation. She had but a few days in Paris, and she made out two for us; she took us to the Conciergerie to see, by lamp-light, the dungeon where the poor Queen and Madame Elizabeth were confined, now fitted up as little chapels. In the Queen's is an altar inscribed with her letter to the King, expressing forgiveness of her enemies. Tears streamed from the eyes of the young Comtesse de Vaudreuil, the daughter-in-law, as she looked at this altar, and the place where the Queen's bed was. Who do you think accompanied us to this place? Lady Beauchamp, Lady Longford's mother, a great friend of Mme de Vaudreuil's, with whom we dined the next day, and who procured for us the Duc de Choiseul's box at the Théâtre Français, when the house was to be uncommonly crowded to see Mlle Duchesnois in Athalie[2] 'avec tous les Choeurs', and a most striking spectacle it was! I had never seen Mlle Duchesnois to perfection before.

(MS. missing—printed from *Mem.* ii. 126–7]

Harriet Edgeworth to Louisa Beaufort

Hôtel Vauban, 366 Rue St. Honoré, 14th November, 1820

. . . Maria has not been at all well this last week, though she has been out almost every day except two which we most virtuously passed with Mme de Roquefeuil at Versailles where everything and everybody scorns to have existed since the days of Louis 14th and everybodys ideas seem to have remained in the same train unaltered by revolution, ruin and exile. The whole society is old croaking dowagers, or rheumatic battered old counts and all the conversation, the weather, the Princes hunts, and dinner, which

[1] This refers to a review (by J. W. Croker) of the *Memoirs of* R. L. *Edgeworth* in *Quarterly Rev.* xxiii (1820). For a discussion of this and its indirect influence on ME's writing, see Marilyn Butler, *Maria Edgeworth,* 410–13.

[2] Racine's play, first acted in 1691.

makes a great and brilliant era in their days. Mme de Roquefeuil's mother, Mme de Calan is a melancholy spectacle wheeled in and out in an armchair and squalling out the same question a hundred times over in every hour in a voice which Maria says sounds as if it came through a butter squirt. I think the whole town the most melancholy place I ever beheld—the immense palace with its gilded domes and vast galleries totally deserted exhibits a spectacle of fallen grandeur but little calculated to increase the ideas of Louis the 18th's grandeur. But it is astonishing what worship the ultras pay to the Bourbons. A captain of the guard told us he passed the whole night of the Duc de Bordeaux' birth in kissing his hand and indeed so romantic is this gentlemans affection for the little Princesse that he is said to blush whenever her name is mentioned. I hope that you have seen the account of the little Dukes birth for the Duchesse de Berry has shewn herself a most heroic character. We heard her dame d'honneur the Duchesse de Reggio lamenting the other night over the number of people to whom she was obliged to refuse admittance every day. Indeed the Princesse must have been dead before this time if every body was let in who goes to her door for it is every day besieged with crowds of carriages which seem to be in ever renewing succession, as we pass and repass the Place du Carousel in going from one side of the town to the other. The Duchesse de Berrys picture by Kinson[1] is very interesting. She is represented sitting on a sofa holding her little daughter who is stretching out her arms towards her fathers bust on a pedestal supposed to be beside her. The Duchesses countenance though far from handsome is without being the least flattered very charming from the look of suppressed grief and calm resignation which it expresses. At the time of her sons birth, while she was waiting for the arrival of Marshal Suchet the officer who was to witness the birth—the physician suddenly perceived that she was just gone and that five seconds delay might be fatal to to her. She saw him change colour and said, 'You are afraid.' 'I am,' said he, 'you are in great danger.' 'No matter' exclaimed she, 'You say the child is safe. His life is what I desire. Mine is of no concern.' The day after, she wrote a note to the King requesting that the first day of her sons life should be marked by a pardon worthy

[1] The original picture by François Kinson is lost, but a copy is in the Museum at Versailles. A print is reproduced in Mario Praz, *Conversation Pieces*, pl. 180.

of a future Henry, the pardon of the two wretches who attempted to frighten her by horrible noises under her windows before the childs birth. They have accordingly been pardoned. A lady of our acquaintance Mme de Pomaret, sent some very beautiful lines on the Duc de Bordeaux birth, which the Duchesse answered by an alabaster vase, bearing on one side the flower called Immortelle, for her husband, on the other the scabius the widows flower, for herself, and on the third the lily for her son. This was of course answered by an elegant impromptu and has served many an empty ultra with conversation since.[1]

Very different from this picture of the Duchesse de Berry is the Corinne of M. Gérards which we saw a few days ago. She is most beautiful and completely realises ones idea of her. She is represented sitting on a rock the sea in the distance and Vesuvius beyond. She is half turned from you her left hand resting on a lyre her head rather thrown back and her eyes fixed upwards with the complete [ ] of inspiration. She is drest in a pale yellow gown a scarlet scarf floating on her shoulders and a yellow turban twisted through her black hair. Nothing can be more beautiful than the idea and the execution of her figure but just close to her, stepping upon the rock is the bewildered figure of Oswald who in a scarlet uniform and green pantaloons, presents one booted leg to Corinne without even looking at her, but staring forward as if frightened by a cow. His hair is of a sandy color and his pale face is just what his character was. Behind him, are a number of other figures, all, particularly a young Greek, beautiful in themselves but placed too close to her to have the effect of a detached group and too unconnected with her to add any interest to her abstracted appearance. If the picture were cut in two it would be perfect but as it is we all agreed that Madame de Staël would have felt that was Corinne. It seems her children do so for they have ordered a copy of it.

I had no idea that Bonaparte had feared Mme de Staëls talents, or her love of meddling in politics to the degree he must, when she and all her friends were watched with such unrelenting jealousy.

[1] Lady E. Stuart wrote to Lady Hardwicke (30 Oct. 1820): 'to hear the *details* of the accouchement and all the circumstances! I assure you one is glad for decency sake to turn the conversation to the Queen [of England] and Bergami.' (*Two Noble Lives*, ed. Hare, 108). The hearing of witnesses in the divorce proceedings of Queen Caroline began on 21 Aug. and it was not until 10 Nov. that the Bill was abandoned.

At the time that she was publishing Allemagne[1] the first volume was printed and she went down to the country to finish the MS and to correct the proofs of the other vols. She was accompanied by Mme Récamier Miss Randall her friend and her 3 children. A few days after her arrival she went with Mme Récamier and her youngest son and daughter to see an estate of M. de Montmorency. She was to stay two days. A few hours after her departure Auguste de Staël who remained came in to Miss Randall and said that he had just received intelligence of the book being seized and that his mother must escape from France or that she would be seized also as she was ordered out of the country. Miss Randall immediately set about to collect the scattered proof sheets, and to pack up all their baggage. As there were spies in every direction, as soon as it grew dark at night Miss Randall and Mme de Staëls maid got out into a wood near the house and buried the whole book. Then she returned and spent the night in arranging all the letters and all those which could be suspected she took down at about five o'clock in the morning and put into hidden recesses, which the master of the house had shewn her the day before behind the book shelves and then having every thing ready she prepared to meet the Gens d'armes—and she walked out before the house where very soon arrived two gens d'armes on horseback.

They stopped when they saw her and one of them said 'Have I the honor to address Mme la Baronne de Staël?' 'Yes sir' said Miss Randall taking care of every word least her English accent should be noticed. They did however perceive it and said one to the other, 'What an accent she has—what can that mean?' 'Oh don't you know it is that Mme de Staël is German—you know her name is quite German.' 'Pray sir' continued Miss Randall 'what may your business be with me?' 'It is' said one of the men 'to thank you for the kindness you shewed to my son when he was wounded five years ago—and to beg you to leave this place while you can.' This advice was followed—the MS was packed up with all possible secrecy and sent by Bordeaux to England—the baggage was sent off to Mme de Staël—her son joined her, and they arrived at

[1] *De l'Allemagne* (1810). Mme de Staël went in August to Fossé, belonging to M. de Salaberry. The events mentioned below took place at the end of September. The latter part of the story, the escape from Geneva, belongs to the end of May 1811.

Coppet in Switzerland before Gens d'armes appeared who were less grateful and more dutiful.

Miss Randall in the mean time was in a great hurry to get to Paris to settle various affairs there and then get to Geneva with all possible speed but the police officers where she was would not give a passport to an English woman, in time of war and so she wrote her name and gave the place of her birth the village where she was born in England as if it was some town in Switzerland which the police officers being very comfortably ignorant never perceived and she arrived in Paris. The day after as she was walking downstairs to go and visit her friends, she met a gentleman who stopped her and asked who lodged in the next floor. She replied that she did not know. The person then said 'I must beg Miss Randall that you will remain at home all day.' 'Sir' said she astonished at this order and perceiving that his first question had only been to discover her English accent—'Sir I do not perceive why I should not go out if I chuse it.'. Upon this he threw open his coat and displayed the uniform of the Police. At this she thought it prudent to obey and she returned to her own room. For three days she remained at home but at last she set off and paid several visits but the next day she received a summons to the Police office. She went, her passport was demanded. The officer with civil contempt remarked the attempt to deceive by writing only the place of her birth, told her every person she had been to see the day before, declared she could not possibly have her passport and asked what she wanted to do at Paris. She replied that she came to see friends and that she had no other object. She was dismissed but day after day passed and no passport could be obtained. At last she demanded to see Fouché himself—at that time the head of the Police. She was admitted to him—declared that she was in the utmost haste to get back to Geneva to see her sister who was going to Italy and dying. 'That is your only motive? You do not go to see Mme de Staël—you do not intend to have any communication with her?' 'I go to see my sister.' 'Evasions are of no use' said Fouché taking out a letter she had written the day before to her sister. 'You say here that the moment you have seen her your first object will be to see Mme de Staël. You cannot now expect a passport.'

Among the clerks of this office there was a young Irishman who struck with compassion at seeing her ineffectual efforts repeated day after day, at last advised her to send all her heavy baggage out of Paris by the diligence and then endeavor to pass the gates in a remise with apparently nothing but what she should want for a visit at Versailles or St. Cloud. This advice she followed but the moment she reached the Barrière her carriage was stopped and her passport demanded. She had none to produce and was obliged to return. She went again to her Irish friend, who said that as a last resort he would make out her passport and get it laid before the war minister the day he signed the orders for leaves of absence, billeting etc. and that it might perhaps be signed unnoticed. He did so and the next day she had received her passport signed by a minister who had nothing to do with it but still it was signed—and with this she arrived safely at Geneva but her sister was gone, and she died soon after in Italy.

Mme de Staël was indeed out of France and in safety but she was watched at every turn and could not go into Geneva without having every part of her carriage searched. She could not write a letter that was not opened and she was refused passports for any part of Europe. At last however she contrived to elude them. She ordered her carriage one morning and said she was going to Nyon a town about five miles from Coppet on the lake of Geneva. Her daughter came down to beg to go with her and twice was refused and at last she took her with her in only a shawl the more to deceive her watchers—and she said she was only gone to dine out. She took no trunks with her and was accompanied only by her daughter and youngest son Albert. Every body who came to the chateau that day was told that she was at Nyon and on the following days that she was unwell. To further the deception a number of letters were to be written to Schinznach a bathing place in Switzerland which as they were to be stopped and read by the police were of course most guardedly written but still as if she was at this bathing place while in reality she got a passport from a Swiss prefect at Nyon and passing through the Tyrol arrived safely in Italy. But the first news of her having left Coppet was given by M. Bonstetten her particular friend who having come to the Château was unwisely allowed to know that she was not there. He told it at a soirée at Geneva and early the next day the old porter at Coppet came up to Miss Randall and said that a person had brought a pacquet for a polish gentleman of his mistresses acquaintance and that he would give it no one but Mme la Baronne herself. Miss Randall desired to see him and the moment he came into her apartment he came nearer and nearer to the table on which were lying her letters directed to Schinznach and all the time he was pretending to give orders about the poles letter he was reading the directions of the pacquets to Mme de Staël. The next day a dragoon arrived with a large parcel for M. de Staël in which he was desired to give directly precise information as to his mother. Monsieur de Staël was gone on a shooting party to the other side of the lake and so fortunately no answer could be sent and before the police had had time to send to and receive an answer from Schinznach the object of their pursuit was out of their reach. They sent the moment the pretended pole had executed his mission to the Post Office at Schinznach—soon found that she was not there and then discovering that a passport had been given by the Nyon perfect they perceived that they were fairly tricked. This story is curious from the wonderful pains and deceit made use of by Napoleons emissaries in persecution of one woman.

Last saturday we saw Mlle Mars in a very pretty little piece called the Jaloux sans amour[1] a very interesting character and afterwards in one as different as possible Betti in La Jeunesse de Henri 5[1] which is as droll an idea of English manners in the time of Henry the 4th as can well be imagined in which Rochester is Henrys favorite companion and in which he is represented as married before his fathers death, but Mlle Mars is charming. On Sunday we went in the morning to see a beautiful picture of Mme de la Vallière[2] at the house of her great great grand-daughter the Duchesse d'Uzès, whose husband is premier Duke and who is herself daughter to the Duc de Châtillon—is everything that can be conceived of superbe—has the finest private hotel in Paris, but she is a poor little old crumpled woman with a crooked mouth and about 4 feet 10 high but she is very obliging and has charming manners. We dined that day with Mme de la Briche who is a rich old widow who lives with her son in law Count Molé and is herself a tidy little woman—always looks just fresh out of a band box and

[1] (1781), a play by Barthélemy Imbert.

[2] *La Jeunesse d'Henry V* by Alexandre Duval was first performed in 1806.

[3] The mistress of Louis XIV.

has a fish bone in her throat which has been sticking there these 20 years but which seems to be no way disagreeable except that she always has a little cough and seems rather frightened if any thing goes wrong in her swallow. From her house we went to that of Mme de St. Aulaire who is stepmother in law to the Duc Decases and who said that he writes over that he is astonished at the comforts of an English country house, and amazed that one can be so well in the country in such weather. Along with this lady was a certain Comte de Ségur a great believer in Animal magnetism[1] and once when he was in Switzerland and his father at Paris, he came into the room one morning all éploré and as white as death. 'My father' said he 'has been seized with a fit of apoplexy and he is dying.' 'What' said every body 'have you heard from Paris?' 'Heard from Paris? Oh no but I feel it an inward voice tells it to me.' He threw himself on a sofa and remained in this deplorable state till 12 o'clock at night when he suddenly started up exclaiming that his father was well—this inward voice having informed him of this happy change. The next day of course came a letter from Paris giving an account of his fathers illness and recovery. From Mme de St. Aulaires we went to the Duchesse D'Escards where were Pozzo di Borgo Marmont and various other sublime personages but we there heard a very pretty story of a frenchwoman who murdered her husband by running an awl into his side in the night, then cut him into bits and salted and packed him up in a box under the bed . . . I told Harriet the last time I wrote a very pretty example of French charity and I now inform you of one of their very refined pieces of crime and with this agreeable impression I leave you . . .

Maria Edgeworth to Mrs. Edgeworth

15th November, 1820 Hotel Vauban, Rue St. Honoré,

Thank you my dearest mother for your wish to save me the pain of seeing the Reviews. They have been here for some time but I have read only the Edinburgh[2] and shall never read any

[1] An early term for mesmerism.

[2] *Edinburgh Rev.* xxxix (1820) contains a review of *Memoirs of RLE.* A 2nd edition of the book came out in 1821.

other. Our really kind friend Mr. Creed has read them all expressly for the purpose of determining whether there was anything in the second edition which I ought to alter. He has assured me that as far as he could see there is nothing I can or ought to alter except what I have done already in the list of corrections of which you have a copy. As to the rest you would scarcely believe my dear friends the calm of my mind and the sort of satisfied resignation I feel. I can scarcely believe it myself. I suppose I had during the two years of doubt and extreme anxiety I endured exhausted all my power of doubting. I *know* that I have done my very best—that I have done my duty without shrinking from any personal consideration and I firmly believe that if my dear father could see the whole he would be satisfied with me . . .

Of *la bonne compagnie* we have as much as ever we can desire. By the by en petit comité the other night at la Duchesse D'Escards, present la duchesse de la Force, La marquise d'Herbouville and Marquis—La Marquise Nadaillac (the duchess's daughter in law) —Comte Alphonse d'Agoult—Marmont duc de Ragusa and Pozzo di Borgo and our dear selves, a discussion took place about the bon or mauvais ton of different expressions. It was ruled that to speak of being *en bonne société* is une expression bourgeoise—it must be *en bonne compagnie*. You may say que *la haute* société se rassemble en telle ou telle maison but never la bonne société. Voilà *des nuances* as Mme D'Escards observed which it is impossible for strangers to know. They laughed much at some book of a M. Craufords,[1] which I have never seen which pretends to teach the English these niceties of expression and it was apropos to his using the words *bonne société* that the conversation began. She says that there is some story he tells of a lady in which he uses terms that would be la risée de l'antichambre. Such an amazing jabbering as all these grandees made about these small matters. The conversation put me in mind of one in the World[2] about good company which we all used to admire. . . . The day we came back from Versailles we dined at home. I went in the evening to Princess Potemkins, who is only a Princess (take notice all manner of men!) by courtesy—for she is married to a Potemkin who is

[1] Perhaps Quintin Craufurd's *Essais sur la littérature française écrits pour l'usage d'une étrangère* (1818). This book went into three editions.

[2] *The World, by Adam Fitzadam*, probably no. 151 (20 Nov. 1755).

not a prince and though [by birth] a Princess daughter of Princesse Galitzine she loses her rank according to the Russian customs by marrying one of inferior rank. The same custom prevails in France and French and Russians are with reason surprised at the superior gallantry of our customs which say once a Lady and always a lady. But whether Princess or not Princess our Mme Potemkin is most charming and you may all bless your stars that you are not obliged to read a page of panegyric upon her. NB She was as much delighted to see us as we were to see her. She was alone with Mme de Noisseville—that happy mixture of my aunt Fox and dear Mrs. Latuffière.[1] We went from Mme Potemkin's to Comtesse d'Haussonville whom I hope you do not forget is one of our fashionable *dears*. With her we found Mme de Bouillé playing at billiards just in the attitude in which we had left her 3 months ago the last night we saw her before we went in quest of Mont Blanc—no difference in her but the change of thin muslin for demi-saison chinese-crape and besides Mme de Bouillé were sundry men very important on the hearth and in the circle of their own conceit but with whose names I need not trouble you . . .

Fanny told you about the delightful dinner at Mme de Rumfords where all intellectual and epicurean delicacies of the season were united. Since that time Friday last we have been at a concert at her house which I am told was very good. They were not public performers but Italian and French amateurs. I can answer for the excellence of the ices having swallowed two in about 5 minutes *Saturday*—I had a great headache and many visits in the morning and much working to get a box at the théatre François and at last in consequence of my superabundant activity had two upon my hands with the fear that my head would not permit me to enjoy or let my dear F and H enjoy either. La Duchesse D'Escards gave me 3 places in la loge des Gentilhommes de la chambre and F. Delessert sent me a ticket for a box of 4 places and I was on my back on my bed racking with pain when these arrived. But by keeping still for 3 or 4 hours and eating as much as a sparrow at first and as a reasonable woman at last the head cleared up and then I wrote and wrote notes and drove and drove to fill these places with proper friends. Went to Mme Potemkins—much

[1] The mistress of the first school ME attended, in Derby.

obliged but after many dubitations her physician who is mighty like Don Snatchaway would not let her go. One of her gentlemen in waiting went with us lodged us in our box des gentilhommes de la chambre—rattled off to the Creeds with my offer of the other box for them and himself—*Much* obliged—came—saw—and enjoyed the delightful Mlle Mars and most comic Michaut . . . Monday—We spent the whole morning with Mme de Roquefeuil who came to breakfast with la Duchesse d'Uzès where we met her and thence carried her to M. Mounier—one of the ministers—Directeur général de la police. Mme Mounier is bedridden but only in consequence of having lately produced a little girl. She was in a superb bedchamber—bed recessed in a large alcove hung with rich drapery of crimson velvet and gold fleur de lys. She [was on] a chaise longue elegantly undressed—and had a cradle beside her with green silk hood and a pretty child rocking or rather s[winging] it—It being suspended you know how—at least if you don't I cant teach you. Mme Mounier a very agreeable unaffected woman doatingly fond of us and all our education books—her sister in law Mme Achard (not like our dear and your hated Mme Achard) very little very thin—very literary and moreover well bred and most gracious to us. Mme de Roquefeuil is really all heart and seemed to take much delight in introducing us to her friends. These Mouniers are *true* to her in their prosperity. Mme de Roquefeuil then took us to another friend of hers—the Marquis de Nicolay—whom we found also in a superb house but tortured with the gout in his armchair. Though suffering he was most amiable and aimable[1] and talked of Voltaire and Rousseau and all former times. The manners of these remains of former times are very different indeed from the manners of these politicians &c of the present day—the ease and playfulness of their conversation and their attention to others appear still more pleasing than they could without the contrast.

We dined at Mme Potemkins—met there the violent Juno-eyed Duchesse de la Force—who has no sense and talks on right or wrong about what she would do to the Libéraux if she had but the power. She is Grammonts sister and high as human veneration can look but she exacts no veneration for she has not common sense. But to make amends we met here the Princess Galitzine

[1] 'Friendly and agreeable.'

aunt to our beauty a thin, tall, odd clever very clever woman who is the daughter of Prince Shouvaloff to whom Voltaire wrote eternally. She is *imbued* with all the anecdotes of that time—very well-bred and quick in conversation. Mme Potemkin declares that this aunt of hers has been for 20 years wishing to see Maria E. If this is a fib it is not my fault—indeed she was most kind to her—very *pleasant* and *superb* dinner!—with the following persons Princess Galitzines daughter married to M. de Caumont a very handsome man who was amusing enough—Princess [ ] who scrambled with M. de Caumont about [some] bank notes—she shutting her hand with a note of [ ] francs and he shutting his with a little crumpled bit. 'Will *you take what I have for what you have*?' was the play [ ] quite Russian!—and there was an ugly bride who had married the family physician and other *personnages muets*. About half after 8 the common hour for departure on dinner visits we went away the Princess Galitzine having first engaged us to dine with her on thursday and the spending the evening with her on friday.

Before I let this Princess Galitzine slide out of my magic lantern I must however make you see what manner of person she is. Then Gentlemen and Ladies, or Gentleman and Ladies (for I suppose Pakenham is the only gentleman now among you) Gentleman and Ladies, you see in the Princess Galitzine a tall thin figure of a gentlewoman of all countries—d'un certain âge—about 50 be the same more or less with a head as small as Honora's and a face more like Lady Dufferin's and Lady Ferrard's mixed than any other I can name—But after all not at all like either. On her head please see a velvet cap and feathers mighty like what I used to wear—but under it a white cap with a full hanging blonde lace border. The velvet cap she thinks an invention of her own and she wears it constantly because she fancies and has fancied for these last 20 years that she is in such delicate health that she should catch cold and die the next day if she did not wear this cap and wrap herself up in half a dozen cachemires and pelisses in going from house to house and room to room. À cela près she is a reasonable woman! She fell to work talking to me without losing one moment and was intimate in 5. Something led to mentioning Tom *Jones* (*Shones*) and immediately she told me that she had been charmed to find by *Ormone* that we agreed in opinion about the moral effect of that book.[1] She had read that passage to her son. It was lucky for me that while she was summoning up the youth to present him to me I recollected what she meant to allude to in Ormone and afterwards made out in time the various allusions she made to King Corny[2] whose name no English mortal could have made [out] by her pronunciation. She seemed to have all we have written quite by heart.

She talked a great deal of Mme de Staël's Delphine and Corinne. When she was with Mme de Staël at Coppet she said to her one day after talking of *Rocca* &c—and pointing to her daughter 'Mais ma chère l'éducation d'Albertine et les romans et les amans comment—?' 'Ah' interrupted Mme de Staël 'avec Mlle Randall et Schlegel tout cela se concilie.'

After leaving Mme Potemkins we went to see—who do you think? Guess all round the breakfast table before you turn over the leaf and if anybody guesses right, I guess it will be Aunt Mary—Mme de la Rochejacquelein.[3] She had but just arrived from the country and we found ourselves in a large hotel in which all the winds of heaven were blowing and in which as we went upstairs and crossed antichambers all was darkness save one candle which a servant carried but what manner of man he might be we could only guess. In a small bedroom well furnished and with a fire just lighted we found Mme de la Rochejacquelein lying on a sofa—her two daughters at work one spinning with a distaff and one embroidering muslin by the fireside. Madame is a fat large woman with a broad round fair face with a most open benevolent expression, as benevolent as Molly Bristow's or as Mrs. Brinkley's[4] countenance—hair cut short and perfectly grey as seen under her cap—the rest of her face much too young for such grey locks. She has not the hard weather beaten look which had been described to us. She *is* Molly Bristow with Mrs. Brinkleys intelligence of expression and though her face and bundled form and dress all *squashed* on a sofa did not at first promise much of gentility you could not hear her speak 5 minutes or see her 3

[1] ME's *Ormond: Tales and Novels* (1833), xviii. 79–81.

[2] Cornelius O'Shane in *Ormond* was known as King of the Black Islands from the name of his estate.

[3] Authoress of the well-known *Mémoires* describing the revolt in the Vendée.

[4] Molly Bristow was an old English servant of the Edgeworths. Mrs. Brinkley was the wife of Dr. John Brinkley.

minutes without perceiving that she is well bred and well born. She had hurt her leg which was the cause of her lying on the sofa in this condition. It seemed a grievous penance to her for she appears of as active a temper as ever. She says her health is perfect but a nervous disease in her eyes has nearly deprived her of sight. She could hardly see my face though I sat as close to her as chair and knees could go to sofa.

'I am always sorry when any stranger sees me' said she, 'parceque je sais que je détruis toute illusion. Je sais que je devrais avoir l'air d'une héroine et surtout je devrais avoir l'air malheureux ou épuisé au moins. Rien de tout cela! Hélas!' She is much better than a heroine of romance—she is benevolence and truth itself—and in hearing her speak we felt that we loved and esteemed and admired her and were convinced that there was no exaggeration or literary manufacture in anything she has written. Her two daughters are simply [simple—inserted above] girls from a convent. She begged them to take us into the great salon to shew us some pictures which she thought might interest us. She apologised for the cold of those rooms and well she might. When the double doors were opened I really thought Eurus[1] himself was puffing in our faces and I made F H and self shawl and cloak ourselves before we ventured in. The salon has at one end the picture of M. de Lescure at the other of Henri[2]—both full length and large as life—by Guérin and Girodet—both presents from the King copies of those which were done for him. These pictures were *made out* from the likenesses of relations. The picture of M. de Lescure was drawn from M. Marcellus a deputy who resembled him in an extraordinary manner. The picture of Henri was drawn from his nephew. Both are as Mme de La Rochejacquelein assured us very like the originals—Very fine military figures! Fanny shall try and make a sketch of them—So I will spare ineffectual pen and ink description. In an inner boudoir was a full length also of M. de la Rochejacquelein—much the finest of all the figures. She never has yet looked at this picture. Upon the whole far from disappointing she gratified all my expectations . . .

[1] The east wind.

[2] M. de Lescure was Mme de la Rochejacquelein's first husband. Both he and his great friend Henri de la Rochejacquelein were killed in the Vendée. Henri de la Rochejacquelein was brother to the marquis de la Rochejacquelein, her second husband.

Harriet Edgeworth to Mrs. Edgeworth

Paris, 18th November, 1820

. . . Thursday the day Maria wrote, we had a ticket given to us for the Opera and we had engaged two gentlemen to go with us but in the morning we went to visit Lady Elizabeth Stuart and she said that one of the foolish performers had had the impertinence to lose her grandmother and so we drove over half Paris to see the advertisements and at last found that no opera should we have that night. We therfore consoled ourselves by dining with the Princess Galitzine at the unheard of hour of 4½. She is as you may perceive by her name Russian—she has a great Tartar lip but she is very clever and perfectly in love with Maria; she had been reading Ennui[1] that morning and she was so delighted with it, she could talk of nothing else. She was charmed with the description of Lady Geraldine making Miss Tracy put on something of everybody[2] and she [ ] into French people. She has children settled in all parts of the world—her son married in Russia—one daughter in Italy—another in Germany and her third in France—to M. de Caumont a very entertaining man who is to be Duc de la Force and has immense moustaches. His aunt the Duchesse de la Force is a most tremendous person with immense black eyes but nothing ever comes of her. She keeps saying and saying the same thing over and over again but Mme Galitzine says she really means to say something different but that the same words always come out in spite of her. The Princesse is now living on a small fortune at Paris because she gave up her seventh part of her husbands property which it seems is the widows right in Russia, to her sons when they married. She is very odd and has been her whole life imagining that she is to die every next day—for which reason she is now under the tyranny of a most brutal Russian, an ugly likeness but a very strong likeness of Alexander himself, with bushy sandy colored whiskers and all marked with the small-pox—and who endeavored to prove to us that it would be quite foolish in the French in acting Marie Stuart to call Leicester any-

[1] ME's story published in *Tales of Fashionable Life*, 1st series (1809).

[2] *Ennui: Tales and Novels* (1833), vi. 104–5. Lady Geraldine as a practical joke persuaded Miss Tracy that it would be fashionable to combine the most striking features of the dress of all the other ladies in the house; the result was 'a perfect monster, formed of every creature's best'.

thing but Leic*est*er—for they always make three syllables of it with a great accent at the end. They do the same in say[ing] Rochester in the Jeunesse de Henri 5 where they make him, the famous Ld Rochester, Henrys intimate friend.[1] I am sure they think half the charm of these plays is in the beautiful manner in which they send forth these names. When Kotzebue came to Paris and saw his two brothers[2] acting he found them mangling the German names so that he never would listen to them till they learnt better.

There dined with the Princesse that day Mme Méhégan the widow of Chevalier Méhégan who wrote a book[3] of which Maria seems amazingly fond but of which I know not even the title—but Mme Méhégan is more than eighty with a heap of rings on her hands, a nice little old face with two narrow lines of black eyebrows carefully painted and a perfectly well plaited white cap and blue ribbon the precise dress which Mme de Graffigny has in the beginning of the Peruvian Letters.[4] However she is a very nice little old woman and she and the Princesse agreed that they were astonished when they saw Maria for that they had always supposed her to be exceedingly tall and very severe and grave. They seemed however to be very soon satisfied of the contrary. Everybody is in a great rage against the Emperor Alexander because, instead of making an opposition, instead of continuing to be the magnanimous he has now become the despotic Alexander and instead of trying to civilise his barbarous subjects, he has classed them all in [ ] of battalions and formed military colonies of them all over his dominions each village containing 100 houses painted red and built on the same model under the inspection and government of an all powerful taskmaster. These slaves are all armed their wives and children join them and they remain submitting only to superior force, not only with the will but with the power to avenge their misfortunes and overturn the government. Alexander himself passes his whole time winter and summer in parades. They go on day after day for hours together, without any regard to heat or cold wet or dry. All the conversation at Petersbourg is of these

[1] The title of Rochester only dates from the seventeenth century. The famous Lord Rochester was John Wilmot, 2nd earl (1647–80), poet and rake.

[2] *Die Versöhnung*, translated as *Les Deux Frères*.

[3] Guillaume Alexandre de Méhégan, *Considérations sur les révolutions des arts* (Lettre sur l'éducation des femmes—dialogue) (1755).

[4] Mme de Graffigny, *Lettres d'une Péruvienne* (1747).

reviews, of cards, and of the movements of the Empresses and Archdukes.

After the dinner at Mme Galitzines we went to Mme de Pastoret, whose old wiggy M. Pastoret himself appeared a very unusual circumstance and the daughter in law who was a Mlle Alexandre, a little always very well dressed woman with excessively black hair and eyes. She is very goodnatured and has a nice little daughter Marie, with whom old Mme Pastoret walks about in a very sentimental grandmotherly manner. Amadis whom you remember is bien instruit, very tall and gentlemanlike, as grand as he can be wearing his red scrap of the Legion of honor particularly conspicuous always talking of the King and the Council and the Elections—but he is exceedingly well informed and very agreeable—that is, lately he has become very agreeable to us but in the summer he kept aloof from us whenever we met—but I believe the reason really was that Maria never did by any chance know him and always looked rather aghast when he spoke to her. One of his great perfections with Fanny at least, is that he plays at billiards remarkably well.

We young people were placed at a table to look over some very good costumes of the dresses in France since 1300. Upon these much could be said and M. Jullien said a good deal. He is *the* M. Jullien that you knew in former times always at Mme Pastorets. I suppose eighteen years have rather changed his appearance—he is now quite bald and looks a little battered. There were besides Cuvier with his great wild head of tawny hair and his uncertain countenance mighty busy looking over a book of elections, which M. Pastoret had – not nearly so elegant as the County of Longford Poll book—but all the Ultras and the Royalists say the elections are very good, and the liberals look rather unhappy about it, so that it appears the ministers have gained something by their great fighting last summer about the law of elections.[1] While the good and bad deputies were discussing there came in a most beautiful woman, Mme de Barante, who has dark hair black eyes and eyebrows, a straight nose the end cut sharp and smooth, a novel shaped face and something rather too sweet in the corners of her mouth. She draws beautifully and has made a very pretty drawing of herself—but once seen you have

[1] See above, p. 152.

done with her. Her countenance has but little expression and except about some little bits of bread and butter I did not see any appearance of animation in her countenance, but the little bits of bread and butter were discussed and eaten with great vehemence by young Mme. Pastoret and by a woman who had a face exactly like what Sophy would draw on a Sunday evening and whose name is d'Houdetot. Whether she belongs to Rousseaus old squinting Mme d'Houdetot or not nobody would tell me. It was a wonderful thing to see anything eatable at Mme Pastorets for often as we have been there I never saw anything, but some spinach and salad which she and her daughter were eating one morning for breakfast!

Friday we dined at Passy where there was nobody but François, the poor [ ] egg colored Étienne and I do not know who his companion. Poor François is so fond of his children that he jumps with delight whenever they say or do anything nice. Mme Gautier looks much better than she did last summer and is particularly gay and agreeable . . . After having galloped about with the children and heard Caroline and little Benjamin sing some very nice little couplets on the return of Étienne—we left them and went to a party at the Princesse de Craon, where a certain M. Marchangy a lawyer declaimed and very eloquently on the romantic style of tragedy and the excellencies of the Vague.[1] After he had said many words and a great many ideas Mr. Lattin, old Jacky Lattin who used to dance with Lady Ferrard came up with an unpolluted (I beg Lucys pardon) Irish brogue—and settled it all up in five or six very droll sentences. But before we could hear more of his drollery or M. Marchangys eloquence we were obliged to go home dress and go to a concert at Lady Elizabeth Stuarts where the music was very delightful and the company singularly select, and where everybody was beautifully drest. Lord Sandon is always to be seen near Miss Edgeworth—Lord Francis Gower is also when he can summon up courage. Lord Gower is also at Paris. He and his friend Lord Valletort, the brother of the man who laced himself to death last year[2]—were

[1] The reference is to Chateaubriand, *Génie du christianisme*, 2e partie, III. ix. *Du vague des passions: . . . 'un état d'âme qui . . . est celui qui précède le développement des grandes passions, lorsque toutes les facultés jeunes, actives, entières, mais renfermées, ne sont exercées que sur elles-mêmes, sans but et sans objet . . .*

[2] Lord Valletort's brother, William Richard Valletort, died in Oct. 1818.

considered as very handsome and there were altogether a most choice set of English nobility and some very nice French. Captain [ ] is always very glad to see us, and always entertaining —and ready to tell us everybody . . .

Harriet Edgeworth to Mrs. Edgeworth

Paris, 30th November, 1820

. . . We have spent a very gay month here, we have many agreeable acquaintances and some kind friends—but we feel that four months at Paris has been sufficient and notwithstanding the surprise we excite by going just when winter and the gaieties begin, Maria settled when she came, to go the 1st and we are off the 2d . . .

Maria Edgeworth to Honora Edgeworth

Tuesday, 5th December, 1820

Calais, morn 10 o clock just arrived—wind not fair—morning tide would serve but I will never go on board without a fair wind . . . Thank you my dear for all your care of Rosamond. We were all 3 of us conceited enough to think you would like Blind Kate better on a second reading than the first and we are proud to find it has been so and delighted to hear that dear Aunt Mary was pleased with the souvenir bracelet.[1] I wonder what part of blind Kate you have cut out that you think it is a favorite of mine. If it be the pricking of the map I confess it was and is a favorite idea and *we* think it ingenious and like Rosamond to think of it. You know it is the real way in which the blind are taught to read—therefore in this respect it cannot be too childish. Besides it is the characteristic of Rosamond to be half childish and half sensible or rather to be alternately sensible and foolish 'By turns averse and joyful to obey'[2] the power of reason. You see I am a true Irish-

[1] The Bracelet of Memory, ii. 150–72; Blind Kate, ii. 173–231. The pricked map was omitted.

[2] Matthew Prior, *Henry and Emma* (*Poems on Several Occasions* (Cambridge, 1941), 145).

woman—After leaving it all to your Honor—and protesting I should be satisfied *with anything at all your Honor pleased*—I am going over it all again. You say I shall see *it* but I don't clearly comprehend how—when—or where. Do you mean in proof sheets? Whenever I know where I am to be—at Em's[1] or elsewhere —I will write to Hunter to desire all the letters he may have for us may be forwarded and also desire him in future to send proof sheets to me . . .

Maria Edgeworth to Mrs. Edgeworth

Calais, 5th December, 1820—arrived at Dessin's hotel after a prosperous journey in which no sort of accident happened to us and during which not the slightest thing was deranged in our carriage except one pin in our limonière. By the by I got two new hind wheels before I left Paris that I might not tempt Fortune too far with our old ones, which had done so much more already than was expected from them. Though opinions even among judges were divided about their future powers of endurance all agreed that they would do no more than carry us safely to London and as we are to go to Bristol probably without *touching at London* and as we must have procured new wheels for our stay and journeying in England and home I thought it best to get them at once at Paris —perhaps a little more clumsy than English wheels but stronger— and now my liver and conscience have been spared and will be spared all eating cares and convulsive twitches. Setting out of the question my own natural portion of love for my own limbs and my own (imputed) large portion of cowardice, my anxiety about my two dear precious charges would have been too great. The idea of being left like Mrs. Freeman[2] in the middle of the road in the middle of the night in a broken chaise while the French or English postillion should ride back for assistance often haunted me and now can haunt me no longer. See what it is to be '*the*

[1] With her sister Emmeline King at Bristol.

[2] This refers to an episode in 'The Freeman Family', a story composed and told aloud to his family by RLE in 1788 or 1789. It formed the basis of ME's *Patronage* (1814).

essence of good sense'. How reviewers have changed since they wrote that.

But to come back to our Muttons—the wind not being fair we did not sail to [Dover but we] are in hopes it will change before tomorrow—mean time have the solace of writing to you coming back to this very place—the same room in which we were 7 months ago when we first landed at Calais. The whole to me and my companions seems like a dream . . . Without a wish unsatisfied abroad, without a regret for anything we leave behind in Paris—except *friends* and those wherever we go if we are happy enough to make them we must be sorry to leave. This is the common pain of travellers. Happy they—happiest they who have the most of it . . .

APPENDIX: FRENCH TRANSLATIONS OF EDGEWORTH BOOKS

THE firms of Truchy, Baudry, and Galignani published in Paris many English editions of Maria Edgeworth's books. The first I have found is an edition of *Ennui* by Galignani which came out in 1813 but it was not until the 1820s that large numbers appeared, presumably partly for the benefit of travellers. French translations of parts of the Edgeworths' books were first published in the Genevan periodical *La Bibliothèque Britannique* (later *La Bibliothèque Universelle*) between 1798 and 1820, and Maria Edgeworth's books for children continued to be reissued throughout the nineteenth century. The following list, however, is limited to those which appeared before her death in 1849. It is based on the catalogues of the British Library and the Bibliothèque Nationale and on B. C. Slade's *Maria Edgeworth. A Bibliographical Tribute* (1937). It is intended to show the range of Edgeworth books available to the French reader, but it does not pretend to be complete. It excludes, for example, many reprints of short stories, incomplete collections and most combinations of stories from different books. It may be noted that there were no translations of the colloquial Irish *Castle Rackrent*, but versions of were produced of the Irish novels *Ennui, The Absentee*, and *Ormond*.

[*The Parents' Assistant*, 1796].
Petites contes moraux, tr. Mme L. Sw. Belloc, Paris, 1820.
L'Ami des parens, Geneva, 1827.
Le Livre des familles, tr. Mlle A. Sobry, Paris, 1833.
Contes des familles, tr. E. Garnier, Paris, 1837, 1838, 1840.
[*Practical Education*, 1798].
Éducation pratique. Traduction libre . . . par Charles Pictet de Genève, Paris and Geneva, 1800, 1801.
[*Belinda*, 1801].
Bélinde, tr. Octave de Ségur, Paris, 1802.
[*Moral Tales*, 1801].
Choix de nouveaux contes moraux offerts à la jeunesse, tr. T. P. Bertin, Paris, 1813.
Contes moraux, tr. E. Garnier, Paris, 1837, 1840, 1842.
Forester, tr. Mlle Tourte Cherbuliez, Paris, 1821.
    tr. Laroche, Paris, 1830.
    tr. Mme E. Niboyet, Paris, 1836.

[*Early Lessons*, 1801; *Continuation of Early Lessons*, 1814; *Rosamond. A Sequel*, 1821; *Frank. A Sequel*, 1822; *Harry and Lucy Concluded*, 1825].
Leçons d'enfance, tr. L. C. Chéron, Paris, 1803.
Contes choisis pour des enfants, traduits de l'anglais. Imprimés sur l'édition de Paris, Edinburgh, 1817, 1823.
Les Jeunes Industriels, tr. Mme L. Sw. Belloc, Paris, 1826.
Éducation familière, tr. Mme L. Sw. Belloc and Mlle A. de Montgolfier, Paris, 1829–34.
Éducation familière, tr. Mlle A. Sobry, Paris, 1833.
Les Jeunes Savans, imité de l'anglais de Miss Edgeworth par Mme Viltardant, Paris, 1838.
[*Popular Tales*, 1804].
Contes à mon fils, tr. T. P. Bertin, Paris, 1813.
Conseils à mon fils, tr. T. P. Bertin, Paris, 1814.
Contes populaires, tr. Mmes Élise Voyart et Read, Paris, 1823.
Nouveaux contes populaires, tr. Mme Élise Voyart, Paris, 1835.
Contes populaires, tr. E. Garnier, Paris, 1837 (2 edns.), 1840.
[*The Modern Griselda*, 1805].
Les Deux Grisélidis, Paris, 1813.
[*Leonora*, 1806].
Léonore, tr. C. Chenel, Paris, 1807.
[*Tales of Fashionable Life*, 1st series, 1809, and 2nd series, 1812].
Scènes de la vie du grand monde, tr. P. L. Dubuc: includes *L'Absent* [*The Absentee*], *Émilie de Coulanges* and *Vivian*, Paris, 1813.
L'Ennui ou mémoires du comte de Glenthorn, tr. Mme E. de Bon, Paris, 1812.
La Mère intrigante [*Manoeuvring*], Paris, 1811.
Vivian ou l'homme sans caractère, tr. J. Joly, Paris, 1813.
[*Patronage*, 1814].
Les Protecteurs et les protégés, tr. J. Cohen, Paris, 1816.
[*Harrington and Ormond*, 1817].
Harrington, tr. C. A. Defauconpret, Paris, 1817.
Ormond, tr. A. J. B. Defauconpret, Paris, 1817.
[*Helen*, 1834].
Hélène, tr. Mme L. Sw. Belloc, Paris, 1834.
[*An Essay on the Construction of Roads and Carriages*, by R. L. Edgeworth, 1811].
Essai sur la construction des routes et des voitures, Paris, 1837.
[*Memoirs of the Abbé Edgeworth*, by C. Sneyd Edgeworth, 1815].
Mémoires de M. l'Abbé Edgeworth de Firmont, Paris, 1815 (2 edns.), 1817.

INDEX OF SUBJECTS AND PLACES

INDEX OF PERSONS

Biographical information is limited to what is necessary to identify persons of interest (where possible) and to elucidate the narrative.